The Form of Sociology—

Paradigms and Crises

The Form of Sociology—
Paradigms and Crises

S.N. Eisenstadt *with* M. Curelaru

A WILEY-INTERSCIENCE PUBLICATION

JOHN WILEY & SONS, New York • London • Sydney • Toronto

Published by John Wiley & Sons, Inc.

Copyright © 1976 by S. N. Eisenstadt

Library of Congress Cataloging in Publication Data:

Eisenstadt, Shmuel Noah, 1923-
    The form of sociology.

    "A Wiley-Interscience publication."
    Includes bibliographical references and indexes.
    1. Sociology.   2. Sociological research.   3. Soci-
ology—History.   4. Intellectual life—History.
I. Curelaru, M., joint author.   II. Title.
HM24.E35   301   76-7602
ISBN 0-471-23472-9

Printed in the United States of America

10 9 8 7 6 5 4 3 2 1

Preface

This book is an effort to analyze two different but closely related problems. First, it tries to evaluate the present state of sociological theory and analysis in the light of major trends in its historical development. Here it attempts to analyze to what degree there emerge, out of the many contemporary theoretical debates, some possibilities of convergence in the paradigms of social order, the major analytic concepts, and the problems of sociological analysis, as well as their relationship to major areas of sociological research. Second, it attempts to relate past trends and present possibilities to the structure of the sociological community.

The relationship between the two problems as presented here is rooted in the varied origins of this book. Perhaps the most important has been the course in sociological theory I have been giving for many years at the Hebrew University of Jerusalem. Since 1968, Miss Miriam Curelaru has participated actively in developing this course, and we thought it might be helpful to put these lectures down in written form, either as several essays or as a book. At the time we became involved in this effort, the outcry of "crisis" in sociology erupted. Thus we faced a paradoxical situation: At the same time that we were exploring possible convergences among different schools in sociology, the controversies about the crisis of sociology arose, depicting the field as consisting of completely closed, "totalistic" paradigms which differed not only in their analytic premises, but also in their philosophical, ideological and political assumptions. This view minimized the possibility of scholarly discourse about problems of common interest, and predicted the possible demise of sociology—or at least of sociology as it has been known until now. Was this concurrence of two aspects of development—constructive advances in analysis and outcries about crisis and the demise of sociology, purely accidental? Or were there reasons for their occurring at the same time?

In addressing ourselves to this problem, we remembered that announcements of crisis in sociology were hardly new. They could be found (as Allessandro Pizzorno pointed out in 1971[1]) in earlier periods of development, after the breakdown of the great evolutionary schemes of the nineteenth century, for example, and in many controversies of the 1920s and 1930s, above all, but not exclusively, in Germany. Such outcries generally accompanied important breakthroughs in the development of sociology. Thus it seemed worthwhile to explore the possibility that the present constructive developments and concerns about crisis did not appear by accident. Rather, there might be something in the nature of the analytic and institutional development of sociology which created the possibility of this paradoxical convergence.

To explore this possibility, we addressed ourselves to several broader problems: first, the relationship of sociology to philosophical, ideological, and political orientations and analyses; and second, the relationship of developments in sociological analysis to the development of the institutions of sociological work.

These two themes, the development of theory on the one hand, and its relationship to broader intellectual and institutional settings on the other, are the major focus of this book and are interwoven in its analysis. The work does not propose to provide a detailed and systematic history either of sociological analysis or of the institutional developments of sociology. There are by now many good works on the development of sociological theory, such as Raymond Aron's *Main Currents in Sociological Thought,*[2] Lewis Coser's *Masters of Sociological Thought,*[3] Robert Nisbet's *The Sociological Tradition,*[4] and Randall Collins' and M. Makowski's *The Discovery of Society.*[5] There are fewer works on the analysis of the institutional development of sociology. Here we would mention the pioneering works of Edward Shils[6] and Robert K. Merton,[7] and the more recent studies by Terry Clark,[8] Anthony Oberschall,[9] and Edward Tiryakian.[10] Recently, several books and readers analyze the more contemporary major theoretical approaches and paradigms in sociology.[11]

We have not attempted to supplement the books on the history of theory or on contemporary theories, and we assume that the reader has some basic acquaintance with the major sociological theories and the broad contours of the scope of sociological work. Nor have we undertaken detailed and systematic research of the relationship between the development of theory and research and the general intellectual history of the respective periods or the institutional development of sociology. Systematic work, as distinct from broad generalization, on these problems is still very new. We have used whatever materials were available but have not undertaken additional systematic research ourselves.

Some of the analyses of contemporary situations in various sociological communities are necessarily personal and impressionistic—but not, I hope, inaccurate.

Bearing in mind the limits of space, we have included in the footnotes only the most important and illustrative indications of all these developments, and even these proved to be numerous.

What we have attempted is an exploratory commentary, an essay of interpretation, on the relationship between the development of sociological analysis, its broader intellectual framework, and the institutional development of sociological work. We also indicated what seems to us to be the present situation of theory and analysis, its possibilities and promises. We hope this discussion may also be of use in the planning of teaching and research.

The discussion presented here is tentative and exploratory. It is less fully documented with respect to the structure of the sociological community. The relations between the aspects examined in this book should be seen as a series of tentative hypotheses which, hopefully, will be of interest for further research.

In the last chapter, I have also attempted to propose, in a preliminary way, a direction for the development of sociological theory and to indicate some possible research programs. Both will be amplified in a future publication.

The debts in the preparation of this work are many and considerable. My interest in the development of sociological theory dates back to my studies with the late Professor Martin Buber, under whose supervision I wrote my doctoral dissertation on "The meaning of the term 'social' in modern sociology." In his teaching and, above all, his private conversations, Buber presented a unique perspective on the place of sociology in the contemporary intellectual framework and on the development of sociology in some of its formative periods. He was, moreover, a unique type of participant observer in this endeavor. Many of his activities, among them his editorship of the paperback series, "Gesellschaft," in the first decade of this century, attest to his involvement.

My interest in sociological theory was reinforced by my association with the late Professor Morris Ginsberg at the London School of Economics. My nearly 30-year association with Professor Edward Shils has added a special dimension to this interest; my debt to him is even greater than my frequent reliance on his seminal papers in the history of sociology suggests.

I have been also influenced, beyond what is evident in the footnotes, by the work of Professor Robert K. Merton, with whom I have several recent, extremely interesting, discussions. In these we discovered a very high degree of convergence of interest and orientation.

Several colleagues have read all or parts of the manuscript and have made very useful comments: R. Baum, D. Bell, J. Ben-David, P. Clark, T. Clark, Y. Ellemers, Y. Elkana, Y. Ezrachi, C. Lammers, J. Goudsblom, G. Germani, E. Goody, T. McCormack, K. H. Silvert, E. Shild, and E. Tiryakian, with whom I had many fruitful discussions on problems discussed in this book, or who have commented on versions of the manuscript. I am especially grateful to Evelyn Geller for her superb work in editing the manuscript and to Eric Valentine, Valda Aldzeris and Marcia Trencher of John Wiley & Sons for their scrupulous care in the various stages of production. We thank Z. Richter for help in index preparation.

Several generations of students at the Hebrew University who have participated in the courses and seminars on sociological theory and history have provided continuous stimulation and criticism, as have the participants in lectures and seminars I have given elsewhere, particularly at Harvard, Yale, Zürich, and Bern.

The basic concept of the book was conceived and several chapters principally written by me. Miss Curelaru fully participated in the working out of the analysis in Chapters 8 to 10, which developed out of the courses in sociological theory mentioned above, and in the writing of chapters 2, 5, 6, 8, 9, and 10. She also read, commented on, and closely criticized all the other chapters as well as the broad conception of the book. All have greatly benefited from her comments. Miss Curelaru kindly undertook the technical aspects of preparing the manuscript and footnotes as well.

The work on this book was facilitated by a grant from the Ford Foundation and by the facilities provided in Jerusalem, by the Department of Sociology of the Hebrew University and by the Jerusalem Van Leer Foundation.

The penultimate draft of this book was written while I was a fellow at the Netherlands Institute for Advanced Study in Wassensar, Holland during the first half of 1973. I would like to record my thanks to the Institute for its facilities and splendid atmosphere.

S. N. EISENSTADT

The Hebrew University
Jerusalem
March 1976

Notes

1. A. Pizzorno, "Una crisi che non importa superare," in Pietro Rossi (ed.), *Ricerca Sociologica e Ruolo del Sociologo,* (Bologna: Mulino, 1972) pp. 327-357.

2. R. Aron, *Main Currents in Sociological Thought* (London: Penguin, 1968, 1970), 2 vols.

3. L. A. Coser, *Masters of Sociological Thought: Ideas in Historical and Social Context* (New York: Harcourt, Brace, and Jovanovich, 1971).

4. R. Nisbet, *The Sociological Tradition* (London: Heinemann, 1967).

5. R. Collins and M. Makowski, *The Discovery of Society* (New York: Random House, 1972).

6. E. Shils, "The calling of sociology," in T. Parsons, E. Shils, K.D. Naegele, and J.R. Pitts (eds.), *Theories of Societies,* Vol. 2 (New York: Free Press, 1961), pp. 1405-1448; E. Shils, "The trend of sociological research," paper presented at the 8th World Congress of Sociology at Evian; to be published in the *Proceedings* of the Congress; E. Shils, "Tradition, ecology, and institution in the history of sociology," *Daedalus,* Vol. 99, No. 4 (fall 1970), pp. 760-825.

7. R. K. Merton, "Social conflict over styles of sociological work," *Transactions of the 4th World Congress of Sociology* (Louvain: International Sociological Association, 1961), pp. 21-44; R. K. Merton, "The precarious foundations of detachment in sociology," in E. A. Tiryakian (ed.), *The Phenomenon of Sociology* (New York: Appleton-Century-Crofts, 1971), pp. 188-199; R. K. Merton, "Insiders and outsiders; a chapter in the sociology of knowledge," *American Journal of Sociology,* Vol. 78, No. 1 (1972), pp. 9-47.

8. T. N. Clark, *Prophets and Patrons: the French University and the Emergence of the Social Sciences* (Cambridge, Mass.: Harvard University Press, 1973).

9. A. Oberschall (ed.), *The Establishment of Empirical Sociology; Studies in Continuity, Discontinuity, and Institutionalization* (New York: Harper & Row, 1972); A. Oberschall, *Empirical Social Research in Germany: 1848-1914,* (Paris: Mouton, 1965).

10. E. A. Tiryakian (ed.), *op. cit.*

11. To mention only a few: A. Boskoff's *Theory in American Sociology* (New York: T. Y. Crowell, 1974); probably above all, J. H. Turner *The Structure of Sociological Theory* (Homewood, Ill.: Dorsey Press, 1974); the somewhat earlier reader edited by Walter L. Wallace *Sociological Theory* (Chicago: Aldine, 1969); the more recent one on *Theories and Paradigms in Contemporary Sociology,* edited by S. Denisoff, D. Callahan, and M. H. Levine (Ithaca: Ill.: F. H. Peacock, 1974); and G. Ritzer, *Sociology, A Multiple-Paradigm Science* (Boston: Allyn and Bacon, 1975).

Author's Note

Recent works, published after the text of this book had been set in type, touch on some of the central aspects of the book's analysis—especially on the "crisis" of sociology and its background. I would like to draw the reader's attention particularly to the following literature:

Raj. P. Mohan and Don Martindale (eds.), *Handbook of Contemporary Development in World Sociology* (Westport, Conn.: Greenwood Press, 1975), which contains a series of useful surveys of the developments in sociology in many countries of the world.

T. Bottomore (ed.), *Crisis and Contention in Sociology,* Sage Studies in International Sociology, Vol. 1, 1975.

E. Crawford and S. Rokkan (eds.), *Sociological Praxis—Current Roles and Settings,* Sage Studies in International Sociology, Vol. 3, 1976.

H. J. Krejsmanski and P. Marwedel (eds.), *Die Krise in der Sociologie, Ein Kritischer Reader zum 17 Deutschen Sociolgentag* (Köln: Paul Reigenstein Verlag, 1975), which contains an extreme idiological-Marxist criticism of "established" sociology. Book is available only in German.

S.   N.   E.

Contents

xi

The Form of Sociology—

Paradigms and Crises

1

The Intellectual and Cultural Background of the Development of Modern Sociology

The Historical Ancestors and Specific Modern Background

1.   The term "sociology" was coined by Auguste Comte, but many components of sociological analysis were heralded long before Comte described this "new department of the comparative method" in the fourth volume of his *Cours de Philosophie Positive* (1830–1842).[1] Its more remote ancestry lies, of course, in the discussions of social and political issues in virtually all intellectual traditions of human society,[2] especially the "Great Traditions." Discussions containing important elements of what has eventually become sociology have included: first, descriptive accounts of the customs and institutions of various societies, especially far-off, distant peoples; second, philosophical or theological speculations about the nature of social order in various traditions–e.g., in the Bible, the Greek classics, or the writings of Confucius, Lao Tse, the Buddha, Aquinas, Maimonides, or Averroes[3]; third, political or administrative speculations on the appropriate conduct of rulers, notably the various "Mirrors of Princes"[4]; and last, the somewhat more rare attempts to probe societies analytically, best illustrated by the work of such speculative historians as

1

Thucydides in Greece,[5] Polybius in Rome,[6] and, perhaps most important, Ibn Khaldoun.[7] Of the various Great Traditions, the one which is most directly relevant to the development of modern sociology is the Western tradition, more specifically that of Greek philosophy, particularly as expressed in the works of Plato and Aristotle,[8] as it was transmitted through medieval culture.

Only with the start of the modern era, however—perhaps from the Renaissance on, can one discern the beginnings of the "secular" type of analysis out of which sociology, among other intellectual and, later on, academic, disciplines, developed.

Modern sociological thought emerged in the late eighteenth and early nineteenth centuries, in conjunction with several major cultural and social changes attendant on the modern era in Europe.[9] The cultural changes involved, first, a new critical perception of the problem of social order, based on the philosophical discussions of the sixteenth, seventeenth, and eighteenth centuries and expressed in many intellectual areas. The second cultural change involved the emergence of the scientific approach and its subsequent extension to the study of human and social existence. Both trends contributed to the development of a tradition of critical scholarly-scientific inquiry into human and social affairs. Sociological theory and analysis were part of these broader intellectual trends, but it was in sociological inquiry above all that the problems of social life became objects not only of critical appraisal, but of systematic scientific research.

The modern philosophical and political orientations, whose roots can be traced to the Renaissance, crystallized in the period of the Enlightenment and Rationalism around the ideas of "progress" and "reason." The new political and philosophical orientations accompanied the transformation of religious orientations, especially in Protestantism, and the development of "secular" opposition to them. Out of these developed new intellectual traditions with philosophical, scholarly, ideological, and scientific components. The incorporation of these idea-systems into the central symbolic and institutional spheres of European society, produced a new social and cultural order presenting a continuous confrontation between existing social reality and the critical observation, analysis, and evaluation of this reality.

2.   These intellectual developments were predicated above all on the new conceptions of social, cultural, and political life which produced the revolutionary movements creating the modern political order—the "Great Rebellion" and "Glorious Revolution" in England, the American and French Revolutions in the eighteenth century. From its start, modern

civilization has been connected with revolutionary imagery and symbolism, and even reformist and conservative orientations developed in modern settings have been set within the framework of such revolutionary imagery.

Central to these conceptions was a new attitude toward political, social, and cultural change. Unlike the processes of change or rebellion in premodern societies, the revolutionry conceptions and movements which produced the modern political orders were more or less consciously oriented to changing the basic contours of these orders. They sought a transformation of the basic premises of the social and cultural order, its societal and cultural centers, and patterns of participation and access to them.

Implicit in these orientations was an increasing tendency to secularize the central societal symbols and to challenge the "givenness" and sanctity of cultural traditions, their cultural centers and symbols, and their guardians. With the breakthrough to modernity, the traditional legitimation of these symbols and centers was weakened; the major social groups tended to question the premises of the social order and to participate in the formation of new cultural traditions which took an active critical stance toward most aspects of political, social, and cultural traditions, and to societal life itself.

Moreover, the developing scientific explanation of the world embodied a new vision of man and the universe, a vision whose emergence led from Copernicus through Darwin to Freud. This vision, on the one hand, dethroned man from his position under God as the center of creation; rejecting the notion of divine preordainment of the social order, it subjected man and the social order, at least potentially, to "natural" law. On the other hand, it also made possible the perception of the sociocultural order as in part created by man. Thus the problem of the potential and limitations of human creativity was posed very sharply.

These social and cultural trends converged in the conception of European modernity. This conception, already present in the Renaissance, was developed more fully under the combined impact of the Reformation, Counter-Reformation, and Age of Reason, and the great scientific-technological advances that began in the seventeenth century. The notion of modernity was based on the assumption that man and society could not only explore the expanding human and natural environments, but could also, by conscious effort, direct and even master them. The exploration of nature by man was seen an "open" enterprise through which a new cultural order could be created: continuous expansion of scientific and technological knowledge might transform both cultural and social orders by creating environments to be explored by man and at the same time be harnessed to his intellectual vision and technical needs.

Such exploration and potential mastery of the environment was conceived in more than a narrow technological sense. The notion was extended to the social sphere in general, and the conception of the sociopolitical order in particular. It was based on the belief that, along with cognitive scientific development, the scope of human participation in society, and of society's mastery of its own fate, would also expand through increase in economic wealth, continuous expansion of the cultural and social environment, and increasing participation of various social groups in society.[10]

The Transformation of Themes of Protest in the Modern Social and Cultural Orders; New Perceptions of the Major Problems of Social Order

3.   These premises of modern civilization served to transform the major themes and movements of protest which developed, with the emergence of modern Europe, out of the contradictions and tensions between its symbolic ideological premises and the institutions presumably based on them. The orientations and movements of protest shared many characteristics with similar movements in other, "traditional" societies,[11] and, indeed, all societies, since these face perennial internal tensions.

Among such universal themes and orientations, the most important are, first, the emphasis on the contradiction between the complexity and fragmentation of human relations entailed in any division of labor, and the possibility of some total, unmediated participation in the social and cultural order. Parallel to this is the tension between the desire for present gratification and its deferment for the sake of future benefit. Hence, many protest movements would negate the structural and organizational division of labor to realize the ideal of "communitas," of direct, unmediated participation in the social and cultural orders. They would eliminate the tensions between "productivity" and "distribution" by merging the two through some basic commitment to unconditional participation in the community.

Another set of tensions around which protest orientations develop contrasts the model of the ideal society and its principle of distributive justice with the reality of institutional life; contrasts the ideal of equality and the actual distribution of power. Other protests have focussed on the tension between the personal, autonomous self and the requirements of social roles; between finding full self expression through social and cultural life and having to achieve this, rather, by retreat from public life.

Thus, movements of protest have often stressed the suspension of tension between time dimensions—past, present, and future as they relate to the allocation of rewards, and between the needs of the inner self and the demands of role performance.

These themes of protest are in all human societies related to the problem of participation in the social order and its distribution of power and resources. They have often demanded the incorporation of new dimensions of human existence into the central parameters of the given tradition, or of broader groups into the more central zones of a society, or for widening the scope of participation by such groups. Hence, the institutional-symbolic foci of such themes have tended to be: first, the bases and centers of authority; second, the system of stratification, which combines the symbolic dimensions of hierarchy with structural features, involving the division of labor and the distribution of resources; and third, the family as the primary locus of authority, socialization, and restrictions (even if these are necessary or creative limitations) on individual impulse and activity, on the basis of such primordial data as differences in age and sex.

At the start of the modern period, the various themes of protest were articulated in a great variety of ways, again resembling the orientations of protest prevalent in other civilizations, particularly in situations of change: chiliastic, millenarian movements, intellectual speculations and heterodoxies, and the various movements of protest and rebellion themselves. As is the case in many other situations of change, the protest themes that accompanied the beginnings of modernity developed first within the more original religious heterodoxies and protest movements and the more speculative and "rationalistic" intellectual movements—all of which had existed in "premodern" Europe in relatively segregated institutional enclaves.

Yet whatever these generic similarities, the orientations of protest of the modern era had their own distinguishing characteristics. First, because of the development of the premises of modernity analyzed above, protest was expressed not only in segregated, secondary institutional enclaves, but in the more central spheres of the evolving social orders and cultural traditions and the new intellectual and scientific traditions. They became manifest in ways that greatly went beyond the usual incorporation of heterodoxies into "traditional" institutions. Of crucial importance in this transformation of the locus of protest were the religious movements, such as the Puritan, which provided the motivational and ideological impetus for interweaving the orientations of protest with the central symbols of the emerging social and cultural orders.[12]

4.   The transformation of the themes of protest was linked to the reformulation of broad philosophical and sociopolitical problems in terms of new perceptions of human existence and of social order. There were two major philosophical problems. The first was that of potential human creativity and innovation in shaping social and cultural life—the possibility that organized social life and cultural creativity could result from the free activity of individuals or groups, as against the constraints imposed by biological characteristics, the environment, the necessities of social organization and the division of labor, or the basic "givens" and ordering of cultural life.[13] The second central problem, as Reinhard Bendix has shown, was the place of reason in human affairs: its trustworthiness and its role in society, particularly modern society.[14]

The more concrete perception of social order that developed within this intellectual framework focused on several themes—themes that would be crucial to the development of sociological analysis. The first was the dialectical dissociation between the transcendental moral order and actual sociopolitical orders and patterns of individual behavior and belief. Closely related to this theme was the recognition that the range of possible personal orientations and commitments to both the transcendental moral realm and to social norms, customs, and institutions was extremely diverse; that these commitments, like other components of individual behavior, developed within particular social and cultural settings; and that their variations could therefore not be explained in terms of individual differences alone. The second major theme centered on the awareness that no single institutional arrangements could fully epitomize any transcendental or ideal moral order, and hence that various types of social or political regimes could not easily be scaled in terms of their conformity to such ideal types.[15]

The main representatives of the early expression of these ideas were, of course, Hobbes and Rousseau, and, to a lesser extent, Locke.[16] By posing the question of the very possibility of different types of social order, rather than assuming some "natural" order as given, they formulated this question in modern terms even while their specific answers remained tied to older conceptions. The Scottish moralists, Ferguson, Millar, and above all Adam Smith, explored the various relationships between moral sentiments and types of social organization, as well as the great diversity of social institutions,[17] further developing this theme and approaching the modern *Problemstellungen*.

Within the framework of these new formulations of the problems of social order, the perennial themes of protest became central components of an emerging intellectual tradition of continuous critical evaluation of social and political reality. Through this process, intellectual interests and orientations were infused with more concrete sociopolitical orientations, while themes of protest were transposed to a more abstract analytical level. The synthesis of these orientations of protest and intellectual concerns coincided also with their increasing concentration on specific characteristics of modern social life, its problems, and its contradictions.

5. Although the protest themes of modern Europe were based, like those in all societies, on the generic contradictions between the symbolic premises and the institutional arrangements of the social order, modern societies have been peculiarly subject to the continuous development of such contradictions.

Social, economic, and cultural developments in the modern world, particularly the West, did not bear out the assumptions that continual expansion in the various spheres of life would have automatic beneficent results. Expansion was neither automatic nor symmetrical: expansion in one sphere did not entail parallel expansion in another, nor did it ensure increasing participation of various groups and strata in the social and cultural order. Rather, complex tensions were created between these developments—especially in the economic and technological, but also the political spheres—and the revolutionary premises of the new sociopolitical orders.

Most important was the contradiction between the promises of these revolutionary assumptions, and of industrial development and economic improvement, on the one hand, and the realities of the Industrial Revolution, on the other. The various revolutionary and Enlightenment premises of political equality, participation, and progress contrasted sharply with the new inequalities, divisions, and conflicts produced by the Industrial Revolution and the rise of the bourgeoisie.[18] These tensions were constantly reinforced by the dynamics of modern societies, the major social and economic processes mobilized by these symbolic and structural characteristics.

Major Types of Evaluation of the Emerging Institutional Order

6. Within the emerging intellectual sociopolitical traditions, the contradictions between the symbolic premises and the institutional developments of modern, especially European, societies were formulated largely in terms of several basic dilemmas seen as inherent in the modern social order.[19]

The first of these was that of *liberty versus authority*. The modern social order was conceived as one in which the scope of liberty was continuously being extended, necessarily creating the problem of maintaining stable, legitimate authority.

The second dilemma was that of *stability and continuity versus change.* Change, whether termed "progress" or "development," and whether revolutionary or gradual, was perceived as a basic tendency of modern society to which a positive value could often be attached. Modern polities and societies were thus seen as facing the problem of combining such change with some degree of institutional and moral stability or continuity.

The third dilemma was the tension between *equality and participation* in the social and cultural orders on the one hand, and *hierarchy* on the other. The quest for equality was one basic premise of modernity, which stressed the importance of equal access to the centers of society. At the same time, the increasing concentration of resources and power intensified the strength of bureaucratic principles in modern societies.

Fourth was the tension between *rationality and values* and the fear that the extension of rationality would undermine the "nonrational" value components of human life—moral commitments to a societal and cultural order, justice, and solidarity—even if these new societal situations allowed greater scope for rationality and epitomized man's control of his environment. It was often stressed that as a result of the extension of rationality, man, freed from the constraints of either common values or self-control, would be prey to his own unregulated or aberrant instincts or the vagaries of changing, conflicting interests.

Fifth, and closely related to these problems, was the contradiction between man's *mastery* of the internal and external environments and *subjugation* to the very products he created—those frameworks and centers of power developed in the very process of controlling the environment.

These analyses and evaluations of the emerging reality were concerned above all with the specific institutional complexes which had developed in Europe from the beginning of the nineteenth century, particularly the increasing autonomy of the major institutional spheres, above all the political and the economic, on the one hand, and the increasing tendencies to centralization of power on the other; and the changing tensions between symbolic premises of modernity and its evolving institutional structure. Thus, in the late eighteenth and early nineteenth centuries, analyses focused on the problem of an autonomous civil society and its relationship to the state; on the problems of the industrial capitalistic economic order and the new inequalities and conflicts it had produced; and on the relationships among these processes.

Later, these orientations concentrated on the analysis of industrialization and the development of large-scale organizations and centers of power; the development of nation-states and of constitutional regimes; social movements and their institutionalization; increasing bureaucratization; and the growth of mass education as a basic resource for access to social positions. Still later, as modern economic, political, and cultural movements and institutions spread beyond Europe, and as worldwide frameworks were created, impinging on non-European societies, new versions of these problems appeared. The ways in which the different themes of protest and analysis developed within the continuously expanding Western social and cultural structure varied greatly with the actual processes of institutional expansion and change.

7. The analyses of these dilemmas were combined in different ways with the modern themes of protest to produce different types of evaluation of the social order. Throughout modern history, first in Europe and later in other parts of the world, the various types of evaluation wavered between the affirmation of modernity and its negation; between accepting the compatibility of different aspects of modernity and insisting on their irreconcilability.

Several major trends of protest and analysis developed from these combinations. One, the "anti-modern," denied the premise that the extension of rationality to human and social affairs necessarily increased meaningful participation by broader groups, or that it would permit the fullest expression of the aesthetic or mythical dimensions of life. Antimodernity was most fully articulated in various traditionalistic and/or romantic ideologies, and to some degree in anarchist, such as the more recent radical, movements[20]

In contrast were those protest movements which accepted the extension of rationality in all spheres of human endeavor, protesting only that such expansion was not completely institutionalized. They demanded broader channels of access to the centers of societies and the scope of participation in them.[21] Common to these movements was the quest for participation in the broader social and political order, and the belief that this quest for participation by those in the periphery was displayed largely in the search for access to the emerging centers.

Different institutional reforms might be stressed in each of these themes of protest—whether aimed at solidarity or freedom.[22] The quest for solidarity could center on the establishment of new collectives, or on liberation from them; on accepting the premises of modernity, or on rejecting them. The quest for community could stress the romantic evaluation of primordial ties and groups, or the attempt to withdraw from such ties, or the effort to transcend them in new interpersonal ties unlinked to institutional settings. Orientations of protest could evaluate the extension of individual autonomy in different ways, some demanding its further extension, some negating it in the name of traditional communal values or of new "modern" solidarity.[23]

8.   The protest orientations differed in their evaluations of the qualities and problems of the modern social order, and the basic characteristics of the emerging social structure. First they differed in evaluating the dilemmas of modern societies. Conservatives tended to stress the maintenance of order, authority, and tradition, whereas the change-oriented and rational position of liberals or revolutionaries, placed priority on liberty and rationality.[24]

Second, these orientations differed in the degree to which they saw the emerging social structure as the embodiment of the new qualities of the social order. For conservative, liberal, and revolutionary ideologies alike, the emerging institutional order exemplified modernity; and this was exactly the reason for its condemnation by conservatives and praise by liberals, and for a more ambivalent attitude on part of the revolutionaries. For many liberals, it was not only the great liberator from the shackles of feudalism and absolutism, but the apex of human evolution.[25] For revolutionaries, however, it represented only the first indication of these liberating possibilities and was itself basically restrictive.[26]

These evaluations were often linked to varying appraisals of the internal contradictions in the modern order and the possibilities of resolving such dilemmas. Liberal, "utopian," or "revolutionary" ideologies denied the ultimate incompatibility between order and justice, on the one hand, and liberty and rationality on the other. They differed, however, in their conceptions of how these conflicts were overcome. Within the liberal tradition, one school, linked with aspects of the Greek tradition, held that liberty was meaningless beyond the existing political order.[27] Its proponents approved the emerging political community and civil society, maintaining that internal contradictions would be resolved through the play of various autonomous forces.

By contrast, the revolutionary ideologies, acknowledging such contradictions within civil-bourgeois or industrial and/or bureaucratic societies, held that they would be resolved in the course of history. Extreme revolutionary groups, whether Jacobin or Communist, held that a great revolutionary act would establish a political order that, by definition, would resolve these dichotomies.[28] Closely related to these revolutionary orientations, although sharply opposed on concrete political or social issues, were the various utopian views which also envisioned a social order, based on a true, voluntary consensus, in which the polarities of authority versus liberty, of rationality versus solidarity, and of progress versus resistance to change would disappear.[29]

9.
All these orientations of protest and analysis have been incorporated into the central intellectual and cultural traditions of modern life. First, they have been incorporated into major political-ideological orientations. Second, and especially important from the point of view of our analysis, these general orientations to the social order, particularly the concern with problems of analysis, were shared, albeit in varying degrees, by all the major modern intellectual movements and scholarly traditions oriented to the analysis of social life. This concern was the main focus of the emerging tradition of social criticism.

On the political level, several views or orientations developed around these themes of protest, especially in Europe. One orientation, usually called "rightist," was rooted in the feeling by various strong groups that they, and their values were being ousted or replaced; consequently, they developed demands for the maintenance or restoration of traditional order and values.[30] The second extreme, which may be called "leftist," was oriented to changing the social structure and basic principles of allocation to favor groups or classes allegedly deprived of advantage or full political participation.[31] These groups could be social classes, occupational categories, regional groups within a given society, or special national or tribal subgroups within a broad imperial/colonial or international social and political order.

Both orientations could stress the need for direct, "pure," unalienated human relations and attachments to primordial symbols. Traditionalists would claim that such relations were possible only under stable, ordered conditions, undisrupted by the forces of increasing differentiation, democratization, and mass society.[32] Political radicals, on the other hand, could claim that such relations could be achieved only by overthrowing such an order and establishing a new one whose institutional arrangements would entirely coalesce with nonalienated relations.[33] Other, less political, radicals could claim that such relations could be attained only outside of both traditional and modern formalized power orders.

New Intellectual Concerns, Activities, and Disciplines

10.
These major themes of protest and analysis provided not only the foci of modern political orientation but also the basic conceptual

framework within which there developed, within the broader tradition of criticism in social matters, several intellectual concerns and orientations. Most of these concerns had roots in the past, but were transformed in the new framework. Through this transformation, they served as a background for the development of several new intellectual trends in general, and of the social sciences and sociology in particular.

One category of intellectual tradition included the work of speculative historians and philosophers of culture, of whom Giovanni Battista Vico is probably the most important.[34] The second trend often connected with the first, was the revival of the secular systematic analysis of politics; its breakthrough in the beginning of the modern period is expressed in the work of Nicolo Machiavelli.[35] A third trend was the gradual redefinition of the philosophical problem of social order through the works stemming from the Wars of Religion (i.e., in such tracts as the *Vindiciae contra Tyrannos*[36]), and culminating in the reformulations of the problem of social contract by Thomas Hobbes, John Locke, and Jean Jacques Rousseau.[37] Fourth was the renewal and intensification of interest in the institutions of foreign people, which became connected with the growth of historical studies. Fifth, and closely related to some of these philosophical speculations, political analyses and interest in history and in foreign institutions, was a new concern with the comparative study of institutions and their moral bases, developed in the work of the Scottish moralists, Adam Ferguson and J. Millar, and perhaps above all by Montesquieu.[38] A sixth orientation in the modern intellectual tradition was systematic statistical inquiry into contemporary conditions,[39] often stemming from the attempt to establish a rational or scientific basis for public economic policy. Among the more important examples are the attempts of William Petty (1623-1687) to establish the art of political arithmetic, and similar efforts among such mercantilist or physiocrat intellectuals as François Quesnay or Turgot, who were forefathers of modern economic analysis.[40]

Out of these broad intellectual interests and orientations there crystallized some more organized types of intellectual activities. Most important were the growth of critical journalism and political analysis, and the development of new historical, juridical, and ethnographic comparative studies based on the critical evaluation of sources. The former was most fully represented by such writers as de Toqueville and Lorentz von Stein[41]; the latter trend, which ultimately crystallized into academic disciplines, was characterized by a relatively nonmoralistic stance toward the subjects of study; it was best exemplified by Barthold Niebuhr, Friedrich de Savigny, and Michelet.[42] At the same time, and related to the increasing use of quantitative methods in studying social affairs, a trend developed toward the use of practical, policy-oriented statistics, field studies, and observations of actual patterns of contemporary social life.[43]

These new intellectual orientations shared two types of analytical concepts which emerged from the combination of the themes of protest with the new problematics of social order. One type consisted of concepts rooted in the normative tradition of political philosophy—concepts such as "equality" and "justice." The other type included seemingly descriptive concepts, such as "state," "society," "community," "class," and others oriented to the characteristics of the emerging social structure. A special characteristic of the modern critical tradition was the continual juxtaposition of these normative and descriptive concepts to produce new concrete analyses and evaluations of the evolving social reality. But the ways in which this juxtaposition and analysis were performed varied greatly among the different components of this tradition—the philosophical, ideological, historical, and sociological. We shall refer to some of these differences later.

The Common Problems of Modern Intellectual Traditions of Analysis of Social Order; the Emergence of the Modern Sociological Tradition

11.   The modern sociological tradition was related to all these intellectual traditions, trends, and developments. The one most closely related to sociology was perhaps the philosophic. It affected the social sciences first through positivistic utilitarianism, which attempted to develop a new social ethics and economics on the basis of a rational calculation of human wants. This tradition retained its influence later in evolutionism, as it was developed in the works of Herbert Spencer.[44] Another important influence on the development of sociology were the various romantic philosophies connected primarily with the names of Fichte, Hegel, and Schlegel, and later on with such philosophers of culture as Wundt or Dilthey.[45]

A second important influence was that of social reform and reconstruction, which developed in different degrees of proximity to the philosophical tradition. This movement was concerned above all with ameliorating, or transforming, through revolution, the outcomes of the industrial revolution and capitalism. Its most important representatives were utopian socialists, such as the Saint-Simonians in the 1830s, to whom Comte was closely related, and different types of social reformers, philanthropists, and revolutionaries, such as St. Simon, Fourier, and above all, Marx.[46]

Sociology was also linked to the journalistic tradition and to such protoacademic and academic disciplines as history, ethnology or comparative jurisprudence.

Modern sociology, as it emerged in the nineteenth century, shared many central problems with these traditions. With the broad sociophilosophical traditions it shared the attempt to explain the basis and nature of social order: How was social order possible at all? How was it related to basic wants of individuals? And what were its basic characteristics and problems? It also shared several particular concerns: the extent to which social order or life was harmonious or conflict-ridden; the relationship of individuals to social life, and to the good or common social order; the extent to which these characteristics were common to all human societies—that is, the degree to which they were something basically "human" or varied from place to place. Finally, these two traditions shared a concern with the degree of "givenness" of social and cultural order, as rooted in "nature" or in some divine command, and, in contrast to such givenness, the possibility of creativity and change.

Sociology shared with the philosophers of culture the quest for "objective" laws of development of human society. With the social reform tradition, it shared an interest in the critical evaluation of some major characteristics of modern society, the conditions of modern social life, and the study of the possibility of changing these conditions through ameliorative or revolutionary programs. With modern political thinking and publicism, sociology shared the concern with such problems as class structure and political behavior; the nature and working of different political systems—particularly the social bases of liberty and tyranny, democracy or autonomy; and the analysis and description of modern city life.

Sociology shared with history, ethnography, and some areas of political analysis a concern with understanding, in a scientific, critical, and detached manner, the conditions and laws of development of single societies or political orders, the institutions and customs of different people, and perhaps the laws of historical development. With the more practical and policy-oriented forms of economic and statistical research, it shared a concern with the observation of actual patterns of contemporary social life (e.g., family life, patterns of consumption) and their implications for the understanding of modern problems; with the collection of data which could shed light on these patterns; and to some extent with the development of statistical and other methods of inquiry.

These various influences affected the work of all the major and minor figures of the emerging sociological tradition, especially in its initial stages[47]: Comte, Marx, Toqueville, and von Stein; the great evolutionists Tylor, Spencer, and Hobhouse; later, the works of the two major Founding Fathers of scientific traditions in sociology, Durkheim and Weber; and later still Mannheim and, to some degree, Alfred Weber. Close links could also be found in the work of the Founding Fathers of American sociology—Ward, Ross, Cooley, and William I. Thomas, as well as many minor American sociologists.

Such ties were not only intellectual, but to some degree institutional and organizational. Most of the early sociologists were closely related (albeit in ambivalent and often marginal ways) to older academic traditions, newer groups of social reformers, new groups of journalists, and various political and religious intellectuals. For a long period of time these groups constituted their principal, though often ambivalent, audiences.

12. Moreover, sociologists also shared with these intellectuals some basic philosophical and ideological positions and orientations of protest toward the emerging order. These orientations varied, of course, among countries, and this variation was shaped primarily by the differing experiences in the development of modern political and social structures in each country. Although a full and systematic analysis of these patterns or of the social conditions producing them is not feasible here, some broad outline of those conditions especially pertinent to the development of sociology may be in order.

The elements of the modernizing experience of different countries which were most decisive in shaping these orientations of protest were the relationships between political centers and the emerging middle strata in the processes of economic and political modernization, especially in such phases as the forming of new nation-states and civil society, and the incorporation of the working classes into political centers.[48]

Of special importance was, first, the degree of autonomy and cohesion of the various social strata and the middle strata in particular, and their ability to undertake political, economic, and social modernization in conjunction with the state; second, the relative openness of the political centers to the participation of the middle strata in their construction; and, third, the relative flexibility of the middle class in responding to the demands of the working classes.

The greater the autonomy of middle strata and the openness of the center toward them, as in England, Scandinavia, and, in its special way, the United States, the greater was the cooperation between them in the process of modernization, the less their tendency to take extreme ideological stances or become pessimistic about modernization.

In France, the relatively strong autonomous middle classes were, because of the French Revolution, split on accepting different aspects or processes of modernization. So, too, was the center. Thus there developed a continuous oscillation between modern, revolutionary orientations, on the one hand, and a strong concern with maintaining the social order in the face of more radical revolutionary tendencies, on the other.

In Germany the emerging middle strata were too weak to undertake the process of modernization on their own. This process was promoted under the aegis of a conservative and relatively closed center, which protected the middle classes from the emerging working class but at the same time minimized their autonomy. As a result, the major strata and political centers were characterized by great ambivalence toward the major aspects of modernization, accepting its technical and economic aspects, but either negating its social and political dimensions or remaining extremely ambivalent toward them.

The Emergence of a Distinctive Sociological Tradition

13.   Despite these common concerns and orientations, there appeared, hesitantly, some of the characteristics which would distinguish modern sociology from other intellectual traditions.

This distinctiveness was not attained merely by combining the various intellectual traditions in a "superscience." Indeed, the efforts of combining these traditions in a mechanical way, usually under the aegis of some scientific laws borrowed from other disciplines, had little long-term impact; they were not incorporated into sociological tradition, as it developed. Rather, the characteristics of sociology crystallized gradually in its early phases through the selection and distinctive transformation of several aspects of these varied intellectual traditions, focusing them on broad *Problemstellungen* and concrete problems derived from them, and coping with these problems with the methods of scientific scholarly criticism.

The most important characteristic of sociological analysis, as it emerged in the late eighteenth century, was the attempt to combine in scientific analysis the explanation of crucial aspects of modern societies with the general problems of social order and the developmental trends of societies. It attempted to do so by analyzing the seemingly most fragile, but perhaps most promising, type of social order—the modern social order—in order to discern the basic, general characteristics of social order, and the bases of such order, its cohesion, and its patterns of change.

But these developments were halting and intermittent; only gradually did sociology attain its distinctiveness. As was the case with other scientific disciplines, the attainment of such distinctiveness depended on some combination of intellectual and organizational or institutional processes. The ways in which this distinctiveness was attained greatly influenced the concrete shape of developments in sociology.

Notes

1. A. Comte, *Cours de Philosophie Positive* (Paris: A. Costes, 1908–1934), 6 vols.
2. For some general reviews of the development of early social thought see H. Becker and H. E. Barnes, *Social Thought from Lore to Science*, 3rd ed. (New York: Dover, 1961), 3 vols.; E. Shils, "The calling of sociology," in T. Parsons, E. Shils, K. D. Naegele, and J. R. Pitts (eds.), *Theories of Society* Vol. 2 (New York: Free Press, 1961), pp. 1405–1448; "Introduction—the development of social thought and institutions," by various authors, in E. R.A. Seligman and A. Johnson (eds.), *Encyclopedia of the Social Sciences* Vol. 1 (New York: Macmillan, 1930), pp. 3–228; F. Jonas, *Geschichte der Soziologie* (Hamburg: Rowohlt, 1968–1969), 4 vols.; Imogen Seger, *Introduction to Sociology: Theory, Methods, Practice* (London: Rupert Hart Davis, 1972).
3. Plato, *The Republic of Plato* (New York: Oxford University Press, 1953); Aristotle, *The Politics of Aristotle* (Oxford: Clarendon Press, 1952); St. Thomas Aquinas, *Summa Theologica,* English translation by the Fathers of the English Dominican Province (London: 1911–1922.
   For general analyses see E. Barker, *Greek Political Theory* (London: Methuen, 1960); G. H. Sabine,*A History of Political Theory* (London: George G. Harrap, 1949), Part 1 and Ch. 13; Confucius, *The Analects of Confucius* (New York: Paragon, 1968); Lao-Tse, *The Tao Tê Ching* (Taipei: Ch'eng-Wen, 1969); Tung Yu-Lan, *The Spirit of Chinese Philosophy* (London: Kegan Paul, 1947); P. A. Pardue, "Buddhism," in *International Encyclopedia of the Social Sciences* (New York: MacMillan, 1968), Vol. 2, pp. 165–184.
   For fuller texts and discussions see W. T. de Barry *et al.* (eds.) *Sources of Chinese Tradition* (New York: Columbia University Press, 1960); R. Tsunoda *et al.* (eds.), *Sources of Japanese Tradition* (New York: Columbia University Press, 1958); W. T. de Barry *et al.* (eds.), *Sources of Indian Tradition* (New York: Columbia University Press, 1958); J. Guttmann, "Maimonides Moses," in *The Encyclopedia of the Social Sciences, op. cit.,* Vol. 10, 1933, pp. 48–49; L. Strauss,*Philosophie und Gesetz: Beiträge zum Verständnis Maimunis und Seiner Vorläufer* (Berlin: Schocken Verlag, 1935); J. Guttmann, *Philosophies of Judaism,* (Garden City, N.Y.: Doubleday, 1966); R. McKeon, "Averroes," in *The Encyclopedia of the Social Sciences, op. cit.,* Vol. 2, 1930, p. 338.
4. See for example R. Levy, *A Mirror for Princes* (London: Cresset, 1951).
5. Thucydides,*History of the Peloponnesian War* (New York: Harper and Brothers, 1893).
6. Polybius, *The Histories* (Cambridge, Mass.: Harvard University Press, n.d.).
7. Ibn-Khaaldun, *The Muqaddimah* (London: Routledge & Kegan Paul, 1958). On Ibn-Khaaldun see also M. Mahdi,*Ibn Khaaldun's Philosophy of History* (Chicago: University of Chicago Press, 1957).
8. See note 3 of this chapter. For an attempt to relate the Greek traditions to modern sociological models see A. Gouldner, *The Coming Crisis of Western Sociology* (New York, London: Basic Books, 1970) especially Ch. 11; see also E. Shils "The calling of sociology," *op. cit.*
9. On the major characteristics of modernity in general and as it has emerged in Europe,

and on various controversies about its definition, see S. N. Eisenstadt, *Tradition, Change and Modernity* (New York: Wiley, 1973), especially Part 1.

10. This faith in human progress and in the power of science for furthering it was shared by some Forerunners of sociology, including Comte and Marx.

Comte's views are to be found in his works *The Positive Philosophy*, freely translated and condensed by H. Martineau (London: Trübner, 1853), 2 vols.; *Positive Polity*, translated by F. Harrison, E. S. Beesley and J. H. Bridges (London, 1875–77).

For a summary and interpretation of Comte's views see also R. Aron, *Main Currents in Sociological Thought* Vol. 1 (Gretna, La.: Pelican, 1968), pp. 63–109.

For the place of science in Marx's utopian classless society, see the interesting interpretation by A. Giddens, *Capitalism and Modern Social Theory: an Analysis of the Writings of Marx, Durkheim and Max Weber* (London: Cambridge University Press, 1971), pp. 62–64.

11. This theme is developed further in S. N. Eisenstadt, *Tradition, Change and Modernity, op. cit.*, Ch. 6.

12. For this see S. N. Eisenstadt, "Introduction," in S. N. Eisenstadt (ed.), *The Protestant Ethic and Modernization: a Comparative View* (New York: Basic Books, 1968).

13. The importance of these themes in the development of sociological thought has been stressed by many scholars; see for example the introduction in the *Encyclopedia of the Social Sciences* quoted in note 2, as well as R. Aron, *Main Currents in Sociological Thought, op. cit.;* D. Atkinson, *Orthodox Consensus and Radical Alternative* (London: Heinemann, 1971); E. Shils, "The calling of sociology," *op. cit.;* R. A. Nisbet, *The Sociological Tradition* (London: Heinemann, 1967); T. Parsons, "Unity and diversity in the modern intellectual disciplines; the role of the social sciences," *Daedalus*, Vol. 94 (1965), pp. 39–65; L. Coser, *Masters of Sociological Thought—Ideas in Historical and Social Context* (New York: Harcourt Brace Jovanovich, 1971); R. Collins and M. Makowski, *The Discovery of Society* (New York: Random House, 1972).

14. For this see R. Bendix, "Sociology and the distrust of reason," *American Sociological Review*, Vol. 35, No. 5 (1970), pp. 831–843.

15. For a review of the various intellectual traditions which dealt with these problems contributing to the emergence of sociology, see R. M. MacIver, "Sociology," in *The Encyclopedia of the Social Sciences, op. cit.*, 1934, Vol. 14, pp. 232–247; E. Shils, "The calling of sociology," *op. cit.*

16. For this see T. Hobbes, *Leviathan, or the Matter Form and Power of a Commonwealth, Ecclesiastical and Civil* (Oxford: Blackwell, 1956); J. J. Rousseau, *The Social Contract* (London: Sonnenschein, 1895); J. Locke, *Two Treatises of Government* (Cambridge: Cambridge University Press, 1960).

17. A. Ferguson, *An Essay on the History of Civil Society*, 8th ed. (Philadelphia: A. Finley, 1819); J. Millar, "The origins of the distinction of ranks," in W. C. Lehmann, *John Millar of Glasgow* (Cambridge: Cambridge University Press, 1960), pp. 165–322; A. Smith, *The Theory of Moral Sentiments* (London: G. Bell and Sons, 1892).

For a concise review of the many-sided contributions of the Scottish Moralists to sociological thought see also L. Schneider (ed.), *The Scottish Moralists on Human Nature and Society* (Chicago: University of Chicago Press, 1967); and especially G. Bryson, *Man and Society: The Scottish Inquiry of the 18th Century* (Princeton: Princeton University Press, 1945).

18. On the content and patterns of these conflicts as they developed in various European countries see S. N. Eisenstadt, *Modernization: Protest and Change* (Englewood Cliffs, N.J.: Prentice-Hall, 1966), especially Chs. 2, 3, 4.

19. For an exposition of most of the dilemmas discussed below, their formulation in various European intellectual traditions, and their influence on sociological thought, see R. A. Nisbet, *The Sociological Tradition, op. cit.;* S. Landshut, *Kritik der Soziologie* (München und Leipzig: Verlag von Duncker & Humblot, 1929); F. Jonas, *Geschichte der Soziologie, op. cit.;* G. Gurvitch, "Brève esquisse de l'histoire de la sociologie," in G. Gurvitch (ed.), *Traité de Sociologie* (Paris: Presses Universitaires de France, 1958), pp. 28–65.

20. On this see R. A. Nisbet, *The Sociological Tradition, op. cit.;* R. Bendix, "Sociology and the distrust of reason," *op. cit.;* I. Zeitlin, *Ideology and the Development of Sociological Theory,* (Englewood Cliffs N.J.: Prentice-Hall, 1968). See also A. Salomon, *In Praise of Enlightenment, Essays in the History of Ideas* (Cleveland and New York: World, 1963), especially Chs. 5, 6; A. Pizzorno, "Una Crisi Che Non Importa Superare," in P. Rossi (ed.), *Ricerca Sociologica e Ruolo del Sociologo* (Bologna: Il Mulino, 1972), pp. 327–357; R. Aron, *De la Condition Historique du Sociologue* (Paris: Gallimard, 1971); G. Gurvitch, "Brève esquisse de l'histoire de la sociologie," *op. cit.*

21. S. Landshut, *Kritik der Soziologie, op. cit.;* F. Jonas, *Geschichte der Soziologie, op. cit.,* especially Vols. 1, 2.

22. R. A. Nisbet, *The Sociological Tradition, op. cit.;* F. Jonas, *Geschichte der Soziologie, op. cit.,* especially Vols. 1, 2; For a general, still valuable, survey see also some of the introductory papers in the *Encyclopedia of the Social Sciences,* quoted in note 2.

23. On this see W. Ebenstein (ed.), *Man and the State: Modern Political Ideas* (New York: Rinehart, 1947), especially selections from Parts 1–3.

24. For this see R. A. Nisbet, "The French Revolution and the rise of sociology in France," in E. A. Tiryakian (ed.), *The Phenomenon of Sociology,* (New York: Appleton-Century-Crofts, 1971), pp. 27–36; S. Landshut, *Kritik der Soziologie, op. cit.;* W. Ebenstein (ed.), *Man and the State, op. cit.,* selections from Parts 1–3.

25. On this see, for example, Comte's and Spencer's evolutionary approaches, R. Fletcher, *The Making of Sociology: a Study of Sociological Theory,* Vol. 1 (London: Michael Joseph, 1971), pp. 165–196, 250–338. See also H. J. Laski, "The rise of liberalism," in *Encyclopedia of the Social Sciences, op. cit.,* 1930, Vol. 1, pp. 103–124; H. J. Laski, *The Rise of European Liberalism* (London: G. Allen & Unwin, 1936).

26. For this see T. B. Bottomore and M. Rubel (eds.), *Karl Marx: Selected Writings in Sociology and Social Philosophy* (Baltimore: Penguin, 1965) pp. 175–185, 236–245, 249–263; K. Marx and F. Engels, "The Communist Manifesto," in A. P. Mendel (ed.), *Essential Works of Marxism* (New York: Bantam, 1961), pp. 13–44. see also: M. Buber, *Paths in Utopia* (London: Routledge & Kegan Paul, 1949).

27. For these trends in political-philosophical thought see H. J. Laski, "The rise of liberalism," *op. cit.*

28. For this see the items cited in note 26.

29. J. L. Talmon, *The Origins of Totalitarian Democracy* (New York: W. W. Norton, 1970); M. Buber, *Paths in Utopia, op. cit.*

30. W. Ebenstein (ed.), *Man and the State: Modern Political Ideas, op. cit.,* Part 2

31. On the variety of modern social and especially socialist thought see A. Fried and R. Sanders (eds.), *Socialist Thought* (New York: Doubleday, 1964).

32. On this see G. H. Sabine, *A History of Political Theory, op. cit.,* especially Ch. 29; R. A. Nisbet, "The French Revolution and the rise of sociology in France," *op. cit.*

33. On this see T. B. Bottomore and M. Rubel (eds.), *Karl Marx: Selected Writings in Sociology and Social Philosophy, op. cit.,* pp. 175–185, 236–245, 249–263.

34. G. Vico, *Principe d'une Science Nouvelle Relative à la Nature Commune des Nations* (Paris: Nagel, 1953). See also: T. G. Bergin and M. H. Frisch (eds. and translators), *The New Science of Gambattista Vico* (Ithaca, N.Y.: Cornell University Press, 1958).

35. N. Machiavelli, *The Prince and the Discourses* (New York: Modern Library, 1950); for discussion see G. H. Sabine, *A History of Political Theory, op. cit.*, Ch. 17.

36. See the English translation, with an introduction by H. J. Laski of *A Defence of Liberty against Tyrants* (London, 1924).

37. T. Hobbes, *Leviathan, or the Matter Form and Power of a Commonwealth, Ecclesiastical and Civil, op. cit.*; J. Locke, *Two Treatises of Government, op. cit.*; J. J. Rousseau, *The Social Contract, op. cit.*

38. A. Ferguson, *An Essay on the History of Civil Society, op. cit.*; J. Millar, "The origins of the distinction of ranks," in W. C. Lehmann, *John Millar of Glasgow: His Life, Thought, and His Contributions to Sociological Analysis, op. cit.* For a relatively new concise presentation of the Scottish moralists see L. Schneider (ed.), *The Scottish Moralists on Human Nature and Society, op. cit.*

    For Montesquieu see C. Montesquieu, *The Spirit of the Laws* (New York: Hafner, 1949). On Montesquieu's contribution see E. Durkheim, *Montesquieu et Rousseau—Précurseurs de la Sociologie* (Paris: Marcel Riviere, 1953); R. Aron, *Main Currents in Sociological Thought*, Vol. 1, *op. cit.*, pp. 17–62.

39. For a concise review of statistical studies undertaken in European countries until the nineteenth century see B. Lécuyer and A. R. Oberschall, "Sociology: the early history of social research," in the *International Encyclopedia of the Social Sciences, op. cit.*, 1968, Vol. 15, pp. 36–53.

40. For a concise exposition of these early economic doctrines see H. Becker and H. Elmer Barnes, *Social Thought from Lore to Science, op. cit.*, Vol. 2, pp. 514–522; J. Schumpeter, *History of Economic Analysis* (London: Allen & Unwin, [1954], 1972), especially Ch. 4; E. F. Heckscher, *Mercantilism* (London: Allen & Unwin, 1955).

41. A. de Tocqueville, *Democracy in America*, (New York: Knopf, 1945), 2 vols.; A. de Tocqueville, *The Old Regime and the French Revolution* (Garden City, N.Y.: Doubleday, 1955); L. von Stein, *Staat und Gesellschaft* (Zurich: Rascher, 1934).

42. For best illustrations of their work see B. Niebuhr, *The History of Rome*, (Cambridge: J. Smith for J. Taylor, 1831–1832), 2 vols.; F. K. de Savigny, *Geschichte des Römischen Rechts im Mittelalter*, (Darmstadt: H. Gentner, 1956), 7 vols.; J. Michelet, *Histoire de France* (Paris: Chamerot, 1861–1866), 17 vols.

43. For this see B. Lécuyer and A. R. Oberschall, "Sociology: the early history of social research," *op. cit.*; P. F. Lazarsfeld, "Notes on the history of quantification in sociology: trends, sources and problems," *Isis*, Vol. 52, no. 2 (1961), pp. 277–333.

44. For the influence of the utilitarian tradition on Spencer's work see, for example, L. A. Coser, *Masters of Sociological Thought, op. cit.*, pp. 89–127; R. Collins and M. Makowski, *The Discovery of Society, op. cit.*, pp. 63–70.

    The classic exposition of utilitarian premises in early sociological thought is T. Parsons, *The Structure of Social Action* (New York: Macmillan, 1937, reprinted by Free Press, 1949). See also T. Parsons, "Unity and diversity in modern intellectual disciplines", *op. cit.*; F. Jonas, *Geschichte der Soziologie, op. cit.*

45. These philosophical traditions were especially influential in the development of German sociology; for this see K. Mannheim, *Essays on Sociology and Social Psychology* (London: Routledge & Kegan Paul, 1953), Ch. 6; A. Mitzman, *Sociology and Estrangement: Three Sociologists of Imperial Germany* (New York: Knopf, 1973), Parts 2 and 3; M.

Jay, *The Dialectical Imagination: a History of the Frankfurt School and the Institute of Social Research, 1923–1950* (Boston: Little, Brown, 1973), especially Ch. 2; T. Parsons, "Unity and diversity in modern intellectual disciplines," *op. cit.;* F. Jonas, *Geschichte der Soziologie, op. cit.,* especially Vols. 1, 4.

46. For the various reformistic and utopian movements see H. Becker and H. E. Barnes, *Social Thought from Lore to Science, Vol. 2, op. cit.,* Ch. 16.

   On St. Simon's influence on Comte see R. Collins and M. Makowski, *The Discovery of Society, op. cit.,* pp. 20–31.

   For the influence of various reformistic and utopian traditions on Marx's thought, and for his personal involvement in such movements, see L. A. Coser, *Masters of Sociological Thought, op. cit.,* pp. 43–87.

   On the tradition of social reform as related to the development of sociology in different countries, see P. Abrams, *The Origins of British Sociology: 1834–1914* (Chicago: University of Chicago Press, 1968), pp. 8–153; R. C. and G. J. Hinkle, *The Development of Modern Sociology: its Nature and Growth in the United States* (New York: Doubleday, 1954), Ch. 1; L. Bramson, "The Rise of American Sociology," in E. A. Tiryakian (ed.), *The Phenomenon of Sociology, op. cit.,* pp. 65–80; A. Oberschall, "The institutionalization of American sociology," in A. Oberschall (ed.), *The Establishment of Empirical Sociology: Studies in Continuity, Discontinuity and Institutionalization* (New York: Harper and Row, 1972), pp. 187–251; A. Oberschall, *Empirical Social Research in Germany, 1848–1914* (Paris, The Hague: Mouton 1965); T. N. Clark, *Prophets and Patrons: The French University and the Emergence of the Social Sciences* (Cambridge, Mass.: Harvard University Press, 1973), Ch. 3

47. These connections are illustrated and analyzed in many works; see for instance the items quoted in notes 44–46 and also R. Aron, *Main Currents in Sociological Thought* (Gretna, La.: Pelican, 1968, 1970), 2 vols.

48. For this and the following discussion see S. N. Eisenstadt, *Modernization: Protest and Change, op. cit.,* pp. 55–75.

2

The First Two Stages of Institutionalization:
The Forerunners and the Founding Fathers

Introduction: Stages of Development in Sociology

1. The areas of sociological research show a general, though gradual, trend of development from quite low levels of professional and/or academic institutionalization—or, to use Edward Shils' term, "density,"[1] in the nineteenth century and the first two decades of the twentieth, toward increasing institutionalization and density.

This trend is often described as having taken place in several stages, designated in somewhat different ways by different scholars. Shils' analysis, for example, implies a distinction between four stages: that of the forerunners (Comte, von Stein, Marx, Spencer); that of the "founding fathers" of modern sociology (Weber, Durkheim, Tönnies, G. Simmel); the period following, between the two World Wars; and that of the institutionalization of sociology, from World War II to the present.[2] On the whole, these stages are parallel to, though not identified with, those designated by Merton and Terry Clark. Merton has distinguished the stages of development of sociology in terms of the formation of intellectual disciplinary boundaries, designating the stage of differentiation from other disciplines, that of the institutional legitimacy of sociology, and that of reconsolidation with other disciplines.[3] Clark's distinctions are largely between different types of organization and the institutionalization of scientific work—between the solitary scientist, the amateur scientist, emerging academic science, established science, and "Big" Science.[4]

Although the components in each stage—the degree and type of institutionalization, the various aspects of intellectual analysis—did not always develop in parallel fashion, together, some broad common tendencies can be discerned, especially in such centers as France, England, Germany, and later the United States. These common characteristics were evident in the ways in which sociologists defined the intellectual distinctiveness of sociology—its subject matter and problems, related themselves to other intellectual traditions in the process of disciplinary differentiation and developed the various aspects of sociological analysis—the different types of sociological theories, the more concrete problems of analysis in social research, and the various traditions of empirical research.

The First Stage: The Forerunners

2. The first stage was characterized institutionally by the lack of a definited role for the sociologist, of an academic base or of recognition of the discipline. The forerunners were largely, to use Clark's terms,[5] solitary and amateur scholars or scientists who carried on their intellectual sociological activities with almost no institutional support. Most sociological activities were conducted at this stage by either a few great thinkers with national or international reputations, or by very narrow, local communities or would-be sociologists. These thinkers imparted, developed, and disseminated their ideas through small circles of disciples, organized informally, or at best in *ad hoc* scientific groups which dissolved after their central figures died.

Many activities which would become common to sociology were centered at this time in a few learned bodies or scholarly periodicals, and in informal groups of academics, public servants, and freelance intellectuals. The place of theee activities and groups, in the academic world or the general intellectual community, was insecure, unstable, and often marginal.

Rarely were those who saw themselves as "practicing" sociologists defined as such. Most arrived at "sociology" by diverse routes. Some were interested mainly in political economy, others in social administration, philosophy, ethnology, history of law or jurisprudence; and it was through these areas that their work touched on sociological problems. Thus at this stage of development, the intellectual and institutional links among various potential components of sociological analysis were weak and variable.

Macrosociological concerns were usually pursued within the framework of other academic disciplines, and only a few areas in practically oriented sociological research were academically accepted. Similarly, investigators concerned with the more practical or applied aspects of sociological research were rarely defined as sociologists within the political, philanthropic, socioreformist, or administrative settings in which they operated. Many intellectuals, scholars, or publicists—de Tocqueville, de Maistre, von Stein, and Marx—who provided the most powerful analyses of contemporary sociopolitical problems, centered their activities in political, journalistic, or freelance scholarly frameworks, seldom engaging in other potentially sociological endeavors; and seldom (with the partial exception of von Stein, Comte, and Spencer) did they identify themselves as sociologists.[6] Only later were some of them, notably de Tocqueville and Marx, incorporated into the sociological tradition.

The intellectual components of what was to become sociology were not only institutionally, but also intellectually dissociated at this stage, even if many of these ideas involved the analysis of the emerging industrial society. The central intellectual foci of sociological endeavor were either grand theories of social evolution, or, as in the case of von Stein and Marx in Germany, critical analyses of the emerging modern bourgeois order and industrial society.[7]

The broad theories of society were largely of two types. On the one hand, there were the grand schemes of Thomas Henry Buckle, Paul Lilienfeld, Albert Schäffle, E. de Roberty,[8] and others, which presented discussions of society as an organism or as subject to various forces, often culminating in rather shallow and complicated typologies of human society or in ambitious general deterministic laws enunciated by various geographical and biological schools.[9] Some of these works have left almost no mark on the development of sociology, although many contained ideas about the influence of social factors on behavior and cultural creativity which later were analyzed more systematically.

Side by side with these schemes developed the far more influential theories of Comte and Spencer,[10] and such anthropological theories as those of Engels, E. B. Taylor, Lewis H. Morgan, and J. J. Bachofen, which elaborated basic laws of development of human society.[11] These theories were based primarily on studies of comparative institutions and, though they are methodologically weak, they profoundly influenced the development of sociology, and delineated the intellectual contours of the new-discipline.

Various substantive areas and traditions of empirical research began to develop at this stage, notably through studies of social conditions and problems: poverty, delinquency and crime, or of ecology, folklore, and stratification. These tended to be dissociated from the broad concerns of the builders of the great analytical schemes. For a long period, most of these areas of research—social surveys, studies of patterns of consumption and mobility—touched only marginally on the emerging central problems of sociological analysis. They were based on somewhat different concerns. Some were derived from the utopian problem of organizing society, some from reformist or philanthropic interest in social problems, some from the growing needs of the emerging state and bureaucratic organizations for quantitative (census) data. They usually employed separate analytical concepts and nomenclatures, and most were isolated from broader analytical or theoretical considerations.[12]

Most of this type of research—even when based on broad classificatory schemes—consisted of the simple enumeration of various traits (see Chapter 4) or on the application of physical or biological models. Hence even those studies which seemed to be oriented to sociological analysis produced very few coherent middle-range theories. Although some of these schemes—such as those of Quetelet, who studied the regularities ("laws") in statistics of crime, birth, death, or of Le Play who, by careful analysis of the expenditures of workers in different countries, attempted to arrive at some general laws of social life[13]—had an important impact on sociology, this influence was largely on research technique and the tradition of empirical and statistical research of contemporary conditions, rather than on the application or development of the "laws" (such as Quetelet's laws of social physic[14]) which they proposed.

The most important middle-range hypotheses or theories developed in that period were by political analysts, thinkers like de Tocqueville, W. H. Riehl, and von Stein[15]; as we observed earlier, few conceived of themselves as sociologists or oriented themselves to general sociological theories. Only in the work of Marx were such middle-range analyses connected with a broad paradigmatic analysis of social life and order.[16] Studies of customs and institutions were also embedded in distinct traditions of descriptive historical or juridical research, but these were generally undertaken by those interested in comparative institutions.[17]

Those scholars who identified themselves as sociologists at this stage were often preoccupied with the attempt to differentiate the subject matter of sociology from other disciplines, especially philosophy and history, and to formulate its methodological bases, above all by applying some positivist "scientific method" to the analyses of social matters.[18] The most prominent of these scholars—Comte in particular—tried to portray sociology as a comprehensive "scientific," "secular" guide for behavior in the modern world, in other words, as a kind of secular religion of progress, reason, and humanity.[19]

At this stage, few institutional foundations of sociological work existed; thus, few continuous research programs were initiated or carried out. The most important contributions consisted rather in the attempts to define the scope, nature, and analytical uniqueness of sociology. Macrosocietal comparative, historical, evolutionary institutional theories emerged as the major focus of this intellectual identity and of theoretically relevant research.[20]

It was also in these areas of sociological analyses that several analytic concepts crucial to sociology developed, such concepts as "class," "civil society," "liberty," "authority."[21] They developed from the intellectual concerns of the Enlightenment and the ideological and political concerns attending the political and economic revolutions of the eighteenth and nineteenth centuries. Now they were transformed from normative or descriptive concepts into more analytical ideas which described or defined the major components of the social/institutional orders in general, and of modern society in particular.

It was also at this stage that some broader intellectual sociological orientations developed in different ways in different countries, depending on these countries' historical experiences of modernization and on the nature of the intellectual disciplines from which sociology dissociated itself.

German sociology, as illustrated by the works of von Stein and especially Marx, began to dissociate itself from philosophy but remained strongly influenced by it, especially by the Hegelian view of the dynamics and contradictions of the historical process.[22] This conception carried a strong critical and even revolutionary view of modern society. This criticism, fully articulated during the philosophical controversies about Hegelian philosophy, was strengthened by socialist political orientations of French origin, and in the case of Marx, by his confrontation of the assumptions of English political economy with the realities of the early stages of capitalism as he observed them in England.[23]

In France, sociology, as represented by Saint-Simon and, even more, by Comte and his contemporaries, was strongly influenced by the Enlightenment philosophy and by the political and social reforms of the French Revolution which attempted to realize its ideals.[24] Sociology owed to the Enlightenment its strong emphasis on positivism as well as its reformistic orientation, rooted in the belief that society could be reconstructed by scientific means.

At the same time it also evinced, especially in the works of Comte, a strong preoccupation with the problem of social stability, a preoccupation which, critical of the existing social order, was still, because of the manner in which the problem was stated and solved, conservative in its political implications.

This conservative orientation, probably influenced by the instability attending the revolutionary experiences of the French, was also reflected in the reformistic empirical research-oriented studies of the working classes conducted by the school of Le Play.[25] Some of these studies were also influenced by the moralistic orientations and comparative analysis of Montesquieu.

In England, early social thought and empirical research developed from several sources[26]: from the new science of economics developed by Adam Smith, from its philosophic-utilitarian extensions and later from Darwinism. They were also greatly influenced by the relatively peaceful, reformist social and political development of English society.

Spencer's evolutionism reflects the influence of Darwinism combined with a vision of development modelled after the peaceful transformations of English society. The utilitarian-individualistic assumptions of his sociology, and even its systemic conception of society, can be attributed to the influence of Smith's analysis of the division of labor.

On the other hand, the tradition of the empirical social survey had its roots in the intellectual and political reorientations which emerged from the confrontation of the utilitarian and liberal laissez-faire politics with the social realities of early industrialization. Basically interventionistic and reformistic in nature, these reorientations sought to alleviate and combat some of the undesirable effects of industrialization, and thus initiated and supported studies into the causes of these phenomena.

These broad orientations, which earlier sociologists shared with other intellectual groups in their societies, continued to be influential in later periods of development in sociology, in the choice of many research problems and in the analytical tools which were developed.

The Second Stage: the Founding Fathers and the Formation of Incipient Institutional and Intellectual Boundaries of Sociology

3.   The second stage—the stage of the Founding Fathers, of the struggles for academic recognition, of the first steps of academic entrenchment—was the most formative in the development of sociology. In terms of the young discipline's intellectual direction, this stage showed some continuity with the earlier one. It was dominated by a series of "schemes" or systems of sociology that attempted in a variety of ways to depict the true nature of society and identify the laws explaining the regularities of social life and the development of human society.

In Germany, the scholars who became involved in this work and dominated the field were Wilhelm Wundt, Moritz Lazarus, Ludwig Gumplowicz, Gustav Ratzenhofer, Weber, Tönnies, Werner Sombart, Simmel, and later on, Alfred Vierkandt. In France and French-speaking Belgium, major figures were Alfred Fouillé, Emile Solvay, Gabriel Tarde, René Worms, Gaston Richard, and above all Durkheim and Maurice Halbwachs. English scholars included Leonard Hobhouse and Edward Westermark. In Italy, Scipio Sighele, Pasquale Rossi, and above all Pareto and Mosca represented the emerging discipline. Spanning these two stages of the development was the towering figure of Marx. Though Marx did not define himself as a sociologist, his works constituted not only a basic contribution to the emerging sociological tradition but also posed an important challenge to many other scholars, particularly in Germany and Italy.[27]

The most distinctive feature of this stage, however, was not the mere multiplication of schemes but a crystallization (though halting and gradual) of forceful analytical theories which contrasted with the schematic classifications of the first stage. The most important of these theories were by Durkheim in France,[28] by Weber, Tönnies, and to a lesser degree Sombart and Franz Oppenheimer in Germany,[29] by Hobhouse and Westermarck in England,[30] and later, in a more peripheral way, by Pareto and Mosca in Italy.[31]

The second important aspect of the analytical developments of this stage was the attempt to integrate the various levels or aspects of sociological analysis. Thus, the various traditions of empirical study of social conditions and problems—poverty, delinquency, and crime; the analyses of concrete patterns of social organization, such as family and kinship, of ecology, of folklore and of stratification, began to be brought together. Though their orientation to broader sociological concepts and problems was still halting and partial, they were related more closely to the systematic analyses of problems of modern societies, such as those of bureaucracy, elites, class relations, or of the conditions of life in modern settings, and to concerns with political or social analysis and comparative study, such as the works of Mosca, Pareto, and Michels in Italy,[32] or of Maxim Kovalevsky and Nikolai Kareyev in Russia.[33] The same was true of several traditions of juridical and historical study: the work of Foustel de Coulanges in France[34]; the classical studies of Gilbert Murray and Jane Harrison as they were related to the anthropological studies in England[35]; the comparative analyses of Kareyev in Russia.[36]

Along with these developments in analytical-theoretical work scene, which will be analyzed in Chapter 4, the most distinctive characteristics of this stage were attempts to find firmer institutional bases, both academic and professional, for the pursuit of sociological work. Within each field of sociological analysis, there developed stronger internal nuclei and some degree of institutionalization—above all in slowly emerging quasicenters of research associated with reformist and administrative purposes, such as the London and Manchester Statistical Society and the Laboratory of Eugenics in England,[37] the *Verein fur Sozialpolitik* and Central Statistical Bureau in Germany,[38] the *Société d'Economie Sociale, Musée Social,* and statistical bureaus of the ministries in France.[39] Similarly, first attempts were made to institutionalize social research in some autonomous framework related to other parts of sociological endeavor and relatively free from administrative or philanthropic settings. Examples were the social research centers at Columbia and Chicago and the *Institut d'Ethnographie* in France, all established in the early 1920s,[40] as well as the group of Durkheim's collaborators at *L'Année Sociologique.*[41] The first national or seminational sociological associations, such as the *American Sociological Society* and the *Société de Sociologie de Paris,* were also established in this period, as was the first international sociological association, the *Institut International de Sociologie.* At this stage, too, the first stable and widespread sociological journals and collections began to be published—*American Journal of Sociology, Sociological Review, L'Année Sociologique, Archiv für Sozialwissenschaft und Sozialpolitik.*

Despite these efforts, which were crucial to the development of different patterns of institutionalization in different countries, overall institutionalization remained at low levels and academic bases were particularly weak, though beginnings in these directions had taken place in most major, and some minor, centers of sociological discourse. The effect of these beginnings of institutionalization and unification of components of sociological work became evident, if only momentarily, in the work of several Founding Fathers—such as Durkheim's study of suicide[42] and Weber's unique combination of historical studies, studies of social conditions, and broader comparative and typological studies—in which the various "partial" fields were closely linked to the central concerns of sociology.[43] Although there were similar tendencies in England at the beginning of the century, they did not crystallize to the same degree in the work of any individual or group.[44]

Throughout this stage, several important shifts in the foci of discussion took place. The problems of the intellectual identity of sociology were conceived more in terms of academization, and of broad critical orientations to modern society, less in terms of direct political and ideological involvement. The growing preoccupation with academic establishment gave rise to disputes about the definition of sociology and its subject matter as distinct from other, more established, academic disciplines; to philosophical controversies about the presuppositions of sociology, its philosophical bases, the philosophical bases of its methodology, the possibility of a sociological method, and its relationship to various scientific approaches; and to fierce debates about whether sociology was a humanistic or a natural science. It was in this period that H. Poincaré voiced his famous dictum that "sociology speaks more about the proper method than about its results."[45]

The most important disputes were those which developed after the breakdowns of the first great attempts in sociological synthesis—the evolutionary, positivist, Marxist, and to some degree the "culturalist" schemes.[46] Later, these disputes recurred following the high level of politization of scholarly life in the 1920s and 1930s in Germany.[47] The major discussions were those of the famous *Methodenstreit* and around the relationship between values and scientific sociological analysis; in both, Weber played a central role.[48] Other serious polemics in the various sociological communities dealt with the very possibility of sociology as an autonomous discipline. This was, indeed, one of Durkheim's major preoccupations, as he attempted to define the specific characteristics of the "social fact" *(fait social),* as distinct from natural or psychological facts.[49]

The Development of Sociology in Different Countries

4.   In all these aspects of institutional development, important differences existed among major countries. They emerged above all with respect to the major intellectual and role orientations of sociologists; the intellectual cohesiveness of the sociological communities; the degree and type of the institutionalization of sociological work; and the major types of disputes.

Germany.   Germany was characterized by the development of strong, distinct intellectual orientations, strong intellectual cohesiveness among sociologists, and important nuclei of a broad sociological community that nevertheless was weakly institutionalized and had a poor academic base. This development was also marked by a dissociation between the different aspects of sociological work.

German sociology evinced a distinct intellectual orientation with strong philosophical-evaluative elements, not unlike those found in the works of the forerunners. At the same time, it lacked their optimism and faith in the possibility of social progress and the role of sociology in furthering it.[50]

Analytically, the major preoccupation was with the contrast between modern and traditional societies in general, and the development and problems of capitalism and civil society in particular. On the whole it was marked by a strong tendency, not unrelated to the political tenor of German intellectuals, to emphasize the destructive forces of modern society—the weakening of social bonds and the impoverishment and alienation of personality as a result of industrialization and capitalism. In the work of Tönnies and Sombart, this criticism was also combined with a denial of the possibility of regeneration of capitalist society even by socialism, and with a neo-Romantic view of the traditional past.[51]

German sociology also evinced a strong historical perspective, a critical reanalysis and reassessment of the Marxist model, and a preoccupation with theoretical problems in the light of the legacy inherited from the German philosophers.[52]

At the same time important elements of a sociological community began to develop. One basis for this lay in the field of publications. Notable among the new efforts was the *Gesellschaft* series edited by Martin Buber. It consisted of short monographs on a variety of broad sociological topics, including, among others, Sombart's book on the proletariat, Tönnies' on custom, Fritz Mautner's on language, Simmel's on religion, Franz Oppenheimer's on the state, and Gustav Landauer's on revolution.[53] These series, among others, also featured monographs on more concrete topics, such as the large department store, the newspaper, sports, and the stockmarket.[54] The latter were empirically oriented, though they placed much less emphasis on direct observation than the later monographs on similar topics by the Chicago school. Later, a more concentrated publication venture was made with the *Grundiss der Sozialekonomik,* which focused on the analysis of the broad trends of contemporary capitalist society; here, Weber's *Wirtschaft und Gesellschaft* was published posthumously. Perhaps most important was the *Archiv fur Sozialwissenschaft und Sozialpolitik,* established in 1904 and edited initially by Weber and Sombart, which became a central organ for the publication of social and historical studies.

Most of these publications were not specifically sociological in any strict sense, and the very variety of topics attested to the vague definition and weak institutional bases of sociology. Yet despite these weaknesses, some signs of an emergent sociological community, with its mutual influences, were evident in the intellectual works of this period. Thus Michels' analysis of political parties, especially his contrast between the structural positions and orientations of the leaders and those of rank-and-file members, reflects, in addition to the influence of Marx, that of his older contemporary, Weber.[55] Sombart's analysis of modern and traditional societies in *Der Moderne Kapitalismus* and in *Das Proletariat* is based on some of Tönnies' theoretical concepts and assumptions, while his analysis of the origin of the spirit of capitalism in *Der Bourgeois* is explicitly oriented to Weber's thesis in *The Protestant Ethic.*[56]

At the same time, sociology suffered a relative lack of academic recognition. Although some of the great figures—Weber, Simmel, Sombart, and Tönnies—held academic positions, they were not professors of sociology. Others, like Michels, were, for political reasons, completely excluded from the academic world.[57] This situation created a dissociation between teaching and creative theoretical work; this dissociation was paralleled by that between empirical research and the theoretical paradigms developed by sociologists.

The institutional bases for continuous sociological research were weak, for the discipline, still entangled in struggles for legitimation, could not find support for research within the universities. Partial support was given by the *Verein fur Sozialpolitik,* a research institute directed by professors and administrators, which conducted empirical research on contemporary social problems with a strong social reform orientation. However, this Institute, in which Weber and Sombart were active from time to time, had goals that did not coincide with the intellectual interests of the sociologists. It could not serve, in the long run, as a source of research funds that would support a permanent program of sociological research.

Many empirical studies of modern social life were conducted during this period, but not by people who called themselves sociologists or who were perceived as such by others. These studies were of working conditions, mobility, and political attitudes of the lower classes; the outcomes of elections; the transmission of elite status; or higher education (such as rates of students' enrollment, social background, and academic preferences). They were carried out by diverse bodies and persons, some with academic training. But most of this research was dissociated from theoretical sociological orientations. Differing in aims and interests, it could not contribute to the institutionalization of a unified tradition of sociological research.[58]

Weber tried to find an institutional base for empirical research within the framework of the German Sociological Society and through the support and cooperation of its members, but he failed. This failure can be attributed in part to the main intellectual interest of German sociology, an intellectual heritage or orientation to history and philosophy, which resulted in reluctance to legitimate research, in a divorce between such research and the theoretical paradigms, and in a narrow range of empirical research undertaken by sociologists.[59]

Such dissociation between empirical research and broader theoretical considerations could also be found to some degree in the work of the major figures. Thus, while some of Weber's early empirical studies, especially those on the stock exchange market and on the agricultural situation in East Prussia, can be seen as connected to his later theoretical concern in the studies of religion,[60] his study of factors determining workers' productivity, conducted for the *Verein fur Sozialpolitik*, is less directly related to theoretical problems.[61]

Similarly, Tönnies' studies of the determinants of crime and suicide, and of working-class conditions, were not explicitly deduced from, or related to, his main theoretical work.[62]

Debates about the proper definition and scope of sociology preoccupied Sombart, Weber, Tönnies, Simmel and many others,[63] as did preoccupation with the distinction between models of explanation in the social and natural sciences, around which there developed the famous *Methodenstreit*.[64] This controversy was rooted in Dilthey's distinction between the natural and social sciences.[65] According to his distinction, the natural sciences *explain* phenomena by abstracting regularities from raw data; the social and cultural sciences, by contrast, interpret, understand *(verstehen)* phenomena in a direct, immediate manner. Understanding in this sense is always subjective, since it is based on the ability of the individual social scientist "to experience" or "live into" the phenomena he investigates. Thus Dilthey's formulation did not accept the positivist claim of the possibility of an objective social science.

The controversy over this problem became salient as sociology in Germany attempted to gain legitimacy as an autonomous science, and the issue continued to preoccupy German sociologists until well after World War II.[66]

Parallel to this controversy, and also related to the attempt of sociology to legitimate itself as an autonomous intellectual and scholarly discipline, was the concern about the possibility of a value-free approach to scholarship on social problems. The relationship between the political and philosophical values of the sociologist as a person, and his values and activities as a scientist, were analyzed in Weber's famous essays "The objectivity of socioscientific and sociopolitical knowledge," written in 1904,[67] and "Science as a vocation," originally given as a speech at the University of Munich in 1918.[68] In these he argued fiercely those German scholars who saw scientific knowledge as a tool of ideological commitment and political action. Defending the separation of personal and scientific values, Weber argued that the main objective of science was the attainment of universal truths, not the formulation of value judgments about political and social phenomena, since the latter belong to the realm of values, which are always relative. At the same time he recognized that the scientist can be motivated, in his choice of problems and even his analytical tools, by the commitment to some values. Thus he emphasized the tension between this commitment on the one hand and scientific truth on the other as one of the major predicaments of modern science, and of social science in particular.

France.   In France, too, sociology displayed some degree of common intellectual orientation in this period. But it had far less intellectual cohesiveness; nor was there a broad sociological community, though there developed around Durkheim a rather strong academic nucleus.

The major intellectual orientations of sociologists in France continued to be closely related to positivism and to the traditions of social reform. Thus the work of LePlay displays the earlier stance of strong reformistic orientation combined with a conservative critical stand toward modern French society.[69]

Durkheim's major works, too, were critical in their analysis of modern society and of France in particular,[70] but Durkheim's critical orientation differed both from that of his compatriots and from that of his colleagues in Germany. While sharing with them, especially with Tönnies, similar analyses of modern versus traditional society and the critique of the effects of modernity,[71] Durkheim remained committed to the modern social order and to that of France in particular.[72] Unlike many German sociologists, he was not alienated from modern society; nor did he extol—as did the school of LePlay, the traditional mode of life in romantic or utopian terms.

In France, as in Germany, sociology lacked institutional academic recognition until World War I. In spite of this basic similarity, however, there were important differences. Some groups of social scientists associated with the emergence of French sociology may have been at the fringe of the academic system or completely outside it; these include the LePlayists, the physical anthropologists, and the group around Worms. Others, however, like Tarde, taught sociology, though they did not hold the position of professor of sociology.[73] And Durkheim did succeed in attaining a semiacademic legitimacy for the discipline which stood in sharp contrast to the situation that prevailed in Germany.[74] His success in establishing an academic base for sociology was due, no doubt, not only to his powerful intellect and entrepreneurial ability, but also to a sociopolitical climate—the crisis of the Third Republic and the Dreyfus affair—that was receptive to his attempts to integrate general sociological analysis with pressing moral and social concerns. Some of the subjects he taught at the Sorbonne, as for instance *Morale et Sociologie,* were recognized as topics for dissertations in philosophy, and the chair of education he occupied at the

Sorbonne from 1902 on was renamed the chair of education and sociology in 1913.

These institutional successes, though significant in themselves, were only partial. Sociology, dispite Durkheim's great academic influence as a *patron universitaire*, did not attain full-fledged academic status. No formal degrees were given in sociology, and no formal academic careers were open to aspiring sociologists as sociologists. The full implications of this structural weakness were to become evident only after Durkheim's death. During his lifetime, thanks at least in part to his influence in the academic world, his younger collaborators succeeded in attaining promising academic positions, though not as sociologists, and formed a strong sectarian nucleus.

In France, as in Germany, there was an institutional split between empirical research and teaching, as well as a rather low degree of institutionalization of research activities themselves, though the beginnings of such institutionalization appeared. These tendencies were evident both in groups of social scientists outside the academic system and among Durkheim's associates. A remarkable amount of empirical research was being conducted by the statisticians in the official bureaus of the ministeries, but it was not, at least at first, connected with teaching. In such teaching institutes as the *Collège Libre des Sciences Sociales*, research activities were nonexistent. A much closer association between teaching and research developed among the followers of LePlay, but this was effected on the personal rather than the institutional level, since this tradition was transmitted mainly by means of private lectures. Only the empirical studies conducted by the followers of LePlay had a firmer institutional basis in the institute of the *Société d'Economie Sociale*, and to some extent in the philanthropically supported *Musée Social*.

This pattern, interestingly enough, also characterized the work of Durkheim and his collaborators at *L'Année Sociologique*. As has been noted, this group performed the traditional functions of a research institute, but it did so outside the university framework, and it lacked even the organizational and material resources of the LePlayists.

Durkheim's group, in contrast to Durkheim himself, also tended to dissociate theoretically oriented developments and empirical quantitative data. Although Durkheim and some of his collaborators, including François Simiand and Maurice Halbwachs, did integrate empirical data into their theoretical works, this tendency on the whole was peripheral to their main work.[75] Nevertheless the Durkheim group did attain a much stronger integration of comparative and institutional studies, using largely secondary ethnographic, anthropoligical, and historical data.[76]

Thus in France, as distinct from Germany, there developed a fairly cohesive institutional nucleus, that of Durkheim and his group, with the beginning of a foothold in academic life. However, the sectarian relationship between these and other groups of sociologists inhibited the development of a broader sociological community.

The same pattern holds for the institutionalization of other professional activities. The tradition of professional publication began in this period. Besides Durkheim's *L'Année Sociologique,* there appeared *La Science Sociale,* the publishing organ of the LePlayist school; the *Revue Internationale de Sociology,* the organ of the first international sociological association; and the series of the *Bibliothèque des Sciences Sociales.* These latter two publications appeared under the initiative of Worms. Because of personal rivalries and the differing academic status of the several clusters of French social scientists, especially along the line of "ins" and "outs" at the university, each cluster developed strong sectarian tendencies in its publishing organ, a fact which hindered the exchange of ideas and the synthesis of viewpoints. Durkheim and his associates also boycotted the International Sociological Association, founded by Worms, and the *Société de Sociologie de Paris* which had been established through Worms' initiative.[77]

At the same time, the strong tradition of political journalism and debate in France was not integrated into the sociological tradition, although all sociologists participated in the wider circles of French intellectuals and in their debates, some, like Durkheim and Gustave Le Bon, very intensively.

Closely related to the institutional position and intellectual orientation of sociology was the development among most French sociologists of a strong leaning to the academic-scholarly role, with a marked classicist emphasis and some critical-intellectual orientation, but only a minimal orientation to the practical or professional aspects of this role. A strong preoccupation with the definition of the subject matter and boundaries of sociology also emerged in this period; it was prominent especially in Durkheim's debates with Tarde and Worms on the relationship of sociology to the other social sciences.[78]

Yet French sociologists at this stage were less concerned with the content and self-image of the sociologist's role than the Germans. Thus, where Weber showed a direct and explicit concern with the potential conflict in this role—conflict related to the presumed contradictory orientations rooted in personal and scientific values, such concern was less central, though not entirely absent, for Durkheim, as some of the problems in *Les Règles* attest.[79]

England.   In England, sociologists developed a relatively homogeneous outlook, but little intellectual cohesiveness. Development of a sociological community, and the institutionalization of sociological activities, were weak.

The homogeneous outlook of English sociologists or would-be sociologists was rooted in the fact that the impetus to the emergence of sociology in Britain was related to the crisis in the prevailing philosophical and intellectual traditions during most of the nineteenth century. That crisis lay in the confrontation between the basic assumptions of the young discipline of political economy, as expressed in utilitarianism and *laisser-faire* politics, and the social realities of industrialization—poverty, crime, and social conflict, which created the demand for a better explanation of the functioning of society. The new social realities made dubious some basic assumptions of the utilitarian intellectual tradition, such as the unproblematic and harmonious nature of the social order, and the basic compatability between individual self-interest and social well-being. At the same time, the types of social research related to these traditions (e.g., social statistics), which were basically informative and not explanatory, became inadequate as a tool for solving social problems.

The first British institutional nucleus of sociology, the London Sociological Society, established in 1903, and its publication, the *Sociological Review,* were the first attempts at organization by those who identified themselves with sociology and hoped it would respond to the intellectual and social crises of the time. The preoccupations of the Society, whose central figures were Patrick Geddes and Leonard Hobhouse, reflected the basic orientations of sociology at that time.

The publications and activities of this group show that sociology, dispite its dissociation from the positivist-utilitarian tradition, continued to exhibit a relatively positive evaluation of modern society; this is apparent in the tradition of social surveys represented by Geddes and in Hobhouse's theoretical works, including *Social Development.*[80] Sociologists of this period maintained that modern society contained incipient elements of progress toward a social order in which reason, cooperation, and individual freedom and self-fulfillment would be realized, although, unlike the earlier utilitarians, they did not assume that this progress would be the automatic consequence of the interplay of individual self-interest.

Although these orientations were attuned to the prevailing ideological and intellectual mood in Britain, this fact did not help to institutionalize sociology.

Its development was probably blocked as suggested by Shils[81] and others, by the disinclination of British elite circles to subject British society itself to a critical examination.

The difficulties in institutionalization were reinforced by several tendencies in British academic life, and by developments within the sociological community itself.

Early sociology in Britain encountered problems of legitimation in the institutionalized academic world, although it was to some degree accepted as a part of a broad intellectual discourse. This pattern of institutionalization was closely related to the controversies about the intellectual boundaries of sociology in relation to other disciplines. Hobhouse and Geddes, Charles Booth and B. Seebohm Rowntree, the fathers of the social survey, and Francis Galton, the leader of the eugenic school, all held rather similar views about the task of sociology. But they disagreed about the focus, scope, and application of sociological laws, and these views in turn affected their conception of the sociologist's role. Here the differing views of Hobhouse and Geddes became paradigms for the further development of British sociology. Geddes' view stressed the commitment to solving immediate social problems; for Hobhouse, the central task of the sociologist was to develop analytical tools for the general understanding of human society and the course of its development.

This division among sociologists heightened the reluctance of the older universities to accept a newcomer whose scientific identity was controversial and undefined even to its most ardent supporters. Another factor was sociology's rivalry with the closely related but better established discipline of anthropology.[82] Thus, by the end of World War II only one chair of sociology proper had been created in Britain. This chair, established in 1902 at the London School of Economics,[83] was occupied jointly by Hobhouse and Westermarck from 1907 until the late 1920s, and by Morris Ginsberg after that.

The beginning of academic institutionalization sharpened the divisions among types of sociological activities which had been apparent in the Sociological Society controversies.

Hobhouse's intellectual concerns, rooted in Spencer and Comte, focused on the evolution of human society and its ethical implications. His emphasis on these problems created a situation in which the institutional kernel of academic sociology for which he had become responsible was dissociated from empirical research; his teaching and scholarly work at the London School of Economics were based on historical and anthropological data. So, too, with the exception of his field work in Morocco, Westermarck's studies and teaching on the development of the institutions of marriage and of morals were not empirically oriented.[84]

The attempts to integrate sociological analysis with comparative ethnographic or historical data were more successful, as the works of Hobhouse, Ginsberg, and Gerald C. Wheeler show.[85] They did not, however, attain the momentum that developed around Durkheim —largely because anthropological scholarship, as epitomized in the work of Tylor, Frazer, and R. R. Marett,[86] was more autonomous and better established than sociology. Thus, while sociologists, anthropologists, and anthropologically oriented historians shared many intellectual concerns, these did not produce coherent, sustained research programs in sociology. Some of the nuclei of such research programs were taken up in academic life by geography, a discipline promoted by Halford Mackinder at Oxford,[87] which also "usurped" the potential place of sociology in these intellectual areas.

Empirical research was conducted, as in France and Germany, and for partly similar reasons, outside of academic sociology, or was dissociated from its specific theoretical concerns. It also had weak institutional basis.[88] In the Laboratory of Eugenics at the London School of Economics, the effects of heredity on ability and social success were studied; but these studies were divorced from the concerns of sociologists of the School. Only later did they awaken sociological interest in the theory and research of social stratification. Philanthropically oriented studies of the social conditions of the poor were undertaken by the Statistical Societies of Liverpool and London from the nineteenth century on; these programs showed some institutional continuity, at least until the late 1920s, when S. T. Simey took over the Department at Liverpool, but were removed from the concerns of academic sociology.

The many influential social surveys of this period were also divorced from analytic sociological interests. Amelioristic in orientation, and privately sponsored by philanthropists, they marked an important departure from the methods of social statistics of the nineteenth century, since they aimed not only to provide data on the conditions of the poor but also to account for the structural causes of poverty. This tradition, however, best exemplified in the works of Booth and Rowntree, differed from academic sociology not only substantively but in its weak theoretical base. This is even more true for the later social surveys conducted and sponsored by Geddes. Initially intended to overcome the theoretical weakness of the earlier surveys by applying and developing Le Play's approach theoretically and methodologically, they deteriorated into mere data-gathering because of lack of manpower and interest in accomplishing Geddes's intentions.

Interestingly, the strong tradition of policy-oriented social statistical analyses and surveys which the Fabian society, above all, Sidney and Beatrice Webb,[89] sponsored was not integrated into the sociological tradition either, despite the fact that the Webbs were among the founders of the London School of Economics. Indeed, this tradition was more fully entrenched in the Departments of Social Administration (Social Work), which were administratively and intellectually distinct from sociology.

The United States.   Sociology in the United States took a different path from European sociology, and some of its characteristics could already be discerned in the early stages of development. Here, too, there was a strong dissociation between theory and research. Unlike the situation in most European countries, however, this disjunction was accompanied by a high degree of institutionalization of sociology in academic settings, which later on in turn created an impetus toward combining research and theory.

In the first phase of development, leaders in American sociology were scholars like Ward, E. A. Ross, Giddings, Sumner, and Cooley, all of whom were influenced by the European tradition of social thought. All developed theoretical schemes of social processes, and of the functioning and change of societies as wholes.[90] Although most of the first American sociologists had strong reformist orientations, their schemes were unrelated to the empirical studies that were conducted in this period to help in the solution of contemporary social problems.

The strong reformistic orientation of the first American sociologists stemmed from their religious concern with human welfare and their rural or small-town backgrounds both of which predisposed them to criticize the social problems created by industrialization and urbanization.[91] Their criticism, however, was not alienative, socialist, or Marxist, and it reflected, as in France and above all in England, a basic acceptance of the existing social order.

Seen from the perspective of the prevailing ideological and political orientations of the time, Social Darwinism and *laisser-faire,* their criticism can be termed liberal-radical. With the exception of Sumner, who was an ardent supporter of *laisser-faire* politics, they endorsed a controlled capitalism, favoring state intervention in the regulation of conflict between workers and capitalists, the right of workers to unionize, and a more equal distribution of wealth. The most radical of these sociologists, Ross, was fired near the beginning of his academic career by the trustees of Stanford University because of his political views. But because most universities competed for personnel and did not universally endorse the dominant *laisser-faire* doctrine, he did not encounter difficulty in obtaining other academic appointments.

This orientation, characteristic of most prominent figures of the period—Ward, Ross, Albion W. Small, and Giddings, was reflected in both their personal ties with reformist movements and their works, which are, on the whole, characterized by faith in progress and a conviction that sociology should provide the tools for understanding social processes as well as the means for overcoming social obstacles to progress by intelligent human intervention.

Although these broad intellectual orientations did not differ greatly from those prevalent in some European countries, above all in England, they were accompanied by a very strong institutionalization of sociological activities in general and in universities in particular, as well as by the development of a widespread sociological community.

In this respect, American sociology far surpassed Europe. While in Europe, chairs or departments of sociology were scarce as late as World War II, sociology courses were taught in some 400 institutions in the United States by the end of the first decade of the twentieth century. There were 50 full-time professors of sociology active in about 72 academic departments, some of these autonomous departments of sociology, others joint departments of sociology and other social sciences.[92]

Several factors seemed to have been responsible for this success.[93] One was the strong association, nonexistent or weak in Europe, between would-be American sociologists and the various religious and secular reformist movements whose goals were to fight the social ills produced by rapid industrialization and urbanization. Social reformers, some of these influential members of the middle and upper classes, were willing to provide material resources for social research and to influence or pressure university boards of trustees to establish the new discipline, in return for the "scientific" legitimation they hoped to obtain for their reformist activities.

Closely related to this aspect was the structure of American universities, which also differed from the European system. In Europe, universities were centrally controlled by ministries of education, or were internally dominated by the professors of the established disciplines. Both of these, for different reasons, could, and for a long time did, resist sociology's claims to academic legitimation. In the United States, however, decisions about such academic innovations as the opening of new departments, or the establishment of new chairs, were in the hands of laymen—the university and college boards of trustees. Their decisions depended largely on successful pressures, and these, for the above-mentioned reasons, could be mobilized by sociologists.

The last factor contributing to the more successful institutionalization of sociology in the United States was the rapid expansion of higher education in this period. This expansion, accompanied by extremely strong competition among universities, not only eased the process of differentiation between disciplines, such as economics and political science, accelerating their autonomous academic consolidation but made institutions of higher learning more receptive to academic innovations. Both factors helped in the institutionalization of sociology.

Moreover, the pattern of institutionalization of sociology in American universities differed greatly from that of most European countries. Because of its strong organizational and intellectual ties with the reform movements,[94] sociology from the start was oriented to empirical research based on direct and first hand observations.[95]

In the majority of institutions where chairs of sociology existed, including Chicago and Columbia, the future centers of American sociology, teaching activity centered on courses that trained students for vocational social work and on empirical research, sponsored generously by charity organizations and social reformers. Most of this research was considered a tool for social action and change, as were also the studies conducted outside the universities by reform movements and organizations. The studies covered a variety of problems, such as the conditions of the poor in cities, and the adaptation of immigrants to the urban environment and to American culture.

Thus in the United States, unlike Europe, empirical research was closely associated with the academic setting. This factor probably contributed to strengthening the tradition of empirical research in American sociology in comparison to Europe, where such research of this kind, although intensive, was generally conducted outside the universities.

Yet despite the early institutional association of empirical research with the universities, one encounters here, as in Europe, a lack of mutual orientation between research and theory. Most of the studies, following the pattern of Booth's community surveys, lacked theoretical foundation. This was due to the difficulty of transforming the analytic concepts of the broad theoretical schemes into working hypotheses, and probably to the inadequacy of research tools themselves.[96]

Another factor was institutional and geographic in nature. The geographic location of Columbia and Chicago in areas where social problems were concentrated may have spurred these future centers of sociology to engage intensively in empirical research. Other universities in which most of sociology's Founding Fathers worked, however, were far from such areas; and this remoteness may have created a cognitive "blindness" to the need for providing operative explanations to concrete contemporary social problems.

The remarkable and early academic acceptance of American sociology entailed several problems which were reflected in the discussions of that period. One was the preoccupation, encountered also in Europe, with the intellectual boundaries of sociology and its points of differentiation from other social sciences,[97] a preoccupation itself indicative of the still vulnerable and unsettled academic position of sociology, and of the aspirations of the first sociologists to clarify the scientific uncertainties of their discipline in order to consolidate its academic legitimation. The controversies about the content and orientation of the sociologist's role, which continued and even sharpened after World War I, reflected the same uncertainties and aspirations, as well as a peculiar paradox: the strong reformist orientation of early sociology, while accelerating its institutional acceptance in the academic world, had also bestowed upon it an "unscientific image" which made problematic its full academic legitimation. It was this paradox which heightened the awareness of potential conflict in the sociologist's role. This awareness would persist in the future and actually push to a solution that would in turn become the focus of new controversies—namely, the choice of a "value-free" sociological orientation.

These intellectual and institutional processes thus produced a strong academic orientation in American sociology, but one that was strongly connected with reform orientations and concerns about the practical and professional problems of sociologists. These orientations were even more fully crystallized in the period after World War I.

5.   Despite different patterns of development in sociology in each country, some major features of this stage were shared by all of them: the search for intellectual boundaries and an institutional foundation, the first attempts at combining the various components of sociological activity. The more exciting developments of this stage took place in only some countries which were "first-comers" in the development of sociology —England, France, Germany, and, to a much smaller extent, Russia.[98] They did not characterize "late-comers" to the same degree—Italy or Spain,[99] for example, or the more provincial parts of France and Germany. Rather, the late-comers' first attempts at intellectual crystallization of sociology, except for the efforts of such figures as Mosca or Pareto, resulted in more rigid classifications, methodological and general historiosophical discourses, or "primitive" or specialized (that is, demographic) types of research which often resembled the first stage of institutionalization in more advanced countries. Yet even in the stronger sociological centers, this second-stage was not a continuous evolution, though it laid the foundation of such a development.

The Nuclei of an International Sociological Community

6.   The more exciting, formative aspects of the second stage of sociological development took place in different countries, and it is remarkable how many parallel developments did occur in the major centers, despite great differences in the details. Although these parallel developments did not produce a viable international sociological community, some attempts at the crystallization of such a community were made as early as 1893, when, through Worms' initiative, the *Institut International de Sociologie* was formed in France.[100] This group, composed of social scientists from different fields, began publication of the *Revue Internationale de Sociologie*. Members of the *Institut* and contributers to the *Revue* belonged to the most important centers of Europe and the United States, giving the organization and publication a truly international character.

Under the sponsorship of the *Institut,* the first International Congress of Sociology was held in Paris in 1894. Additional meetings were held in other European cities, establishing a tradition that continued until 1940 and the interruption of World War II, and was renewed in 1948. Worms also initiated the *Bibliothèque des Sciences Sociales,* a series of sociological publications which included collections of essays or translated works of various social scientists, including Tarde, Gumplowicz, Ward, and Michels.

The programs of the *Institut* and the *Revue* reflected the aspiration to establish a viable international sociological community more than they showed substantive accomplishments. There was little evidence of an intellectual community in these activities; above all there were few confrontations between sustained research programs and various theoretical orientations. For the most part, the congresses attracted those sociologists who were least committed to such research programs. Nor were scholars who participated in this work professional sociologists. They came largely from other disciplines, and the conception of sociology reflected in the discussions still involved large schemes of social evolution, general "laws," and broad philosophical considerations of its nature. Concrete research that was presented rested on diverse traditions, sharing no common analytic concerns.

It is significant that those contemporary sociologists who would become most influential in the further development of sociology were largely unknown to each other and beyond their own countries. In most cases they did not participate in these common debates, and there was little intellectual intercourse—sometimes little mutual awareness—among them.

Durkheim, for example, was not well known to his British and American contemporaries, and remained obscure long after his death, though he was somewhat better known in Germany.[101] Weber hardly enjoyed a better fate; in his lifetime, and even afterwards, he was virtually unknown to other European (i.e., non-German) and to American sociologists. Tönnies and Simmel fared better, but this was due to personal rather than institutional channels: both were introduced to France through Durkheim's *L'Année Sociologique*. Yet it was Durkheim himself who was responsible for the halt in the publication of their works.[102] Whatever the details of mutual awareness among the major figures of sociology at this stage, there was little sustained intellectual discourse among them.

Notes

1. For this see E. Shils, "The trend of sociological research," paper read at the 8th International Congress of Sociology, Evian, 1966.

2. See E. Shils, "Tradition, ecology, and institution in the history of sociology," *Daedalus*, Vol. 99, No. 4 (Fall 1970), pp. 760–825; E. Shils, "The trend of sociological research," *op. cit.*

3. R. K. Merton, "Social conflict over styles of sociological work," *Transactions of the Fourth World Congress of Sociology*, Vol. 3 (Louvain, Belgium: International Sociological Association, 1961), pp. 21–44.

4. T. N. Clark, "The stages of scientific institutionalization," *International Social Science Journal*, Vol. 24 No. 4 (1972), pp. 658–671.

5. For this and some of the following discussion of institutional frameworks in which the Forerunners carried on their intellectual activities, see T. N. Clark, "The stages of scientific institutionalization," *op. cit.;* E. Shils, "Tradition, ecology, and institution in the history of sociology," *op. cit.;* R. Collins and M. Makowski, *The Discovery of Society* (New York: Random House, 1972), pp. 22–31, 32–62, 67–70.

6. R. Collins and M. Makowski, *The Discovery of Society, op. cit.;* H. Becker and H. E. Barnes, *Social Thought from Lore to Science* (New York: Dover, 1961), Vol. 2, pp. 490–494; S. Landshut, *Kritik der Soziologie* (München und Leipzig: Verlag von Duncker & Humblot, 1929), especially Chs. 4, 5.

7. On L. von Stein see L. von Stein. *Staat und Gesellschaft*, (Zürich: Rascher, 1934).
   On Marx see K. Marx, *Capital* (New York: Kerr, 1906); also the following works, which contain good selections from Marx's major writings: K. Marx, *Early Writings*, ed. T. B. Bottomore (New York: McGraw-Hill, 1963); K. Marx, *Selected Writings in Sociology and Social Philosophy* ed. T. B. Bottomore and M. Rubel (Penguin, London 1965).

8. On these scholars and their major works see T. H. Buckle, *History of Civilization in England* (London, J. W. Parker & Son, 1857–61), 2 vols.; P. Lilienfeld, *Gedanken über die Sozialwissenschaft der Zukunft* (Mitau: E. Behre, 1873–81), 5 vols.; P. Lilienfeld, *La Pathologie Sociale* (Paris, V. Giard & E. Briere, 1896); P. Lilienfeld, *Zur Verteidigung der Organischen Method in der Soziologie* (Berlin, 1898); A. Schäffle, *Bau und Leben des Socialen Korpers* (Tübingen, H. Lauppsche Buchhandlung, 1875–78), 4 vols.; E. de

Roberty, *Nouveau Programme de Sociologie* (Paris, 1904); E.de Roberty, *Sociologie de l'Action* (Paris, 1908).

9.   For these schools and approaches see P. A. Sorokin, *Contemporary Sociological Theories* (New York: Harper & Row, [1928], 1964) Chs. 3, 4.

10. On Comte see A. Comte, *The Positive Philosophy* (London: Trübner, 1853), 2 vols.; A. Comte, *System of Positive Polity* (London: Longmans, Green and Co., 1875–77); R. Aron, *Main Currents in Sociological Thought* Vol. 1 (Penguin, 1968), pp. 63–109; L.A. Coser, *Masters of Sociological Thought*, (New York: Harcourt, Brace Jovanovich, 1971), pp. 3–41.

     On Spencer see H. Spencer, *The Principles of Sociology*, (New York: Appleton, 1925–1929), 3 vols.; H. Spencer, *On Social Evolution*, ed. and with an introduction by J. D. Y. Peel (Chicago: University of Chicago Press, 1972); L. A. Coser, *Masters of Sociological Thought, op. cit.*, pp. 89–127; R. Fletcher, *The Making of Sociology; a Study of Sociological Theory*, Vol. 1 (London: Michael Joseph, 1971), pp. 250–338.

11. On this see F. Engels, *The Origin of the Family, Private Property and the State* (New York: International Publishers [1884], 1942); E. B. Tylor, *Researches into the Early History of Mankind and the Development of Civilization* (London: Murray, 1878); E. B. Tylor, *Primitive Culture: Researches into the Development of Mythology, Philosophy, Religion, Art and Custom* (Gloucester, Mass.: Smith, 1958), 2 vols.; L. H. Morgan, *Ancient Society* (Cambridge, Mass.: Belknap Press, Harvard University Press, 1964); J. J. Bachofen, *Das Mutterrecht und Urreligion* (Leipzig: A. Kröner, 1939).

12. For this and the other characteristics of the social research of this period, discussed above, see B. Lécuyer and A. R. Oberschall, "Sociology: the early history of social research," in *International Encyclopedia of the Social Sciences*, Vol. 15 (New York: Macmillan and Free Press, 1968), pp. 36–53; A. Oberschall, *Empirical Social Research in Germany: 1848–1914* (Paris, The Hague: Mouton, 1965); P. Abrams, *The Origins of British Sociology: 1834–1914* (Chicago: University of Chicago Press, 1968), pp. 8–153; A. Oberschall, "The institutionalization of American Sociology," in A. Oberschall (ed.), *The Establishment of Empirical Sociology: Studies in Continuity, Discontinuity and Institutionalization* (New York: Harper & Row, 1972), pp. 187–251; T. N. Clark, *Prophets and Patrons: The French University and the Emergence of the Social Sciences* (Cambridge, Mass.: Harvard University Press, 1973) Chs. 3, 4; H. Maus, "Zur vorgeschichte der empirischen sozialforschung," in R. König (ed.), *Handbuch der Empirischen Sozialforschung* Band 1 (Stuttgart, F. Enke, 1973), pp. 21–57.

13. For this see A. Quetelet, *Physique Sociale*, (Bruxelles: C. Muquardt, 1869), 2 vols.; F. LePlay, *Les Ouvriers Europeens* (Tours: Alfred Mamé et Fils, 1879), 6 vols.

14. On the appraisal of Quetelet and LePlay as pioneers in the development of social science research techniques, see P. F. Lazarsfeld, "Notes on the history of quantification in sociology: trends, sources and problems," *Isis*, Vol. 52, No. 2 (1961), pp. 277–333.

15. Middle-range hypotheses about the relationship between equality, freedom, and forms of political institutions were developed by Tocqueville; for this see: A. de Tocqueville, *Democracy in America*, (New York: Knopf, 1945) 2 vols.; A. de Tocqueville, *The Old Regime and French Revolution* (Garden City, N.Y.: Doubleday Anchor, 1955). See also W. H. Riehl, *Die Bürgerliche Gesellschaft* 10th ed. (Stuttgart: J. G. Colta [1861], 1907); L. von Stein, *Staat und Gesellschaft, op. cit.*

16. Such is, for example, Marx's theory of stratification. On this see K. Marx and F. Engels, "The Communist Manifesto," in A. P. Mendel (ed.), *Essential Works of Marxism* (New York: Bantam, 1961), pp. 13–44; R. Bendix and S. M. Lipset, "Karl Marx's

theory of social classes," in R. Bendix and S. M. Lipset (eds.), *Class, Status and Power* (Glencoe, Ill.: Free Press, 1953, pp. 26–35.

17. See for example P. Vinogradoff, *Growth of the Manor* (London: G. Allen & Unwin [1911], 1951); P. Vinogradoff, *English Society in the 11th Century* (Oxford: Clarendon Press, 1908); P. Vinogradoff (ed.), *Oxford Studies in Social and Legal History*, (1909–1927), London: Oxford University Press, 9 vols.; P. Vinogradoff, *Common Sense in Law*, 3rd. ed. (London: Oxford University Press, 1959); J. J. Bachofen, *Das Mutterrecht und Urreligion, op. cit.*

    For a general survey of the emergence of comparative study of customs and institutions during the eighteenth and nineteenth centuries see also M. Harris, *The Rise of Anthropological Theory: a History of Theories of Culture* (London: Routledge & Kegan Paul, 1968), especially Chs. 1–8.

18. On the process of differentiation of sociology from other disciplines see R. K. Merton, "Social Conflict over Styles of Sociological Work," *op. cit.*

    On Comte's attempts to formulate the methodological bases of sociology see L. A. Coser, *Masters of Sociological Thought, op. cit.*, pp. 3–6.

19. On Comte see L. A. Coser, *Masters of Sociological Thought, op. cit.*, pp. 3–41.

20. For this see A. de Tocqueville, *Democracy in America, op. cit.*; A. de Tocqueville, *The Old Regime and the French Revolutionl op. cit.*; H. Spencer, *The Principles of Sociology, op. cit.*; H. Spencer, *On Social Evolution op. cit.*; A. Comte, *The Positive Philosophy, op. cit.*; A. Comte, *Positive Polity, op. cit.*; K. Marx, *Selected Writings in Sociology and Social Philosophy, op. cit.*

    See also F. Jonas, *Geschichte der Soziologie*, Vol. 2 (Hamburg: Rowohlt Verlag, 1968) 4 vols.

    For a summary statement of the intellectual distinction of sociology as it had emerged in this stage, see also R. Fletcher, *The Making of Sociology*, Vol. 1, *op. cit.*, pp. 601–642.

21. For this see S. Landshut, *Kritik der Soziologie op. cit.*; R. A. Nisbet, *The Sociological Tradition* (London: Heineman, 1967); A. Salomon, *In Praise of Enlightenment: Essays in the History of Ideas* (New York: Meridian Books, 1963), especially Ch. 7.

22. K. Mannheim, *Essays on Sociology and Social Psychology* (London: Routledge & Kegan Paul, 1953) Ch. 6; F. Jonas, *Geschichte der Soziologie*, Vols. 1, 2, *op. cit.*

23. On the various intellectual orientations which influenced Marx's thought see R. Aron, *Main Currents in Sociological Thought*, Vol. 1, *op. cit.*, pp. 111–182; L. A. Coser, *Masters of Sociological Thought, op. cit.*, pp. 43–87.

24. On this see R. A. Nisbet, "The French Revolution and the rise of sociology in France," in E. A. Tiryakian (ed.), *The Phenomenon of Sociology* (New York: Appleton-Century-Crofts, 1971), pp. 27–36.

25. On this school see P. F. Lazarsfeld, "Notes on the history of quantification in sociology," *op. cit.*; T. N. Clark, *Prophets and Patrons: the French University and the Emergence of the Social Sciences, op. cit.*, Ch. 3.

26. For the various sources which influenced English social thought and research discussed below, see P. Abrams, *The Origins of British Sociology: 1834–1914, op. cit.*; J. Rex, *Discovering Sociology: Studies in Sociological Theory and Method* (London, Boston: Routledge & Kegan Paul, 1973), Ch. 5; K. Mannheim, *Essays on Sociology and Social Psychology, op. cit.*, Ch. 6; L. A. Coser, *Masters of Sociological Thought, op. cit.*, pp. 89–127.

27. On Marx's general influence on German sociology see K. Mannheim, *Essays on Sociology and Social Psychologyl op. cit.*, Ch. 6.

About the challenge posed by Marxism for various scholars in Germany see S. Landshut, *Kritik der Soziologie, op. cit.*, especially Chs. 2, 3; A. Mitzman, *Sociology and Estrangement: Three Sociologists of Imperial Germany* (New York: Knopf, 1973); R. Bendix, *Max Weber: an Intellectual Portrait* (New York: Doubleday, 1960), Ch. 15; A. Mitzman, *The Iron Cage: an Historical Interpretation of Max Weber* (New York: Grosset & Dunlap, 1971), especially pp. 181–191; K. Mannheim, *Essays on the Sociology of Knowledge* (London: Routledge & Kegan Paul, 1952), pp. 1–32 (P. Kecskemeti's introduction); M. Jay, *The Dialectical Imagination: a History of the Frankfurt School and the Institute of Social Research, 1923–1950* (Boston: Little, Brown, 1973).

On Marx's influence on Italian social thinkers see for example H. S. Hughes, *Consciousness and Society*, (New York: Vintage Books, 1958), especially Ch. 3.

28.   E. Durkheim, *The Division of Labor in Society* (New York: Free Press, 1964); E. Durkheim, *The Rules of Sociological Method*, (New York: Free Press, 1964); E. Durkheim, *Suicide* (New York: Free Press, 1966); Emile Durkheim, *On Morality and Society*, ed. and with an introduction by R. N. Bellah (Chicago: University of Chicago Press, 1973); E. Durkheim, *Selected Writings*, ed. with an introduction by A. Giddens (Cambridge: Cambridge University Press, 1972).

For general interpretations of Durkheim's sociology see

T. Parsons, *The Structure of Social Action* Vol. 1 (New York: Free Press, 1968), Chs. 8–12; R. A. Nisbet, *The Sociology of Emile Durkheim* (London: Heinemann, 1975); R. Aron, *Main Currents in Sociological Thought*, Vol. 2 (Penguin, Harmondsworth, 1970), 2 vols., pp. 21–107; S. Lukes, *Emile Durkheim—His Life and Work: a Historical and Critical Study* (London: Allen Lane, 1973).

29.   The following English translations provide a good idea of Weber's contribution to sociology: M. Weber, *The Protestant Ethic and the Spirit of Capitalism* (New York: Scribner, 1958); M. Weber, *The Religion of China* (New York: Free Press, 1951); M. Weber, *The Religion of India* (New York: Free Press, 1958); M. Weber, *Ancient Judaism* (New York: Free Press, 1952); M. Weber, *Economy and Society* (New York: Bedminster Press, 1968), 3 vols.; M. Weber, *Essays in Sociology* (New York: Oxford University Press, 1946); M. Weber, *The Methodology of the Social Sciences* (Glencoe, Illinois: Free Press, 1949).

For selections from Weber's works see also M. Weber, *On Charisma and Institution Building*, ed. with an introduction by S. N. Eisenstadt (Chicago: University of Chicago Press, 1968).

For general interpretations of Weber's sociology see R. Bendix, *Max Weber: an Intellectual Portrait, op. cit.*; A. Mitzman, *The Iron Cage, op. cit.*; A. Giddens, *Politics and Sociology in the Thought of Max Weber* (London: Macmillan, 1972); T. Parsons, *The Structure of Social Action*, Vol. 2, *op. cit.*; R. Aron, *Main Currents in Sociological Thought*, Vol. 2, *op. cit.*, pp. 185–258; W. Mommsen, *Max Weber, Gesellschaft Politik u. Geschichte* (Frankfurt am Main: Suhrkampf, 1974).

On Tönnies see F. Tönnies, *Community and Society* (Gemeinschaft und Gesellschaft), translated and edited by C. P. Loomis (East Lansing, Mich.: State University Press, 1957); F. Tönnies, *On Sociology: Pure, Applied and Empirical*, selected writings, edited and with an introduction by W. J. Cahnman and R. Heberle (Chicago and London: University of Chicago Press, 1971);

For an evaluation of Tönnies' sociology see W. J. Cahnman, (ed.), *F. Tönnies: a New Evaluation: Essays and Documents* (Leiden: E. J. Brill, 1973); A. Mitzman, *Sociology and Estrangement, op. cit.*, Part 2.

On Sombart see W. Sombart, *Der Moderne Kapitalismus* (Leipzig: Duncker und Humblot, 1916), 3 vols.; W. Sombart, *Der Bourgeois* (Munich: Duncker und Humblot, 1913), also translated in English by M. Epstein as *The Quintessence of Capitalism* (New

York: Dutton, 1915); W. Sombart, *Das Proletariat* (Frankfurt: Rütten & Loening, 1905).
For an evaluation of Sombart's sociology see A. Mitzman, *Sociology and Estrangement, op. cit.,* Part 3;
On Oppenheimer see F. Oppenheimer, *System der Soziologie* (Yena: G. Fischer, 1922–35) 4 vols.

30. L. T. Hobhouse, *Social Development: its Nature and Conditions* (London: Allen & Unwin, 1924); E. A. Westermarck, *The History of Human Marriage* (London: Macmillan [1891], 1921) 3 vols.; E. A. Westermarck, *The Origin and Development of the Moral Ideas,* (London: Macmillan, [1906–1908], 1924–1926), 2 vols.
For a general survey, especially on Hobhouse's contribution to the emergence of British sociology, see also P. Abrams, *The Origins of British Sociology, op. cit.*

31. V. Pareto, *The Mind and Society* (New York: Harcourt Brace, 1935), 5 vols.; G. Mosca, *The Ruling Class* (New York: McGraw-Hill, 1939).
For an evaluation of these scholars' work see J. H. Meisel (ed.), *Pareto and Mosca* (Englewood Cliffs, N.J.: Prentice-Hall, 1965); F. Jonas, *Geschichte der Soziologie,* Vol. 3, *op. cit.*
For Pareto see also T. Parsons, *The Structure of Social Action,* Vol. 1, *op. cit.,* especially Chs. 5–7; R. Aron, *Main Currents in Sociological Thought,* Vol. 2, *op. cit.,* pp. 109–183; L. A. Coser, *Masters of Sociological Thought, op. cit.,* pp. 387–426.

32. On Mosca and Pareto see the items cited in note 31. On Michels see R. Michels, *Political Parties* (New York: Collier, 1962); A. Mitzman, *Sociology and Estrangement, op. cit.,* Part 4.

33. M. Kovalevsky, *Russian Political Institutions* (Chicago: The University of Chicago Press, 1902); M. Kovalevsky, *Modern Customs and Ancient Laws of Russia* (London: D. Nutt, 1891); M. Kovalevsky, *Sociology* (in Russian) St. Petersburg, (1910); M. Kovalevsky, *Contemporary Sociologists* (in Russian) (St. Petersburg, 1905); N. Kareyev, *History of Western Europe,* 6 vols (in Russian) (St. Petersburg: Tip M. M. Stasiulevicha 1892–1913); N. Kareyev, *Basic Questions of the Philosophy of History* (in Russian) (2 vols. Moscow: Izd. L. F. Panteleeva, 1883); N. Kareyev, *Introduction to the Study of Sociology* 2nd ed. (1907, St. Petersburg: Tip. M. M. Stasiulevicha).

34. F. de Coulanges, *Histoire des Institutions Politiques de L'ancienne France: La Monarchie Franque* (Paris: Hachette, 1888–1901), 6 vols.; F. de Coulanges, *La Cité Antique* (Paris: Hachette, 1923), translated as *The Ancient City* (Garden City, N.Y.: Doubleday Anchor Books, 1956).

35. G. Murray, *Five Stages of Greek Religion* (London: Watts, 1935); J. E. Harrison, *Themis: a Study of the Social Origins of Greek Religion* (Cambridge: Cambridge University Press, [1912] 1937); J. E. Harrison, *Ancient Art and Ritual* (New York: Oxford University Press, [1913] 1951).

36. See the items quoted in note 33.

37. On this see B. Lécuyer and A. R. Oberschall, "Sociology: the early history of social research," *op. cit.;* P. Abrams, *The Origins of British Sociology, op. cit.;* Donald G. MacRae, "The development of sociology in Britain," *Ideology and Society: Papers in Sociology and Politics* (London: Heinemann, 1961), pp. 16–30.

38. On this see B. Lécuyer and A. R. Oberschall, "Sociology: the early history of social research," *op. cit.;* A. Oberschall, *Empirical Social Research in Germany, op. cit.,* especially pp. 21–27; S. P. Schad, *Empirical Social Research in Weimar Germany* (Paris, The Hague: Mouton, 1972), especially pp. 13–17; H. Maus, "Zur vorgeschichte der empirischer sozialforschung," *op. cit.*

39. On this see T. N. Clark, *Prophets and Patrons, op. cit.,* Chs. 3, 4.

40. On the research centers of Columbia and Chicago see A. Oberschall, "The institutionalization of American sociology," *op. cit.*
    On the Institut d'Ethnographie see T. N. Clark, *Prophets and Patrons,* op. cit., p.120.

41. On L'Année Sociologique, Société de Sociologie de Paris, and Institut International de Sociologie, see T. N. Clark, *Prophets and Patrons, op. cit.,* Chs. 5, 6.
    On the American Sociological Society see: A. Oberschall, "The institutionalization of American sociology," *op. cit.*

42. E. Durkheim, *Suicide, op. cit.*

43. For this see, for example, Weber's studies of religion, cited in note 29, and also R. Bendix, *Max Weber: an Intellectual Portrait, op. cit.*

44. On this see P. Abrams, *The Origins of British Sociology, op. cit.*

45. R. K. Merton, *Social Theory and Social Structure,* (Glencoe, Illinois: Free Press, 1957), p. 87.

46. Actually the theories of some of the great Founding Fathers, as for instance those of Durkheim and Weber, emerged as a reaction to these disputes. For this see T. Parsons, *The Structure of Social Action,* especially Vol. 1, Ch. 12, and Vol. 2, Ch. 18, *op. cit.*
    On Weber see also R. Bendix, *Max Weber: an Intellectual Portrait, op. cit.* especially Chs. 14, 15; F. Jonas, *Geschichte der Soziologie,* Vol. 4, *op. cit.*

47. On this see R. König, *Studien zur Soziologie* (Frankfurt am Main und Hamburg: Fischer Bücherei, 1971) pp. 9–37; A. Vierkandt, *Gesellschaftslehre* (Stuttgart: F. Enke, 1923); A. Vierkandt, *Handwörterbuch der Soziologie* (Stuttgart: F. Enke Verlag, 1931); M. Jay, *The Dialectical Imagination, op. cit.*

48. On the *Methodenstreit* see S. P. Schad, *Empirical Social Research in Weimar Germany, op. cit.,* pp. 44–46.
    On Weber's position on the relationship between values and scientific-sociological analysis see Max Weber, *Essays in Sociology* (New York: Oxford University Press, 1958), pp. 129–156; Max Weber, *The Methodology of the Social Sciences, op. cit.,* especially pp. 1–112.
    For a relatively recent reevaluation of Weber's position by various sociologists see O. Stammer (ed.), *Max Weber and Sociology Today* (Oxford: Basil Blackwell, 1971); A. Giddens, *Politics and Sociology in the Thought of Max Weber, op. cit.;* Allan N. Sharlin, "Max Weber and the origins of the idea of value-free social science," *Archives Européennes de Sociologie,* Vol. 15, No. 2 (1975), pp. 337–353. A.. Giddens (ed), *Positivism and Sociology* (London: Heinemann, 1974).

49. On Durkheim's definition of "social facts" see E. Durkheim, *The Rules of Sociological Method, op. cit.,* especially Ch. 1. The echo of the polemical stand which Durkheim had taken toward other definitions can be found also in his study on suicide. See E. Durkheim, *Suicide, op. cit.,* Book 1.

50. On this see A. Mitzman, *Sociology and Estrangement, op. cit.;* L. A. Coser, *Masters of Sociological Thought, op. cit.,* especially pp. 189–193; A. Mitzman, *The Iron Cage, op. cit.;* F. Jonas, *Geschichte der Soziologie,* Vol. 4, *op. cit.*

51. On this see A. Mitzman, *Sociology and Estrangement, op. cit.,* Parts 2, 3.

52. On this see K. Mannheim, *Essays on Sociology and Social Psychology, op. cit.,* Ch. 6.

53. W. Sombart, *Das Proletariat* (Frankfurt am Main: Rütten & Loening, 1907); F. Tönnies, *Die Sitte* (Frankfurt am Main, Rütten & Loening, 1909); F. Mautner, *Die Sprache* (Frankfurt am Main: Rütten & Loening, 1908); G. Simmel, *Die Religion*

(Frankfurt am Main: Rütten & Loening, 1906); F. Oppenheimer, *Der Staat* (Frankfurt am Main: Rütten & Loening, 1907); G. Landauer, *Die Revolution* (Frankfurt am Main, Rütten & Loening, 1907).

54. F. Glaser, *Die Börse* (Frankfurt am Main, Rütten & Loening, 1909); R. Hessen, *Der Sport* (Frankfurt am Main, Rütten & Loening, 1906); P. Göhre, *Das Warenhaus* (Frankfurt am Main, Rütten & Loening, 1907): T. T. David, *Die Zeitung* (Frankfurt am Main: Rütten & Loening, 1906).

55. On this see R. Michels, *Political Parties, op. cit.;* R. Collins and M. Makowski, *The Discovery of Society, op. cit.,* pp. 186–190.

56. On this see A. Mitzman, *Sociology and Estrangement, op. cit.,* Part 3.

57. E. Shils, "Tradition, ecology and institution in the history of sociology," *op. cit.,* p. 766; R. Collins and M. Makowski, *The Discovery of Society, op. cit.* pp. 186–190; A. Mitzman, *Sociology and Estrangement, op. cit.,* Part 3.

58. On the characteristics of the social research in this period which have been discussed above see A. Oberschall, *Empirical Social Research in Germany, op. cit.* pp. 76–145.

59. *Ibid,* pp. 140–145.

60. R. Bendix, *Max Weber: an Intellectual Portrait, op. cit.,* Ch. 2.

61. For a review of this study and Weber's related publications see A. Oberschall, *Empirical Social Research in Germany, op. cit.,* pp. 113–131; P. F. Lazarsfeld and A. R. Oberschall, "Max Weber and empirical social research," *American Sociological Review,* Vol. 30, No. 2 (April 1965), pp. 185–199.

62. For a review of Tönnies' studies and his numerous related publications see A. Oberschall, *Empirical Social Research in Germany, op. cit.,* pp. 51–63; W. J. Cahnman and R. Heberle (eds.), *Ferdinand Tönnies on Sociology: Pure, Applied and Empirical* (Chicago: University of Chicago Press, 1971), especially the introduction and Part 4.

63. For Sombart, especially for his distinction between the social and natural sciences, see A. Mitzman, *Sociology and Estrangement, op. cit.,* especially pp. 234–238.

For Weber's definition and conceptualization of sociology and its scope see for example *Max Weber on Charisma and Institution Building, op. cit.,* especially pp. 3–10; Max Weber, *The Methodology of the Social Sciences, op. cit.,* pp. 1–112.

For Tönnies see W. J. Cahnman (ed.), *Ferdinand Tönnies: a New Evaluation, op. cit.,* especially Part A.

For Simmel see K. H. Wolf (ed.), *The Sociology of Georg Simmel* (Glencoe, Ill.: Free Press, 1950), especially the introduction and Part 1; D. Levine (ed.), *Georg Simmel on Individuality and Social Forms,* (Chicago: University of Chicago Press, 1971), especially the introduction and Parts 1, 2.

64. On this see note 48 and also F. Jonas, *Geschichte der Soziologie,* Vol. 4, *op. cit.*

65. For a brief and useful account of Dilthey's approach see H. Stuart Hughes, *Consciousness and Society,* (New York: Vintage Books, 1958), pp. 192–200; M. Truzzi (ed.), *Verstehen: Subjective Understanding in the Social Sciences* (Reading, Mass.: Addison-Wesley, 1974), especially pp. 8–17.

66. For this see T. Adorno, u.a., *Der Positivismusstreit in der Deutschen Soziologie* (Neuwied und Berlin: Luchterhand, 1969); T. Adorno, W. Hochkeppel, and H. Albert u.a., (Hrsg.), *Soziologie zwischen Theorie und Empirie* (München: Nymphenburger Verlagshandlung, 1970); E. Topitsch, *Logik der Sozialwissenshaften* (Köln: Kiepenheuer & Witsch, 1972) sweiter teil, vierter teil.; M. Jay, *The Sociological Imagination, op. cit.,* especially Ch. 2; K. Mannheim, *Ideology and Utopia,* (New York: Harcourt Brace, 1936).

67. With a slightly changed title this paper appears in M. Weber, *The Methodology of the Social Sciences, op. cit.,* pp. 49–112.

68. M. Weber, *Essays in Sociology, op. cit.,* 1958, pp. 129–156.

69. For the conservative and reformistic orientations of the Leplayist school see T. N. Clark, *Prophets and Patrons, op. cit.,* Ch. 3; P. F. Lazarsfeld, "Notes on the history of quantification in sociology," *op. cit.*

70. For this see E. Durkheim, *Suicide, op. cit.;* E. Durkheim, *The Division of Labor in Society, op. cit.;* S. Lukes, *Emile Durkheim—his Life and Work, op. cit.,* especially Ch. 7, 9; R. A. Nisbet, *The Sociology of Emile Durkheim, op. cit.,* especially Ch. 4–9.

71. For analytical similarities between Durkheim's and Tönnies' analysis of traditional and modern societies compare F. Tönnies, *Community and Society, op. cit.;* E. Durkheim, *The Division of Labor in Society, op. cit.*

    For Tönnies' general criticism of modernity see A. Mitzman, *Sociology and Estrangement, op. cit.,* Part 2.

    For Durkheim's criticism of modernity see E. Durkheim, *Suicide, op. cit.;* E. Durkheim, *The Division of Labor in Society, op. cit.,* especially pp. 1–31 and Book 3, Ch. 1.

72. For the nature of Durkheim's commitment to modern society in general and to French society in particular see R. N. Bellah, "Introduction," in E. Durkheim, *On Morality and Society,* selected writings edited by R. N. Bellah (Chicago: University of Chicago Press, 1973); T. N. Clark, *Prophets and Patrons, op. cit.,* Ch. 6; S. Lukes *Emile Durkheim: his Life and Work, op. cit.,* especially Ch. 17; R. A. Nisbet, *The Sociology of Emile Durkheim, op. cit.,* Ch. 9.

73. For these groups of social scientists and Tarde see T. N. Clark, *Prophets and Patrons op. cit.,* Ch. 3, 5.

74. For this and the following discussion on Durkheim's success and its limitations in institutionalizing French sociology, as well as on the relations between teaching and research, and on the institutional bases of research, see T. N. Clark, *Prophets and Patrons, op. cit.,* Ch. 3, 4, 5, 6.

75. The combination of quantitative data with theoretical perspectives is found, of course, in Durkheim's study on suicide; for this see E. Durkheim, *Suicide, op. cit.*

    For illustrations of the same trend in Simiand's and Halbwachs' works see F. Simiand, *Le Salaire des Ouvriers des Mines de Charbon en France* (Paris: Cornély, [1904] 1907); M. Halbwachs, *La Classe Ouvrière et les Niveaux de Vie* (Paris: Alcan, 1913). T. N. Clark, *Prophets and Patrons, op. cit.,* Ch. 4.

76. For brief surveys of these studies see C. Lévi-Strauss, "French sociology," in G. Gurvitch and W. E. Moore (eds.), *Twentieth Century Sociology* (New York: Philosophical Library, 1945), pp. 503–537. H. Becker and H. E. Barnes, *Social Thought from Lore to Science,* Vol. 3, *op. cit.,* Ch. 22.

77. For these sectarian trends see T. N. Clark, *Prophets and Patrons, op. cit.,* Ch. 5, 6.

78. On this, *Ibid.,* Ch. 6.

79. Such is, for example, Durkheim's discussion on the distinction between the "normal" and the "pathological" and its relevance in assessing social situations by the policy makers; for this see E. Durkheim, *The Rules of Sociological Method, op. cit.,* especially Ch. 3; also the introduction in A. Giddens (ed.), *Emile Durkheim: Selected Writings* (Cambridge: Cambridge University Press, 1972).

80. The intellectual background which was conducive to the emergence of British sociology, its first institutional nuclei, and the initial role orientations of British sociologists are discussed in P. Abrams, *The Origins of British Sociology, op. cit.,* pp. 8–153; J. Rex,

Discovering Sociology, op. cit., Ch. 5. See also L. T. Hobhouse, *Social Development: its Nature and Conditions, op. cit.*

81. E. Shils, "On the eve," *The Twentieth Century,* Vol. 167, No. 999 (May 1960), pp. 445–459;

82. A. J. Reiss, "Sociology: the field," in *International Encyclopedia of the Social Sciences* Vol. 15 (New York: Macmillan and Free Press, 1968), pp. 1–23.

83. E. Shils, "Tradition, ecology and institution in the history of sociology," *op. cit.*

84. For Westermarck's principal studies on marriage and morals see E. A. Westermarck, *The History of Human Marriage, op. cit.;* E. A. Westermarck, *The Origin and Development of the Moral Ideas, op. cit.*

85. For this see L. T. Hobhouse, G. C. Wheeler, and M. Ginsberg, *The Material Culture and Social Institutions of the Simpler Peoples: an Essay in Correlation* (London: Routledge [1915] 1965); E. A. Westermarck, *The History of Human Marriage, op. cit.;* E. A. Westermarck, *The Origin and Development of the Moral Ideas, op. cit.*

86. For some of their major works see E. B. Tylor, *Researches into the Early History of Mankind and the Development of Civilization, op. cit.;* E. B. Tylor, *Primitive Culture: Researches into the Development of Mythology, Philosophy, Religion, Art and Custom, op. cit.;* J. Frazer, *The Golden Bough,* (New York: St. Martins; London, Macmillan [1890] 1955), 13 vols.; R. R. Marett, *The Threshold of Religion* (London: Methuen [1900] 1929).

   A general survey can be found in M. Harris, *The Rise of Anthropological Theory—a History of Theories of Culture, op. cit.,* especially Ch. 6, 7.

87. On this see P. Abrams, *The Origins of British Sociology, op. cit.,* especially pp. 104–106.

88. For these aspects of empirical research and the details discussed below see E. Shils, "Tradition, ecology and institution in the history of sociology," *op. cit.;* P. Abrams, *The Origins of British Sociology, op. cit.;* B. Lécuyer and A. Oberschall, "Sociology: the early history of social research," *op. cit.;* J. Rumney, "British sociology," in G. Gurvitch and W. E. Moore (eds.), *Twentieth Century Sociology, op. cit.,* pp. 562–585.

89. D. Bell, "Socialism," in *International Encyclopedia of the Social Sciences,* Vol. 14, *op. cit.,* pp. 506–532; M. Cole, "Webb, Sidney and Beatrice," *ibid,* Vol. 16, pp. 487–491, and its bibliography.

90. L. Ward, *The Psychic Factors of Civilization* (Boston: Ginn, 1893); L. Ward, *Outlines of Sociology* (New York: Macmillan, 1898); L. Ward, *Pure Sociology* (New York: Macmillan, 1903); E. A. Ross, *Social Control* (New York: Macmillan, 1915); F. H. Giddings, *The Principles of Sociology* (New York: Macmillan, 1896); W. G. Sumner, *Folkways* (Boston: Ginn, 1906); C. H. Cooley, *Social Organization* (New York: Scribner, 1929); C. H. Cooley, *Social Process,* New York: Scribner, 1907).

91. On the nature of the reformist orientations of the American sociologists discussed below see R. Collins and M. Makowsky, *The Discovery of Society, op. cit.,* pp. 70–75; R. C. Hinkle and G. J. Hinkle, *The Development of Modern Sociology: its Nature and Growth in the United States* (New York: Doubleday, 1954), Ch. 1; L. Bramson, "The rise of American sociology," in E. A. Tiryakian (ed.), *The Phenomenon of Sociology, op. cit.,* pp. 65–80; A. Oberschall, "The institutionalization of American sociology," *op. cit.*

   For a radical criticism of these orientations see H. Schwendinger and J. R. Schwendinger, *The Sociologists of the Chair: a Radical Analysis of the Formative Years of North American Sociology, 1883–1922,* (New York: Basic Books, 1974).

92. A. Oberschall, "The institutionalization of American sociology," *op. cit.,* pp. 212–213.

93. These factors are analyzed by E. Shils, "Tradition, ecology, and institution in the

history of sociology," *op. cit.;* A. Oberschall, "The institutionalization of American sociology," *op. cit.*

94. On these alignments see A. Oberschall, "The institutionalization of American sociology," *op. cit.*

95. On the nature of empirical research discussed below see A. Oberschall, "The institutionalization of American sociology," *op. cit.*

96. E. Shils, *The Present State of American Sociology* (Glencoe, Illinois: Free Press, 1948), especially pp. 56–58; A. Oberschall, "The institutionalization of American sociology," *op. cit.*

97. On this process of differentiation and the conflicting role orientations of sociologists discussed below, see A. Oberschall, "The institutionalization of American sociology," *op. cit.;* L. Bramson, "The rise of American sociology," *op. cit.*

98. On Russia see M. M. Laserson, "Russian sociology," in G. Gurvitch and W. E. Moore (eds.), *Twentieth Century Sociology, op. cit.,* pp. 671–702.

99. On Italy and Spain see C. Panunzio, "Italian sociology," in G. Gurvitch and W. E. Moore (eds.), *op. cit.,* pp. 638–652; A. Mendizabal, "Spanish sociology," *op. cit,,* pp. 653–670; F. Jonas, *Geschichte der Soziologie, op. cit.,* Vol. 3.

100. T. N. Clark, *Prophets and Patrons, op. cit.,* Chs. 5 and 7.

101. E. Shils, "Tradition, ecology, and institution in the history of sociology," *op. cit.,* especially pp. 786–789.

   On the knowledge of Durkheim in Germany, especially by Tönnies, see W. J. Cahnman (ed.), *F. Tönnies: a New Evaluation, op. cit.,* pp. 239–256.

102. E. Shils, "Tradition, ecology, and institution in the history of sociology," *op. cit.,* especially pp. 782–783.

3

The Emergence of a Distinctive Sociological Tradition

The Intellectual Preconditions of a Distinctive Sociological Tradition

1.   The developments that took place at the second stage were the most formative for the development of sociology. Some basic components of its institutional and intellectual identity and distinctiveness were crystallized then, and with them the major problems it has continued to face up to the present.

It was at this stage above all that sociology began to attain its distinctiveness from the closely related disciplines and the traditions of philosophy, social reform and reconstruction, critical journalism and political analysis, policy-oriented economics and statistics, and scientific quantitative methods in the study of human affairs.

The achievement of a distinctive sociological mode of analysis depended first on attaining a certain intellectual distance from philosophical, ideological, and political movements, and such distance was apparent fairly early. As Tiryakian[1] has stressed, most sociologists were ambivalent toward political ideologies in general, and toward liberalism and socialism in particular. Perhaps even more important, the same sociological theories could be used for different political and ideological ends. Thus, the developing sociological tradition tended to distinguish sociolo-

55

gical theories and their philosophical and ideological counterparts; there was a particularly noticeable weakening of ties with philosophical or ideological optimism, as espoused by revolutionaries or evolutionary liberals, and with the pessimism of many Romantics, particularly as applied to problems of social order and to modern society in particular.[2]

The development of a distinct perspective also depended on achieving some distance from the tradition of social reform. This was especially true in England and the United States, where strong traditions of social reform existed, and in France, where the reformist tradition of St. Simon, later adopted by LePlay and his disciples, had lasting influence.[3] The increasing distance between sociology and these traditions was apparent in the abandonment of zeal and optimism in favor of a more objective and detailed analysis of modern social life.

The most·interesting shift occurred between some Forerunners and Founding Fathers of sociology. The early evolutionists in Europe and America, as well as Karl Marx and his followers, generally identified themselves with philosophical and ideological movements and certain attitudes toward social melioration,[4] though not all identified themselves with a particular political party or social movement. Even among the Forerunners, however, there were some, especially among such representatives of the new sociopolitical approach as Tocqueville and von Stein,[5] who questioned the viability of such attitudes and of "simple" political choices—liberal, conservative, or revolutionary—directions for modern society.

Such detached, complex, and ambivalent attitudes toward ideological and political visions became more pronounced in the next generation, especially among the European Founding Fathers of the sociological tradition, Durkheim and Weber, Simmel and Tönnies, and even, to some degree, Hobhouse.[6] Certainly all showed great concern with social and political problems, particularly those of modern society, and great commitment to their exploration and solution; indeed, they saw sociological inquiry as a crucial instrument of critical clarification. They could also identify sociology with intellectual trends like rationalism or secularism, and Durkheim even tried to make sociology the basis of a new civic morality of the Third Republic.[7] But they did so much less than did the first generation or even the contemporaries with whom they disputed these problems; and they refused to identify themselves, or the sociological enterprise, with any single ideological trend or political party. Above all, they did not share either the social, philosophic, or reformist optimism or the Romantic pessimism of many Forerunners or some contemporaries. They tended to stress rather, the ubiquity and continuity of tensions between creative and restrictive aspects of modern life, the potential contradictions between liberty and rationality, and those between liberty-rationality and justice-solidarity.

Both Durkheim and Weber saw contradictions as inherent in the human condition and all societies; they saw these contradictions as articulated with increasing sharpness in the development of modern society. Weber's most complete explication of this position was his analysis of charisma versus discipline and of the tension between the two basic aspects of rationality-*Zweckrationalität* and *Wertrationalität*[8]—concepts that Mannheim developed into functional and substantive rationality.[9] Similarly, Durkheim saw anomie in modern society as the concomitant of change and increased individual liberty.[10]

Although later sociologists—Mannheim, and later Marxists, including members of the Frankfurt school, Hobhouse and Morris Ginsberg in England[11]—tried to maintain a new optimism, some hoping that sociology might provide a basis for a new morality based on reason, they were never fully successful in this endeavor, even in their own thinking, which showed strong critical overtones. Moreover, other sociologists took a skeptical attitude toward their optimism. Above all, whatever their personal standing or outlook, they could no longer identify the sociological enterprise as such with any single philosophical, ideological, or political *Weltanschaung*.

But this distance from ideology and movements of social reform was only one precondition of the emergence of a distinctive analytic perspective.

More central to such a development was the conceptual reformulation and transformation of problems which substantially resembled those of other intellectual traditions and academic disciplines. As we have seen above (Ch. 1), sociology in the nineteenth century shared many central problems with all these traditions.

The distinctiveness of sociology from philosophical and ideological orientations emerged through the approaches and problematics it created in attempting to analyze these common problems. It became evident, first, in the effort to transform questions about the nature and bases of social order from philosophical into analytic problems subject to critical, and potentially empirical or testable investigation. Second, unlike social reformers, on the one hand, and political analysts, historians, and observers of contemporary social life on the other, it transformed their concrete problems into more analytical terms directed to the study of the general problems of social order: its nature, conditions, and variability.

More specifically, the distinctively sociological approach involved:

1. The development of specific *Problemstellung* differing greatly from those of philosophic, ideological, and reformist orientations.

2. The development of the "grand" sociological theories: explanatory and analytical paradigms of social order.

3. The development of specific questions or problems about concrete aspects of social life, organization, and behavior, which could be related to the broad paradigmatic problems of social order.

4. The linking of these orientations to scholarly-scientific research and particular analytic concepts.

Each component of the sociological approach will be analyzed further in the sections that follow.

> *The Intellectual Distinctiveness of Sociology: The Emergence of the Sociological Problemstellung; the Major Components of Sociological Theories*

2.   The uniquely sociological *Problemstellung,* as it gradually distinguished itself, was marked by its abandonment of questions about the "natural" conditions or characteristics of social order or the single "best" type of order. Instead, inquiry shifted to the analysis of the conditions and mechanisms of social order and its components, and of continuity and change in the social order in general or in different types of social order. Thus, the basic problem of social order was gradually reformulated. The question of how society was constituted from a presocial base was transformed into how continuous interaction among human beings was possible.

In this way, the central problems of sociological theory became how social order could be attained given (as a kind of basic datum or evolutionary universal) both the interdependence of human beings and the multiplicity of their goals; and how the organization of such order—i.e, what in sociology came to be known as the "institutional framework"—coped with these two basic problems of social life. Through this reformulation, the general problem of social order was also associated with more concrete problems.[12]

It is true that sociologists did continue, to formulate the Hobbesian problem of social order in terms of a transition from a presocial, individual state to some social bond,[13] especially when they put the problems in social-philosophic terms. Despite this tendency, however, the major advances in sociological analysis gradually transferred the locus of this problem to the institutional sphere itself, to the construction of human society. Thus, Marx stressed that alienation was rooted in the very nature

of the—class—division of labor.[14] Similarly, Durkheim's critique of the
conceptual inadequacy of purely contractual ties in explaining social
relationships stressed that it was the organizational aspects of the division
of labor which created the central problem of social order.[15] And Weber's
emphasis on the significance of legitimation of material, power, or ideal
interests made a similar point.[16]

3. The major analytic components of so-called sociological
theories—i.e., the basic questions to which most sociological theories
addressed themselves—emerged out of these problem formulations.
Most of these theories attempted to provide answers to problems of the
nature of social life, its regularities, and its patterns of stability and
change.

The first problem was the nature of the basic unit, or "starting point,"
of society. In the development of sociological theory, four major aspects
of social and cultural life were singled out as possible bases[17]: the individual with his goals and desires; society with its special organizational
characteristics and needs; the cultural order with its specific laws; or the
givens of the ecological environment.

The second problem dealt with the nature of the regularities of social
life. Particularly it attempted to define the degree to which social order
and social interaction exhibited systemic qualities—that is, the degree to
which what is called "society" had the properties of distinctive boundaries,
differentiated parts exhibiting functional interdependence, and special
boundary-maintaining mechanisms. It asked also to what degree such
interrelations were rigid or flexible.

The third problem, or focus of attention, was the basis (or bases) of
individual acceptance or legitimation of social order—coercion,
identification, or self-interest, and the mechanisms by which that
order—its cohesion, solidarity, activity, and functional interdependence
of parts—was maintained.

The fourth problem asked whether social life was basically harmonious
or discordant. That is, did consensus or conflict provide the basic principles of the mechanisms of integration of societies?

*The Developing Perception of Social Order, Disorganization, and
Change; Variability in the Sociological Problemstellung and Theories*

4. It was around these problems, or poles, that the major types of
analytical paradigms or "grand" sociological theories developed. They
have made up the core of the distinctiveness of sociological analysis.

These problems or starting points, however, were in many ways shared by sociology and older types of speculation.

The particular contribution of sociological analysis and theory was the attempt to treat them systematically in terms of the specific reformulation of the problems of social order discussed above, particularly through inquiry into the conditions and mechanisms of social order, rather than the general characteristics of society as a "natural" or moral order.

The impact of this reformulation became most fully manifest in the gradual transformation of several problems which were of central interest in most sociological theories: the problems of social disorder, disorganization, and change. The reanalysis of these concepts, which are present in classical and modern philosophical speculation, was part of the attempt to construct general laws about the conditions of social order and of its transformation in different societies.

The existence of social disorder, the ubiquity of internal conflict, and the demise of sociopolitical systems have been recognized at least since the time of Plato and Aristotle[18] as a basic facet of any society or polity. Hobbes took these phenomena as the point of departure for analysing the possibility of social order.[19] Sociological analysis developed by making these phenomena the starting point for understanding the mechanisms of social order and the conditions of its stability, functioning and change, both generally and in terms of various types of society.

This perspective did not view social disorder as prior to, and hence different from, social order, but saw it rather as one particular constellation of elements which could produce a stable social order. Still other combinations of the same elements could produce change within that order, or societal transformation. In other words, the phenomena of disorder were to be analysed in the same terms as those of social order.

Views of social order and disorganization as dichotomous did persist in certain sociological formulations—such as the distinction between the normal and the pathological as developed by Durkheim,[20] or between statics and dynamics, as developed by Spencer.[21] But the major thrust of sociological analysis was away from such an approach.

The new approach to social disorganization became very closely tied to the reformulation of the problems of social change, a reformulation based on the use of the same concepts in the analysis of social change as in that of social order. The ubiquity of social change has also been recognized since classical times.[22] The modern sociological breakthrough was the recognition that social and cultural systems might transform themselves, producing out of their own forces the capacity and impetus for the creation of new social and cultural orders; and that this capacity for transformative capabilities might in fact be related to some phenomena of disorder themselves. Most important, these transformative propensities of social systems were not external or random events, but were also major aspects of the phenomena of social order.

This approach to disorganization and change characterized some of the greatest figures and most important breakthroughs in sociological analysis. The first of these was Marx's analysis, especially his crucial concept of alienation,[23] which he saw as potential in the very construction by man of his environment, and as activated in specific types of social conditions. Of central importance was Marx's insistence on the ubiquity of alienation and conflict in "class" society and on the close interrelationships of alienation, conflict, and social change. Marx's weakness lay in assuming that alienation and conflict were specific to "class" society, and that they would disappear in the "classless" situation. Hence he concentrated on aspects of conflict which might produce the supposed conflictless society.

A second breakthrough was Simmel's specific contribution—his insights into the perenniality of conflict in social life.[24] But Simmel's view was limited in perspective, focusing on the purely "formal" or general aspects of social interaction that were present in all types of social interaction.

Two further conceptual advances were made by Durkheim and Weber. Both analysed the phenomena of disorganization as a possible central focus for the deeper understanding of conditions and mechanisms of the functioning of social order and for their systematic comparative analysis. Durkheim's analysis of anomie was the counterpoint of his preoccupation with social integration, especially on the level of "organic solidarity,"[25] For Weber, confrontation between the institution-building and institution-destroying tendencies of charisma in various societal settings was a central focus of analysis.[26] Durkheim and Weber, like Marx, saw the possibility of change and conflict as given in the very constitutive aspects of social order. Unlike him, however, they left the ubiquity of such conflict an open question. Hence they were much more flexible in indicating the various different structural conditions under which this possibility could be realized to different degrees and in different ways.

Closely related to the analysis of disorganization was the increasing recognition of the great variety of types of social order or of societies. This recognition, at least in the analysis of political orders, is present in Aristotelian thought, as is the attempt to relate different political orders to different types of individual moral postures and civic attitudes.[27] In these two respects, modern sociological analysis is very much in the Aristotelian tradition. However, it goes beyond the Aristotelian tradition, first, by refusing to equate the social and political orders, seeing greater variety in their possible interrelationships; and second, by stressing the variety of interrelationships between moral and transcendental orientations and types of social order.[28] In this respect, as Edward Shils has pointed out,

"Sociology has partially closed the gap left by Aristotle between the *Ethics* and the *Politics*."[29] Modern sociology also goes beyond Aristotle in seeing temporal development as one major mechanism of the variety and changeability of social orders, and by focusing on the internal transformative capacities of social orders as well as major changes.

This recognition and curiosity about the great variety of forms of social life and institutions was shared by ethnographers, historians, and social statisticians, but sociology differed from ethnographic description by attempting to place the concrete descriptions within the analytic framework of its explanatory paradigms. The interest in the variability of social institutions led to emphasis, both in sociology and such related fields as anthropology on environmental factors (geographical, climatic) as systematically influencing the working of social order and the development of a variety of types of society.[30] The first major modern figures in the study of comparative institutions were Montesquieu and some of the Scottish moralists, particularly Adam Ferguson and J. Millar. Later, various ethnologists and anthropologists, including E. B. Taylor, took up such studies, as did, still later, the various evolutionary schools of the nineteenth century.[31] These were followed in the twentieth century by the great surge of comparative studies in the social sciences of the 1940s.[32]

This shift in explanatory tools, characterizing the modern perception of the problems of social life, encouraged the gradual sociological reformulation of the basic problems of social order and its explanation of regularities in social life—in the development of societies, various macrosocietal or institutional patterns, or of patterns of social behavior—as well as the constraints and possibilities of creativity within them. The shift in problem definition and the analysis of social organization and change created another crucial aspect of sociological analysis: the application of these problem-formulations and approaches to different levels of social life, ranging from macrosocietal analysis to patterns of daily informal behavior, and to study of the interrelationships among them. Through such extension, the specific sociological *Problemstellung* became accessible to different types of research beginning to develop in ethnography, social surveys and statistics, and in political journalism and publicist writing.[33]

The First Central Areas and Concepts of Sociological Theory: Comparative Macrosocietal Analysis and the Analysis of Modern Societies

5.   The differentiating intellectual characteristics of sociology first became visible in several leading areas of research in the emerging sociological tradition. One major area was that of macrosocietal analysis: compara-

tive analysis in general, and the analysis of modern social order in particular. Another was the search for general "numerical" or "mathematical" laws of society.[34]

Macrosocietal analysis centered on three major problems: first, the general characteristics of "societies" in terms of the theoretical problems specified above; second, the comparative analysis of different types of societies and institutional complexes; third, the explanation of typological variation in terms of social or "natural" forces or mechanisms.

The first major concern of comparative macrosocietal analysis, which was central to modern sociology from its inception, was the understanding of the peculiar "qualitative" and "descriptive" characteristics of premodern Europe and non-European societies in relation to (especially in contrast with) modern—initially European—societies. In sociological and anthropological analysis, concern with the characteristics of modern society was linked to the description and analysis of structural and organizational aspects of different types of societies. This provided the impetus to the development of comparative studies in sociology.

Many Forerunners and, even more, Founding Fathers of sociology undertook such comparisons, although they varied in stressing general macrotheoretical or comparative approaches as against the detailed analysis of the modern social order; or general laws of society or social development as against the historical specificity of different concrete societies or of modern society. Thus such eighteenth-century thinkers as Montesquieu, Ferguson, and the Scottish philosophers were more interested in comparative structural studies than in the qualitative characteristics of modern societies.[35] By contrast, Marx, and to some extent Tocqueville, were far more interested in analyzing the specific characteristics of modern societies, although they too especially Marx, never ignored the comparative or the general analytical perspective.[36]

The first great combinations of general macrosocietal, comparative studies and analyses of the specific characteristics of modern social orders emerged in the evolutionary schools. The great figures of evolutionary thought, Comte and Marx, tried to synthesize these emphases by showing, through comparative analysis of customs or institutions, what seemed to them to be the universal trend of development of human society toward the extension of liberty, rationality, and progress.[37]

Long after the breakdown of the various evolutionary syntheses, whether positivist (i.e. Comtean or Spencerean) or Marxist, comparative evolutionary analysis remained the central analytic focus in sociology. Even Durkheim, who was one of the most severe critics of positivist evolutionary sociology, retained this comparative and evolutionary perspective in his distinction between mechanical and organic solidarity.[38]

The same perspective was also reflected in Tönnies' distinction between *Gemeinschaft* and *Gesellschaft*,[39] concepts that designated not merely ideal types of social order, but an evolutionary sequence. This perspective later took the form of the distinction between "traditional" and "modern" societies.

The most articulated "post-evolutionary" formulation of this approach is found in Weber. Instead of postulating one general and universal evolutionary trend for all societies and using comparative analysis for illustration, he used comparative study to illustrate a certain particular dominant trend in one society or group of societies, assuming that the analysis of such a trend could then throw light on similar or opposite tendencies in other societies. Yet throughout these studies he was, implicitly or explicitly, concerned with the nature of modern societies and with the relationship between their qualitative and descriptive characteristics.[40]

Weber's most famous analysis of this kind was that of the economic orientations of the great world religions, which he used as a background for analyzing specific religious constellations in Europe, particularly the rise of the Protestant Ethic, which he saw as central to the development of modern capitalism. But his work abounds in other comparative analyses, from his study of types of charismatic authority and the routinization of charisma to his discussion of the trend toward bureaucratization within modern societies.

6.   Many of the analytic tools which guided these comparative studies, and which were central to the development of sociological theory, were formulated through the combination of comparative approaches with the analysis of the predicaments of modern society. Most of the conceptual tools of sociology—that is, such concepts as "class," "state," "civil society," "liberty," "authority," and "law," as well as concrete problems of sociological analysis—developed from the intellectual concerns of the Enlightenment and the ideological issues of political and economic revolutions of the eighteenth and nineteenth centuries. As we have seen, they were transformed from normative or descriptive into presumably analytical or analytical-descriptive concepts that defined the major components of the social and institutional order, or of aspects of modern societies.

Most of the analytic concepts used to depict the working and developmental trends in them, were also derived from a comparative perspective—such tools as the "societal division of labor," "structural differentiation," "rationalizattion," "bureaucratization," and "mechanical" or "organic" solidarity. These concepts illuminated major characteristics of modern social life, trends of development of society, and the basis of social cohesion in different types of society.

From these concepts in comparative analysis, or the analysis of modern society, some of the major themes of sociological speculation developed in turn—such themes as the tensions between society and community, power and autonomy, status and class, sacred and secular, progress and alienation—which have been singled out by Robert Nisbet as the major themes of modern sociology.[41]

These tools were used, in varying emphases, either for the construction of "grand theories," for broad comparative analyses, or for the analysis of the historical specificity of particular societies. Whatever the emphases, however, the work and the specific *Problemstellung* of the first generations of sociologists, above all the Founding Fahters, were guided by these concepts in various combinations. These concepts have affected all subsequent developments in sociological thought and analysis.

7. The effort to link the sociological *Problemstellung* and descriptions of contemporary life, with numerical or mathematical laws of social behavior was first displayed in the works of Adolphe Quetelet and of Frédéric LePlay.[42]

Because of weak analytic formulation and its institutional isolation however, the mathematical tradition had only tenuous relations to broader research programs, and never became part of the central sociological tradition.[43]

The other areas of research mentioned in the preceding chapter—the study of contemporary conditions of life, of family, stratification, social mobility, were also incorporated into major sociological analyses only gradually. Some of them crystallized in the peripheral disciplines of demography and "social biology."

In the period between that of the Founding Fathers and the late 1940s, these concerns displaced macrosociological analysis as a central focus of attention. Later, macrosociological issues moved back into the center of sociological analysis, along with other areas of research.

Methodological advances in observation, field work, and quantification, are another area that was incorporated into the sociological tradition only at a later time.[44]

The Distinctiveness of Sociology; Emerging Relationships Between Sociology and Other Intellectual Traditions

8. The development of a specifically sociological Problemstellung and a stable research tradition was enhanced insofar as sociology attained its distinctiveness from closely related disciplines. Its differentiation from philosophical and ideological orientations lay in the attempt to transform philosophical questions about the nature and bases of social order into analytic problems which could be tested empirically. Its distinction from the perspectives of social reformers, political publicists, and historians, ethnographers, and sociographers consisted in the transposition of the concrete problems it shared with these disciplines to the framework of a more general concern with the nature and problems of social order—the search for regularities in the structure of societies, institutions, and social behavior, the use of more general and analytic concepts, and the effort at scientific verification.

Although a unique tradition and *Problemstellung* with research implications were emerging, the impetus generated by sociological inquiry also provided a major focus and rallying point for the broader developing tradition of critical self-appraisal. The sociological enterprise continued to be part of the self-critical, intellectual tradition that had developed in Europe since the early seventeenth century, sharing many concerns and problems with other parts of this tradition.

Thus, sociology was in constant competition with other intellectual traditions in trying to provide, in terms of its own *Problemstellung,* the appropriate scholarly and critical perspective on social life, especially modern social life. Its distinctiveness in the period of the Founding Fathers, therefore, was not attained by isolation of sociology from other intellectual traditions or an accepted interdisciplinary division of scientific labor. It became distinct, rather, insofar as the problems it shared with other orientations were transformed in terms of its particular problem formulations.

Since the components of sociological analysis, however, were rooted in different traditions, they could develop fairly independently of each other, maintaining or "reopening" connections with "parent" or "sister" disciplines that were often stronger than the links to other components of the new sociological tradition. Thus, sociological theories could be closely tied to philosophical schools and certain ideological orientations.[45] More specific, middle-range problems could be closely related to the new traditions of publicistic writing, political analysis, or history and ethnography, while many concrete research programs and methodological problems could be related to statistical and demographic inquiry. Indeed, for a long period of time, the various traditions of speculative analysis and different types of research, from which the major components of sociological analysis emerged, went their separate ways,[46] coming together only in "passing" situations and in the work of only a few people.

Although the pull of these intellectual and institutional traditions has been strong, other developments permitted contact among them and the gradual crystallization of "sociology." There was no single "royal way" to such a synthesis. In different situations and phases of development, the components united in different combinations. Any combination of components, when reformulated in terms of the sociological *Problemstellung*, could become, as the history of sociology shows, the basis of an initial, and sometimes permanent, institutionalization of some type of sociological analysis. The most fruitful source of such combinations was, as we shall see, the synthesis of the sociological *Problemstellung* with certain types of research—historical, ethnological, comparative, statistical, field work, and contemporary survey—and the continual testing of analysis by these research techniques.

Even where sociology developed fairly autonomously, it was not dissociated from other approaches and intellectual traditions. Moreover, where the different components of sociology crystallized in a concrete situation, tensions among them developed, competing with other parts of the broader tradition from which sociology was becoming differentiated.[47] Thus, as it emerged as a distinct orientation, its intellectual and institutional relationships with other modern intellectual traditions were continually problematic and tension-ridden. These tensions shaped some of the major foci of discussion within the sociological camp and around it.

Foci of Tension and Discussion Between Sociology and Other Intellectual Traditions; the Definition of the Intellectual Identity of Sociology and Role Orientations of Sociologists

9. These tensions and problems were expressed in several types of discussions, and debates which were most fully articulated in the second stage of the development of sociology. First was the discussion of the definition of the intellectual and institutional self-identity of sociology and the major components or reference orientations of the sociologist's role. Second were discussions of the definition of sociology's subject matter as distinct from that of other academic disciplines. Third were discussions about major methodological and metaanalytical problems and questions which were continually raised about sociology.

The attempt to attain distinctiveness in the modern intellectual tradition, however, confronted professed sociologists with more than the question of the *content* and boundaries of sociology. It also posed the problem of sociology's *place* in the new intellectual-scientific tradition that had been emerging since the eighteenth century. These problems did not trouble scholars or intellectuals like Tocqueville, who did not identify themselves as sociologists and who were only later incorporated into the sociological tradition. Nor did they concern Marx, for whom the special identity of sociology was of no interest at all—although the ways in which he developed his distinctiveness from Hegelian-idealist philosophy (with the partial exception of emphasis on *praxis* or direct ideological involvement) resembled the way in which many sociologists tried to define the distinctiveness of sociology.[48]

The question of the intellectual identity and place of sociology, however, was of great concern to the Forerunners of sociology, like Comte and Spencer. To a somewhat lesser degree, it also troubled scholars like von Stein, Albert Schäffle, Gustav Ratzenhofer, Ludwig Gumplowicz, and Franz Oppenheimer.[49]

The initial dissociation of sociology from philosophy and the stress on its ability to formulate the laws of human society were often combined with pretensions to provide a new over-all "scientific," "secular" guide to behavior in the modern setting. Sociologists tried to portray their discipline as a kind of secular religion, part of the basic manifestation of the religion of progress, reason, and humanity. Indeed, in these initial attempts to define the scope and intellectual place of sociology, the scientific, critical, moral, and practical—that is, policy-oriented—aspects of sociology were closely combined,[50] and were subsumed under a general vision of sociology as a secular or scientific substitute for religion or philosophy, as the apex of the humanistic sciences.

Gradually, the different elements of the self-image of sociologists were decomposed, and these pretensions were subjected to increasing criticism among those who called themselves sociologists. A skepticism emerged among the Founding Fathers—Durkheim, Weber, Simmel, and Tönnies—toward the "philosophical" optimism or pessimism of the Forerunners.[51] This sceptical view was even more apparent in the work of Pareto and Mosca,[52] who were even less sanguine about the possibility of combining the various orientations—scientific, moral, critical, and practical—under the single intellectual canopy of sociology. The philosophical impulse, the concern with the existential and moral dimensions of modern society, and the commitment to upholding the moral fabric of society were still very strong for all of these scholars. But they doubted sociology's ability to provide panaceas for the ills of the modern world. Even when (as Durkheim did) they tried to overcome these doubts, these scholars tended increasingly to sense the tensions among their own scholarly orientations, their own moral commitments and orientations, and the variety of critical orientations to social reality—tensions which only increased their commitment to sociology as an objective scholarly analysis, combined with a distant and critical orientation to modern society.

Out of these sceptical attitudes and the effort to find a base in academic life, there developed in sociology first, the scholarly emphasis; second, varying types of commitment to a critical evaluation of society; and third, the practical concern as a component of the sociologist's role. Based on the discipline's slowly evolving definition, these three areas also embodied internal disagreements.

The scholarly scientific attitude and the critical orientation could be congruent as well as antithetical. Their common core was the nonacceptance of any social reality or explanation of it as given, and the consequent search for a critical, objective analysis of society. These orientations diverged, however, insofar as the critical orientation could become identified with ideology or politics denying the possibility of disinterested scholarly analysis. Parallel tensions also developed between the scholarly and practical, and between the practical and critical orientations,—especially around the problem of "total" vs. piecemeal approach to social affairs, and on the appropriate degree of political involvement.

In conjunction with the institutionalization of sociology, these issues became poles of tension about the conception of sociology and the sociologist's role.

One pole of tension involved the "prophetic" vs. "priestly" orientation. Should the critical or "prophetic" component of the sociologist's role be stressed, along with his participation in ideological, reforming, political, or intellectual communities or publics? Or should sociology be seen as an "objective," scholarly enterprise, with roots in the academic institutions and publics and with a stronger "priestly" component?[53] Within the critical role a further tension developed between the prophetic conception of sociology as a sort of secular substitute for religion and a more detached, less utopian, but nevertheless political stance. Still another conflict arose between the practical or applied component of the sociologist's role and the scholarly or critical component.

Within the policy orientation there developed, in turn, as Shils has shown, the tension between manipulative, alienated, and consensual sociologies. The third term refers to the use of sociology as part of the process of transforming the relationship of authority and subject through the enhancement of self-understanding and a sense of affinity. The distinction implied in the first and third terms resembles the "enlightenment" and "engineering" models analyzed by Janowitz.[54]

With the institutionalization of sociology, each orientation produced many suborientations, to be analyzed later. Moreover, many "crossings" occurred between these poles or role-references. The salience of each pole varied greatly in different stages and situations. All of them, however, have been constant, if often latent, components of the sociologist's self-image, activated in different situations, and affecting several important aspects of the intellectual development of sociology.

*The Major Points of Metaanalytic Disputes: the Scope and Identity of
Sociology, Sociological Method, and the Problems of Value-Free
Sociology*

10. The tensions involved in attaining distinctiveness from other
intellectual traditions shaped discussions not only of the intellectual identity of sociology and the sociologist's role, but also matters of intellectual
content. One of course was precisely the problem of its intellectual distinctiveness from other academic disciplines, a problem reinforced by its
academic aspirations. What was its subject matter as distinct from that of
history, social philosophy, or ethnography, and from other social sciences, such as economics and political science? This search for an unique
subject matter led initially to a wavering between a view of sociology as the
apex of the social sciences, and a search for a narrower analytic focus on
"formal" elements in social life, such as the element of "sociability."[55]

The problem of subject matter was often related to discussion of the
proper method of sociology. The core issue in these methodological
debates was whether the human and social sciences could develop along
the pattern of the natural sciences, given the special nature of the data of
human social experience, as well as the intimate involvement of social
research in social and cultural life itself. Accordingly, these debates centered on several points.[56] Among the most persistent foci were views of
sociology as nomothetic vs. ideographic, as a positivist vs. a humanistic
science; of the respective validity of cause and seemingly deterministic
analyses patterned after natural science as against explanations based on
Verstehen and the imputation of meaning to people's activities; and of
causal and comparative generalization as against explanation in terms of
unique historical situations. Closely related to these issues were also the
first major discussions of "reductionism" and collectivist vs. individualist
explanations of social phenomena; and of the methodological and
philosophical implications of the social investigator's inseparability from
the objects of his research.

11. Cutting across these metaanalytic problems, and echoing the tension between the ideological and scholarly role orientations of
sociologists, was the debate about the possibility of a value-free sociology.
Closely related to this debate was the problem of the major analytic
concepts in sociology.

The problematics of a value-free sociology developed in greatest force,
as we have seen, at the time when the great evolutionary and positivistic
approaches were in decline. Although the issue has been identified with
Weber's discussion, it had already assumed importance before then and
has continued to develop since.[57]

The methodological and metascientific debates on the central concepts of sociological analysis were intimately related to the redefinition of problems of social order that constituted the sociological *Problemstellung.* As we have seen, this redefinition involved major concepts taken from ideological and philosophical movements, particularly concepts which were based on the major themes of protest and on the analysis of the institutional realities of modern society.

The basic vocabulary of sociology took over such normative concepts as "liberty," "equality," "society," and "community," and descriptive terms like "authority," "state," "class," and "social organization." In doing so, however, it transformed them from being normative or descriptive concepts into purportedly analytic or analytic-descriptive terms that described or defined the major components of the social and institutional order, and different aspects of emerging modern structures.

The major problem in such a redefinition, however, was this: whatever the success of these concepts as analytic "objective" terms, they could not be completely divorced from their original evaluative connotations and from the concrete reality to which they addressed themselves. As Reinhard Bendix and Bennett Berger have shown,[58] the very choice of some concepts—such as socialization vs. individualization; class vs. status; rational (bureaucratic) vs. traditional authority; primary vs. secondary relations—implied certain views of society and greatly influenced the concrete propositions derived from them. Moreover, any definition of a concept—class, family, and so on—was often influenced and limited by the particular institutional setting to which it was oriented.

Hence, sociological analysis has always faced the possibility of "petrification" or "reification" of its concepts. Consequently, it has experienced a constant need to reexamine and redefine its concepts, often breaking them up into new components.

The relative importance of these metaanalytic problems and those involving the intellectual identity of sociology, varied in different periods and situations of institutionalization.[59] Some of these problems, especially those pertaining to the proper subject matter of sociology, have almost disappeared as different research areas have developed and sociology has attained academic institutionalization. Others, particularly the metaanalytical, philosophical, and methodological ones, have reemerged, albeit in new forms, in periods of growing consolidation in sociological analysis.

These controversies kept the internal tradition of sociology open to those intellectual forebears from which it was differentiated: philosophy, whether in the form of social philosophy, theory of scientific method, or theory of knowledge; to history; to political analysis; and ideological and political movements and orientations. Such openness was generally only latent. But in some situations they were reactivated, and in those cases they exerted great influence on sociological analysis and research.

12.   Some consequences of this openness to parent traditions was evident in the discussions analyzed above. In Germany, these debates, in which Weber was a central figure, took place among the "Socialists of the Chairs," or on the famous *Methodenstreit*. In France, somewhat similar discussions were taken up by Durkheim, Gaston Richard, René Worms, and others.[60]

It was in these discussions that the first "crisis" of sociology developed, first involving these problems which would be recurrent and even more prominent in later periods: the problem of the identity of sociology, its intellectual bases, and its relationship to bordering disciplines. These controversies also entailed an examination of the validity, limits, and possibilities of prevaling sociological concepts; the "nature" or "standing" of sociology; the real and presumed methodological weakness of sociological research; the weaknesses in the sociological enterprise; and the relationship between theory and research.

Incipiently the problem of impact of "crises" in sociology on its development also emerged. This impact might be productive or destructive.

The constructive potential of these crises showed itself in the broadening and deepening of intellectual activity. This included the development of different and more sophisticated sociological theories; broader scope of research related to such theories; the development of more sustained research programs; and increasing mutual orientations among different sociological groups.

Crises could have negative outcomes too. One of these was the increasing compartmentalization of "schools," each with its own paradigms and research programs, and the tendency of such schools to develop metaphysical and ideological closure. Another was the bifurcation of sociological analysis into dogmatic-metaphysical assertions about the nature of society and sociological inquiry, and the emphasis on purely technical aspects of sociological research which could be used in administrative affairs.

13.   An extremely interesting aspect of development of sociology that first became apparent at this stage involved the impact of external intellectual influences on the internal development of sociological theory and research. Within various sociological communities or sectors, the components of the sociological tradition (e.g., philosophical speculations, comparative research, empirical research) were combined in different patterns and stressed in different ways. Various intellectual orientations also developed in the definition of sociological work, especially "critical," "conservative," and reformist orientations, and consensual vs. conflictual views of social life.

Such differences, occurring in sectors that shared similar analytic and institutional developments, were closely related to trends in the major intellectual circles. As we have seen, sociologists were closely related to these intellectual circles, and these external influences greatly affected the general tenor of sociological discussion, the choice of concrete research problems, and often the selection of conceptual tools. Although much systematic work—in contrast to the speculations of recent controversies[61]—must still be done to analyze the precise impact of these "external" forces on various aspects of sociological work, there can be no doubt about their great influence on sociological analysis.

Along with these influences, however, some areas of agreement gradually emerged on common concepts, problems, and analytic approaches. Grounded in the specific sociological *Problemstellung,* this agreement cut across the various intellectual modes. While these common approaches were still quite tenuous at this stage, they became apparent in the work of the Founding Fathers and in the discussions and controversies over their works. Their future development was greatly influenced by the outcomes of the first "crisis" in sociology, and some of these possibilities became evident in the subsequent stage of development, between the two World Wars. Before proceeding to this stage, however, the most central analytic aspect of sociology, so-called sociological "theory" or "theories," must still be analysed.

Notes

1. E. A. Tiryakian, "Introduction to the sociology of sociology," in E. A. Tiryakian (ed.), *The Phenomenon of Sociology* (New York: Appleton–Century–Crofts, Meredith, 1971), especially pp. 6–9.
2. The studies on the development of sociology from philosophy are of course too numerous to cite. For some earlier analyses which contain useful information on the relationship of sociology to the development of history, jurisprudence, see the surveys on the development of sociology in different countries in the *Encyclopedia of the Social Sciences,* Vol. 1 (New York: Macmillan, 1930), pp. 231–349. See also H. Becker and H. E. Barnes, *Social Thought from Lore to Science,* (New York: Dover, 1961), especially Vol. 2; T. Parsons, "Unity and diversity in the modern intellectual disciplines; the role of the social sciences," *Daedalus,* Vol. 94 (1965), pp. 39–65; F. Jonas, *Geschichte der Soziologie* (München: Rowohlt Verlag, 1968), 4 vols; S. Landshut, *Kritik der Soziologie und Leipzig:* Verlag von Duncker & Humblot, 1929); E. Topitsch, *Sozialphilosophie zwischen Ideologie und Wissenschaft,* (Berlin: Luchterhand, Neuwied, 1966); I. Zeitlin, *Ideology and the Development of Sociological Theory* (Englewood Cliffs, N.J.: Prentice-Hall, 1968); A. Salomon, *In Praise of Enlightenment: Essays in the History of Ideas* (Cleveland and New York: World, 1963), especially Chs. 6, 7; A. Pizzorno, "Una crisi che non importa superare," in P. Rossi (ed.) *Ricerca Sociologica e Ruolo del Sociologo* (Bologna: Il Mulino, 1972), pp. 327–357; R. Aron, *De la Condition Historique du Sociologue* (Paris: Gallimard, 1971); G. Gurvitch, "Brève esquisse de l'histoire de la sociologie," in G. Gurvitch (ed.), *Traité de Sociologie* (Paris: Presses Universitaires de France, 1958), pp. 28–65.
3. On the tradition of social reform in these countries and in Germany, see P. Abrams, *The Origins of British Sociology: 1834–1914* (Chicago: University of Chicago Press, 1968), pp.

8–153; R. C. and G. J. Hinkle, *The Development of Modern Sociology: its Nature and Growth in the U.S.* (New York: Doubleday, 1954), Ch. 1; L. Bramson, "The rise of American sociology," in E. A. Tiryakian (ed.), *The Phenomenon of Sociology, op. cit.,* pp. 65–80; A. Oberschall, "The institutionalization of American sociology," in A. Oberschall (ed.), *The Establishment of Empirical Sociology: Studies in Continuity, Discontinuity, and Institutionalization* (New York: Harper & Row, 1972), pp. 187–251; T. N. Clark, *Prophets and Patrons: The French University and the Emergence of the Social Sciences* (Cambridge, Mass.: Harvard University Press, 1973), Ch. 3; A. Oberschall, *Empirical Social Research in Germany, 1848–1914* (Paris, The Hague: Mouton, 1965).

4. On these attitudes, see the items cited in note 3 and also H. and J. R. Schwendinger, *The Sociologists of the Chair: a Radical Analysis of the Formative Years of North American Sociology, 1883–1922* (New York: Basic Books, 1974); R. A. Nisbet, "The French Revolution and the rise of sociology in France," in E. A. Tiryakian (ed.), *The Phenomenon of Sociology, op. cit.,* pp. 27–36; A. Giddens, *Capitalism and Modern Social Theory: an Analysis of the Writings of Marx, Durkheim and Max Weber* (London: Cambridge University Press, 1971), Part 1.

5. On Tocqueville see among others A. Salomon, *In Praise of Enlightenment, op. cit.,* Ch. 7; J. M. Zeitlin, *Liberty, Equality and Revolution in Alexis de Tocqueville* (Boston: Little, Brown, 1971).

   On L. von Stein see S. Landshut, *Kritik der Soziologie, op. cit.;* L. von Stein, *Staat und Gesellschaft* (Zürich: Rascher, 1934).

6. The literature on these scholars is, of course, too extensive to cite. What follows are some of the best analyses.

   On Durkheim see R. Aron, *Main Currents in Sociological Thought,* Vol. 2 (London: Penguin Books, 1970), pp. 21–107.

   On Weber see O. Stammer (ed.), *Max Weber and Sociology Today* (Oxford: Basil Blackwell, 1971); R. Bendix, *Max Weber: an Intellectual Portrait* (New York: Doubleday, 1960), Ch. 14; A. Giddens, *Politics and Sociology in the Thought of Max Weber* (London: Macmillan, 1972); W. Mommsen, *Max Weber—Gesellschaft, Politik und Geschichte* (Frankfurt an Main: Suhrkamp, 1974).

   On Tönnies see A. Mitzman, *Sociology and Estrangement: Three Sociologists of Imperial Germany* (New York: Knopf, 1973), pp. 39–131.

   On Simmel see D. N. Levine, "Introduction," in *Georg Simmel on Individuality and Social Forms,* selected writings edited by D. N. Levine (Chicago: University of Chicago Press, 1971).

   On L. T. Hobhouse, see M. Ginsberg, "L. T. Hobhouse," in *The International Encyclopedia of the Social Sciences,* Vol. 6 (New York: Macmillan, 1968), pp. 487–489.

7. T. N. Clark, *Prophets and Patrons, op. cit.,* Ch. 6; R. N. Bellah, "Introduction," in *Emile Durkheim on Morality and Society,* edited by R. N. Bellah (Chicago: University of Chicago Press, 1973).

8. On this see *Max Weber on Charisma and Institution Building,* selected papers, edited and with an introduction by S. N. Eisenstadt (Chicago and London: University of Chicago Press, 1968), pp. 6, 18–42, 48–77.

9. For this see K. Mannheim, *Man and Society in an Age of Reconstruction* (London: Routledge and Kegan Paul, 1940), especially pp. 51–60.

10. On this see E. Durkheim, *The Division of Labor in Society* (New York: Free Press, 1964); E. Durkheim, *Suicide* (New York: Free Press, 1966); R. N. Bellah, "Introduction," in *Emile Durkheim on Morality and Society, op. cit.*

11. On Mannheim see K. Mannheim, *Man and Society in an Age of Reconstruction, op. cit.;* K. Mannheim, *Diagnosis of Our Time* (London: Routledge and Kegan Paul, 1943); K.

Mannheim, *Freedom, Power and Democratic Planning* (London: Routledge and Kegan Paul, 1961); G. W. Remmling, *The Sociology of Karl Mannheim* (London: Routledge and Kegan Paul, 1975).

On the Frankfurt school, see M. Jay, *The Dialectical Imagination: a History of the Frankfurt School and the Institute of Social Research, 1923-1950* (Boston: Little, Brown, 1973).

On Hobhouse see L. T. Hobhouse, *Social Development: its Nature and Conditions* (London: Allen and Unwin, 1924); M. Ginsberg, "L. T. Hobhouse," *International Encyclopedia of the Social Sciences, op. cit.*

On Ginsberg see M. Ginsberg, *Reason and Unreason: Essays in Sociology and Social Philosophy* (London: London School of Economics, 1947), especially Chs. 1, 6, 15, 16; M. Ginsberg, *On Justice in Society* (London: Penguin, 1965); J. Gould, "On Morris Ginsberg," *The Jewish Journal of Sociology* Vol. 16, No. 2, (December 1974), pp. 123-133.

12. One set of such problems has been recently enumerated by Percy Cohen:

a. Why do members of social groups and systems continue to participate in them? For example, why don't the citizens of one state, or the members of one tribe, clan, or lineage, or the officeholder of one organization, leave it for another?

b. Why do the sections or segments of a social unit, or collectivity, hold together? Why do they not secede from the whole of which they are parts? Why do lineages not split off from tribes, and tribes from states? Why do sects not become separate churches, or factions become different parties? Why do conjugal family units remain part of joint family units? This is the problem of cohesion.

c. Why do members of a social group, quasigroup, or collectivity continue to recognize themselves as an entity, distinct from other such entities, and why are they prepared under some conditions to act as an entity? This is the problem of solidarity.

d. Why do the participants in a social system or subsystem of a society adhere to or conform to its norms? These are the problems of compliance, commitment, conformity, and consensus.

e. Why do the different acts of men in social systems continue to complement, reciprocate, support, or correspond to one another? This is the problem of mutuality.

On this see P. Cohen, *Modern Social Theory* (London: Heinemann, 1968), p. 129.

13. This aspect of development of sociological thought is analyzed in S. N. Eisenstadt, "The development of sociological thought," *The International Encyclopedia of the Social Sciences,* Vol. 15, *op. cit.,* pp. 23-35.

14. K. Marx, *Early Writings,* edited by T. B. Bottomore (New York: McGraw-Hill, 1963), pp. 168-188, 189-194; K. Marx, *Selected Writings in Sociology and Social Philosophy,* edited by T. B. Bottomore and M. Rubel (London: Penguin Books, 1965), pp. 175-185.

15. E. Durkheim, *The Division of Labor in Society, op. cit.,* especially Book 1, Ch. 7, Book 3, Ch. 1.

16. Some of the pertinent materials on this have been collected in Max Weber, *On Charisma and Institution Building, op. cit.,* especially pp. 11-12, 46-47, 54-61.

17. For this and the problems discussed below, see S. N. Eisenstadt, "The development of sociological thought," *op. cit.*

18. For the relation of sociology to the Aristotelian tradition, see E. Shils, "The calling of sociology," in T. Parsons, E. Shils, K. D. Naegele, and J. R. Pitts (eds.) *Theories of Society* Vol. 2 (New York: Free Press, 1961), pp. 1405-1448.

19. On the place of the Hobbesian problem in sociology, see the classical statement of T. Parsons in *The Structure of Social Action,* Vol. 1 (New York: Free Press, 1968), pp. 89-94.

20. E. Durkheim, *The Rules of Sociological Method,* (New York, Free Press, 1964), Ch. 3.

21. See J. D. Y. Peel (ed.), *Herbert Spencer on Social Evolution* (Chicago: University of Chicago Press, 1973), pp. 17–33; R. Fletcher, *The Making of Sociology: a. Study of Sociological Theory* Vol. 1 (London: Michael Joseph, 1971), pp. 250–338.

22. For a comprehensive review of conceptions of social change since antiquity, especially stressing the distinction between historical vs. progressive-evolutionary change see R. A. Nisbet, *Social Change and History* (London, New York: Oxford University Press, 1969); E. Shils, "The calling of sociology," *op. cit.*

23. On the concept of alienation and its relation to "class" society, conflict, and change, as discussed below, see K. Marx, *Early Writings, op. cit.*; K. Marx, *Selected Writings in Sociology and Social Philosophy, op. cit.*, pp. 175–185, 236–245, 249–263.

   On the concept of alienation in Marx and its derivatives see also B. Ollman, *Alienation: Marx's Conception of Man in Capitalist Society* (Cambridge: Cambridge University Press, 1971); J. Israel, *Alienation from Marx to Moderns Sociology—a Macrosociological Analysis* (Boston: Allyn & Bacon, 1971); R. Schacht, *Alienation* (London: George Allen & Unwin, 1971); S.Avineri, *The Social and Political Thought of Karl Marx* (Cambridge: Cambridge University Press, 1968), Ch. 4.

24. See G. Simmel, *Conflict and the Web of Group Affiliations* (New York: Free Press, 1964), especially Chs. 1–3; D. N. Levine, "Introduction," in *Georg Simmel on Individuality and Social Forms, op. cit.*

25. E. Durkheim, *Suicide, op. cit.*; E. Durkheim, *The Division of Labor in Society, op. cit.*

26. *Max Weber on Charisma and Institution Building, op. cit.,* pp. 18–27; 48–65.

27. G. H. Sabine, *A History of Political Theory* (London: George G. Harrap, 1959), especially Chs. 5, 6.

28. This approach can be best illustrated by Max Weber's works. On the purely analytical level, it is implied in the ideal types of the orientations of social action as well as in the general types of orientations to social order. Some of the relevant materials for this point have been gathered in Max Weber, *On Charisma and Institution Building, op. cit.,* pp. 3–6, 11–12.

   For a broader review of Weber's historical-comparative works in this connection, see also R. Bendix, *Max Weber: an Intellectual Portrait, op. cit.*; W. Mommsenn, *Max Weber, Gesellschaft, Politik und Geschichte, op. cit.*

29. E. Shils, "The calling of sociology," *op. cit.*, p. 1419.

30. For this see P. A. Sorokin, *Contemporary Sociological Theories* (New York: Harper & Row, 1928), Ch. 3.

31. On Montesquieu, see C. Montesquieu, *The Spirit of the Laws* (New York: Hafner, 1949); A. Salomon, *In Prise of Enlightenment, op. cit.*, pp. 117–140.

   On the Scottish Moralists see G. Bryson, *Man and Society: The Scottish Inquiry of the Eighteenth Century* (Princeton: Princeton University Press, 1945).

   On Taylor and other anthropologists see E. B. Taylor, *Researches into the Early History of Mankind and the Development of Civilization* (London: Murray, 1878); E. B. Taylor, *Primitive Culture: Researches into the Development of Mythology, Philosophy, Religion, Art and Customs,* (Gloucester, Mass.: Smith, 1958), 2 vols.; H. Becker and H. E. Barnes, *Social Thought from Lore to Science, op. cit.,* Vol. 2, pp. 748–757.

   On evolutionism, especially that of Comte and Spencer, see A. Comte, *The Positive Philosophy* (London: Trübner, 1853), 2 vols.; A. Comte, *Positive Polity* (London, Longmans, Green and Co., 1875–1877); H. Spencer, *The Principles of Sociology* (New York: Appleton, 1925–1929), 3 vols.; J. D. Y. Peel, (ed.), *Herbert Spencer on Social*

Evolution, op. cit.; R. Fletcher, *The Making of Sociology,* Vol. 1, *op. cit.,* pp. 165–196, 250–338.

32. For a brief survey of these developments see S. N. Eisenstadt, "Social institutions: comparative study," *International Encyclopedia of the Social Sciences,* Vol. 14, *op. cit.,* pp. 421–29.

33. For brief surveys on the emergence of these traditions of research, see B. Lécuyer and A. R. Oberschall, "Sociology: the early history of social research," *International Encyclopedia of the Social Sciences,* Vol. 15, *op. cit.,* pp. 36–53; P. Lazarsfeld, "Notes on the history of quantification in sociology: trends, sources and problems,"*Isis,* Vol. 52, No. 2 (1961), pp. 277–333.

34. On the beginning of research oriented to discovery of mathematical laws in society, see P. Lazarsfeld, "Notes on the history of quantification in sociology," *op. cit.*

35. For Montesquieu and the Scottish philosophers see the items cited in note 31.

36. For Marx, see relevant materials gathered in Karl Marx, *Selected Writings in Sociology and Social Philosoohy, op. cit.,* especially Parts 2, 3; A. Giddens, *Capitalism and Modern Social Theory, op. cit.* Part I.
    For Tocqueville see A. Salomon, *In Praise of Enlightenment, op. cit.,* Ch. 7.

37. For Comte, see the relevant items cited in note 3.
    For Marx, see the materials gathered in Karl Marx, *Selected Writings in Sociology and Social Philosophy, op. cit.*
    For these social thinkers, see also R. Aron, *Main Currents in Sociological Thought* Vol. 1 (London: Penguin Books, 1968), pp. 63–182.

38. On this see E. Durkheim, *The Division of Labor in Society, op. cit.;* E. Durkheim, *The Rules of Sociological Method, op. cit.,* especially Chs. 4, 5; R. Aron, *Main Currents in Sociological Thought,* Vol. 2, *op. cit.,* pp. 21–107; R. N. Bellah, "Introduction," in *Emile Durkheim on Morality and Society, op. cit.*

39. F. Tönnies, *Gemeinschaft und Gesellschaft,* translated in English as *Community and Society,* (East Lansing, Mich.: State University Press, 1957); W. J. Cahnman (ed.), *Ferdinand Tönnies, a New Evaluation* (Leiden: E. J. Brill, 1973), especially pp. 103–124.

40. For the methods employed by Weber in his comparative studies, and for his critical stand against unqualified evolutionary assumptions, see T. Parsons, "Introduction" to M. Weber, *Sociology of Religion,* (Boston: Beacon Press, 1963), pp. xix–xxvii; R. Bendix, *Max Weber: an Intellectual Portrait, op. cit.,* Ch. 8. Bendix's work provides also a good analysis of Weber's comparative studies, mentioned below, and of their contribution to the understanding of the qualitative characteristics of modern Western societies.

41. R. Nisbet, *The Sociological Tradition* (London: Heinemann, 1967).

42. For a review of their works see P. Lazarsfeld, "Notes on the history of quantification in sociology," *op. cit.*

43. For this, especially concerning the LePlayist tradition, see T. N. Clark, *Prophets and Patrons, op. cit.,* Chs. 3, 6.

44. On these trends see E. Shils, "The trend of sociological research," paper read at the 8th International Congress of Sociology, Evian, 1966.

45. For this see the items cited in note 2.

46. For this see E. Shils, "The trend of sociological research," *op. cit..*

47. E. Shils, "The calling of sociology," *op. cit.*

48. On the relationship between Marx's sociological analysis and the Hegelian philosophy see, among many works, R. Aron, *Main Currents in Sociological Thought,* Vol. 1, *op. cit.,*

pp. 111–182; A. Giddens, *Capitalism and Modern Social Theory, op. cit.*, Part 1; S. Landshut, *Kritik der Soziologie, op. cit.,* Ch 3; K. Löwith, *Meaning in History* (Chicago: University of Chicago Press, 1949), Ch. 1, 3.

49. R. Fletcher, *The Making of Sociology,* Vol. 1, *op. cit.*, pp. 165–196, 250–338; F. Jonas, *Geschichte der Soziologie, op. cit.,* Vol. 1, Ch. 3; Vol. 2, Ch. 5; Vol. 4, Ch. 8. On this see also the discussion in I. Seger, *Introduction to Sociology* (London: Rupert Hart-Davis, 1972), especially Chs. 7, 8.

50. For this see the items cited in note 3.

51. For this see, for example;
    On Durkheim, R. N. Bellah, "Introduction" to *Emile Durkheim: on Morality and Society, op. cit.*
    On Weber, see R. Bendix, *Max Weber: an Intellectual Portrait, op. cit.*, Ch. 14; A. Mitzman, *The Iron Cage: an Historical Interpretation of Max Weber* (New York: Grosset & Dunlop, 1969).
    On Tönnies, see A. Mitzman, *Sociology and Estrangement, op. cit.*, pp. 39–131.
    On Simmel, see L. A. Coser, *Masters of Sociological Thought* (New York: Harcourt Brace Jovanovich, 1971), pp. 177–215; D. Levine, "Introduction," in *Georg Simmel on Individuality and Social Forms, op. cit.*

52. J. H. Meisel, "Pareto and Mosca—Introduction," in J. H. Meisel (ed.), *Pareto and Mosca* (Englewood Cliffs, N.J.: Prentice-Hall, 1965), pp. 1–44; H. S. Hughes, *Consciousness and Society* (New York: Vintage, 1958), Ch. 7.

53. On this and other tensions between different orientations in the sociologist's role (discussed below), see R. K. Merton, "Social conflict over styles of sociological work," *Transactions of the 4th World Congress of Sociology,* Vol. 3 (Louvain, International Sociological Association, 1961), pp. 29–44; I. L. Horowitz, "Mainliners and marginals: the human shape of sociological theory," in L. Gross (ed.), *Sociological Theory: Inquiries and Paradigms* (New York: Harper & Row, 1967), pp. 358–383; M. Janowitz, "Professionalization of sociology," in *Varieties of Political Expression in Sociology* (Chicago, University of Chicago Press, 1972), pp. 105–135; R. W. Friedrichs, *A Sociology of Sociology* (New York: Free Press, 1970) especially Chs. 3, 4, 5.

54. On this see E. Shils, "The calling of sociology," *op. cit.;* M. Janowitz, "Professionalization of sociology," *op. cit.*

55. Illuminating in this connection is the difference between Durkheim's "imperialistic" and Simmel's "narrow" definition of sociology.
    For Durkheim see E. Durkheim, *The Rules of Sociological Method, op. cit.* especially Ch. 1; T. N. Clark, *Prophets and Patrons,* op. cit., Ch. 6.
    For Simmel see K. H. Wolff (ed.), *The Sociology of Georg Simmel* (Glencoe, Ill.: Free Press, 1950), especially the introduction and Part 1; D. Levine (ed.), *Georg Simmel on Individuality and Social Forms, op. cit.,* introduction and especially Parts 1, 2.

56. Some of the earlier and later debates over these problems have been brought together or summarized in the following books and collections: T. Adorno et al., *Der Positivismusstreit in der Deutschen Soziologie* (Berlin: Luchterhand und Neuwied, 1969); E. Topitsch, *Sozialphilosophie zwischen Ideologie und Wissenschaft, op. cit.;* W. Hochkeppel, *Soziologie zwischen Theorie und Empirie* (München: Nymphenburger Verlagshandlung, 1970), pp. 13–48, 135–154, 179–195; E. Topitsch, *Logik der Sozialwissenschaften* (Köln: Kiepenheuer & Witsch, 1972), Parts 2, 4, 8; A. Giddens (ed.), *Positivism and Sociology* (London: Heinemann, 1974).
    For some of the relevant material which illustrates the positions of Durkheim and Weber on these problems, see E. Durkheim, *The Rules of Sociological Method, op. cit.*,

especially Chs. 1, 2, 4, 5; Max Weber, *On Charisma and Institution Building, op. cit.,* especially pp. 3–8; Max Weber, *On the Methodology of the Social Sciences* (Glencoe, Ill.: Free Press, 1949); R. Bendix, *Max Weber: an Intellectual Portrait, op. cit.,* especially Chs. 8, 15; R. Aron, *Main Currents in Sociological Thought,* Vol. 2, *op. cit.,* pp. 21–107, 185–258.

57. For Weber see Max Weber, *On the Methodology of the Social Sciences, op. cit.,* especially pp. 1–112; J. Torrance, "Max Weber: methods and the man," *Archives Européennes de Sociologie,* Vol. 15, No. 1 (1974), pp. 127–165.

    For earlier debates on this problem and their reemergence after Weber, see the discussion in Chs. 5, 9, 11, 12, and the relevant material quoted there. See also the introduction and the materials collected in A. Giddens (ed.), *Positivism and Sociology, op. cit.*

58. R. Bendix and B. Berger, "Images of society and problems of concept formation in sociology," in L. Gross (ed.), *Symposium on Sociological Theory* (New York: Harper & Row, 1959), pp. 92–118.

59. For this see the detailed discussion in Chs. 5, 6, 9, 11, 12 and the material quoted there.

60. On the *Methodenstreit* see S. P. Schad, *Empirical Social Research in Weimar Germany* (Paris, The Hague: Mouton, 1972), pp. 44–46.

    On Weber see, among other works, the items quoted in note 57.

    For France see T. N. Clark, *Prophets and Patrons, op. cit.,* Chs. 6, 7; F. Jonas, *Geschichte der Soziologie,* Vol. 4, *op. cit,* Ch. 8; materials in A. Giddens (ed.), *Positivism and Sociology, op. cit.*

61. On this see the discussion in Chs. 9, 11, 12.

4

The Development of Sociological Theory
The Major Types of Explicative Paradigms

The Major Types of Sociological Explanation and Theory

1. The specific sociological tradition, particularly in analysis and theory, developed through a continuous reformulation of the major problems stipulated by the basic sociological *Problemstellung* and through their transformation into more specific types of theories.

As is well known, it is difficult to define the analytic nature of sociological theories, and the problem of what can be called "theory" has been debated since sociology emerged. Hence Henri Poincaré's famous dictum that sociology abounds more in discussions of proper methodology than in substantive matters.[1] Indeed, sociology has been more prolific in developing classificatory schemes and what George C. Homans calls "nonoperating definitions" and "orienting statements," which "tell us what we ought to look into further or how we ought to look at it," than in developing strict analytic propositions and theories.[2] Since its beginning, sociological analysis has produced classifying statements and would-be theories and propositions. Theories in the strict sense of deductive hypothetical explanations, however, have developed only slowly and intermittently, and many doubt whether they need be the only way to conduct theoretical discourse in sociology.

Whatever their exact analytic standing, several major types of theories and explanations have developed in the history of sociological analysis. The most important among these have been: broad explicative paradigms of social order; "middle-range" theories focused on more concrete areas of social life, (e.g., types of institutions, groups, patterns of behavior) and based on specific, relatively restricted analytic variables; research programs; and, last, empirical generalizations.

The broad explicative or conceptual paradigms attempt, as Raymond Boudon[3] puts it, to provide valid explanations of social order or its major aspects through their generalizing and heuristic powers. They have been central to the development of sociological analysis, deriving from and defining its basic Problemstellung, and providing a framework for the refinement of concepts, theories, including middle-range theories, and researchable hypotheses.

Among "middle-range" theories[4] in sociology, at least three different types may be distinguished. One type analyzes specific concrete topics that are theoretically important—the conditions of democracy and of liberty, the different types of class formation in modern societies, and the like. The second type involves the analysis of broad areas of social life: institutional spheres such as kinship and stratification systems; major types of social groups; and types of social behavior. The third, and analytically more sophisticated, type of middle-range theory centers on analytic variables and propositions, such as "relative deprivation," "reference group" theory, and the like, which in principle may cut across specific institutional or organizational areas or patterns of behavior. Middle-range theories, in being applied constantly to different problems of social analysis, and insofar as they are related to, or based on, broader assumptions inherent in explicative paradigms, may be transformed into more specific research paradigms or research programs.

Research programs are continuous programs of sociological research. Their continuity is based either on a common reference, in specific projects, to certain theories, and/or on sustained work on a particular institutional sector, type of organization, or pattern of behavior.

Less analytically sophisticated than the first types of explanation are empirical generalizations—"isolated propositions summarizing observable uniformities of relationships between two or more variables,"[5] and descriptive analyses and classifications.

All of these approaches can be applied to research areas of different scope, ranging from macrosocietal to the most "narrow" and microsocietal studies. They differ not in empirical scope but in their degree of analytic explication—that is, not in generality but in level of abstraction. In descriptive analyses, classifications, or empirical generalizations, analytic components have usually been the least articulated, indicating at most general orientation to analytic problems. Middle-range theories vary in their degree of analytic explication, but are usually more analytic than "pure" empirical generalizations or classifications. It is in the explicative paradigms above all, and in the broader research programs, that sociological problems have received their most analytic formulation.

The chances for such anticipation have been greater insofar as explicative paradigms or sociological theories have been related to, or combined with, various research programs.

The Central Place of Explicative Paradigms in the History of Sociological Analysis

2. Explicative paradigms or paradigmatic models have been the backbone of sociological theory, and the internal development of such paradigms, particularly in relation to the development of research, the crux of sociological analysis. They have served as the major analytic frameworks within which concepts, theories, and potentially researchable propositions have been developed in sociology, notably in the works of the Forerunners and Founding Fathers: Schäffle and Ratzenhofer; Comte, Spencer, and Marx; and above all Durkheim, Weber, Tönnies, and Simmel.

Most of the models were built around the analytic problems or poles drawing from the basic sociological *Problemstellung,* the problems seen as essential for understanding the working of societies and patterns of social behavior.

The major sociological theories tried more than to answer questions about the nature of social order. On the basis of these answers, they attempted to explain the major problems deriving from the sociological *Problemstellung.* Thus they attempted, first, to define the basic units of analysis, or bases, of social life: the individual with his goals, social organizations, the cultural order, and the ecological environment. They aimed also at explaining the regularities and systematic variability in the functioning of the social order (i.e., instituional groups and individual behavior), analyzing its continuity and change, and determining the mechanisms through which its components were combined and the laws governing these mechanisms.

The analytic fruitfulness of these paradigms, depended greatly on the ways in which they dealt with the basic problem of social order as it had been reformulated in the sociological *Problemstellung:* How could order be attained in social life, given both the multiplicity and interdependence of individual goals? And how did the organization of this social order, or, in more recent terminology, institutional framework, cope with these two basic problems?

The most important aspect of these explanations was their analysis of the emergent qualities of the institutional order—that is, the relationship of this order to its basic components, the individual, society, culture, and environment, and of their interrelationships. Were these components of institutional order to be seen as concrete entities external to one another, each constituting part of the other's given environment? Or, were they to be defined as analytic constructs in which each was a basic component of the others? In other words, to what degree were the emergent qualities of institutional life, and the ways in which they dealt with problems of social order, just "reflections" of any concrete component? To what degree did they constitute, rather, a fairly autonomous sphere through which these components, defined as analytic constructs, were continuously interlinked?

Because of the crucial importance of this problem, the various paradigms tried not only to identify the basic dynamics of the components of social order—that is of individuals, groups, cultural symbols and the environment—but to analyze the specific mechanisms through which these components were combined in networks of social relationships, and the rules which governed such mechanisms. Since specification of these dynamics and mechanisms was critical in explaining the emergent qualities of different levels of social life, it was the crux of sociological analysis and theory.

Approaches to the problem of social order could also be purely phenomenological, of course. That is, they could confine themselves to definitions of the various characteristics or aspects of social order. This was especially true of the first generations of sociologists, such as Albert Schäffle, Gustav Ratzenhofer, and René Worms. Their work culminated in elaborate classifications and "systems of sociology," each attempting to depict the true "nature" of society.[6]

The nature or "essence" of society was defined, in these schemes, in terms of basic forces or traits; society was defined, for example, as an organization, or as a reflection of geographical forces. These traits or forces were often seen as natural, metaphysical "givens."

Even the most formal or analytic classifications, however, had to relate their explanations of societies to concrete, researchable data. Hence most analytic paradigms addressed themselves to some degree to the analysis of the mechanisms of institutional life. The emphasis on such mechanisms permitted the paradigm to lend itself to various types of research and to the development of middle-range theory.

The ways in which sociologists dealt with these problems depended greatly on their often implicit assumptions about some of the metaproblems of sociological analysis—that is, the degree to which social life and behavior were predetermined by various forces or open to creativity; the institutional loci of determinism or creativity; and the importance of "causal" explanations as against those focused on the attribution of meaning to social behavior. Similarly, each paradigm addressed itself, implicitly or explicitly, to the question of generally human, as against the specific and "local," characteristics of social and cultural orders, and to the concomitant problems of the degree of historical uniqueness or specificity of societies and the possible trends of their development. Above all, each paradigm generally addressed itself to the Hobbesian problem of the roots of social order, the degree to which social interaction was basically conflicting or harmonious, stable or in flux.

These assumptions were in turn influenced by the relationship of these paradigms to the two main philosophical traditions so important in the development of modern social thought: the Utilitarian and the Romantic traditions.[7] The success of the various paradigms in dealing with problems of sociological analysis, however, also depended, as we shall see in greater detail, on their ability to dissociate themselves from these traditions.

In principle, the theoretical paradigms could be applied to research programs of differing scope and to different topics, ranging from macrosocietal analysis to the study of the most informal patterns of behavior. As we have seen, however, they were originally applied to the analysis of macrosocietal institutional or behavioral problems. Research stemming from compilations of statistics or social surveys, or from the tradition of political analysis, was only gradually synthesized with such broad analytic considerations. It remained at a low level of analytic sophistication or was confined to restricted intellectual spheres. Gradually, these areas, some of which did develop great methodological sophistication, were brought into the framework of the broader analytic paradigms and the research programs derived from or related to them. The combination of the two lines of development—analytic paradigms with areas of research and their concomitant development—is the center of the history of sociological analysis.

The Major Individualistic, Sociologistic, Cultural, and
Environmental Paradigms

3. We can attempt only a brief analysis of the major types of explicative paradigms in the development of sociological research and analysis. The typology used, which is a modification of the classification developed by Pitirim Sorokin in his *Contemporary Sociological Theories*,[8] distinguishes four kinds of paradigms: individualistic, sociologistic, cultural or culturalistic, and environmental. The distinction is based on the particular component of social order that is used as the point of departure for the explanation of social life—the individual and his goals, social organizations, the cultural order, or the ecological environment.[9] Each will be analyzed in greater detail in the following sections.

"Individualistic" approaches in the history of sociological thought have explained social order in one of several ways. One variant, the psychologistic, explains social order in terms of individual drives and habits, as do the earlier approaches of William MacDougall and Gabriel Tarde.[10] A more sophisticated version interprets social order in terms of various kinds of generalized goals of individuals; these may be W. I. Thomas' "wishes," Pareto's "residues,"[11] or ends couched in terms of power, love, or some "deeper" personality variables or in terms of basic mechanisms of cognition.[12] More recently, such "psychologistic" assumptions can be found to some degree in the exchange model as developed by Homans, and in works in social psychology.[13] The parallel development of psychoanalysis has provided another powerful impetus to various "individualistic" approaches, giving rise to a wide range of speculation and research in sociology. Its influence is illustrated by the various attempts to apply psychological categories to macrosociological phenomena, as in Harold D. Lasswell's attempts to analyze political behavior in terms of psychoanalytic personality theories; by Erik Erikson's work on the psychological bases of sociohistorical dynamics, as in his study on the development and establishment of Lutheran Protestantism; and in the "national character school" (a combined psychologistic-culturalistic approach) exemplified by the work of Ruth Benedict and Geoffrey Gorrer.[14]

Another category of individualist approach which has stressed the structure of social interaction among individuals, includes two versions: the symbolic interactionist approach of Mead, Schutz, Blumer, and Goffman; and various analyses patterned on the models of game theory or coalition theory.[15] Both approaches can also be related to such formal sociologistic approaches as those of Simmel and the anthropological theories of Elizabeth Bott, Jeremy Boissevan and Frederic Barth, which have stressed the importance of networks and coalitions.[16]

Most scholars in the symbolic interactionist school stress the ways in which any social situation is built up through interaction among its participants, and through the process by which individuals give interaction appropriate meanings, constructing its definition. Coalition and network theories, the second version, developed much later—in the 1950s and 1960s. They emphasize the ways in which individuals, in pursuing their goals, develop different patterns of interaction with other individuals and try to manipulate them. Out of the exigencies of such interaction there develop different types of continuous channels, networks, and groups; the exigencies of such interaction also place certain limits on the activities of the individual.

Most individualistic paradigms, quite naturally, were closely related to developments in psychology, particularly social psychology and to such adjacent research areas as studies of the patterns of social behavior; the impact of psychological forces on institutional settings and behavior; and the study of small and primary groups, interpersonal relations, and less formalized aspects of collective behavior, "mobs," and "crowds." These paradigms, however, could also affect macrosocietal analysis through their attempts to explain institutions, societies, and cultures in psychological terms.

4.   Sociologistic paradigms have used social groups and institutions as the key variables in explaining the conditions and mechanisms of social order. Within this category, three major approaches can be distinguished in terms of the way they view groups and institutions, stressing different aspects of this component of social order.

One approach is found in the formal school of sociology, particularly the work of Simmel; to some degree Tönnies, Alfred Vierkandt, and, later on, Theodor Geiger, Leopold von Wiese, and Hans Freyer; and, in the Anglo-Saxon world, the earlier works of Robert M. McIver.[17] The formal school attempted to define and study basic formal characteristics of social interaction: the social distance or proximity between individuals and groups; the number of members participating in interaction; and above all the quality of the relationship that develops among group members (e.g., "associational" or "communal"); and the characteristics which cut across different institutional spheres and types of organization (e.g., political or economic) and cultural contents.

The second major type of sociologistic explanation stresses the systemic properties of groups, institutions, and macrosocietal orders, their internal organizational and structural characteristics or dynamics, and possibly, their interrelationships. It has tended to define social units as systems or organizations with specific structures and needs. Some earlier biological-organic models, such as those of Paul von Lilienfeld, Schäffle, Worms, and Alfredo Niceforo,[18] probably belong to this type, as do the most powerful earlier sociological analyses of Marx, Comte, Spencer, and Durkheim.[19] Among the most recent variants of this approach are the models which have been the main focus of contemporary controversy: the various structural and structural-functional schools in anthropology and sociology, associated with the names of Radcliffe-Brown and Malinowski in anthropology, and later with Parsons, Merton, and Shils in sociology, all of whom were greatly influenced by Durkheim and Weber and, paradoxically, by Marx as well.[20]

A third type of sociologistic approach sees conflict and ecological interrelations among groups as central factors in social order. Among these are the theories of Ratzenhofer, Gumplowicz, and Franz Oppenheimer, and in the United States those of Albion W. Small, Lester F. Ward, and, to a large extent, Robert Ezra Park.[21] These theories stress such mechanisms of social interaction as "competition" and "adjustment" as the sole determinants of social life and order. Elements of such approaches can be found also in Weber's work; among their latest exponents are Reinhard Bendix and Randall Collins.[22]

Sociologistic models, using a "societal" point of departure, have been especially predisposed to macrosocietal and comparative research. These models, however, especially the formal approach, have also influenced small group research and, more recently, the sociology of organizations. Similarly, in the case of some formal schools of sociology, these paradigms have been the source of important insights into the structural properties of social situations, which in turn have had great influence on the study of role-sets, reference groups, and the like.[23]

5.   Social order has also been explained in terms of major cultural forces, defined often in terms of autonomous, immanent laws. Here, social order and its variations are seen as manifestations of a "world spirit," or of the rules of the human mind, as manifested in any of the major spheres of cultural creativity: religion, art, language, and law.

The major early approaches of this type were developed in the evolutionary-culturalistic and historicist schools. They are represented in Moriz Lazarus' and Wilhelm Wundt's *Völkerspsychologie,* and most importantly in Wilhelm Dilthey's approach to analysis of history. Later, the work of Oswald Spengler on the decline of the West, and the much more systematic work of Alfred Weber on the sociology of cultures and the differences between culture, civilization, and society, used this orientation.[24] These approaches were also close to some earlier approaches, like those of A. Fouillée and Gustave Le Bon, to the study of the national character and psyche.[25] Most recently, the major thrust of these approaches appears in certain developments in linguistic studies, and above all in the work of Claude Levi-Strauss and other modern structuralists.[26]

Of the environmental theories, the most important (if we discount simplicist biological racist approaches[27]) were the geographic-sociological approaches, starting with the simpler forms of geographical determinism exemplified in the work of Thomas Buckle.[28] The environmental approach has come to flll flower in the more sophisticated ecological theories, such as Otis Dudley Duncan's, and such neoevolutionary anthropological approaches as those of Julian Steward and, to some degree, Marshall Sahlins, which conceive social order in terms of ecosystems.[29]

These environmental approaches can also, in principle, be closely related to those of Gumplowicz and Collins.[30] These, unlike the more systemic emphases or orientations, tend to view social order as based largely on ecological interaction or the struggle of various groups and societies over "material" and "nonmaterial" resources.

Analytic Properties of Explicative Paradigms

6. Classifying sociological paradigms and theories in terms of the different starting points or "basic units" of social life is only a first step in analysis. Each approach could vary in its treatment of the basic problems, or poles, of sociological analysis. Each type of paradigm embodied various analyses of the nature of the regularities of social life and behavior, of the systemic nature of societies, and of the relative importance of instrumental rewards, coercion, and persuasion as the major mechanisms for maintaining social order. Similarly, any one of these models could embody a great variety of thematic emphases, on conflict or harmony, on acceptance or rejection of tradition, and the like.

Although some approaches showed a greater predilection for one particular combination than for others, this was only a matter of degree. Of the approaches analyzed above, for example, the societal has been the most strongly systemic, emphasizing the systemic characteristics and qualities of social order. It has tended often to postulate a system with distinctive boundaries and, more important, the maintenance of boundaries through regulative mechanisms.

Even within paradigmatic models starting from the-societal base, however, an environmental or ecological "group" approach developed. This is seen in the early work of Gumplowicz or Ratzenhofer, and, more recently, in a transformed and partial way, in the works of Bendix and Collins. The ecologic "group" approach basically denies the existence of a systemic social division of labor, with its implications of systemic properties and needs of social life, stressing instead ecological coexistence and competition among different groups.[31]

Similarly, within the individualistic approach one can discern a tendency to disregard the systemic qualities of social life. Psychological approaches, whether based on stimulus-response theories, the psychology of learning, or psychoanalytic theory, have tended to take the social system as a sort of external given. They have also, however, depicted it as a kind of system, though stressing that it reflects some basic psychological forces.[32]

Thus, whatever the different starting emphases of paradigms seem to imply, any concrete model can combine these components or starting points of sociological analysis in different ways. The ways in which they have done so, and hence explained the problem of social order in various ways, have been critical in theoretical development.

The historical importance of the models, however, did not rest on the *combinations* per se of these "poles" of the problem of social order. It hinged, rather, on the ways in which they analyzed the emergent properties of the institutional framework as the organizational focus of social order; the basic dynamics of each of its components; the specific mechanisms combining individuals, groups, and societies in networks of social relations and systems; and the rules governing such mechanisms. The specific *ways* in which the components were fruitfully combined and operationalized varied with the level of analytic sophistication and openness in each approach, and with its ability to incorporate and develop various research traditions.

The Analytic Modes of Explanation of Social Order: Discrete, Closed-System, and Open-System Explanations

7.   The three major analytic modes of explanation which developed in sociology can be classified as discrete, closed-system, and open-system.[33] They differ in the way they see the analytic nature of each component of

social order and the nature of their interrelationships, particularly whether these are fixed or variable.

The first type, the "discrete" mode, views individual activities and various social or cultural arrangements and settings in terms of separate and relatively discrete concrete entities or traits which tend to coalesce either randomly or in terms of some "external"—physical, biological, or "spiritual"—model.

The second type of explanation, the closed-system approach, was an analytic breakthrough with respect to the discrete approaches. It saw the components of the social order—the personal, social, and cultural starting points, and the environmental forces impinging on them—as both concrete entities and analytic constructs depicting different modes of organization of human activity, each with its own structure and mechanisms of self-maintenance and change. Each, however, was closely and systematically related to the others, and the different components of social order did not have equal explanatory power. Usually one was chosen as predominant because of its analytic qualities; the others, whatever systemic qualities they had, were subsumed under the "laws" or dynamics of the predominant entity.

Such analytic closure could also be applied to the conception of the systemic qualities of social life. That is, societies could be seen as entirely closed systems, or as exhibiting unsystemic qualities except for the general interaction of groups in a common ecological framework; they were not seen as open systems. And closure could characterize the analysis of conflictual and consensual aspects of social order when either of these was seen as the sole basis of social order.

In somewhat greater detail, closed-system approaches were usually characterized by at least some of the following analytic and methodological characteristics:

1. The perception of the components of social order, of the major units of social interaction (of a group, of any given society, or of humanity as a whole), as each having some systemic properties;

2. The predominance of one sphere, component, or aspect of social order over the others;

3. The positing of relatively fixed relationships between components of the dominant and subsidiary spheres;

4. The concomitant view that any of the "bases" of acceptance of social order was the single "basic" explanation of its dynamics;

5. The view of the social system either as systemically closed or as entirely "unsystemic," never as an open system.

Any single paradigm or theorem could incorporate various combinations of these aspects of systemic closure, as well as different emphasis on one or several of the components of social order.

The third mode of explanation can be called the open-system approach. Its major characteristic is the opening up of one or more of the analytical closures that characterize the closed-system models. It could do so by:

1. Seeing the elements or constituents of social order as autonomous and yet variable components or referents of each other;
2. Distinguishing, to some degree at least, between these components as concrete entities and as analytic constructs;
3. Giving up the idea of fixed relationships between them, "softening" the vision of society as a closed system;
4. Changing the analytic place of any basis of acceptance of social order, or of consensual or conflictual aspects, as the single explanation or mechanism of social order.

The crucial aspect of the opening of closed systems was not the recognition of all the components of social order as important, or as related in terms of vague "interdependencies" or mutual "interconnections." This was found in some form in the "discrete" analytic approach. Rather, it entailed, first, attempts to formulate the interrelationships among the components of social order, or between the bases of its acceptance, in such a way that each element, although relatively independent or autonomous, also constituted a basic systemic referent of the other components. Second, this approach entailed giving up the assumption of some type of fixed relationship between the subcomponents of social order. Third, it entailed the recognition that the crucial focus of sociological analysis was the examination of the internal systemic dynamics, interconnections, and continuous feedback processes among the components of social order. Thus the search for the principles regulating these dynamics was the central analytic concern.

Trends in the Development of the Major Types of Paradigms and the Development of Sociological Analysis

8.   These different modes of explanation developed in a complex manner. Their development follows no simple, natural, chronological trend, but exhibits, rather, considerable temporal and operative overlap-

ping of the several approaches. Nevertheless, one important, if irregular, trend did affect the emergence of a sociological *Problemstellung* and tradition: the move toward open-system approaches.

The crystallization of the sociological *Problemstellung* and a distinctively sociological mode of analysis was greatly reinforced by—indeed was probably predicated on—the displacement of discrete and closed-system by open-system approaches as the dominant paradigms for explaining the bases of social order, and the macrosocietal order. At the same time, however, discrete and closed-system approaches came to dominate the specialized fields of sociological analysis.

The relationship between this process and the crystallization of a distinctively sociological *Problemstellung* and analysis can be better understood through a more detailed examination of the possibilities and limitations of the three approaches as they were developed in sociological analysis and research.

Discrete Analytic Approaches: Their Place in the Development of Sociological Analysis

Many illustrations of "discrete" approaches to the explanation of macrosocietal phenomena and the bases of social order are found in the early stages of development in sociology. The explanation of criminality in terms of discrete biological traits, as attempted by Cesare Lombroso; the explanation of social life as derived from different instincts, as attempted by McDougall; the more schematic classificatory approaches of formal sociology, such as those of Vierkandt; the attempts of Ratzenhofer, Gumplowicz, and others to explain social order in terms of the struggle of different groups for existence; Buckle's geographical deterministic theories[34]; and many others were long accepted as sociological theory. They were often elaborated into classificatory schemes and systems, and often copied models derived from physics, biology, or simplicist psychology.

In most discrete approaches, the basic units of analysis—whether individuals, formal social relationships, groups, societies, or cultural artifacts—were usually conceived as concrete entities and described in terms of discrete traits, such as various ecological properties, size of groups, and racial or psychological characteristics. The major "dynamic" concern of these approaches was to explain regularities and variations in the distribution of such traits. These regularities or differences were usually explained in simplistic "deterministic" terms—that is, in terms of "external" nonsocial forces (such as biological traits or geographical forces), and were often formulated in terms of principles like "attraction," derived from the would-be basic sciences of physics or biology, or in terms of such broad social forces as "power," "greed," technology, or the "human spirit." These forces were reified as over-all explanatory principles of social life, or metaphysical forces, often seen as constituting both the mechanisms of social life and the principles which governed the working of these mechanisms.

Given this conceptualization of the components or bases of social life, as discrete, it was difficult to explore the internal dynamics of each component or their systemic interrelationships. Thus, discrete approaches left little room for the analysis of the emergent properties of social interaction and the institutional order; these were usually subsumed under the discrete traits or "forces." Nor was there much room for the analysis of innovation or creativity in the social realm; if analyzed at all, it was usually attributed to bursts of genius or to unexpected external forces. These approaches abounded in schematic classifications, general typologies, and grandiose pronouncements about sociology, without being able to generate continuous research programs.

Similarly, discrete approaches, when used to explain the bases of social order, adopted positivist or behaviorist utilitarian premises about the nature of human wants, or cultural assumptions about the manifestations of the human spirit. The Hobbesian problem of social order was conceived largely in presocial, individualistic terms: in terms of original asocial individual tendencies which were curbed by external physical or cultural forces.

These simplistic, discrete approaches permitted only the most preliminary advances in a sociological *Problemstellung*. It is not surprising that only small portions of these "theories" were incorporated into the sociological tradition. Their relevance for the development of sociological analysis lay more in the specification of objects of research, in the quest for scientific explanation, and in discrete insights, than in their direct contribution to such analysis. But if the discrete approach produced a simplicist determinism in explaining the bases of social order, its methodology could still be usefully applied to more limited areas and explanations. Indeed, it has persisted and proved valuable in many areas, including social surveys and attitude research.[35] In these fields, discrete approaches are fruitful for what Stinchombe calls "demographic" analysis of social phenomena,[36] such as changes in fertility rates, or in proportions of supporters of political parties, in a given population—phenomena that permit analysis in terms of simple causal structures.

The Transition to Closed-System Approaches in the Formative Period;
Their Place in the Further Development of Sociological Analysis

9.   The simplest discrete approaches, as exemplified in the works of
scholars like McDougall, Ratzenhofer, Buckle, and many others, had no
significant impact on the development of sociological analysis and the
sociological tradition. This is in marked contrast to the first great schemes
of comparative sociology; those of the Forerunners, Montesquieu, the
Scottish Moralists, and especially—the first great system-builders, the
positivist evolutionists St. Simon, Comte, and Spencer.

Most of these systems, especially those of Comte and Spencer,[37] which
were so important in delineating major problems in sociology, were
"mixed" analytically, being intermediate between discrete and closed-
system approaches, albeit with a strong predilection to the latter. Unlike
discrete approaches, they did not speak in terms of any single component
of social order, such as the individual, society, or culture, but subsumed
them under a broad category like "human society," "spirit," or "mind."
The latter, however, were not always distinguishable from the traits or
laws of the discrete approaches; they were seen as ruled by their own
internal dynamics, which in turn accounted for the nature of social
organization and development.

The approximation to the closed-system approach lay in these
theorists' great effort (like that of earlier Forerunners like Montesquieu
and the Scottish philosophers[38]) to delineate systematic interrelationships
between aspects of social life, with heavy emphasis on the description of
social institutions and their analytic qualities, hence on the systemic qualities of social order. This orientation to a closed-system, as against discrete
approach, was further strengthened by their emphasis on the
mechanisms of the interrelationship between components of social order
and between institutions, and by their attempts to relate these
mechanisms to systemic aspects of social life, especially to structural
differentiation and the evolution of societies.

Full-fledged closed-systems appeared during the formative stages of
sociology, the period between the Forerunners and the Founding Fathers
and the formative period of the Founding Fathers. Their characteristics
are exhibited partially in Spencer's work, and even more strongly in many
of the differentiated sociologistic, individualistic, and culturalistic
paradigms that were central in the development of sociological theory.

Among the sociologistic paradigms using a closed-system approach the
best-known is, of course, the Marxist, especially in Marx's later work and
in that of the so-called "vulgar" Marxists.[39] This approach combined

almost all the characteristics of a closed-system approach, with its particular strengths and weaknesses.

The great analytic strength of the Marxist paradigm lay in the recognition and analysis of the systemic properties of the different components of social order, particularly the societal and cultural levels, but to some degree the individual as well; in the stipulation of the systemic—almost "functional"—relationships among them; in the search for basic rules of the structure and dynamics of society; and in the attempt (only partially successful) to explain the dynamics of social order in the same terms as its stability.

But Marx's approach, and, even more, that of his followers, had the flaws of the closed-system approach. Societal forces, defined as forces of production and relations of production, provided the basic "hidden" structure of the society, which was organized on the basis of power relations. This view, especially in its more simplistic versions, assumed relatively fixed relationships between the basic structure and the various superstructures. It also failed to distinguish the components of social order as concrete entities and as analytic constructs.

Similarly, "formal" sociology, (in contrast to classificatory approaches, which resembled "discrete" models) also delineated systemic interrelationships in the various patterns and configurations of social life, and individuals' social orientations, showing their influence on the working of groups and societies and the construction of social reality by individuals.

The most important of the formal approaches were Simmel's many perceptive analyses of patterns of social interaction and their development in different societal settings[40]; Tönnies' transformation of the formal characteristics of social interaction into bases of macro-sociological typologies, *Gemeinschaft* and *Gesellschaft;* and Tönnies' more detailed works on custom and on public opinion in modern society.[41]

In the works of Simmel and Tönnies, later in Geiger and Freyer, and then in some of Merton's and Lazarsfeld's work, particularly that on the processes existent in the formation or disruption of friendship under the influence of various degrees of value similarity,[42] this approach became a powerful tool for analyzing not fully formalized, but very pervasive, aspects of social organization. It analyzed such crucial dimensions of social life as solidarity or instrumentality, which could be identified in different kinds of social settings and at the same time influenced the working of these settings.

Also belonging, in principle, to closed-system approaches are some sociologistic theories, like those mentioned above, those of Gumplowicz and Oppenheimer, and some later versions developed in the United

States, such as that of Edward A. Ross.[43] These concentrated mainly on analyzing one of the bases of social order and particular mechanisms of social interaction, like "competition" or "adjustment," which they saw as the sole key to the understanding of social life. Among the Founding Fathers, at least some characteristics of closure were later exhibited by Durkheim.[44]

Culturalist paradigms displaying closed-system approaches include those of Dilthey and Spengler, which emphasized the internal rules of culture or of human spirit, operating under their own momentum, as the great motive force in human history. To a lesser degree, Hobhouse used this approach in his stress on the development of reason as manifest in societal institutions and cultural spheres.[45]

10.   As these important examples show, the closed-system approaches achieved important methodological and analytic advances over the discrete approaches, and their contribution to the development of sociological analysis was significant.

1. By stressing the potential systemic quality of each component of social life, they made possible a deeper understanding of the dynamics of these components and of their interrelationships, making a preliminary distinction between these components as concrete entities and as analytic constructs.

2. By stressing the systemic interrelationships between the components of social order, they went beyond the simplistic correlations or overarching generalizations of the discrete approaches.

3. By stressing the possibility of "hidden" principles governing such relationships, they highlighted the importance of the mechanisms by which such relationships are maintained.

4. By stressing systemic relationships they tried to locate the principles that explained the working of such mechanisms within social relationships, rather than in external—physical or biological—factors, although they often reified such psychological, sociological, ecological, or cultural mechanisms.

While the least sophisticated of these approaches sought such principles in "extrasociological" explanations or vague metaphysical forces, the more sophisticated looked for explanations in the interrelationships between the components of social order. Similarly, they defined the different bases of acceptance of social order not as vague metaphysical forces, but as aspects of mechanisms of social interaction and orientations. In this way, they also became open to testable research. By virtue of the advances of the more sophisticated approaches, it became possible, within the framework of such closed systems, to transform some classificatory schemes—such as Simmel's sophisticated typology of social relationships, or Tönnies' broad societal types, *Gemeinschaft* and *Gesellschaft*[46]—into researchable components of dynamic analysis.

The analytic advances of the closed-system approaches implied a more qualified stand toward the two major philosophical traditions so influential at the critical points in the emergence of the modern social sciences: utilitarianism and idealism. Both utilitarian assumptions, with their view of human wants as given, and idealistic approaches, with their emphasis on the uniqueness of cultural or societal entities, persisted as major influences in most of the classical approaches in sociology—in Marx, Hobhouse, and Pareto. These approaches, nevertheless, also detached themselves from philosophic traditions.[47] This detachment was reflected most apparently in the treatment of human creativity, the place of reason in the social order, and the emergent qualities of institutional life.

Most closed-system approaches had more complex assumptions than did discrete approaches about the problems of human creativity and determinism within social life, the place of reason in it, and the roots of the problem of social order. Yet, because of their analytic closure and, especially, the tendency to stress one component of social life as the basis of acceptance of social order, these approaches had a deterministic view of social life. Because of its systemic orientation, this determinism was not the simplistic, external type that marked the discrete approaches; rather, it tended to stress the analysis of the internal dynamics and the interrelationships of the components of social order. Thus, it recognized the possibility of creativity, innovation, and freedom in social life, especially in the area of mechanisms connecting the components of social order: the relationship between forces of production and relations of production in Marxism, the imputation of meaning to social situations in symbolic interactionism.[48]

Very instructive from the point of view of the preceding discussion are the shifts in Marxist thought and in Durkheim's work. The original anthropological-philosophical vision of Marx was focused on man's autonomous construction of his environment, and on his continual struggle with the limits placed on creativity by this very process. Although even here, as in utilitarianism, wants were generally assumed as fixed and given, the concept of alienation and the search for a nonalienated society did provide openings for a new analysis of the interrelationship between personality and social structure. Similar openings lay in the more flexible formulations about the relationship between structure—the forces of production, and the superstructure or ideology and culture. However, as Marxism was dogmatized, the construction of the human environment was conceived in terms of a simplistic materialist determinism. Man's potential creativity was relegated to a shallow, semiutopian view of the future, without any impact on the concrete analysis of social structure. The result was that "vulgar" Marxism became a "discrete" approach.[49]

Similarly, Durkheim in his more deterministic moments subsumed individual creativity under "collective representations." In his more sophisticated analysis of the predicaments of modern society, however, the problem of human creativity in society became more central to his concerns, and the construction of society was seen as effected in large measure through a certain type of symbolic activity. Durkheim also became more interested in the distinct analytic qualities of individuals' relationships, attitudes, and moral commitments to society. Thus, while in his more deterministic, sociologistic, moments he explained the symbolic field as a "reflection" of society, in his more "open" moments he stressed the autonomy of the symbolic realm as the very constitutive force through which social order was constructed. Especially in *Suicide*, in parts of *Les Formes Élementaires de la Vie Religieuse,* and in the introduction to the second edition of *De la Division du Travail Social,* he presented a more differentiated picture than in his earlier work of the institutional and organizational spheres of social life, their internal dynamics, and the importance of the symbolic construction of social order as well as individual commitment to cultural symbols in the construction of social order.[50]

The complex attitudes in the closed-system approaches toward the problems of human creativity were paralleled by their attitude to the Hobbesian problem. Here they wavered between seeing its roots in a presocial state of nature or in the process of the division of labor. Less sophisticated approaches assumed that the spiritual or organic forces though which society was constructed "solved," as it were, the basic problems of social order, which were rooted in the presocial nature of man. Marx's far more sophisticated view stressed that the specific human problems of social order—those of exploitation and alienation—were indeed rooted in the very construction of the social division of labor.[51] However, his utopian orientation led him to believe that these problems would be resolved by one type—the postrevolutionary—division of labor, and he sometimes attributed the exploitive division of labor to asocial elements in relationships among people, stemming from a seminatural residue in society.

Durkheim's contribution was to point out, in the *Division du Travail Social,* that the problem of social integration arose not because of the asocial or presocial nature of men, but because it was rooted in the encounter between human nature and the construction of the social division of labor itself.

The closed-system approaches displayed a complex attitude toward the problem of emergent properties of the institutional framework. Their analytic closure tended to neglect the emergent properties of various fields, such as the institutional and cultural fields in the case of psychological paradigms, or the dynamics of personality in the more sociologistic or cultural approaches.[52] The tendency was to conceive such secondary fields as direct emanations of the basic component. In the more sophisticated models, however, this tendency was balanced by the recognition of specific, albeit secondary, emergent systemic properties of these components, and of institutional mechanisms that linked them. One example is the recognition of the internal, though limited, dynamics of political and religious ideologies in Marxism.[53]

Even if they admitted the existence of emergent qualities, however, most of these approaches did not analyze them systematically, assuming that such properties, characterizing secondary fields, were irrelevant to the understanding of the "basic" field. Paradoxically, even the internal dynamics of the basic field was often accepted as given and left unexplored.

11. These characteristics of closed-system approaches explain why, despite advances over discrete approaches, their analyses of the processes of continuity, change, and transformation of the social order, and the comparative study of such orders, often faltered. The obstacles to their development derived from their philosophical and ideological concerns and orientations.

First, it was common for the initial generation of sociologists to assert the scientific legitimacy of sociology by aping what they thought were the models of the established sciences: the mechanistic models of the physical sciences and the organismic models of the biological. Second, the search for, or belief in a conflictless society was important for at least some of them; this quest was deeply rooted in the ideological genesis of sociological theory. Although this search could often sharpen understanding of patterns of conflicts and disorganization in society, it tended to minimize the general analytic application of such approaches. It could also limit recognition of alternative directions of social change and possibilities of transformation, seeing change as directed toward a single end-state.[54]

Similarly, the comparative analysis of social order, disorganization, and change could easily be hindered if the dichotomy between general laws and regularities, and the uniqueness of specific social, cultural, and historical events, was seen as irreconcilable. The idealistic tradition, tending to stress uniqueness, could flourish in both the discrete and the closed-system approaches. Thus, while many concrete analyses of social settings as unique events often produced insights into the dynamics of each setting, these insights were lost or neglected if their general implications were not brought out or examined in a broader context.[55] On the other hand, generalizations which did not try to explain unique constellations of different societal situations often led to "empty," generalized typologies.[56]

Despite these limitations, the closed-system approaches were important in the crystallization of the sociological *Problemstellung*. They were more open than the discrete approaches to the internal dynamics of the components of social order and to their interrelationships, and they saw the bases of acceptance of social order as mechanisms that connected these components.

Their explanations were largely, to use Stinchombe's terms,[57] functional or historicist in nature; because of their emphasis on the mechanisms of social order, they could incorporate or link themselves to middle-range theories—for example, of the development of aspects of modern social order (capitalism, democracy), or of comparative institutional analysis. Thus closed-system paradigms were far more persistent in the development of sociological theory than the more discrete approaches; they have been developing and flourishing up to the present.

The analytic and research potential of closed-system approaches was least important where they tried to explain macrosocietal variations and developmental trends in human society in terms of one predominant component of social order. Such explanation marked the transition between the Forerunners and Founding Fathers of sociology. With the further development of sociology, however, and the development of open-system models, important shifts took place in the importance of these approaches for sociological analysis, as well as in some of their own concepts, which increased their impact on sociological work.

The greater analytic strength of the "later" closed-system approaches lay in their renunciation of over-all explanations of social order in favor of the analysis of more segregated spheres, or analytical aspects, of social phenomena, and in their concentration, as with some of Pareto's work, on the study of mechanisms of social continuity and the bases of acceptance of social order.[58] The analytic assumptions of closed-system approaches were implicit in many research areas which have developed since: in small group and organizational theory, which developed an early emphasis on a societal system approach; in much attitude and survey research seeking the psychological or institutional determinants of patterns of behavior; and in aspects of theories of exchange, conflict theory, or psychological theory, such as the study of culture and personality and national character.[59]

Here the analytic vitality and superiority of closed-system to discrete, especially deterministic, approaches, lay in their exploration of analytic aspects of the systemic interrelationships and of the autonomy of each component of social order and the bases of its acceptance. Analyses of the dynamics of each component, though limited in scope, could be bases for accumulative research. In fact, such vitality was greater by virtue of partial analysis, since any closed-system approach centered on the detailed analysis of only one component of social order or basis of acceptance.

Insofar as these systems were applied to research, whether historical, ethnographical, or field work, their importance for the continuing development of sociological analysis was enhanced. A fruitful relationship between these broad, orienting paradigms and specific research programs and sets of analytic variables and hypotheses began to develop.

Open-System Paradigms and the Development of Sociological Analysis

12.　The most crucial phase of development of modern sociology, nevertheless, has been marked analytically by the shift from closed systems to open-system approaches, and subsequently by the continuing internal development of various open-system approaches. The most important of these will bring us to more recent trends in sociology and the controversies about structural-functionalism.

The first major breakthrough in these types of approach came with the Founding Fathers of sociology: Durkheim and Weber, and, to a lesser extent, Tönnies, Simmel, and Hobhouse, who still evinced many characteristics of the closed-system approaches. Potential openings already existed in Marx's analysis, especially in his recognition of the complex and contradictory relationships between power and economic factors, between objective class positions and class consciousness, and in the concept of alienation as a basic constituent of the social division of labor. But these openings were not pursued by later Marxists. In the conception of Marxist thought which prevailed after the end of the nineteenth century and which could, of course, be fully substantiated by Marx's own writings, the interrelationships between the basic components of institutional life —relations of production, class struggle, and historical change—were taken as constant. This complex subsumed in itself the other components of institutional life and of social order, such as the individual goals and activities, political structures and cultural symbols.

The increasing deterministic petrification of Marxism, which neglected its open system potential, separated it for a long time from the mainstream of the emerging sociological tradition. Only more recently, in such developments of Marxism as the works of Antonio Gramsci, the discussion of the Asian mode of production, and the work of scholars like Lucien Sebag, Maurice Godelier, and to some degree Louis Althusser, have attempts been made again to open the Marxist system.[60]

Similarly, some later evolutionists, especially Hobhouse and Ginsberg, also tried to overcome the "closure" of earlier evolutionist systems, especially those of Comte, Spencer, and Tylor,[61] by recognizing the complex interrelationships between personality, social organization (institutions), and culture. They were not able to do this as successfully as Weber and Durkheim, however, since they were confined by a totalistic concept of "reason" or "mind" whose internal laws of development were seen as guiding the course of institutional development.

13.   The breakthroughs which had the greatest impact on the development of sociological analysis are associated with Durkheim and Weber. Some of the most crucial aspects of these advances have been analyzed by Parsons in *The Structure of Social Action,* where he demonstrates the potential convergence between Weber and Durkheim in their recognition that crucial concepts of sociological analysis—individual goals and wants, norms and values, symbols, groups and institutions, which had been treated separately in closed systems, could be best understood by opening them up to each other and emphasizing their nature as analytical constructs.[62] In this way the basic systemic core of each component of social order, their continuous systemic interrelationships, and the potential variability of these relationships were recognized. Furthermore, the importance of investigating the system-maintaining mechanisms was emphasized, so that all were opened to further exploration.

Durkheim's opening was only partial, for his insistence on the uniqueness of the social as against laws of individual psychology may be seen as representative of a closed "sociologistic" approach. But even in his most sociologistic formulations, Durkheim did not forget the importance of analyzing individuals' orientation to the social order.

Similarly, his work exhibits a continual tension between the recognition of cultural systems as a constitutive element in the construction of society or of the institutional order, placing limits on social organization and individual alike, and the idea that they are just a "reflection" of it.

Moreover, while Durkheim may at one point have seen society—i.e., the overall institutional framework—as a closed, self-maintaining homeostatic system and even as a concrete entity, in his later work he abandoned the idea of fixed relationships among the basic components of the social system, viewing them more as analytic constructs. The tension in his work between the conception of society as an organization or symbolic entity, and the emphasis on the continuous interaction between interests and normative elements, weakened his perception of society as a totally closed system, despite his emphasis on normative elements as the major basis for accepting social order.[63]

The greatest "opener" of the closed-system approach, of course, was Weber. Historically, Weber can be seen as the scholar who "broke up" both the sophisticated closed Marxist system, and the earlier German culturalist paradigm. Analytically, Weber combined all the major types of openings: of the vision of society as a closed system; of the assumption of fixed relationships between different components of social life; of the predominance of a single mode of acceptance of social order.[64] This does not mean, as some interpreters claim,[65] that he negated the systemic view of interrelationships among aspects of social life or of society. Rather, he was more fully aware than others of the great variability of interrelationships between society's components and bases, although because of these concerns and his "fight" against metaphysics in social analysis, he did not deal directly with the systemic aspects of social life.

Weber's breakthrough from the Marxist system consisted not in negating Marxist concepts, but rather in denying the assumption of a *fixed* relationship between various components of social order, and in transforming such relationships from assumptions into problems of research.[66] Only when such a transformation had taken place could the concepts themselves be subject to revision, new questions be formulated about the mechanisms and conditions of interrelationships between them, and further advances be made toward the sociological *Problemstellungen* and deeper perception of the phenomenology of social order.

The intellectual challenge, then, was to demonstrate variability in the relationship among the components of the social order—individual, society, culture. Weber accomplished this task by systematically exploring such variation in several ways. He examined differences in individual perceptions of social structure, stressing different *types* of individual orientation to social structure, the ways in which they are shaped by cultural symbols, and the continuing effects of social structure and individual activity on the legitimating function of cultural symbols, beliefs, and codes. Concomitantly, he explored the mechanisms through which different types of social structures were sustained by individuals with varying interests, and cultural symbols and beliefs. Above all, he explored the various types of social activities used in different structures (communities, class and status categories, political organizations, etc.), as well as the rules according to which these activities and the resources used in them were activated in different structures. He looked for those rules not outside of cultural orientations and social relationships but within them, in their mutual interaction.[67]

In this respect, his comparative analyses of religion, particularly his study of the Protestant Ethic, are of special importance.[68] Their significance lies not so much in the recognition of the importance of "nonmaterial" or "cultural" factors as in the attempt to specify the *mechanisms* by which such cultural factors produce institutional change and transformation. Whatever the accuracy of the details of Weber's theses, about the institutional implications of different world religions in general, and of Protestantism in particular, it is an attempt to explain an entire process of sociocultural transformation through a change in the type of relationship between personal identity and collective and cultural symbols, on the one hand, and institutional and organizational activities, on the other. These analyses are important illustrations of the transition to open system approaches in Weber's work.

Another instructive illustration of the "openings" in Weber is his treatment of the field of so-called "formal sociology," especially his transformation of Tönnies' major formal categories of *Gemeinschaft* and *Gesellschaft.* Tönnies tended to view *Gesellschaft* and *Gemeinschaft*—as did Freyer at a later stage—as concepts designating both total societies and stages of historical development. Weber transformed them from descriptions of total social structures into analytic elements inherent in any social process, *Vergemeinschaftung* and *Vergesellschaftung.*[69] In this way they designated basic types of individual orientation and commitment to social interaction and society, each with some basic or "core" structural implications, but "open" to other aspects or elements of social life, such as different types of individual goals and different institutional spheres. Thus they became amenable to research which could investigate the types and degrees of their connectedness to many other aspects of social life, giving rise, for example, to the entire gamut of primary group research and later to the redefinition of the nature of man's attachment to primordial relations and symbols.[70]

14.   The breakthroughs to open-system approaches were usually closely accompanied by a new attitude toward the problem of the predetermination of social life by "external" forces, and the place of reason and creativity in shaping the social environment. The more open approaches tended increasingly to emphasize the possibility of human creativity in the construction of social and cultural environment, rather than assume the "givenness" of such environments. Because of this, the problematics of creativity and its predicaments could be fully recognized only within open systems.

Similarly, it was the open-system approaches that rooted the problem of social order in the very construction of the social division of labor, as against presocial "givens" of human nature. Of great importance for this advance were, as we have indicated, Durkheim's analysis of normative elements undergirding the social arrangements inherent in the division of labor, and Weber's analysis of the bases of legitimation of social order.[71]

Open-system approaches were also characterized by increasing ambivalence toward the place of reason in the construction of social and cultural order—a denial of both the easy positivism and the gloomy rationalism of the earlier sociologists. The problematics of the place of reason in social and cultural order are expressed in Weber's emphasis on the differences between charisma and institution-building and between the liberating and constricting aspects of rationality. In Durkheim, the same problem is treated in the analysis of the relationship between organic solidarity and anomie.[72]

By these new attitudes toward the place of creativity and of human reason in social order, the open-system paradigm transformed the relationship of sociological analysis to the utilitarian-positivist and idealist traditions. As Parsons has analyzed this process so subtly in *The Structure of Social Action*,[73] its most crucial conceptual advance over utilitarianism was the transformation of the problem of individual "wants" from givens into variables that are greatly influenced by social and cultural factors. The major advance over the idealistic tradition was the transformation of the "cultural givens", so strongly emphasized by this tradition, into an albeit important and autonomous element of social action, which in turn is influenced by the voluntaristic aspects of this action.

Thus open-system approaches, especially once they were crystallized, rather than merely implied, usually entailed greater logical independence of sociological paradigms from philosophical and ideological orientations, and an even less direct relationship between any specific analytic model and a specific metaphysical or ideological counterpart. That is, a particular sociological model did not entail a particular metaphysical position but lent itself to a variety of philosophical applications. Thus, the models developed by Weber and Durkheim could be taken up by scholars with a much wider range of metaphysical and ideological orientations than could the models of the earlier Marxists and evolutionists.[74]

In all these ways, the development of open-system approaches permitted a significant expansion of the analytic and methodological bases of the paradigms of social order, and made these more flexible—open to advances in theory and research. The major analytical, methodological, and substantive developments attending breakthroughs from closed-system to open-system approaches, and within open systems, have always been based on the awareness that the focus of the construction of social order, and of the regularities of social order, lies in the dynamics of interaction among its major components and in the varied systemic interrelationships among them. This has entailed: first, greater emphasis on the analysis of the mechanisms through which the crystallization of interaction takes place—for example, socialization, reference group behavior, and the regulation of power; second, a tendency to stress that such mechanisms are to be found in the interrelations among different components of social life, not in general, external metaphysical forces; and, third, the attempt to relate these mechanisms systematically to the analysis of the processes of social disorganization and anomie, of the development of personality, and the transformation of social and cultural systems.

The crucial analytic step in any such breakthrough, as we have seen in the case of Weber, was a critical reexamination of the assumption of the existence of fixed relationships between the components of social systems. This entailed the redefinition of their analytic qualities, the search for variable relationships among the components, and emphasis on the mechanisms of feedback and interaction among them. In this way, many explanatory typologies were decomposed into their component variables, and the assumptions implicit in the earlier explicative paradigms were transformed into problems of research.

Thus, it was in the breakthroughs to open-system approaches that the specific sociological *Problemstellung,* in all its repercussions and potential development, was gradually crystallized. This process was greatly reinforced by the fact that the analytic and methodological advances within open-system approaches placed great emphasis on emergent qualities of social interaction and institutional order. These systems also attempted to resolve the dilemma between analysis of general trends and of unique events, not by denying the uniqueness of any particular structures or historical constellations or by questioning the possibility of sociological analysis of the historically unique, but by viewing the analyses of particular phenomena as complementary to, and dependent upon, analyses of general systemic tendencies and regularities in social life. In fact, insofar as the uniqueness of any type of social order—feudal or imperial systems, industrial or technological society, different types of organizations and groups—could be analyzed in broad, comparative terms, the possibility of understanding its specific characteristics was heightened.[75] Most important, by their great insistence on the importance of the mechanisms of social life, these approaches generated or facilitated the systematic development or incorporation of many middle-range theories.

15.   Open-system approaches varied greatly, of course, in their analytic fruitfulness. Their utility depended on four factors. First was the degree to which they could account for, and explore, the dynamics of each component of social order—individuals, societies, cultural systems, and environmental forces—in terms of the emergent properties of each such component, and of their openness to each other. Second, the advances possible within any approach depended on the degree to which the components or subsystems, and the mechanisms connecting these components, were accepted as given, or were seen as variables to be investigated. Third was the extent to which such mechanisms were explained in terms of external—presocial, physical or biological—forces, or defined in "internal" terms—i.e., in terms of the components and aspects of social order and their interaction, subsuming external forces under these internal components. Fourth was the degree to which such frameworks produced testable paradigms or research programs. It was, of course, the open-system paradigms that combined these characteristics and were analytically most useful.

But whatever their *analytic* fruitfulness—and here it is of crucial importance that the first two builders of these approaches, Weber and Durkheim, also created two of the most analytically powerful open systems—it was for the above reasons that breakthroughs to open system approaches helped crystallize not only the sociological *Problemstellung*, but also sociology as a field of scholarly endeavor. It was within the framework of open-system approaches that diverse analytic paradigms, theories, and research programs, however analytically or methodologically weak, were able to develop. Above all, it was the open-system approaches that produced the momentum for sustained, cumulative research programs revised through internal analysis and research.[76] Where closed-system approaches had often included what seemed to be final pronouncements about the nature of human society, open-system approaches incorporated the possibility of their own demise, the continual transformation of their specific premises, and their supercession by other theories and research programs.

In this respect, the open-system approaches also had far-reaching implications for these closed systems which were developed after the first overarching open-system paradigms had been created, notably by Durkheim and Weber.

First, the various closed-system approaches that developed after the time of the Founding Fathers, Durkheim and Weber, tended less to claim to provide overall frameworks for broad analysis, because they were already formulated against the background influence—however faint it might have been—of these open systems.

Second, the later closed-system approaches, taking place during the latter part of the second stage of development in sociology and after the period of the Founding Fathers, were more open than the earlier great systems. Broader potential openings are found in the work of scholars like Alfred Weber, Freyer, and above all Hobhouse, despite the strong close-system assumptions of their approach.[77] Similar openings characterized other closed-systemic approaches based on sophisticated personality theories, especially stimulus-response and learning theory and psychoanalytic approaches. Although in both types of approach the social institutional level was initially seen as derivative from psychic forces, both approaches developed a number of interesting hypotheses which could be opened up to accommodate the institutional level. This is also true of the most recent theories in Erikson's work on psychohistorical dynamics which, starting from similar assumptions, contain potential transitions to an open-systemic approach.[78]

Similarly, while symbolic interactionism, as it developed in the work of G. H. Mead and Schutz, exhibited some closed system characteristics, its analysis of the emergent qualities of the institutional sphere included already strong theoretical openings to the social system component. This orientation is apparent in Mead's analysis of the importance of social interaction in the shaping of the "self." Moreover, the emphasis on the symbolic definition of the situation in symbolic interactionism opened it to the cultural sphere.[79]

In the same manner, the more recent ecological theories, in contrast to the earlier, discrete geographic-deterministic approaches, have also shown significant openings to the social sphere while retaining some basic characteristics of the closed-system approach. This is especially true of the theories of Amos Hawley and Otis Dudley Duncan, and of the ecological-evolutionist approaches of Leslie White, Steward, and Sahlins.[80] On the one hand, they usually see the societal, individual, and ecological frameworks as relatively autonomous forces with mutual systemic interrelationships and hence tend to explore the mechanisms through which such interrelationships are maintained. At the same time, however, they also assume that the ecological-environmental component is the predominant factor, and so they do not systematically explore the possible impact of the other components in shaping and constructing the respective environmental settings. On the whole, they have focused on the exploration of the mechanism of ecological equilibrium. In this area, however, they have made significant contributions which can in principle be incorporated into more differentiated, open schemas.

16. In all these ways, the open-system approaches, particularly those of the Founding Fathers, had enormous impact on other approaches and on their incorporation into an expanding sociological tradition. They provided the basic framework for the sustained development of that tradition.

Of course, the crystallizattion of sociology as a field of scientific endeavor did not develop automatically with the first open systems. Needless to say, not all the approaches of that period exhibited the characteristics assuring analytic fruitfulness as did the schemes of Durkheim and Weber. In many cases, such openings were purely formal, schematic, definitional, or at most "phenomenological," and did not contribute to the understanding of either the internal dynamics of the components of social order, or of their interrelationships.

Similarly, the opening of closed-system approaches and the construction of open systems sometimes took place with respect to only one aspect. This aspect might be the degree of closure or openness of each component of social order, and the degree to which relationships among them were fixed; the degree of systemic closure or openness of social order; or the degree to which any single base of acceptance of social order or the nature and degree of conflict and consensus, were seen as exclusive. Moreover, systems which were substantively open, in the sense that they recognized the interrelationships between the components of social order and the bases of its acceptance, could still concentrate on only one of them from a methodological point of view, and often also assumed fixed relationships among them. In this way, even open systems could be closed or become similar, at least methodologically, to closed systems. Thus the structural-functional approach, which in principle had the characteristics of an open system, tended to assume rather fixed relations between values, societal needs, institutions, and roles; thus it was often perceived as a closed system.

However, given the basic analytic premises of the open-system approaches, whatever analytic closure developed within them could to some degree be corrected—either internally, through changes in their own premises, or through their synthesis with "external" problems deriving from the other intellectual traditions analyzed above. Thus in principle the further development of open-system approaches was in a sense unlimited: it contained the possibility of continual exploration of premises, and of the transformation of the "givens" of any paradigm or research program into problems for further research and analysis. In principle, such transformation could develop from any analytic component of a paradigm or research program, from the further "phenomenological" exploration of the basic components of social order, from the assumptions about the relationships among them, or from the relationships among these assumptions. In all these ways, the breakthrough to open paradigms made possible continual, self-sustaining, and self-correcting scientific progress.

The actualization of these possibilities, however, depended not only on the development of new and brilliant, open paradigms. These were, at most, necessary conditions and not sufficient causes of sustained and self-correcting progress in sociology. Scientific advance demanded also the combination of analytic paradigms with research programs, and the continuity in these combinations—factors dependent on the organizational and institutional aspects of sociology.

In the first two stages of development in sociology, the links between sociological theories and research programs were, as we have seen, intermittent and their institutional bases weak. It was mainly in the work of the Founding Fathers that these trends combined briefly. The picture changed somewhat in the period between the two World Wars, and we shall turn now to a brief analysis of these developments.

Notes

1. See R. K. Merton, *Social Theory and Social Structure* (Glencoe, Ill.: Free Press, 1957), p. 87.

2. G. C. Homans, *The Nature of Social Science* (New York: Harcourt, Brace & World, 1967), p. 14 ff.

3. R. Boudon, "The sociology crisis," *Social Science Information*, Vol. 11, Nos. 3-4 (1972), pp. 109–139; R. Boudon, *La Crise de la Sociologie* (Genève: Librairie Droz, 1971), Ch. 6.

4. For the definition of this concept, see R. K. Merton, *Social Theory and Social Structure*, (New York: Free Press, 1963), pp. 5–6.

5. R. K. Merton, *Social Theory and Social Structure*, *op. cit.*, p. 95.

6. A. Schäffle, *Bau und Leben des Socialen Körpers* (Tübingen: H. Laupp'sche buchhandlung, 1875–1878), 4 vols; G. Ratzenhofer, *Wesen und Zweck der Politik* (Leipzig: F. A. Brockhous, 1893), 3 vols; G. Ratzenhofer, *Die Soziologische Erkenntnis* (Leipzig: F.A. Brockhous, 1898); G. Ratzenhofer, *Soziologie* (Leipzig: F. A. Brockhous, 1907); R. Worms, *Organisme et Société* (Paris: Giard, 1896); R. Worms, *La Sociologie, sa Nature, son Contenu, ses Attaches* (Paris: Giard & Brière, 1921).

7. On the importance of these traditions for the development of modern social thought, see T. Parsons, *The Structure of Social Action* (New York: Free Press, 1968), 2 vols; T. Parsons, "Unity and diversity in the modern intellectual disciplines," *Daedalus*, Vol. 94 (1965), pp. 39–65; F. Jonas, *Geschichte der Soziologie* (Hamburg: Rowohlt Verlag, 1968), 4 vols.

8. P. Sorokin, *Contemporary Sociological Theories* (New York: Harper & Row, [1928], 1964). See also T. Geiger, "Soziologie: Hauptrichtungen, Aufgaben, Verfahren," in A. Vierkandt (ed.), *Handwörterbuch der Soziologie* (Stuttgart: F. Enke, 1931), pp. 568–578; H. L. Stoltenberg, "Geschichte der Soziologie," *ibid.*, pp. 579–588.

9. In discussing these different types of theories we shall refer both to those already mentioned in the discussion of the first two stages of development in sociology, and to others, developed later, which will be discussed below in the chapters on the development of sociology between the two World Wars and after World War II.

10. W. MacDougall, *An Introduction to Social Psychology* (London: Methuen, 1922); G. Tarde, *Social Laws* (New York: Macmillan, 1899); G. Tarde, *The Laws of Imitation*, 2nd ed. (Gloucester, Mass.: P. Smith, 1962); T. N. Clark (ed.), *Gabriel Tarde on Communication and Social Influence* (Chicago, The University of Chicago Press, 1969); P. Sorokin, *Contemporary Sociological Theories*, *op. cit.*, Ch. 11.

11. W. I. Thomas and F. Znaniecki, *The Polish Peasant in Europe and America* (Chicago: University of Chicago Press, 1918–1920), 5 vols; V. Pareto, *The Mind and Society* (New York: Harcourt Brace, 1935), 5 vols.
    On Pareto see also T. Parsons, *The Structure of Social Action*, *op. cit.*, Vol. 1, Chs. 5–7; J. H. Meisel (ed.), *Pareto & Mosca* (Englewood Cliffs, N. J.: Prentice-Hall, 1965).

12. See for example J. Dollard and N. E. Miller, *Social Learning and Imitation* (New Haven, Conn.: Yale University Press, 1941); J. Dollard and N. E. Miller, *Personality and Psychotherapy: an Analysis in Terms of Learning, Thinking, Culture* (New York: McGraw-Hill, 1950).

13. G. C. Homans, *Social Behavior: Its Elementary Forms* (New York: Harcourt, Brace & World, 1961), and in greater detail the notes for Ch. 8, below.

14. H. Lasswell, *The Analysis of Political Behavior* (London: Routledge & Kegan Paul, 1949); E. Erikson, *Young Man Luther: a Study in Psychoanalysis and History* (New York: W. W. Norton, 1958); R. Benedict, *Patterns of Culture* (Boston, New York: Houghton Mifflin, 1934); R. Benedict, *The Chrysanthemum and the Sword: Patterns of Japanese Culture* (Boston: Houghton Mifflin, 1946); G. Gorer, J. Rickman, *The People of Great Russia: a Psychological Study* (New York: Norton [1950], 1962).

15. G. H. Mead, *Mind, Self and Society* (Chicago: University of Chicago Press, 1934); A.

Schutz, *On Phenomenology and Social Relations*, edited with an introduction by H. R. Wagner (Chicago, London: University of Chicago Press, 1970); H. Blumer, *Symbolic Interactionism: Perspective and Method* (Englewood Cliffs, N.J.: Prentice-Hall, 1969); E. Goffman, *The Presentation of Self in Everyday Life* (Garden City, N.Y.: Doubleday, 1959). For the early history of symbolic interactionism see R. E. L. Faris, *Chicago Sociology: 1920–1932* (San Francisco: Chandler, 1967), Ch. 6.

For a recent reevaluation of this approach see the papers of P. M. Hall and R. M. Kanter in *Sociological Inquiry*, Vol. 42, Nos. 3-4 (1972), pp. 35–99.

For analyses based on game and coalition theories see, for example, M. Shubik (ed.), *Game Theory and Related Approaches to Social Behavior* (New York: Wiley, 1964); J. S. Coleman, "Foundations for a theory of collective decisions," *American Journal of Sociology*, Vol. 71, No. 6 (1966), pp. 615–627; T. C. Schelling, *Strategy of Conflict* (New York: Oxford, Galaxy, 1963); S. Groennings, E. W. Kelley, and M. Leiserson (eds.), *The Study of Coalition Behavior* (New York: Holt, Rinehart & Winston, 1970); R. Buchler and H. G. Nutini (eds.), *Game Theory in the Behavioral Sciences* (Pittsburgh, Pa.: University of Pittsburgh Press, 1969).

16. For illustrations of Simmel's formal approach see D. N. Levine (ed.), *Georg Simmel on Individuality and Social Forms* (Chicago: University of Chicago Press, 1971), especially Part 2; F. Barth, "Models of social organization," Occasional Paper no. 23, Royal Anthropological Institute of Great Britain and Ireland, 1966; E. Bott, *Family and Social Network* (London: Tavistock, 1957); J. Boissevain (ed.), *Network Analysis: Studies in Human Interaction* (The Hague: Mouton, 1973); J. Boissevain, *Friends of Friends: Networks, Manipulators and Coalitions* (Oxford: Basil Blackwell, 1974).

17. K. H. Wolff (ed.), *The Sociology of Georg Simmel* (Glencoe, Ill.: Free Press, 1950), especially the introduction and Part 1; D. N. Levine (ed.), *Georg Simmel on Individuality and Social Forms, op. cit.*

For the elements of formal sociology in Tönnies' work see W. J. Cahnman (ed.), *Ferdinand Tönnies: a New Evaluation* (Leiden: E. J. Brill, 1973), pp. 125–139; A. Vierkandt, *Gesellschaftslehre* (Stuttgart: F. Enke, 1923); R. Mayntz (ed.), *Theodor Geiger on Social Order and Mass Society* (Chicago: University of Chicago Press, 1969); Geiger's articles "Führung," "Gemeinschaft," "Gesellschaft," and "Revolution," in A. Vierkandt (ed.), *Handwörterbuch der Soziologie, op. cit.*, pp. 136–141; 173–180; 201–211, 511–518; L. von Wiese, *Systematic Sociology: on the Basis of the Beziehungslehre and Gebildelehre*, adapted and amplified by H. Becker (New York: Wiley, 1932); H. Freyer, *Einleitung in die Soziologie* (Leipzig: Quelle & Meyer, 1931); H. Freyer, *Soziologie als Wirklichkeitswissenschaft* (Leipzig: B. G. Teubner, 1930); R. M. MacIver, *Community: a Sociological Study: Being an Attempt to Set Out the Nature and Fundamental Laws of Social Life* (London: Macmillan [1917], 1935); R. M. MacIver, *Society: a Textbook of Sociology* (New York: Farrar & Rinehart, 1937).

18. P. Lilienfeld, *Gedanken über die Sozialwissenschaft der Zukunft* (Mitau: E. Behre, 1873–1881) 5 vols; P. Lilienfeld, *La Pathologie Sociale* (Paris, V. Giard & E. Brière, 1896); P. Lilienfeld, *Zur Verteidigung der Organischen Method in der Soziologie* (Berlin, G. Reimer, 1898); A. Niceforo, *Les Indices Numériques de la Civilisation et du Progrès* (Vienna: E. Strache, 1930). On Schäffle and Worms, see the items quoted in note 6.

19. For selections from Marx's works which provide a good idea of his approach see, for example, T. B. Bottomore and M. Rubel (eds.), *Karl Marx, Selected Writings in Sociology and Social Philosophy* (London: Penguin, 1965), especially Parts 1–4. On Marx, see also R. Aron, *Main Currents in Sociological Thought*, Vol. 1 (London: Penguin, 1968), pp. 111–182; A. Comte, *The Positive Philosophy* (London: Trübner,

1853), 2 vols; A. Comte, *System of Positive Polity* (London, Longmans, Green, and Co., 1875–1877); H. Spencer, *The Principles of Sociology*, (New York: Appleton, 1925–1929), 3 vols; J. D. Y. Peel (ed.), *H. Spencer on Social Evolution* (Chicago: University of Chicago Press, 1972).

On Comte and Spencer see also R. Fletcher, *The Making of Sociology: a Study of Sociological Theory*, Vol. 1 (London: Michael Joseph, 1971), pp. 165–196, 250–338; E. Durkheim, *The Division of Labor in Society*, (New York: Free Press, 1964); E. Durkheim, *The Rules of Sociological Method* (New York: Free Press, 1964); E. Durkheim, *Suicide* (New York: Free Press, 1966); R. Aron, *Main Currents in Sociological Thought*, Vol. 2 (London: Penguin, 1970), pp. 21–107.

20. For illustrations of Radcliffe-Brown's and Malinowski's approaches see, for example, A. R. Radcliffe-Brown, *Structure and Function in Primitive Society* (London: Cohen and West, 1952); B. Malinowski, "Culture," in *Encyclopedia of the Social Sciences*, Vol. 4 (New York: Macmillan, 1931), pp. 621–645.

Structural-functional analysis in sociology is best represented by T. Parsons and E. Shils (eds.), *Toward a General Theory of Action*, (Cambridge, Mass.: Harvard University Press, 1951); T. Parsons, *The Social System* (New York: Free Press [1951], 1964); T. Parsons and N. J. Smelser, *Economy and Society* (New York: Free Press [1956], 1965); R. K. Merton, *Social Theory and Social Structure, op. cit.*, especially Parts 1 and 2.

On Durkheim's and Weber's influence on Parsons, see T. Parsons, *The Structure of Social Action, op. cit.*, and his discussion in many of the essays collected in T. Parsons, *Essays in Sociological Theory*, rev. ed. (New York: Free Press, 1963).

On the influence of Durkheim and Weber on Shils and Merton, see for example E. Shils, "Charisma, order, and status," *American Sociological Review*, Vol. 30 (1965), pp. 199–213; and Merton's analysis of anomie and Chs. 18, 19 in his *Social Theory and Social Structure, op. cit.*, 1963 edition.

On similarities between Parsons' and Marx's approaches see, for example, D. Atkinson, *Orthodox Consensus and Radical Alternative* (London: Heinemann Educational Books, 1971), Ch. 5.

21. On Ratzenhofer see note 6. For the other authors cited see L. Gumplowicz, *Outlines of Sociology*, 2nd English ed. (New York: Paine-Whiteman, 1963); F. Oppenheimer, *The State* (New York: Huebsch, 1922); F. Oppenheimer, *System der Soziologie* (Yena: G. Rischar, 1922); A. W. Small, *General Sociology* (Chicago: University of Chicago Press, 1905); L. F. Ward, *The Psychic Factors of Civilization*, (Boston: Ginn, 1893); L. F. Ward, *Outlines of Sociology*, (New York: Macmillan, 1898); L. F. Ward, *Pure Sociology*, (New York: Macmillan, 1903); R. E. Park and E. Burgess, *Introduction to the Science of Sociology* (Chicago: University of Chicago Press, 1921).

22. On this see R. Bendix, *Max Weber: an Intellectual Portrait* (Garden City, N. Y.: Doubleday, 1960); R. Collins, "A comparative approach to political sociology," in R. Bendix (ed.), *State and Society* (Boston: Little, Brown, 1968), pp. 42–67; R. Bendix and G. Roth, *Scholarship and Partisanship: Essays on Max Weber* (Berkeley, Cal.: University of California Press, 1971), especially Ch. 11.

23. For illustrations of the influence of the formal sociological approach on those areas of research, see for example P. F. Lazarsfeld and R. K. Merton, "Friendship as a social process; a substantive and methodological analysis," in M. Berger, T. Abel, and C. H. Page (eds.), *Freedom and Control in Modern Society* (New York: D. Van Nostrand, 1954), pp. 18–66; D. N. Levine, "Introduction," in D. N. Levine (ed.), *Georg Simmel on Individuality and Social Forms, op. cit.*

24. M. Lazarus' and H. Steinthal's papers in *Zeitschrift für Völkerpsychologie und Sprachwissenschaft*, Vol. 1 (1860), pp. 1–73, 437–477; Vol. 2, (1863), pp. 54–62, 393–453; Vol. 3

(1865), pp. 1–94, 385–486; Vol. 17 (1887), pp. 233–264; W. Wundt, *Völkerspsychologie* (Stuttgart; Kröner, 1912–1921), several vols.
For brief and useful accounts and selections of Dilthey's approach, see H. Stuart Hughes, *Consciousness and Society*, (New York: Vintage, 1958), pp. 192–200; H. A. Hodges, *The Philosophy of Wilhelm Dilthey* (London: Routledge & Kegan Paul, 1952), H. A. Hodges, *Wilhelm Dilthey: an Introduction* (London: K. Paul, Trench, Trubner, 1944); O. Spengler, *The Decline of the West* (New York: Knopf, 1932); A. Weber, *Kulturgeschichte als Kultur Soziologie* (Munich: Piper, [1935], 1950); A. Weber, *Das Tragische und die Geschichte* (Hamburg: Govert, 1943).

25.   A. Fouillée, *La Science Sociale Contemporaine* (Paris: Hachette, 1885); G. LeBon, *La Psychologie des Foules*, translated as *The Crowd* (New York: Macmillan [1895], 1947).

26.   Among Lévi-Strauss' best known works are the following, some of which are translated in English: C. Lévi-Strauss, *Structural Anthropology* (New York: Basic Books, 1963); C. Lévi-Strauss, *Totemism* (Boston: Beacon Press, 1967); C. Lévi-Strauss, *The Savage Mind* (London: Weidenfeld and Nicolson, 1966); C. Lévi-Strauss, *The Elementary Structures of Kinship* (Boston: Beacon Press, 1969); C. Lévi-Strauss, *Mythologiques: Le Cru et le Cuit*, translated as *The Raw and the Cooked* (New York: Harper & Row, 1969); C. Lévi-Strauss, *Mythologiques: Du Miel aux Cendres* (Paris: Plon, 1967); C. Lévi-Strauss, *Mythologiques: L'origine des Manières de Table* (Paris: Plon, 1968); C. Lévi-Strauss, *Mythologiques: L'homme Nu* (Paris: Plon, 1971).
For further bibliography, see Ch. 8, below.

27.   On these see P. Sorokin, *Contemporary Sociological Theories, op. cit.*, Ch. 3.

28.   H. T. Buckle, *History of Civilization in England* (London, J. W. Parker & Son, 1857–1861), 2 vols; J. M. Robertson, *Buckle and his Critics: a Study in Sociology*, (London: Swan Sonnenschein, 1895).

29.   O. D. Duncan, "Social organization and the ecosystem," in R. E. L. Faris (ed.), *Handbook of Modern Sociology* (Chicago: Rand McNally, 1964), pp. 36–82; J. H. Steward, *Theory of Culture Change: The Methodology of Multilinear Evolution* (Urbana: University of Illinois Press, 1955); M. D. Sahlins and E. R. Service (eds.), *Evolution and Culture* (Ann Arbor: University of Michigan Press, 1960).

30.   See the works of these scholars cited in notes 21 and 22.

31.   See the respective works cited in notes 21, 6, 22.

32.   See, for example, some of Homans' works, especially G. C. Homans, *The Human Group* (New York: Harcourt, Brace, 1950); G. C. Homans and D. M. Schneider, *Marriage, Authority and Final Causes* (Glencoe, Ill.: Free Press, 1955).

33.   On this see S. N. Eisenstadt, "Sociology, the development of sociological thought," in *The International Encyclopedia of the Social Sciences*, Vol. 15 (New York: Macmillan, 1968), pp. 23–35.

34.   For the works of these scholars see notes 10, 17, 6, 21, 28; and C. Lombroso, *Criminal Man* (New York: Putnam, 1911).

35.   For illustrations of social surveys and attitude research employed by British and American sociologists, see W. J. H. Sprott, "Sociology in Britain: preoccupations," in H. Becker and A. Boskoff (eds.), *Modern Sociological Theory in Continuity and Change* (New York: Dryden Press, 1957), pp. 607–622; J. Rumney, "British sociology," in G. Gurvitch and W. E. Moore (eds.), *Twentieth Century Sociology* (New York: Philosophical Library, 1945), pp. 562–585; E. Shils, *The Present State of American Sociology* (Glencoe, Ill.: Free Press, 1948).

36. On this see A. Stinchcombe, *Constructing Social Theories* (New York: Harcourt, Brace & World, 1968), Ch. 3.

37. On Comte and Spencer, see note 19.

38. C. Montesquieu, *The Spirit of Laws* (New York: Hafner, 1949).
    On Montesquieu see also R. Aron, *Main Currents in Sociological Thought, op. cit.,* Vol. 1, pp. 17–62; G. Bryson, *Man and Society: the Scottish Inquiry of the 18th Century* (Princeton, N.J.: Princeton University Press, 1945).

39. For Marx see the items cited in note 19. Aron's work cited there also provides a concise review of the more and the less orthodox tendencies which have developed in the Marxist camp.
    For Marx's approach see also A. Giddens, *Capitalism and Modern Social Theory: an Analysis of the Writings of Marx, Durkheim, and Max Weber* (Cambridge: Cambridge University Press, 1971), Part 1.

40. On Simmel see the relevant works quoted in note 17 and G. Simmel, *Conflict and the Web of Group Affiliations* (Glencoe, Ill.: Free Press, 1955).

41. F. Tönnies, *Gemeinschaft und Gesellschaft,* translated as *Community and Society* (East Lansing, Mich.: The State University Press, 1957); F. Tönnies, *Die Sitte,* translated as *Custom: an Essay on Social Codes* (Glencoe, Ill.: Free Press, 1961); F. Tönnies, *Kritik der Offentlichen Meinung* (Berlin: Julius Springer, 1922).
    Good discussions of these works are found in the various papers collected in W. J. Cahnman (ed.), *Ferdinand Tönnies: a New Evaluation, op. cit.,* especially Part A.

42. On Geiger and Freyer, see the relevant works cited in note no. 17. For the other references, see P. F. Lazarsfeld and R. K. Merton, "Friendship as a social process: a substantive and methodological analysis," *op. cit.;* E. Shils, "Primordial, personal, sacred, and civic ties." *British Journal of Sociology,* Vol. 8 (June 1957), pp. 37–52; E. Shils, *Center and Periphery: Essays in Macrosociology* (Chicago: University of Chicago Press, 1975), Part 4 (Chs. 18–20).

43. For Gumplowicz and Oppenheimer, see the relevant works cited in note 21. For Ross, E. A. Ross. *Social Control* (New York: Macmillan, 1901).

44. E. Durkheim, *The Division of Labor in Society, op. cit.;* E. Durkheim, *Suicide, op. cit.,* E. Durkheim, *The Rules of Sociological Method, op. cit.;* R. Aron, *Main Currents in Sociological Thought, op. cit.,* Vol. 2, pp. 21–107.

45. On Dilthey and Spengler, see the relevant works cited in note 24. For Hobhouse, L. T. Hobhouse, *Social Development: its Nature and Conditions* (London: Allen & Unwin, 1924).

46. On this see the items cited in notes 17, 40, 41.

47. For Marx, see R. Aron, *Main Currents in Sociological Thought, op. cit.,* Vol. 1, pp. 111–182; A. Giddens, *Capitalism and Modern Social Theory, op. cit.*
    For Hobhouse, see M. Ginsberg, "Hobhouse, L. T.," in *The International Encyclopedia of the Social Sciences, op. cit.,* Vol. 6 (1968), pp. 487–489.
    For Pareto, see T. Parsons, *The Structure of Social Action, op. cit.,* Vol. 1, Chs. 5–7; R. Collins and M. Makowsky, *The Discovery of Society* (New York: Random House, 1972), pp. 169–173.

48. On this, see for Marxism, R. Aron, *Main Currents in Sociological Thought, op. cit.,* Vol. 1, pp. 111–182.
    For symbolic interactionism, see the works of Mead, Shutz, Blumer, and Goffman cited in note 15.

49. For divergent trends in Marxism which exhibit open- or closed-system approaches to

the problems discussed here, see in addition to R. Aron's interpretation, D. Atkinson, *Orthodox Consensus and Radical Alternative, op. cit.,* Ch. 3; M. Jay, "Some recent developments in critical theory," *Berkeley Journal of Sociology,* Vol. 18 (1973–1974). pp. 27–44; N. Birnbaum, "The crisis in Marxist sociology," in D. Colfax and J. L. Roach (eds.), *Radical Sociology* (New York: Basic Books, 1971), pp. 108–131.

50. On these aspects, see R. Aron, *Main Currents in Sociological Thought, op. cit.,* Vol. 2, pp. 21–107; R. N. Bellah, "Introduction," in R. N. Bellah (ed.), *Emile Durkheim on Morality & Society* (Chicago: University of Chicago Press, 1973).

51. For Marx's analysis of the problem of alienation in class societies and in post-revolutionary society, see the materials collected in T. B. Bottomore and M. Rubel (eds.), *Karl Marx: Selected Writings in Sociology and Social Philosophy, op. cit.,* especially pp. 175–185, 249–263.

52. For the psychologically based systems see, for example, the following criticisms of Homans' approach which are close to the discussion here: P. Ekeh, *Social Exchange Theory* (London: Heinemann, 1974), Chs. 5, 6; H. Turk and R. L. Simpson (eds.), *Institutions & Social Exchange* (Indianapolis and New York: Bobbs-Merrill, 1971).

   For the criticism mentioned here of sociologistic and culturalistic approaches see, for example, G. C. Homans and D. M. Schneider, *Marriage, Authority and Final Causes, op. cit.*

53. On this see the following concise surveys and their bibliographies: A. G. Meyer, "Marxism," in *International Encyclopedia of the Social Sciences, op. cit.,* Vol. 10 (1968), pp. 40–46: C. Gneuss, "Bernstein, Eduard," *op. cit.* Vol. 2. pp. 68–69; J. H. Kautsky, "Kautsky, Karl," *op. cit.* Vol. 8, pp. 356–358.

   For greater detail, see K. Kautsky, *Die Materialistische Geschichtsauffassung* (Berlin: Dietz, 1927), 2 vols; E. Bernstein, *Evolutionary Socialism: a Criticism and Affirmation* (London: Independent Labour Party [1899], 1909); E. Bernstein, "Wie ist Wissenschaftlicher Socialismus möglich?" *Socialistische Monatshefte,* Jahrgang, (v.) 5 (Berlin: 1901); M. Jay, *The Dialectical Imagination: a History of the Frankfurt School and the Institute of Social Research, 1923–1950* (Boston: Little, Brown, 1973).

54. On this see the discussion and criticism of Comte's, Spencer's, and Marx's theories of social change in R. A. Nisbet, *Social Change and History* (London: Oxford University Press, 1969).

55. On this see T. Parsons, *The Structure of Social Action, op. cit.,* Vol. 2, Ch. 13.

56. On this see, for example, Nisbet's criticism of the "comparative method" as developed by Comte, Spencer, and Marx in their analysis of social change, in R. A. Nisbet, "Developmentalism: a critical analysis," in J. C. McKinney and E. Tiryakian, (eds.), *Theoretical Sociology* (New York: Appleton-Century-Crofts, 1970), pp. 168–204.

57. A. Stinchcombe, *Constructing Social Theories, op. cit.,* Ch. 3.

58. On this aspect of Pareto's work see, for example, the papers of N. S. Timascheff, "The social system, structure and dynamics," and M. Ginsberg, "The sociology of Pareto," in J. H. Meisel (ed.), *Pareto and Mosca, op. cit.,* pp. 63–70, 89–107.

59. For small group and organizational theory which are system-oriented see, for example, R. F. Bales, *Interaction Process Analysis* (Cambridge, Mass.: Addison-Wesley, 1950); T. Parsons, "Suggestions for a sociological approach to the theory of organizations," *Administrative Science Quarterly,* Vol. 1, Nos. 1–2 (June, September, 1956), pp. 63–85 and 224–239; E. F. Borgatta, A. P. Hare, and R. F. Bales (eds.), *Small Groups: Studies in the Social Interaction,* rev. ed. (New York: Knopf, 1967).

On attitude and survey researches see, for example, E. Katz and P. F. Lazarsfeld, *Personal Influence* (Glencoe, Ill.: Free Press, 1955); P. F. Lazarsfeld and F. N. Stanton (eds.), *Communications Research, 1948–1949* (New York: Harper, 1949); R. K. Merton, *Mass Persuasion: The Social Psychology of a War Bond Drive* (New York: Harper, 1946). For exchange theory see G. C. Homans, *Social Behavior: its Elementary Forms, op. cit.* For conflict theory see, for example, R. Dahrendorf, *Class and Class Conflict in Industrial Society,* (Stanford, Cal.: Stanford University Press, 1959).

For "culture and personality" and "national character" theories, see the works of Benedict and Gorer, cited in note 14 and the following surveys: G. A. de Vos and A. A. Hippler, "Cultural psychology, . . ." in G. Lindzay and E. Aronson (eds.), *Handbook of Social Psychology,* 2nd ed., Vol. 4 (Reading, Mass.: Addison-Wesley, 1969), pp. 323–417; A. Inkeles and D. J. Levinson, "National character: the study of modal personality and sociocultural systems," *ibid.,* pp. 418–506.

60. L. Sebag, *Marxisme et Structuralisme* (Paris: Payot, 1964); M. Godelier, *Horizons, Trajets Marxistes en Anthropologie* (Paris: Maspero, 1973); L. Althusser *et al., Lire le Capital* (Paris: Maspero, 1965); L. Althusser, *Pour Marx,* translated as *For Marx* (London: Penguin, 1969); A. Gramsci, *The Modern Prince and Other Writings* (London: Lawrence & Wishart, 1957); *The Open Marxism of A. Gramsci* (New York: Cameron Association, 1957); G. A. Williams, "Gramsci's concept of egemonia," *Journal of the History of Ideas,* Vol. 21, No. 4 (December 1960), pp. 586–599; A. Pizzorno, "A propos de la méthode de Gramsci," *l'Homme et la Société,* Vol. 8 (1968), pp. 165 ff.; H. Portelli, *Gramsci et le Bloc Historique* (Paris: Presses Universitaires de France, 1972).

On the Asian mode of production, see K. Marx, *Pre-Capitalist Economic Formations,* with an introduction by E. J. Hobsbawn (New York: International Publishers, 1972); F. Tokëi, *Sur le Mode de Production Asiatique,* Studia Historica Academiae Scientiarum Hungaricae (Budapest: Akadémiei, Kiado, 1966); *Sul Modo di Produzione Asiatico,* a cura di D. Giori (Milano: Franco Angeli, 1972); *Sur le Mode de Production Asiatique,* avec une préface de R. Garaudy (Paris: Éditions Sociales, 1969).

61. For this see L. T. Hobhouse, *Social Development: Its Nature and Conditions, op. cit.;* M. Ginsberg, "Hobhouse, L. T.," *op. cit.;* Julius Gould, "On Morris Ginsberg," *The Jewish Journal of Sociology,* Vol. 16, No. 2 (December, 1974), pp. 123–133.

62. T. Parsons, *The Structure of Social Action, op. cit.,* Vol. 1, Chs, 8–12; Vol. 2, Chs 14–18.

63. For all points stressed in the above discussion, see especially E. Durkheim, *The Division of Labour in Society, op. cit.;* E. Durkheim, *The Elementary Forms of Religious Life* (New York: Macmillan, 1915); R. N. Bellah, "Introduction," in R. N. Bellah (ed.), *Emile Durkheim on Morality and Society, op. cit.*

64. On this see, for example, R. Bendix, *Max Weber: an Intellectual Portrait* (Garden City, N.Y.: Doubleday Anchor, 1962), especially Chs. 8, 15; R. Bendix, "Max Weber," *International Encyclopedia of the Social Sciences, op. cit.,* Vol. 16 (1968), pp. 493–502; R. Bendix and G. Roth, *Scholarship and Partisanship, op. cit.,* especially Chs. 6, 12.

65. T. Parsons, "Introduction," in M. Weber, *Sociology of Religion* (Boston: Beacon Press, 1963), and R. Collins, "A comparative approach to political sociology," *op. cit.;* S. N. Eisenstadt (ed.), *Max Weber: on Charisma and Institution Building* (Chicago: University of Chicago Press, 1968), Introduction.

66. On this see, for example, Weber's theory of stratification and his analysis of the relationship between interests and religion, in M. Weber, *Essays in Sociology* (New York: Oxford University Press, 1958), Chs. 7, 11, 13; R. Bendix, *Max Weber: an Intellectual Portrait, op. cit.,* Ch. 3.

67. On all these aspects of Weber's approach see M. Weber, *Essays in Sociology, op. cit.*, Ch. 7; S. N. Eisenstadt (ed.), *Max Weber on Charisma and Institution Building, op. cit.*, pp. 3–12, 18–27, 46–65.

68. For concise expositions of Weber's analytic achievements in his comparative study of religion, see R. Bendix, *Max Weber: an Intellectual Portrait, op. cit.*, Chs. 3–8; S. N. Eisenstadt, "The Protestant Ethic thesis in an analytical and comparative framework," in S. N. Eisenstadt (ed.), *The Protestant Ethic and Modernization* (New York: Basic Books, 1968).

69. On Tönnies, see the works cited in note 41.
     On Freyer, see the works cited in note 17.
     For the definition of Weber's concepts discussed here, see S. N. Eisenstadt (ed.), *Max Weber on Charisma and Institution Building, op. cit.*, pp. 9–10.

70. On this see E. Shils, "Primordial, personal, sacred, and civic ties," *British Journal of Sociology, op. cit.*; E. Shils, *Center and Periphery; Essays in Macrosociology, op. cit.*

71. On this see E. Durkheim, *The Division of Labor in Society, op. cit.*, Book 1, Ch. 7; S. N. Eisenstadt (ed.), *Max Weber on Charisma and Institution Building, op. cit.*, pp. 11–12; 46–65.

72. On this see S. N. Eisenstadt (ed.), *Max Weber on Charisma and Institution Building, op. cit.*, pp. 28–42, 48–77; A. Mitzman, *The Iron Cage: an Historical Interpretation of Max Weber* (New York: Grosset & Dunlap, 1969); R. Bendix, *Max Weber: an Intellectual Portrait, op. cit.*, Ch. 14; E. Durkheim, *The Division of Labor in Society, op. cit.*, especially Book 3, Ch. 1; E. Durkheim, *Suicide, op. cit.*

73. T. Parsons, *The Structure of Social Action, op. cit.*, especially Vol. 2, Ch. 18; T. Parsons, "Unity and diversity in the modern intellectual disciplines," *Daedalus, op. cit.*

74. As is well known, Parsons' theoretical approach, which is thought by many to be "conservative," owes much to Weber and Durkheim. See, for example, his programmatic papers in T. Parsons, *Essays in Sociological Theory*, rev. ed. (New York: Free Press, [1949], 1963).
     Both Weber and Durkheim also influenced, directly or indirectly, theoretical approaches which by implication are more "radical."
     On Weber see, for example, R. Collins, "A comparative approach to political sociology," *op. cit.*; D. Atkinson, *Orthodox Consensus and Radical Alternative, op. cit.*, especially Chs. 7, 8.
     On Durkheim see, for example, E. A. Tiryakian, "Structural sociology," in J. C. McKinney and E. A. Tiryakian (eds.), *Theoretical Sociology, op. cit.*, pp. 112–135.

75. This was actually Weber's achievement in his use of "ideal types" in comparative analysis. For this see R. Aron, *Main Currents in Sociological Thought, op. cit.*, Vol. 2, pp. 185–258.

76. This can be illustrated, for example, by Weber's thesis on the influence of the Protestant Ethic and by Durkheim's analysis of anomie, which continue to be important foci of research and analysis. For good reviews of these two fields see, for example, S. N. Eisenstadt (ed.), *The Protestant Ethic and Modernization, op. cit.*; M. B. Clinard (ed.), *Anomie and Deviant Behavior* (New York: Free Press, 1964), especially Clinard's review paper, pp. 1–56.

77. On A. Weber and Hobhouse, see the works cited in notes 24, 45.
     On Freyer see the works cited in note 17.

78. On this see E. Erikson, *Childhood & Society*, 2d ed. (New York: Norton, 1963); E.

Erikson, *Young Man Luther, op. cit.;* F. Weinstein and G. M. Platt, *Psychoanalytical Sociology* (Baltimore, Md.: John Hopkins University Press, 1973); T. W. Adorno, *The Authoritarian Personality* (New York: Harper & Row, 1950); A. Kardiner *et al., The Psychological Frontiers of Society* (New York: Columbia University Press, 1946); R. S. Wallenstein and N. J. Smelser, "Psychoanalysis and sociology: articulation and applications," *International Journal of Psychoanalysis,* Vol. 50 (1969), pp. 694 ff.

    On learning theory see the works of Dollard and Miller cited in note 12, and also: A. Bandura and R. H. Walters, *Adolescent Aggression: a Study of the Influence of Child-Training Practices and Family Interrelationships* (New York: Ronald Press, 1959); A. Bandura and R. H. Walters, *Social Learning and Personality Development* (London: Holt, Reinhart & Winston [1963], 1969).

79. On this see G. H. Mead, *Mind, Self and Society, op. cit.;* A. Schutz, *On Phenomenology and Social Relations, op. cit.*

    For similar but more recent developments in symbolic interactionism, see also the papers of P. M. Hall and R. M. Kanter in *Sociological Inquiry,* Vol. 42, Nos. 3–4 (1972), pp. 35–99.

80. O. D. Duncan, "Social organization and the ecosystem," *op. cit.;* J. H. Steward, *Theory of Culture Change, op. cit.;* M. D. Sahlins and E. R. Service (eds.), *Evolution and Culture, op. cit.;* L. White, *The Science of Culture* (New York: Grove Press, 1949); A. H. Hawley, *Human Ecology: a Theory of Community Structure* (New York: Ronald Press, 1950).

5

Sociology Between the Wars

1. The development of sociology after World War I in most countries was distinguished from the period of the Founding Fathers in several respects. In one sense it was a period of recession when compared with the heroic attempts of the Founding Fathers and the vociferous discussions of the nature and problems of sociology which attended these efforts. The Founding Fathers' attempts to combine various types of sociological activities were followed by a period of new dissociation among these activities in most centers of sociological research. The tradition of combining various types or levels of sociological analysis was to some degree continued by some successors of the Founding Fathers, like Maurice Halbwachs[1] in France. However, given the sporadic nature of the academic and professional settings of sociological activity, these efforts did not create a self-generating continuity of the sociological tradition of the type envisaged by the Founding Fathers. Moreover, few towering figures emerged. However, the possibility of uniting various components of sociological activity continued as a latent aspiration, functioning as a catalyst, and the different components of sociological analysis became reference points for those engaged in them. Moreover, within each component, an internal momentum developed which later proved to be an

important base for the sustained and integrated development of the period after World War II. In this chapter we shall survey the developments in the major centers of sociological work, then attempt to assess the entire period.

Sociology in Germany

2. German sociology trends encountered before the First World War continued but with certain intellectual and institutional departures. The combination of continuity with some innovation was apparent both in the major intellectual orientations of sociologists and the major fields of substantive research. The critical-evaluative stance toward modern capitalist democratic society was maintained, but with substantive differences. Where Werner Sombart's or Ferdinand Tönnies' criticisms of modern society in the prewar period had implied a positive evaluation of traditional society and a return to romanticism,[2] postwar critiques showed such important modifications as the liberal democratic posture, best exemplified by Mannheim in his *Man and Society in an Age of Reconstruction,*[3] in which he saw societal planning as a way to solve problems of modern society; and the position of radical Marxism, both dogmatic and nondogmatic, the latter best exemplified by the sociologists of the Frankfurt Institute for Social Research.[4]

Another line of continuity was the strong theoretic orientation of German sociology, and the elaboration of theoretical paradigms as a major concern. Theoretical advances were made in several areas: the elaboration of formal sociology by Alfred Vierkandt, Leopold von Wiese, Theodor Geiger, and to some degree Hans Freyer, who combined formal sociology (in the tradition of Tönnies) with a philosophy of culture orientation[5]; more direct approaches to the philosophy of culture and history in the works of Freyer and Alfred Weber[6]; comparative political, historical, or ethnological work, exemplified by Franz Oppenheimer, Alfred Weber, Richard Thurnwald, and to some degree the comparative historical work of Otto Hintze[7]; and, most important, attempts by Mannheim to develop a new, comprehensive philosophical-analytic paradigm.[8]

Most explicative paradigms developed by these scholars had elements of both closed-system and open-system approaches.[9]

The schemes of formal sociology developed by Vierkandt and von Wiese, though more intricate than Simmel's and Tönnies' classifications, were closed systems. However, the work of Geiger and (to a lesser degree)

Freyer showed important characteristics of systemic openings-toward structural aspects of society in the case of Geiger, toward cultural processes with Freyer.

The paradigms developed by Oppenheimer and Alfred Weber were, in principle, open systems with heavy emphasis on the variable interrelationships between society and culture, although Oppenheimer's emphasis on force as the creator of states and Alfred Weber's emphasis on the internal autonomy of systems of culture, civilization (i.e., technical knowledge), and society, assumed that each of them worked according to its own dynamics without much systematic mutual influence.

Although these theories lacked the richness of Max Weber's theoretical, historical, and comparative analyses, all displayed increasing systematization of sociological analysis and research.

They also showed an increasing preoccupation with historiosophic concerns, couched either in culturalist or semi-Marxist terms. This is true particularly of Freyer, and to some degree Alfred Weber.

The concern with combined theoretical, historical, and philosophical problems was apparent above all in the sociology of knowledge and culture—the most important new theoretical departures in German sociology of this period. The field of sociology of knowledge, formally developed after the war by Max Scheler[10] became the focus of such outstanding works as Mannheim's *Ideology and Utopia*,[11] which triggered widespread interest and criticism. Opposition to Mannheim is best represented by Alexander von Schelting, who rejected Mannheim's extreme relativism and sociologism in the realm of values and thought.[12] Partly independent of Mannheim's thesis, partly referring to it, the subject also preoccupied sociologists of the Frankfurt Institute, especially Max Horkheimer.[13] In a broader historical perspective, and with somewhat differing emphases, it was also the focus of Alfred Weber's work on the morphology of cultures and the relationships among cultures, civilizations (technical knowledge), and social organization.[14]

The keen interest in the sociology of knowledge and culture may explain the preoccupation of German sociologists with a related problem: the possibility of an objective sociology and its place in the intellectual panorama. This concern is especially evident in Mannheim's *Ideology and Utopia* and in the works of the scholars of the Frankfurt Institute.[15] All, in differing ways, criticized Marx's and Max Weber's positions, claiming that intellectuals could transcend the bias of different outlooks to achieve an "objective" and "critical" perspective, and that sociology and critical analysis were major manifestations of such an outlook.

Concern with the development of modern society continued as a central issue in German sociology. In this area, an important reformulation was made of some of the central problems of modern industrial-capitalist society, with emphasis on its potential breakdowns and problems as they developed in the Weimar period, and with the special problems of the new salaried middle classes and large bureaucratic organizations. The new problem in sociological analysis of modern society was that of mass society, and of the possible abdication of societal and individual autonomy in the era of "late" capitalism. This problem was treated in different ways by Geiger, Emil Lederer, and Mannheim on the one hand, and the Marxists, particularly the Frankfurt school, on the other.[16]

This reformulation of the problems of modern capitalist society on the verge of the Hitler era was also a basis for a critical reexamination of Marxism, another continuing focus of German sociology. The centrality of these theoretical issues can probably be best explained by shared intellectual traditions, legacies of the past (i.e., Marx and Max Weber, and German idealism[17])—which continued to produce a certain intellectual coherence among German sociologists.

An important attempt at comparative macrosocietal analysis was made by Norbert Elias in *Uber den Prozess der Zivilisation*. Published in Switzerland on the eve of World War II, however, this work had no direct impact till much later.[18]

Several tentative advances were made in the institutionalization of sociology, and the development of stronger nuclei of sociological work. The group of scholars at the Frankfurt Institute for Social Research was established in 1923, and gained semiacademic legitimation some years later. Like the group of *L'Année Sociologique* in France, the scholars of the Institute[19] were united by a common intellectual endeavor, the critical analysis of Marxism, including a search for factors which would explain the failure of some of Marx's predictions about modern capitalist society.

Other nuclei included the rather loose groupings of students around Mannheim and the more stable group around von Wiese in Cologne, which elaborated his schema of formal sociology and undertook related empirical research.

Sociological publication continued as an active enterprise.[20] Oriented both to the general public and to sociologists, historians, and other specialists, this activity reflected the involvement of sociologists in broader intellectual activities and concerns of this period.

Important shifts in the direction of research and its theoretical bases also characterize this period. Although most research undertaken in a theoretical context was historical or ethnological, a new tradition of empirical research also began to develop, producing studies based on direct observation. Moreover, this type of research was more closely linked to theoretical perspectives than research before World War I. Some studies of this period do lack a strong theoretical base. This is true of research on social mobility and on rural vs. urban conditions. Similarly, Tönnies' investigation of the causes of crime and suicide was not related to his lasting theoretical contributions on *Gemeinschaft* and *Gesellschaft*. Other empirical work, however, did derive from an analytic framework. The field work conducted by von Wiese and his students in the 1920s in villages and ghettoes was intended to test the applicability of his formal sociology to real situations.[21] Lederer and Geiger investigated the new middle class of employees,[22] analyzing its class and status position and its political attitudes in the light of the stratification theories of Marx and Max Weber.

Another serious attempt to relate theory to empirical research was made by the Frankfurt Institute. Preoccupied before their emigration in the early thirties from Germany with the conservative political outlook of the proletariat, which contradicted Marx's predictions, the scholars of the Institute tried to complement Marx's assumptions with Freudian principles to explain the mechanisms by which authority structures are maintained and perpetuated. Developed mainly by Erich Fromm, this theoretical synthesis was "tested" by two empirical studies of the attitudes of workers and of adolescents toward authority.[23]

Of special interest, too, were the attempts to combine research not only with broad theoretical frameworks but also, as in the work of Geiger, Lederer, and Sigfried Kracauer, with the tradition of political analysis of contemporary life.[24] Indeed, many sociologists participated actively in the intellectual debates on democracy and capitalism that characterized the atmosphere of the Weimar Republic.[25] They belonged to all camps, from the liberal to the Romantic neonationalists, often forming small sectarian groups. These tendencies to sectarianism were also reinforced by the tendency of each "school" or person to develop its own research program, with little research contact among the various groups.

Despite these tendencies to sectarianism, contact between different "schools" and persons did increase in meetings and debates. Most of these discussions dealt with ideological or theoretical problems, questions of the nature and limits of sociology, and such pervasive metaanalytic problems as proper methodology and the problem of political and ideological stances in sociology. There was still little comparison of respective research programs,[26] although the beginning of such developments can be discerned.

This situation stemmed from the slow tempo of academic institutionalization of sociology. Notable achievements were gained in the introduction of courses of sociology in most institutions of higher learning. However, few chairs of sociology or independent departments were established,[27] and the official academic conception stressed the philosophic and historical orientations of sociology. Consequently, the problem of academic acceptance continued to preoccupy German sociologists, a fact amply reflected in the discussions of the leading sociological journal in this period, *Kölner Vierteljahrshrift fur Soziologie,* and in the debates of the German Sociological Association.[28]

Sociology in France

3. Emile Durkheim's intellectual and methodological legacy continued as the outstanding sociological tradition in France between the wars,[29] at least until the mid-1930s, and it was the younger generation of the *L'Année Sociologique* who made the best-known developments of this legacy. These contributions, inspired by Durkheim's broad conception of sociology, were not deeply concerned with problems of modern society. Nor were their authors professional or academic sociologists alone. Rather, ethnographers, anthropologists, historians, and economists applied or developed Durkheim's perspective to their respective fields.

Purely sociological works in the Durkheimian tradition included Halbwachs' *Les Cadres Sociaux de la Mémoire,*[30] Paul Fauconnet's *La Responsabilité,*[31] inspired by Durkheim's theory of sanctions, and Célestin Bouglé's work developing Durkheim's theory of values.[32] In sociological ethnography, Durkheim's impact was evident above all in Marcel Mauss' rich anthropological analyses, which in a sense were forerunners of modern structuralism, and in Lucien Lévy-Bruhl's analysis of the primitive mind.[33] In the field of law, Durkheim exercised an important influence on the works of Georges Davy[34]; in history, on Marcel Granet's studies of Chinese civilization[35]; and in economics, on the works of François Simiand.[36]

Important intellectual ties also developed between sociologists and historians who were heavily influenced by sociological trends, although not solely by the Durkheimian tradition. The best examples of these ties are the *Annales* group led by Lucien Fèbvre and Marc Bloch; the collections of *L'Évolution de l'Humanité* and the *Bibliothèque de Synthèse Historique,* edited by Henri Berr; and the meetings of the Centre International de Synthèse.

These works were strongly theoretically oriented and based, as in the past, on historical and secondary ethnographic and anthropological data. Most of the general advances in theory and comparative analysis, especially in the work of Mauss, were developed from these fields. It was indeed in the field of ethnography, which during this period became institutionally differentiated from sociology, that some significant research developments took place. One of these was the beginning of research based on empirical field work; the other was the integration of teaching and research activities. These developments were facilitated by the creation in 1925 of the Institut d'Ethnologie supported financially by the Ministry of the Colonies and directed by Mauss and Lévy-Bruhl.

Sociology did not show parallel developments. Only after World War II was sociological research introduced into the L'École Pratique des Hautes-Études, the French organization for research which had been established in 1868. Academic acceptance of sociology continued to be problematic between the wars, and the achievements attained in this period were not very impressive. Only a few chairs of sociology existed: one at the Sorbonne, occupied by Fauconnet; one at Strasburg, occupied by Halbwachs, and one at Bordeaux. Moreover, only a handful of courses were introduced in other institutions of higher learning.

This lack of official recognition and support was due in part to the rigid, semi-feudal structure of the French academic system. Moreover, Durkheim's death in 1917 added to the difficulty. He had exercised great influence in academic and educational circles and had succeeded, by virtue of his intellectual and organizational abilities, in turning the group of the *L'Année Sociologique* into a viable research institute.[37] But he left no successor as an intellectual leader or academic entrepreneur. In addition, the changed social and political conditions after World War I made obsolete both the ideological elements of the LePlayist tradition[38] and the secular rationalism of Durkheim, causing sociology to withdraw to a more restricted position in the intellectual life of the 1920s and early 1930s than it had assumed before. Durkheim's attempts to establish a new civic religion were seen as an "anachronism," and did not spark intellectual developments or controversy. For similar reasons, and in contrast to the situation in Germany, there were fewer discussions of sociology's intellectual boundaries or its involvement in political and social affairs.

There were few studies in this period based on quantitative data or direct empirical observation, far fewer than in Germany. There were several exceptions, such as Simiand's sociologically inspired works on wages,[39] and Halbwachs' first reexamination of Durkheim's thesis on *Suicide* in the light of new statistical data, and his own study of living conditions of the working class.[40] But these did not basically alter the situation of decline in empirical research, a situation underscored by the decline of the LePlayist tradition, which had been so strong before World War I.

Durkheim's followers, however, did make two attempts to institutionalize research. They revived the work patterns which had prevailed before World War I among scholars associated with the *L'Année Sociologique*, but this was only for a short period (1925–1926) before *L'Année* was replaced. The new publications, the *Bulletin* (published from 1926 to 1934 by the Institut Français de Sociologie) and the *Annales Sociologiques* (which began publication in 1934), both media for Durkheimian scholars, were general scientific publications. Their efforts contrasted with the intensive and coordinated group work and research which had characterized *L'Année* before World War I.

The second attempt was the establishment by Bouglé of the Centre de Documentation Sociale, where seminars were held and some research facilities were provided. This framework, however, was too slight to encompass the activities of a full-fledged research institute.

In the mid-1930s the declining influence of the cluster of international sociologists led before and right after World War I by René Worms[41] also became apparent. The changed political and social atmosphere made this tradition intellectually obsolete; consequently, this school ceased to play a substantive role in French sociology. As a result the international orientation, always important in its activities, became even more prominent for a while, but even this weakened at the end of the 1930s with increased international political tensions.

The mid-1930s were a turning point from another perspective as well, marking a "crisis" in French sociology. Basically, this was a period of intellectual reorientation: a weakening of the Durkheimian tradition and the emergence of new scholarly interests. The crisis in the Durkheimian tradition, the strongest that had yet taken place among French sociological schools, had both intellectual and social roots. Intellectually, this tradition became increasingly unattractive for the younger postwar generation of potential scholars and intellectuals, mainly because its underlying assumptions of rational secularism were seen as obsolete in the face of the events of the war and its aftermath. Nevertheless, the tradition was continued by the young scholars who had worked with Durkheim before World War I. In the 1930s the problem of replacing this aging group became critical, since few potential young scholars were willing to carry the tradition further.

The intellectual lethargy of the mid-1930s was partly overcome by awakening interest in Marxism, until then almost nonexistent in French sociology, mainly through the impact of Russian *émigré* scholars and the Frankfurt Institute, which after its exile from Germany carried on its activities in France, among other European countries. Young scholars like Raymond Aron, Georges Friedmann, and Georges Gurvitch began their academic and intellectual careers under this influence, although only after World War II was this influence elaborated.

Sociology in Great Britain

4. English sociology did not undergo substantive changes or trans-formations in the interwar period, continuing trends apparent before World War I. This was also a period of stagnation, especially with respect to academic institutionalization and legitmacy. The chair of sociology endowed before World War I at the London School of Economics con-tinued to be the only one in the country until after World War II, and only a few new general departments of social sciences were established.[42] The factors which accounted for resistance to the academic acceptance of sociology before the war—namely, the latent rivalry with anthropology, the success of anthropology, and the rigidity of the older universities —continued to play a similar role in this period.

In terms of broad intellectual orientations, British sociology continued to be characterized by reformism and belief in rationality and progress, with little participation in the intense debates of the 1930s on capitalism and socialism. Conceptual links to prewar sociology were also strong. At the London School of Economics, the only center of institutionalized academic sociology, Hobhouse and Westermarck continued the tradition of macrosociology based on the comparative method and the historical and secondary analysis of anthropological data until the late 1920s. Mor-ris Ginsberg, who succeeded Hobhouse at the London School, shared with his predecessor a belief in evolutionary progress and rationality. Ginsberg also continued and elaborated the intellectual tradition (evolutionism, values, and ethics) and the method of research which Hobhouse and his colleagues had initiated.[43] In general, theoretical work in sociology continued to be divorced from empirical research, and Ginsberg's pioneering study on social mobility, conducted in the late 1920s,[44] was an exception to his central theoretical interests.

Empirical research, sponsored partly by government agencies, con-tinued to be oriented to solving immediate social problems; it lacked either a firm institutional basis or intellectual links with broader theoreti-cal concerns.[45] Several problem areas gained increased attention in these studies, among these the study of changes in the national level of intellig-ence. Interest in this topic stemmed from the eugenics controversy on the extent to which intelligence was innate or determined by the social environment,[46] and on the social consequences of differing birth rates and levels of intelligence among the various social classes.

Another focus of practical research was the town and country surveys. Executed largely in the Booth-Geddes-Rowntree tradition, these surveys described the location of industries and public services, the patterns of social intercourse among people in different residential areas, changes in the distribution of wealth and poverty, variations in unemployment, and so on. Other studies examined the social position of various occupational groups, such as professionals and higher-level civil servants, and various aspects of delinquency. The tradition of social research geared to policy problems, so greatly promoted by the Fabians, became increasingly popu-lar in governmental circles, but continued separate from the sociological tradition, with closer ties to social work and administration.

In the late 1930s, a broadening of perspective was reflected in meetings that brought together scholars concerned with sociological studies in the broader sense of the word, as well as sociologists and students of neighbor-ing disciplines. These meetings dealt with the question of sociology's intellectual boundaries, as well as substantive problems (e.g., social class mobility) and methodological questions (e.g., field work, intelligence tests, etc.)[47] Under the influence of some *émigrés,* above all Karl Mannheim, sociologists began to concern themselves with such current problems as class analysis and social planning.

Sociology in the United States

5.   The second period of development in American sociology was characterized institutionally by the further expansion and consolidation of sociology on the academic level; its differentiation into specialized fields; the multiplication of journals and publishing houses specializing in sociological work; and increased employment of sociologists in public and private institutions. Intellectually, it was characterized by a certain with-drawal from grand analytic schemes; emphasis on the study of social life in the United States; only marginal interest in macrosociology; increasing preoccupation with methodology; contact with neighboring disciplines like psychology and anthropology; and the development of many middle-range theories.[48]

The scientific status of sociology continued to preoccupy American sociologists, especially in the 1920s. Indeed, it was this quest for scientific standing that gave rise to two central debates relating to the proper activities and orientations of the sociologist.[49] One debate, which centered on operationalism, was about the extent to which sociology should follow the path of the physical sciences—that is, the degree to which sociologists should choose as subjects of investigations only those social phenomena and aspects of behavior to which rigorous statistical techniques and measurements could be applied. The second issue involved the possibility and desirability of a value-free sociology.

Although neither problem was resolved, the second seems to have been settled in a less ambiguous manner than the first, since the ideal of a value-free sociology became the professional ethos accepted by most American sociologists in the early 1940s. Several factors contributed to this. First, World War I shattered the belief of many intellectuals, among them sociologists, in the possibility of attaining social progress by rational human intervention in social processes. Second, as the academic status of American sociology was strengthened, the alliance with the reform movements which had assisted in its institutionalization seemed to most sociologists unnecessary if not detrimental. Finally, increased possibilities for private nonacademic employment of sociologists and for government-sponsored sociological research,[50] weakened the appeal of direct partisan political involvement.

At the same time, a more radical trend began to develop, epitomized in Robert S. Lynd's *Knowledge for What?*[51] Lynd did not criticize the claims to objectivity of American sociologists, so much as he did their avoidance, in research and theory, of crucial problems—for example, the distribution of power in society. Indirectly, Lynd argued, they became accomplices of the powerful to the detriment of social good. In the mid-1950s this theme of criticism would again be taken by C. Wright Mills in his *The Sociological Imagination.*[52]

Institutionally and intellectually, this period was characterized by the emergence of two strong sociological centers, Columbia University and the University of Chicago,[53] and the proliferation of secondary centers. The emergence of the major centers helped crystallize a core of theoretical orientations at Chicago, and a methodological tradition at Columbia. These gave American sociology at least a partial sense of intellectual unity which had been almost completely lacking in the preceding period, despite its success in organizational and academic institutionalization.

At Columbia in the 1920s, William Ogburn, Stuart Chapin, and others introduced and developed several basic statistical methods and techniques for applied research, some of which were known by then in England.

Through continuous publication, they made these methods known to a large public of sociologists and other social scientists.

At Chicago, W. I. Thomas and later, Ezra Park made major contributions to the crystallization of a tradition of urban sociology. It consisted less in methodological innovation, which could be "imported" from Columbia, than in the break away from the earlier fragmented studies of social problems, which had lacked theoretical grounding and substance. Thus Thomas and Florian Znianecki in their ethnographic study, *The Polish Peasant in Europe and in America*,[54] investigated the processes of social and cultural change undergone by an ethnic minority who immigrated from a rural to an urban environment, within a broad analytic social-psychological framework. Later, Park developed a theoretical framework for the study of most social processes taking place in the city,[55] including in it previous concerns with poverty, immigration, assimilation and disorganization, and race relations. Thus he succeeded partially in bridging the gap between theory and research that had characterized the first period of development. Park's intellectual powers, combined with the material resources the Chicago sociology department was able to mobilize for research and salaries, attracted scholars and students from across the United States. The department also gained national prominence through its graduates, who brought its intellectual orientations to the universities they staffed, and through the influence of its members on the American Sociological Society.[56]

Nevertheless, the theoretical impact of the University of Chicago department of sociology was only partial. Neither symbolic interactionism, explored by Thomas and systematically developed by Mead,[57] nor the stronger ecological tradition of urban sociology became the predominant frame of reference for theory and research in American sociology, although for a period they were the single most important schools. The dominant characteristics of American sociology shifted over time until in the late 1930s, research was fragmented into empirical studies dissociated from a larger theoretical framework.[58] This trend, apparently, was the outcome of the increased institutionalization of sociology, which created pressures for research results that could provide immediate answers to concrete, narrow problems, as well as the nature of the Chicago tradition of urban sociology. That tradition, though theoretically oriented, lacked enough analytic coherence to withstand fragmentation.

The result was a number of relatively unconnected empirical studies conducted in various social spheres: studies of social stratification, especially status groups in small communities, initiated by Lloyd Warner in the 1930s; studies of ethnic groups; studies of the family and changes in its functions attendant on modernization; studies of socialization patterns, and of determinants of marital stability; studies of communication and public opinion; studies of small groups, of factors influencing group structure and performance, and of mechanisms of social control. Most of these studies lacked a theoretical referent or, at best, were based on middle-range hypotheses. The latter was the case with some studies of ethnic groups, families, in which psychoanalytic theory was used to explain ethnic prejudice or the effects of early socialization on adult personality.

There was little interest in macrosociological theory[59] in this period. Compared with the theoretical tradition of urban sociology and the strong tendencies to empiricism, the macrosociological perspectives of Ogburn's theory of social change, and MacIver's refinement of Tönnies' ideas of *Gemeinschaft* or *Gesellschaft* into "Community and Association," had relatively little impact on sociological research, though these scholars, particularly MacIver, were for a long time major exponents of theory in American sociology.[60]

True enough, the various research schools also worked with some broader assumptions about the nature of social order. The Chicago school especially tended to use a Darwinian or ecological approach, while symbolic interactionism dealt with the relationship between the individual and society in terms of its own theoretical emphases on voluntarism and situationally emergent elements of social structure. Both explanations, however, were increasingly unsatisfactory: "primitive" Darwinism in the face of the Depression, aroused social conscience, and the New Deal; symbolic interactionism in the light of the emerging consensus among psychologists and sociologists on the effects of biological, psychological, structural, and organizational constraints on individual action and personality.

Thus in the late 1930s and early 1940s, sociologists felt increasingly the need to establish closer relationships between theory and research and to overcome the flaws of the prevailing paradigms.[61] This interest in *macrosociological* paradigms and in linking research and theory had been evident in some earlier works: Pitirim Sorokin's *Contemporary Sociological Theories, Handbook of Rural Sociology*, and later *Social and Cultural Dynamics;* MacIver's *Society;* and the work of the mid-1930s influx of European, particularly German, scholars.[62] It was also the background for the emergence of the structural-functional school in the mid-1940s (see Chapter 7).

Some implicit macrosocietal orientations can also be found in the collection of studies *Recent Social Trends.*[63] Commissioned by the President of the United States, these studies, investigating over-all changes in American society since 1900, attempted to trace the differing rates of change in various spheres of social life and their reciprocal repercussions. Though displaying little theoretical orientation, they were perhaps the first systematic attempt at a comprehensive "state of the nation" stocktaking.

Empirical, theoretical, and policy concerns were fused more successfully in Gunnar Myrdal's classic study of race discrimination, *An American Dilemma*. [64] This was a major attempt to combine a broad theoretical view with the empirical study of a major problem in American society.

The theoretically oriented research which began to develop at the end of this period included also the small-group studies of Kurt Lewin and his associates, and Paul Lazarsfeld's and Bernard Berelson's *The Peoples' Choice*. [65] The latter was unique among studies of public opinion conducted in this period for its theoretical orientation. To this category also belong the studies on the *American Soldier* [66] conducted during World War II, which displayed a successful combination of new methodological techniques (above all scale and latent structure analysis) and middle-range theories of group behavior, especially theories of reference groups and relative deprivation.

At the end of the war, several *émigré* scholars from the Frankfurt Institute conducted studies on prejudice whose results were published at the end of the 1940s. One of the best known was *The Authoritarian Personality*, conducted by Theodor Adorno with the collaboration of psychologists from Berkeley. [67] Following the earlier theoretical concern of the Institute with the problems and changes of modern mass society, the researchers attempted to identify the basic personality traits which predispose individuals to prejudice and to anti-Semitism in particular. They explained the genesis of such traits in terms of a theoretical framework stressing changes in the nuclear family produced by industrialization and political modernization, and with psychoanalytic assumptions about the effects of early socialization on the adult personality.

This and other studies in the series, such as Bruno Bettelheim's and Morris Janowitz's *Dynamics of Prejudice*, [68] reflected a synthesis of the theoretical and analytic orientations of the European sociological traditions with the methodological sophistication and research tradition of American sociology. This combination heralded the post-World War II era.

These intellectual and theoretical developments had several institutional consequences for the community of American sociologists. As competing perspectives developed, the University of Chicago's intellectual preeminence declined as did its influence in the American Sociological Society. The appearance of the *American Sociological Review* in 1936 was symptomatic of this change for the *Review* was initially conceived as a means for expression of views critical of the Chicago tradition, with which the *American Journal of Sociology* had been associated for many years.[69] This reorientation was strengthened by an increasing openness to other disciplines, especially psychology and anthropology, and the development of interdisciplinary paradigms, such as the psychological model based on learning theory and the "culture and personality" framework.[70]

Some Illustrations of Developments in Sociology in Other Countries

6. Along with developments in the centers of sociological activity, impressive, though quantitatively restricted, advances took place in some peripheral sociological communities—above all Poland, Czechoslovakia, Rumania, and Finland. Although the institutional antecedents and starting points of sociology differed in each country, the main trends resemble those in the major European centers.

Poland. Before World War I, sociology in Poland[71] received no recognition, partly because of its controversial scientific status, but also as a result of difficulties resulting from Poland's loss of political independence in 1794, which was regained only in 1918. Sociological activity did take place, however, especially in ethnographic studies, which explored Polish folklore and tradition, and in theoretical and speculative trends that were largely imitative of similar speculation in the major sociological centers.

In the interwar period, this situation changed significantly. Sociology gained academic recognition, other institutional centers were established and courses of sociology were introduced, first, interestingly enough, in some theological faculties. More important, three chairs of sociology were established, in the universities of Poznan, Warsaw, and Cracow. In 1921 Florian Znianecki, one of the outstanding sociologists of this period, established the first institute of sociological research in Poznan, where he taught sociology, and in 1930 he launched the *Przeglad Sociologiczny*, the first sociological periodical.

Znianecki's most important contributions were in theory and theoretically based research. Both aspects of his contribution are illustrated in the work he coauthored with W. I. Thomas, *The Polish Peasant in Europe and in America.* His analytic insights on the theory of action were further elaborated in *Social Actions* and in *The Social Role of the Man of Knowledge,* written in the United States.[72] Znianecki's main theoretical and methodological approach was taken up in Poland by one of his collaborators, J. Chalasinski, who conducted elaborate studies of rural Poland, and the sociology of education. Sociologists at the Warsaw university were also active in this period, most notably Stanislaw Ossowski, who worked in the fields of sociological theory, sociology of culture, and sociology of class relations; and Stephan Czarnowski, whose studies of religion combined Durkheimian theoretical insights with rich historical and ethnographic data.

Czechoslovakia.   In Czechoslovakia,[73] as in Poland, the first substantive developments in sociology took place in the period between World Wars I and II, when three chairs of sociology were established, at the universities of Brno, Prague, and Bratislava.

Although several reductionistic approaches, psychologistic or biologistic in nature, were developed at this time, developments were in principle more open. Thus the theoretical works and studies of religion and revolution, by Czech sociology's Founding Father, Thomas Masaryk, stressed both the individual and the collectivity as important in the explanation of social phenomena. Masaryk's pupils, especially Arnost Blaha from Brno University, also exhibited an open-system approach. Although Blaha's theoretical sociology had a strong functionalist bent and was heavily influenced by Durkheim, he emphasized the importance of the individual in his analysis.

Blaha was also important in initiating empirical research. Among his best known studies are his work on the city; the monograph on the peasant and worker, which is concerned with stratification; and his study of the social function of the intelligentsia, Although these studies were not systematically based on coherent theoretical frameworks, they made analytic insights. Important beginnings of a similar kind of research were also made by sociologists at Prague University, among them by Zdenek Ullrich, who applied Weber's open methodological approach to the study of Prague's metropolitan influence on its environments.

Rumania.   Similar trends can be discerned in the development of sociology in Rumania.[74] Before World War I, sociology was not recognized as an autonomous academic discipline, but some scattered quasi-sociological activities were taking place. One finds in this period, for example, a remarkable number of surveys of rural life; but they were cut off from other sociological endeavours. Theoretical works included treatises using closed-system approaches, for the most part, and works on the relationship between sociology and history.

After World War I, some substantive changes took place. One was the academic recognition of sociology and the establishment of chairs of sociology at the universities of Bucharest, Cluj, and Iasi. The second was a closer rapproachment between theory and research. Although major sociologists, including C. Sudeteanu, Georghe Marica, Vasile Barbat in Cluj, and Petre Andrei in Iasi, elaborated purely theoretical systems or studied French and German sociologists without being engaged in research, a departure from this trend was also evident in the work of the outstanding sociologist, Dimitri Gusti of Bucharest University. Gusti applied some of his sociological conceptions empirically in the intensive interdisciplinary surveys that he and his students conducted in Rumanian villages. He also institutionalized this tradition of research in the Rumanian Social Institute (for research) which he founded in 1921. Other scholars who tried to relate theory and research included M. Saint-Zeletin, who analyzed the social and political history of the Rumanian bourgeoisie from a Marxist theoretical perspective.

Finland.   In Finland[75] the tradition of sociological analysis developed out of a variety of sources. They include social history, ethnography, and folklore, Romantic Marxism, and Romantic social philosophy.

The central figure in the development of Finnish sociology was Westermarck. He and his students and collaborators, especially Rafael Karsten and Gunnar Landtman, occupied the three chairs of sociology established between the wars and shaped the main intellectual preoccupation of sociology: comparative and evolutionary theory of institutions based on ethnographic data.

A single exception to this trend is found in the work of Heikki Waris, who studied the rise of a working class community in Helsinki in the tradition of the Chicago school. Warris' studies of criminology and alcoholism also constituted an important focus of research.

Institutional Growth: Contacts, Debates, and Codifications

7.   Throughout this period, both the number of sociological activities and communities and the intellectual and organizational institutionalization of sociology increased greatly. There were increasing contacts among different sociological communities, changing patterns of international communication, important attempts at codification of sociology. The flow

of influence among sociological centers or communities, aptly described by Edward Shils,[76] became more regular, giving rise to many attempts to institutionalize the emerging international orientations and activities. Apart from the not too fruitful meetings of the International Congresses which Worms had initiated,[77] sociologists became aware of each other's work. Writers like Sorokin, MacIver, Znianecki, Ginsberg, the young Talcott Parsons and Aron, and the still younger Robert Merton and Shils, became important carriers of these activities and orientations.

Personal factors, rather than institutionalized channels, were largely responsible for these improvements in the international dissemination of sociological ideas after World War I. Sorokin's *Contemporary Sociological Theories,* published at the end of the 1920s, and Parsons' *The Structure of Social Action,* published in 1937,[78] are important not only because they signify the beginning of codification of sociological ideas, but also because their authors, especially Parsons, tried to synthesize various viewpoints which had been intellectually and ecologically isolated. Similarly, personal contacts seemed to be responsible for the introduction by Chapin at Columbia and Ogburn in Chicago of statistical methods developed by British eugenicists.[79]

These signs of growth of an international sociological community had little counterpart in empirical research. Research conducted in a particular country did not become a major concern of sociologists in other countries until after World War II.[80]

8. The increasing institutionalization of sociological analysis was accompanied by a trend to consolidation and codification of different traditions of analysis. Such attempts at codification of theory, and to some degree of research, can be found at this stage in almost all the national sociological communities. However, the nature of this codification differed in terms of the characteristics of the national sociologies—some of which were, in fact, analyzed at the end of this period by Mannheim.[81]

The attempts at codification were evident mainly in the development of textbooks, symposia, and encyclopedias. The textbooks published in this period were of two types. One, most prevalent in the United States and attuned to the needs of college and university teaching, were usually focused on broad principles of sociology, such as interaction, assimilation, and the like, illustrated largely from such areas as urban or family life.[82] Only in MacIver's *Society*[83] was a far more systematic macrosociological, and to some degree comparative, perspective attempted.

The other type of textbook, more prevalent in Europe, is best exemplified by such small volumes as von Wiese's *Soziologie;* the Oppenheimer and Salomon, and the Sombart "readers" in Germany; René Hubert's *Manuel de Sociologie* in France; and Ginsberg's seminal *Sociology.*[84] These works concentrated on the analysis of the boundaries and limits of sociology, such basic concepts as the "individual and society" and their historical and philosophical origins, the history of sociology, the broad comparative analysis of different institutions, and the application of these concepts to contemporary problems. However, they rarely incorporated research in a systematic way; nor were the topics synthesized either in one analytic paradigm or through some common middle-range theories.

Similar features of codification can be found in various encyclopedic ventures, as, for example, the *Handworterbuch der Soziologie,* published in 1932 under the editorship of Vierkandt; the *Study of Society,* edited by Ginsberg, Frederic C. Bartlett and others in England; Bouglé's *Bilan de la Sociologie Française Contemporaine;* Aron's *La Sociologie Allemande Contemporaine,* in France[85]; and above all the *Encyclopedia of the Social Sciences,* published in 15 volumes in the United States between 1930 and 1935. In all these works several similar trends can be discerned despite local difference. All stressed the search for, and delineation of, the proper subject matter of sociology; the differences between schools of sociology; and different general-theoretical approaches, with less emphasis on subfields of sociology or on the relationship of these subfields to macrosocietal or explicit analytic frameworks.

Thus, the *Handwörterbuch der Soziologie* was divided into four broad categories: Sociology of Societies *(Gesellschafts-soziologie);* General Sociology of Culture; Sociology of Specific Cultural Spheres or Types (einzelne Kulturgüten); and, last, Sociology of Specific Cultures or Periods. These broad categories consisted of a mix of articles on trends in sociology, the history of sociology, *ad hoc* fields such as the sociology of occupations, settlements, and the like, and a variety of topics like "Crowd," "Gemeinschaft and Gesellschaft," and "Capitalism and Imperialism." Thurnwald's "Symposium"[86] was concerned with the delineation of the proper scope of sociology by such diverse scholars as Freyer, Sorokin, Ginsberg, Rudolf Steinmetz, Tönnies, Ogburn, and MacIver.

The British *Study of Society* displayed a rather different mix in its articles, testifying to a weaker conception of the sociological field. One finds in this compendium a heavy emphasis on surveys of the methods used in psychological and anthropological research, and on studies which are largely psychological: discussions of intelligence tests and of the development of thinking, emotions, and language in young children.

The range of specifically sociological topics is much narrower. Only a few specialized fields are touched upon—social surveys, urban sociology, small groups in industry, and even these only in a cursory way, without stress on the theoretical background or the problems in the fields. The only discussion that critically reviews and synthesizes research data and theory is Ginsberg's, but the problems analysed in his article (the study of social institutions, of social control, of social morphology), although central to sociology, are seldom related, with the partial exception of social change, to specific fields of research or to middle-range theories.

The *Encyclopedia of the Social Sciences*, like the *Handwörterbuch*, included thinkers of the classic period—Sombart, Hobhouse, Ginsberg, MacIver, and Sorokin, and "newcomers" like Mannheim and Parsons. The *Encyclopedia* covered all social sciences and stressed their mutual relevance, but generally abstained from engaging in interdisciplinary disputes. At the same time, however, it reflected the mixed levels of analytic specification in each discipline. In anthropology, for example, Franz Boas' "eclectic" approach appeared side by side with the more "militant" or paradigmatic Bronislaw Malinowski's article on "Culture."[87] Even more interesting is MacIver's far-ranging article on sociology.[88] Engaged primarily in distinguishing sociology from philosophy and secondarily in examining the schools of sociology, MacIver stressed formal sociology as the major method for developing a distinctive science of sociology, yet scarcely mentioned the various traditions of empirical research. At the same time, newer trends of development of sociological theory were presented. The young Parsons, for example, in his article on "Society,"[89] attempted a more analytic approach to the development of the conceptual tools of sociology.

Many specific articles on topics like Capitalism, Feudalism, Technology, Utopia, Industrialism, Classes, and the like, are of great and continuing intellectual value. Nevertheless, the field of sociology seems disconnected, though often very rich in content and variety, a picture resembling that in the *Handwörterbuch*.

The Uneven Pattern of Institutionalization

9. At the close of the pre-World War II period, sociology evinced a rather mixed picture. Throughout the late 1920s and the 1930s, the separate traditions of research and teaching were strengthened and more fully institutionalized in universities and research institutes. Within the slowly emerging centers, different kinds of research were developing,

each with its own momentum but with little continual mutual association. Around these centers, there developed separate traditions of explicative paradigms; of analytic concepts and tools; and of more specialized fields of inquiry such as social organization, formal organization, stratification, various sociopsychological theories of small groups, attitude and public opinion research, and demographic or ecological research.

Macrosociological and comparative research, the central field of sociological analysis as it had developed in the nineteenth century, continued to focus on different types of social order and institutions. However, it was only partially retained in the emerging centers of sociological study, and, with partial exceptions in the work of von Wiese and members of the Frankfurt Institute, tended to be dissociated from advances in research techniques and work in the new centers of empirical research. The latter, which began to develop in Europe and, more rapidly, in the United States, retained few orientations toward comparative and macrosociological analysis.

Most of the broad explicative paradigms developed in this period hardly advanced analytically beyond the Founding Fathers. They were often more systematic, but were certainly less rich or open to middle-range theory and research. Many were in a sense mere elaborations of points made by the Founding Fathers, without new systematic insights. Their contribution lies in having opened up new fields of inquiry.

Middle-range theories that developed in various fields of research were still *ad hoc* and unrelated to development of broader paradigmatic schemes.[90] Some, however, found a common focus in the discussions of mass society, which were oriented to broader paradigmatic analyses.[91]

Few connections were established between theoretical paradigms and fields of research. Although some—but only a few—of the paradigms were by now oriented toward research, even this research was largely illustrative, and a systematic and continuing discussion of research programs or specific analytic research hypotheses, did not take place.

Commentaries of sociologists on each other's work, especially across countries, focused on principles of sociology or sociological method, rather than on substantive problems of sociological analysis, Definition of the field was still a major topic of sociological discussion. Yet throughout this period, in many of the above-mentioned works, in some of the attempts at codification, in the mutual awareness of sociologists in different countries, and in the encounter between European *emigré* scholars and American researchers, the tendencies to relate different aspects of sociological analysis became stronger. These tendencies were also influenced by developments in other social sciences in this period: social anthropology in Great Britain, psychoanalysis in Germany and later on the United States, and learning theory in the United States.[92]

Among the attempts at such synthesis, we may mention Sorokin's *Social and Cultural Dynamics*,[93] though it focused on broad comparative analysis of macrosocietal and civilizational processes, and MacIver's continuous revision of his macrosocietal comparative analysis.[94] Perhaps the most important of these attempts at synthesis was the work of Mannheim, especially *Man and Society in an Age of Reconstruction*.[95] Here he attempted to bring broader paradigmatic perspectives to bear on specific problems of modern society, especially those involving the possibility of a democratic society in the age of mass society. He sought also to relate research from different empirical fields to these broad problems through the use of middle-range hypotheses. Mannheim's attempt was not very successful for several reasons: his preoccupation with the ideological problems of the Weimar period and the philosophical problems of the German tradition; the writing of the book at the time of the rise of Nazism and his exile to England; the lack of a stable institutional base for his teaching and research. One important institutional outgrowth of his effort, however, was the establishment, under his editorship, of the International Library for Sociology and Social Reconstruction, which served for many years as an important medium of international publication in sociology. Moreover, Mannheim's work, as well as that of many other German emigrants in England and the United States, was of major importance in linking sociology to broader intellectual problems of the war era. And these works bore their first fruits in the changing intellectual atmosphere for sociology which developed after World War II.

Notes

1. M. Halbwachs, *Les Causes du Suicide* (Paris: F. Alcan, 1930); M. Halbwachs, *L'évolution des Besoins dans les Classes Ouvrières,* (Paris: F. Alcan, 1933).

2. On this see A. Mitzman, *Sociology and Estrangement: Three Sociologists of Imperial Germany* (New York: Knopf, 1973), Parts 2 and 3.

3. K. Mannheim, *Man and Society in an Age of Reconstruction* (New York: Harcourt, Brace, 1940). On Mannheim see also G. W. Remmling, *The Sociology of Karl Mannheim* (London: Routledge & Kegan Paul, 1975); E. Shils, "Mannheim, Karl," in *International Encyclopedia of the Social Sciences,* Vol. 9 (New York: Macmillan, 1968), pp. 557–562.
    On the entire period see R. König, *Studien zur Soziologie* (Frankfurt am Main und Hamburg: Fischer Bücherei, 1971), pp. 9–37.

4. For a comprehensive review of their works and criticism, see M. Jay, *The Dialectical Imagination: a History of the Frankfurt School and the Institute of Social Research, 1923–1950* (Boston: Little, Brown, 1973).

5. The major works of these scholars relevant in this connection are A. Vierkandt, *Gesellschaftslehre* (Stuttgart: F. Enke, 1923); L. von Wiese, *System der Allgemeinen Soziologie als Lehre von den Sozialen Prozessen und den Sozialen Gebilden der Menschen*, I Teil: *Beziehungslehre* (Munich: Duncker & Humblot, 1924), II Teil: *Gebildelehre* (Munich: Duncker & Humblot, 1929). For the English adaptation of this work, see L. von Wiese, *Systematic Sociology: on the Basis of the Beziehungslehre and Gelbildelehre*, adapted and amplified by H. Becker (New York: John Wiley, 1932).

For the elements of formal sociology in Tönnies' work see W. J. Cahnman (ed.), *Ferdinand Tönnies: a New Evaluation* (Leiden: E. J. Brill, 1973), pp. 125–139.

On Geiger see *Theodor Geiger on Social Order and Mass Society*, edited with an Introduction by R. Mayntz (Chicago: University of Chicago Press, 1969), especially the introduction. For Geiger's works bearing on this problem, see especially his articles in the *Handwörterbuch der Soziologie*, edited by A. Vierkandt (Stuttgart: Ferdinand Enke Verlag, 1931), especially "Führung" (pp. 136–141), "Gemeinschaft" (pp. 173–180), "Gesellschaft" (pp. 201–211), "Revolution" (pp. 511–518).

On Freyer see H. Freyer, *Einleitung in die Soziologie* (Leipzig: Quelle & Meyer, 1931); H. Freyer, *Soziologie als Wirklichkeitswissenschaft* (Leipzig: Tubner, 1930).

6. H. Freyer, *Soziologie als Wirklichkeitswissenschaft, op. cit.*; H. Freyer, *Einleitung in die Soziologie, op. cit.*; H. Freyer, *Theorie des Objektiven Geistes* (Berlin: Teubner, 1928); A. Weber, *Kulturgeschichte als Kultursoziologie* (Munich: Piper, 1950 [1935]); A. Weber, *Das Tragische und die Geschichte* (Hamburg: Govert, 1943).

7. For this see F. Oppenheimer, *The State* (New York: Huebsch, 1922); F. Oppenheimer, *System der Soziologie* (Jena: Gustav Rischar, 1922); A. Weber, *Kulturgeschichte als Kultursoziologie, op. cit.*; R. Thurnwald, *Die Menschliche Gesellschaft in ihren Ethno-Soziologischen Grundlagen* (Berlin: W. de Gruyter, 1931–1935), 5 vols.; O. Hintze, *Gesammelte Abhandlungen* (Göttingen: Vandenhoeck & Ruprecht, 1962–1967), 3 vols.

8. On this see especially K. Mannheim, *Ideology and Utopia* (New York: Harcourt, Brace, 1936); G. W. Remmling, *The Sociology of Karl Mannheim, op. cit.*; E. Shils, "Mannheim, Karl" *op. cit.*; K. Mannheim, *Essays on the Sociology of Knowledge* (London: Routledge & Kegan Paul, 1952); K. Mannheim, *Systematic Sociology: an Introduction to the Study of Society* (London: Routledge & Kegan Paul, 1957); *From Karl Mannheim*, edited with an introduction by Kurt H. Wolff (New York: Oxford University Press, 1971).

9. On the works of the scholars referred to in the following discussion, see the items quoted in notes 5–7.

For Simmel's formal sociology see K. H. Wolff (ed.), *The Sociology of Georg Simmel* (New York: Free Press, 1950); G. Simmel, *Conflict and the Web of Group-Affiliations* (New York: Free Press, 1955); L. A. Coser, *Masters of Sociological Thought* (New York: Harcourt Brace Jovanovich, 1971), pp. 177–215; D. Levine (ed.), *Georg Simmel on Individuality and Social Forms* (Chicago: University of Chicago Press, 1971).

10. M. Scheler, *Die Wissensformen und die Gesellschaft* (Leipzig: Der Neue-Geist Verlag, 1926). On Scheler see J. R. Staude, *Max Scheler: an Intellectual Portrait* (New York: Free Press, 1967).

11. K. Mannheim, *Ideology and Utopia, op. cit.*

12. See for example A. von Schelting, "Review of Mannheim's Idology and Utopia," *American Sociological Review*, Vol. 1, No. 4, (August 1936), pp. 664–674.

13. For this see M. Jay, *The Dialectical Imagination, op. cit.*, especially Ch. 2 and the detailed bibliography quoted there; and the most important single collective work of the group, M. Horkheimer (ed.), *Studien über Autorität und Familie* (New York: International Institute of Social Research, 1936).

14. A. Weber, *Kulturgeschichte als Kultursoziologie, op. cit.*

15. For this see M. Jay, *The Dialectical Imagination, op. cit.*, especially Ch. 2.

16. The most relevant works of these scholars in this connection are T. Geiger, *Die Masse und ihre Aktion: ein Beitrag zur Soziologie der Revolutionen* (Stuttgart: F. Enke, 1926); E. Lederer, *The Sate of the Masses* (New York: Norton, 1940); K. Mannheim, *Man and Society in an Age of Reconstruction, op. cit.;* M. Jay, *The Dialectical Imagination, op. cit.*

17. On this see K. Mannheim, *Essays on Sociology and Social Psychology* (London: Routledge & Kegan Paul, 1953), Ch. 6.

18. N. Elias, *Uber den Prozess der Zivilisation* (Basel: Verlag Hause zum Falken, 1939), 2 vols.

19. The Institute was closed down in 1933, following the Nazi accession to power, but it continued its activities in some European countries—Switzerland, France, England —and in the United States. After the war it was reestablished in Frankfurt. For its institutional history until 1933, see Martin Jay, *The Dialectical Imagination, op. cit.*, Ch. 1.
    The most outstanding scholars who were associated with the Institute at one time or another were Max Horkheimer, Theodor Adorno, Leo Lowenthal, Erich Fromm, Herbert Marcuse, and Karl Wittfogel.

20 For details see W. E. Mühlmann, "Sociology in Germany: shift in alignment," in H. Becker, A. Boskoff (eds.), *Modern Sociological Theory in Continuity and Change* (New York: Dryden Press, 1957), pp. 666–667; R. König, *Studien zur Soziologie, op. cit.*

21. On the studies of social mobility, and of rural and urban conditons, see S. P. Schad, *Empirical Social Research in Weimar Germany* (Paris, The Hague: Mouton, 1972), pp. 49–55.
    On Tönnies' empirical research see S. P. Schad, *Empirical Social Research, op. cit.*, pp. 72–76; A. Oberschall, *Empirical Social Research in Germany: 1848–1914,* (Paris, The Hague: Mouton, 1965), pp. 51–63.
    For von Wiese's and his students' field studies, see S. P. Schad, *Empirical Social Research, op. cit.*, pp. 58–66.

22. On this see E. Lederer and J. Marschak, "Der neue Mittelstand," *Grundriss der Sozialökonomik* (Tübingen, 1926), Section 9, Part 1, pp. 120–141; T. Geiger, *Die Soziale Schichtung des Deutschen Volkes: Soziographischer Versuch auf Statistischer Grundlage* (Stuttgart: F. Enke, 1932).

23. On this see M. Jay, *The Dialectical Imagination, op. cit.*, Chs. 3, 4. For greater detail see, for example, E. Fromm, "Uber methode und aufgabe einer analytischen, sozialpsychologie," *Zeitschrift für Sozialforschung*, Vol. 1, Nos. 1, 2 (1932); M. Horkheimer (ed.), *Studien über Autorität und Familie, op. cit.*

24. On this see T. Geiger, *Die Masse und ihre Aktion, op. cit.;* T. Geiger, *Die Soziale Schichtung des Deutschen Volkes, op. cit.;* E. Lederer and J. Marschak, "Der neue Mittelstand," *op. cit.;* E. Lederer, *The State of the Masses, op. cit.;* S. Kracauer, *Die Angestellten* (Frankfurt am Main: Societäts-Verlag, 1930).

25. On this see R. König, *Studien zur Soziologie, op. cit.*

26. On this see S. P. Schad, *Empirical Social Research in Weimar Germany, op. cit.*, pp. 44–46; R. König, *Studien zur Soziologie, op. cit.*

27. On this see W. E. Mühlmann, "Sociology in Germany: shift in alignment," *op. cit.*, pp. 665—666.

28. On this see S. P. Schad, *Empirical Social Research in Weimar Germany, op. cit.*, pp. 44–46, 49–50; and for greater detail the discussions in the various volumes of *Schriften der Deutschen Gesellschaft für Soziologie* (Tübingen: Mohr, published since 1910).

29. For the various aspects of the intellectual and institutional history of French sociology,

discussed below, see T. N. Clark, *Prophets and Patrons: the French University and the Emergence of the Social Sciences* (Cambridge, Mass.: Harvard University Press, 1973), Ch. 7.

For the institutional aspects see also E. Shils, "Tradition, ecology, and institution in the history of sociology," *Daedalus*, Vol. 99, No. 4 (Fall 1970) pp. 760–825.

For the intellectual aspects, see also H. Becker and H. E. Barnes, *Social Thought from Lore to Science*, Vol. 3 (New York: Dover, 1961), Ch. 22; C. Lévi-Strauss, "French sociology," in G. Gurvitch and W. E. Moore (eds.), *Twentieth Century Sociology* (New York: Philosophical Library, 1945), pp. 503–537; J. Stoetzel, "Sociology in France: an empiricist view," in H. Becker and A. Boskoff (eds.) *Modern Sociological Theory in Continuity and Change, op. cit.*, pp. 623–657.

30. M. Halbwachs, *Les Cadres Sociaux de la Mémoire* (Paris: Alcan, 1925).

31. P. Fauconnet, *La Responsabilité* (Paris: F. Alcan, 1920).

32. C. Bouglé, *Leçons de Sociologie sur l'évolution des Valeurs* (Paris: A. Colin, 1922).

33. For Mauss, see for example M. Mauss, "Les variations saisonnières dans les sociétés Eskimo," *Année Sociologique*, Vol. 9 (1904–1905); M. Mauss, "Essai sur le don, forme archaique de l'échange," *ibid.*, translated as *The Gift: Forms and Functions of Exchange in Archaic Societies* (Glencoe, Ill.: Free Press, 1954); M. Mauss, "Une catégorie de l'esprit humain: celle de personne . . .," *Journal of the Royal Anthropological Institute*, Vol. 68 (July–December, 1938).

On the structuralistic elements in Mauss' work see Cl. Lévi-Strauss, "Introduction à l'oeuvre de Marcel Mauss," in M. Mauss, *Sociologie et Anthropologie* (Paris: Presses Universitaires de France, 1950), pp. ix–lii; M. Glucksman, *Structuralist Analysis in Contemporary Social Thought* (London: Routledge Kegan Paul, 1974), Ch. 2.

Among L. Lévy-Bruhl's works see for example L. Lévy-Bruhl, *La Mentalité Primitive* (Paris: Presses Universitaires de France, 1960).

34. G. Davy, *La Foi Jurée* (Paris: Alcan, 1922).

35. M. Granet, *La Civilisation Chinoise* (Paris: La Renaissance du Livre, 1929), translated as *Chinese Civilization* (New York: Meridian Books, 1939); M. Granet, *La Pensée Chinoise* (Paris: La Renaissance du Livre, 1934); M. Granet, *Études Sociologiques sur la Chine* (Paris: Presses Universitaires de France, 1953).

36. See for example F. Simiand, *Le Salaire, L'évolution Sociale et la Monnaie* (Paris: Alcan, 1932), 3 vols.

37. On this see T. N. Clark, *Prophets and Patrons, op. cit.*, Ch. 6.

38. On this and the LePlayist tradition of empirical research mentioned below, see T. N. Clark, *Prophets and Patrons, op. cit.*, Ch. 3; P. Lazarsfeld, "Notes on the history of quantification in sociology: trends, sources and problems," *Isis*, Vol. 52, No. 2 (1961), pp. 277–333.

39. F. Simiand, *Le Salaire, L'évolution Sociale, et la Monnaie, op. cit.*

40. M. Halbwachs, *Les Causes du Suicide, op. cit.*; M. Halbwachs, *L'évolution des Besoins dans les Classes Ouvrières, op. cit.*

41. On the international sociologists in the prewar period see T. N. Clark, *Prophets and Patrons, op. cit.*, Ch. 5.

42. On this see E. Shils, "Tradition, ecology, and institution in the history of sociology," *op. cit.*; W. J. H. Sprott, "Sociology in Britain: preoccupations," in H. Becker and A. Boskoff (eds.), *Modern Sociological Theory in Continuity and Change, op. cit.*, pp. 607–622.

43. M. Ginsberg, *Reason and Unreason, Essays in Sociology and Social Philosophy* (London: The

London School of Economics, 1947) especially Chs. 1, 6, 15, 16; M. Ginsberg, *On Justice in Society* (London: Penguin, 1965); M. Ginsberg, *Essays in Sociology and Social Philosophy*, Vol. 1, *On the Diversity of Morals*, Vol. 3, *Evolution and Progress* (London: Heinemann, 1956–1961); J. Gould, "On Morris Ginsberg," *The Jewish Journal of Sociology*, Vol. 16, No. 2 (December 1974), pp. 123–133.

44.   On this study see M. Ginsberg, *Studies in Sociology* (London: Methuen, 1932), Ch. 9.

45.   On this and on the main foci of research conducted during this period and mentioned below, see W. J. H. Sprott, "Sociology in Britain: preoccupations," *op. cit.;* J. Rumney, "British sociology," in G. Gurvitch and W. E. Moore (eds.), *Twentieth Century Sociology, op. cit.,* pp. 562–585.

46.   On this, and on the Booth-Geddes-Rowntree tradition of social surveys, mentioned below, see P. Abrams, *The Origins of British Sociology: 1834–1914* (Chicago: University of Chicago Press, 1968), pp. 8–153.

47.   On this see *The Social Sciences: Their Relations in Theory and in Teaching* (London: LePlay House Press, 1936); J. E. Dugdale (ed.), *Further Papers on the Social Sciences: Their Relations in Theory and in Teaching* (London: LePlay House Press, 1937); T. H. Marshall (ed.), *Class Conflict and Social Stratification* (London: LePlay House Press, 1938); F. Bartlett, M. Ginsberg, E. J. Lindgren, and R. H. Thouless (eds.), *The Study of Society: Methods and Problems* (London: Routledge & Kegan Paul [1939], 1949).

48.   On these aspects see R. C. Hinkle and G. A. Hinkle, *The Development of Modern Sociology: its Nature and Growth in the United States* (New York: Doubleday, 1954), Ch. 2; A. J. Reiss, "Sociology: the field," *International Encyclopedia of Social Sciences*, Vol. 15 (New York: Macmillan, 1968), pp. 1–23; A. Oberschall, "The institutionalization of American sociology," in A. Oberschall (ed.), *The Establishment of Empirical Sociology: Studies in Continuity, Discontinuity, and Institutionalization* (New York: Harper & Row, 1972), pp. 187–251; S. M. Lipset, "Trends in American sociology," *Dialogue*, Vol. 8, No. 3-4, (1975), pp. 3–15.

49.   For the debates on the orientations of the sociologist's role and the factors which contributed to their emergence, see R. C. Hinkle and G. A. Hinkle, *The Development of Modern Sociology, op. cit.,* Ch. 2; A. Oberschall, "The institutionalization of American sociology," *op. cit.;* H. Kuklick, "A scientific revolution: sociological theory in the U.S., 1930–1945," *Sociological Inquiry*, Vol. 43, No. 1 (1973), pp. 3–22.

     The acceptance of the ethos of a value-free sociology did not necessarily mean that sociology in this period became devoid of evaluative elements. However, these evaluative elements or orientations became less directly related to sociological research than in the period of the Founding Fathers, as is illustrated, for example, by the controversial interpretations of Park's ideological commitments. On this see L. Bramson, "The rise of American sociology," in E. A. Tiryakian (ed.), *The Phenomenon of Sociology* (New York: Appleton-Century-Crofts, 1971), pp. 65–80.

50.   There were many examples of nonacademic employment and research of sociologists. Some, however, were especially outstanding. One was the study of social change in American society (published in the collection *Recent Social Trends*), conducted by a committee of social scientists appointed in 1929 by President Herbert Hoover and financed by the Rockefeller Foundation. During World War II, studies of the behavior of the American soldier were sponsored by government agencies. These studies were directed by S. Stouffer and became codified later in the volumes of the *American Soldier*. During the war, too, the Carnegie Corporation financed the study by Gunnar Myrdal and his staff on the position of the American Negro, which was later published as *An American Dilemma*.

51. R. S. Lynd, *Knowledge for What? The Place of Social Science in American Culture* (Princeton: Princeton University Press, 1939).

52. C. Wright Mills, *The Sociological Imagination* (New York: Oxford University Press, 1959), especially Chs. 2, 3, 4.

53. On this see A. Oberschall, "The institutionalization of American sociology," *op. cit.;* R. E. L. Faris, *Chicago Sociology: 1920–1932* (San Francisco: Chandler, 1967).

54. W. I. Thomas and F. Znaniecki, *The Polish Peasant in Europe and America,* (Chicago: University of Chicago Press, 1918–1920), 5 vols.

55. R. E. Park, *Human Communities: The City and Human Ecology,* (Glencoe, Ill.: Free Press, 1952); R. E. Park, "The city: suggestions for the investigation of human behavior in the urban environment," in R. E. Park, E. W. Burgess, and R. D. McKenzie, *The City* (Chicago: Chicago University Press, 1925) pp. 1–46.

56. On this see A. Oberschall, "The institutionalization of American sociology," *op. cit.;* R. E. L. Faris, *Chicago Sociology: 1920–1932, op. cit.,* especially Ch. 7.

57. On Thomas' contribution see R. C. Hinkle and G. J. Hinkle, *The Development of Modern Sociology, op. cit.,* especially pp. 32–33.

     For Mead see G. H. Mead, *Mind, Self and Society* (Chicago: University of Chicago Press, 1934).

58. For these trends and their causes, and for the main topics of research conducted in this period, discussed below, see E. Shils, *The Present State of American Sociology* (Glencoe, Ill.: Free Press, 1948).

59. For this see, for example, K. Mannheim, *Essays on Sociology and Social Psychology, op. cit.,* pp. 185–194.

60. For Ogburn see W. F. Ogburn, *Social Change: with Respect to Culture and Original Nature* (New York: B. W. Huebsch, 1922).

     For MacIver's concepts of community versus association, see R. M. MacIver, *Community: A Sociological Study; Being an Attempt to Set Out the Nature and Fundamental Laws of Social Life* (London: Macmillan [1917], 1935); R. M. MacIver, *Society: a Textbook of Sociology* (New York: Farrar & Rinehart, 1937); R. M. MacIver and C. Page, *Society: an Introductory Analysis* (New York: Holt [1949], 1961), which was one of the major theoretical textbooks in American sociology.

61. On this see H. Kuklick, "A scientific revolution . . .," *op. cit.*

62. P. Sorokin, *Contemporary Sociological Theories Through the First Quarter of the Twentieth Century* (New York: Harper & Row, 1928); P. Sorokin, C. C. Zimmerman and C. J. Galpin (eds.), *A Systematic Source Book in Rural Sociology* (Minneapolis: University of Minnesota Press, 1930–1932), 3 vols.; P. Sorokin, *Social and Cultural Dynamics* (New York: American Book, 1937–1940), 4 vols.; R. M. MacIver, *Society: a Textbook of Sociology, op. cit.*

     For a concise summary of the works of German scholars who emigrated to the U.S., see M. Jay, *The Dialectical Imagination, op. cit.,* especially Chs. 6, 7.

63. *Recent Social Trends in the U.S.: Report of the President's Research Committee on Social Trends,* 1-vol. ed. (New York: McGraw-Hill, 1933).

64. G. Myrdal, *An American Dilemma* (New York: Harper, 1944), 2 vols.

65. For details on the small-group studies of K. Lewin and his associates, see E. Shils, *The Present State of American Sociology, op. cit.,* pp. 7–52.

     For the public opinion study mentioned here see P. F. Lazarsfeld, B. Berelson, and H. Gaudet, *The People's Choice* (New York: Duell, Sloan & Pearce, 1944).

66. S. A. Stouffer et al., *The American Soldier* (Princeton: Princeton University Press, 1949), 2 vols.

67. T. W. Adorno with E. Frenkel-Brunswik, D. J. Levinson, and R. N. Sanford, *The Authoritarian Personality* (New York: Harper, 1950).

68. B. Bettelheim and M. Janowitz, *Dynamics of Prejudice: a Psychological and Sociological Study of Veterans* (New York: Harper, 1950).

69. For the causes responsible for the decline of the Chicago department of sociology, and for its institutional and intellectual consequences, see E. Shils, "Tradition, ecology, and institution in the history of sociology," *op. cit.;* H. Kuklick, "A scientific revolution . . .," *op. cit.*

70. For a reorientation and opening to other disciplines, see E. Shils, *The Present State of American Sociology, op. cit.;* T. Parsons, *Essays in Sociological Theory* (Glencoe, Ill.: Free Press, 1949), Chs. 16, 17.

    For learning theory and culture and personality school, see G. A. de Vos and A. A. Hippler, "Cultural psychology: comparative studies of human behavior," in G. Lindzey and E. Aronson (eds.), *Handbook of Social Psychology*, Vol. 4, 2nd ed. (Reading, Mass.: Addison-Wesley, 1969), pp. 323–417; A. Inkeles and D. J. Levinson, "National character: the study of modal personality and sociocultural systems," *ibid.*, pp. 418–506.

71. For the institutional and analytic trends discussed here and below, see H. Becker and H. E. Barnes, *Social Thought from Lore to Science, op. cit.*, Vol. 3, pp. 1069–1078.; Wladyslaw Markiewicz, "Poland," in J. J. Wiatr (ed.), *The State of Sociology in Eastern Europe Today* (Carbondale and Edwardsville, Ill.: Southern Illinois University Press, 1971), pp. 97–103.

72. On these see W. I. Thomas and F. Znaniecki, *The Polish Peasant in Europe and America, op. cit.;* F. Znaniecki, *Social Actions* (New York: Farrar & Rinehart, 1936); F. Znaniecki, *The Social Role of the Man of Knowledge* (New York: Columbia University Press, 1940).

73. For the institutional and analytic trends discussed here and below, see J. Macku, "Czechoslovakia," in J. J. Wiatr (ed.), *The State of Sociology in Eastern Europe Today, op. cit.*, pp. 59–68; H. Becker and H. E. Barnes, *Social Thought from Lore to Science, op. cit.*, Vol. 3, pp. 1060–1067.

74. For the institutional and analytic trends discussed here and below see M. Cernea and J. Matei, "Rumania," in J. J. Wiatr (ed.), *The State of Sociology in Eastern Europe Today op. cit.*, pp. 139–147; H. Becker and H. E. Barnes, *Social Thought from Lore to Science, op. cit.*, Vol. 3, pp. 1088–1095.

75. For developments in Finland see E. Allardt, "Scandinavian sociology," *International Journal of Sociology*, Vol. 3 (Fall-Winter 1973–1974), especially pp. 9–19; Risto Alaquro et al., *Suomalaisen Sociologian Juuret* (Helinski: Werner Söderstrom Osakeyhtiö, 1973).

76. E. Shils, "Tradition, ecology, and institution in the history of sociology," *op. cit.;* E. Shils, "The trend of sociological research," lecture given at the 8th International Congress of Sociology, Evian, 1966.

77. For this see T. N. Clark, *Prophets and Patrons, op. cit.*, Chs. 5, 7.

78. For these see P. Sorokin, *Contemporary Sociological Theories, op. cit.;* T. Parsons, *The Structure of Social Action,* (New York: Free Press, 1968) 2 vols. (first published in 1937 by McGraw-Hill); E. Shils, "Tradition, ecology, and institution in the history of sociology," *op. cit.*

79. On this see A. Oberschall, "The institutionalization of American sociology," *op. cit.*, pp. 229–230.

80. On this and the causes responsible for the situation, see E. Shils, "The trend of sociological research," *op. cit.*

81. K. Mannheim, *Essays on Sociology and Social Psychology, op. cit.*, Chs. 4, 6.

82. See for example R. E. Park and E. W. Burgess, *Introduction to the Science of Sociology* (Chicago: University of Chicago Press, 1921).

83. R. M. MacIver, *Society: a Textbook of Sociology, op. cit.*

84. L. von Wiese, *Soziologie: Geschichte und Haupt-probleme* (Berlin: Gruyter, 1926); F. Oppenheimer und G. Salomon (eds.), *Soziologische Lesestücke* (1926, G. Braun-Karlsruhe), 3 vols; W. Sombart (mit H. L. Stoltenberg), *Soziologie* (Berlin: Pan Verlag, Rolf Heise, 1924); R. Hubert, *Manuel Elémentaire de Sociologie* (Paris: Delalain, 1935); M. Ginsberg, *Sociology* (London: T. Butterworth, 1937).

85. A. Vierkandt (ed.), *Handwörterbuch der Soziologie, op. cit.;* F. Bartlett, M. Ginsberg, et al (eds.), *The Study of Society: Methods and Problems, op. cit.;* C. Bouglé, *Bilan de la Sociologie Française Contemporaine* (Paris: F. Alcan, 1935); R. Aron, *La Sociologie Allemande Contemporaine* (Paris: Alcan, 1935), translated as *German Sociology* (Glencoe, Ill.: Free Press, 1957).

86. R. Thurnwald (ed.), *Soziologie von Heute* (Leipzig: C. L. Hirschfeld, 1932).

87. F. Boas, "Anthropology," in *Encyclopedia of the Social Sciences,* Vol. 2 (New York: Macmillan, 1930), pp. 73–110; B. Malinowski, "Culture," in *Encyclopedia of the Social Sciences, op. cit.,* Vol. 4 (1931), pp. 621–645.

88. R. M. MacIver, "Sociology," in *Encyclopedia of the Social Sciences, op. cit.,* Vol. 14 (1934), pp. 232–247.

89. T. Parsons, "Society," in *Encyclopedia of the Social Sciences, op. cit.,* Vol. 14 (1934), pp. 225–232.

90. This was the situation especially in the United States; for this see E. Shils, *The Present State of American Sociology, op. cit.*

91. For this see especially the references quoted in note 16.

92. For this see the references quoted in note 70, and also M. Jay, *The Dialectical Imagination, op. cit.* Chs. 3, 7.

93. P. Sorokin, *Social and Cultural Dynamics, op. cit.*

94. R. M. MacIver, *Society, op. cit.;* for different editions, see note 60.

95. K. Mannheim, *Man and Society in an Age of Reconstruction, op. cit.* For the following discussion on Mannheim, see also E. Shils, "Tradition, ecology, and institution in the history of sociology," *op. cit.;* L. A. Coser, *Masters of Sociological Thought, op. cit.,* pp. 429–463.

6

Trends in Sociological Analysis and Activity after World War II

Increasing Institutionalization and Density of the Sociological Community

1. The entire pattern of organization and institutionalization of sociological activity changed greatly after World War II,[1] and this change had far-reaching implications for the development of sociological research and analysis. In the postwar years, and especially from the 1950s on, there developed a relatively high, though uneven, degree of institutionalization in sociological teaching and research in academic centers and research institutions, and a concomitant development of strong national sociological communities and an international sociological community. Sociology became an established academic discipline in universities of many countries—above all the United States, Western Europe, and Japan. Its theories and practice were increasingly applied in government departments, in business, institutions, and research bureaus. In most of these countries, close and sustained relationships developed among the various kinds of sociological activity, and these activities were

usually centered around the teaching of sociology in universities and in a growing number of research institutes. General public interest in sociological work increased, along with interest in the application of scientific methods to social affairs. All these trends contributed to the increased institutionalization of sociologists' roles, though in uneven and diversified ways in different countries.

The growing institutionalization of sociology was facilitated by a change in intellectual temper, as well as by a changing "market" situation for sociologists. In the postwar period a general intellectual atmosphere developed which provided positive encouragement or reinforcement for some of the claims and images of sociology; in addition, a growing number of available resources could be geared to new developments. The immediate postwar era was one in which the belief in science and in its application to social matters again became relatively strong, yet without taking on the simplistic evolutionary or "progressive" implications of the nineteenth century. Among the educated public, there emerged a general belief in scientific method as applied to human affairs, along with an increasing faith in planning and a concomitant growth in various governmental activities in social science and social policy. This belief coincided with disappointment in the great ideological Marxist and evolutionary prognoses and with a weakening of older ideological stances, reinforced by the events of the Stalin era and the Cold War period.

The rise of the welfare state provided important opportunities for the acceptance of sociology as an autonomous approach which could, through the development of its distinctive characteristics, also fulfill broader intellectual functions. A widespread belief arose in the ability of sociology to provide general orientations to socioeconomic problems as well as research that would be relevant both to broader social planning and to the more concrete problems of specific bureaucracies —government departments, business firms, factories, schools, the army, all of which provided funds for research and employment for sociologists. This trend was reinforced by the growing technicality and specialization of philosophical and historical studies, which weakened their position as major intellectual orientations of educated publics, as well as by fascination with the apparent possibilities, promises, and performances of other social sciences, particularly economics.

The greater potential demand for the services of sociologists was reinforced by other institutional processes, principally the spread of higher education, which catered to the heightened social interest of students and created a supply of students as well as pressures for the academic and professional services of sociology graduates. The spread of higher educational facilities provided the resources taken up by various academic entrepreneurs who started to create new departments and research bureaus.

The internal developments in sociology, and the participation of sociologists in various wartime bureaus, provided a latent model which could be spread further. A prime example was the above-mentioned work of sociologists in the Research Branch of the U. S. Army, which resulted in several pioneering studies, such as *The American Soldier*, the studies of *The Authoritarian Personality*, and a number of communications studies.[2] However, both the scope and the concrete patterns of institutionalization varied greatly among countries.

2. During this period, a significant shift took place in the relative importance of major centers of sociological endeavor. The most important new centers developed in the United States, building on the initial institutionalization of sociology in universities and on the great demand for sociological research during the war. These centers were enriched by many European scholars and American sociological cosmopolitans. As a result, a wide range of sociological activity took place in such new academic centers as Harvard, Columbia, Berkeley, and Ann Arbor, and in the many research institutes attached to these universities.[3]

In post-World War II Europe, sociology also developed considerably, but not on the same scale as in the United States. The impetus came from the new social problems brought about by the postwar situation and from the willingness of governments and, to some degree, private sectors, to support sociological teaching and research. These factors, together with the spread of higher education, provided favorable demand and supply conditions for sociological activity and institutionalization.

This development was rather slow during the first decade after the war, especially in European countries where earlier nuclei of research had been institutionally damaged during the prewar and war periods.[4] In Germany,[5] sociology had to rebuild itself completely, since most sociological activities had been interrupted by the Nazi regime and some of the most prominent sociologists had fled abroad. After the war, the proper academic frameworks for training sociologists did not exist. The situation improved constantly, however. Young sociologists were sent to study abroad; the old chairs of sociology were filled and new chairs were established in other universities. Empirical research developed in new institutes often attached to academic frameworks. Sociology became more diversified and specialized: Community studies, for example, became the subject of research in Cologne, sociology of education in Göttingen, political sociology in Berlin, industrial sociology in Saarbrücken. Over time, this research became more theoretically oriented.

In France[6] sociology suffered a heavy blow during the war. Some of the most prominent figures had been killed or had left the country. The teaching of sociology was resumed on a smaller scale than in Germany, and only gradually was it recognized. New chairs were established in Paris and in some provincial universities, and degrees in sociology proper were conferred. Empirical sociological research was undertaken in new research institutes established in Paris and in the provinces—some by public bodies and government agencies with varying degrees of affiliation with the universities. Outstanding among these were the Centre d'Études Sociologiques; the French Institute of Public Opinion; several research bureaus connected with the École Pratique des Hautes Études, such as the Institut des Sciences Sociales du Travail, under the direction of Georges Friedmann, and, later, the Center of Studies of Communication; and various private research organizations. Research and investigation became diversified, covering such subjects as industrial relations, voting behavior, religion, social stratification, small groups, sociology of knowledge, and cultural anthropology.

In Britain,[7] interest in sociology increased in the prewar and immediate postwar period through the impetus of Continental refugee scholars like Karl Mannheim, and later the influence of social changes brought about by the war and Labor government policies. Academic teaching of sociology rapidly broadened its institutional base beyond the London School of Economics, especially in the universities of the provinces, although its acceptance by the prestigious English universities, Oxford and Cambridge, was delayed. Several institutes developed research programs in special fields. The Tavistock Institute for Human Relations, for example, specialized in group dynamics; other areas of research gaining special prominence included social stratification and community studies.

In the British universities, empirical research in the tradition of survey research became more closely related to sociological analysis and theory, though it was not always fully integrated with them.

Similar developments, albeit over different time spans, took place in other European countries and in Japan. In Scandinavia, the Netherlands, and Japan, sociology expanded considerably,[8] in comparison with the situation before the war and with other countries. New chairs and independent departments of sociology were established in many universities, and research activities, partly sponsored by government agencies and strongly oriented to problems of social policy and legislation, were carried out in the universities or in special institutes for research. In Italy, Austria, Spain, and Switzerland, however, the level of institutionalization of sociology remained low,[9] confined to a few solitary chairs with only the beginnings of organized research. But here, too, the number of chairs and institutes steadily increased, even if institutional bases remained weak.

Asia and Latin America[10] also witnessed a growth in sociological research and teaching, based on whatever centers had existed before or,—in African countries;—on new establishments. Among the countries outside Europe and the United States, the greatest upsurge and institutionalization of sociological activity took place, as noted, in Japan. In India, too, several major universities established chairs in sociology. In Israel, the Department of Sociology at the Hebrew University was established in 1947 and expanded after 1949, combining a strong emphasis on theoretical study and comparative institutional analysis with field work and empirical investigation of such problems as absorption of immigrants, collective settlements, youth groups, professions, and industrial sociology. The Israel Institute of Applied Social Research was established in 1949 and has conducted series of surveys and researches in many applied fields of research. Research departments have also been established in several ministries as well as other public bodies.

In all European states and some countries outside Europe, many new professional sociological journals were launched and older ones given a firmer base. A few of the more important were the *Kölner Zeitschrift für Soziologie und Sozialpsychologie* in Germany; the *Cahiers Internationaux de Sociologie, Revue Française de Sociologie,* and *Sociologie du Travail* in France; *the British Journal of Sociology* and *Human Relations* in Great Britain; *Acta Sociologica* in Scandinavia; and *Przeglad Socjologiczny* in Poland.

In almost all these countries, national sociological associations and organizations were gradually established. But even before such associations were formally established, contacts among national sociological communities developed and expanded. The relationships between national and international sociological communities developed in different ways in different countries and time periods. Initially, most new sociological communities were greatly influenced by the older centers in the United States and England or France, the latter influence being especially strong in some Latin American countries. But, gradually at first and more rapidly from the 1960s on, most countries tended to foster their own traditions of sociological analysis and to confront them with perspectives brought in from the outside.[11]

In most of these countries, national centers of sociological activity grew and became mutually oriented and internationalized. Although each sociological community was concerned with the problems of its own country, these problems were no longer seen as isolated, and a continuous mutual interaction and reference orientation developed between these traditions, a trend easily discerned in the patterns of international meetings and in references in professional articles.[12]

International comparative-cooperative research also increased. At first it was sponsored largely by the Research Committee of the International Sociological Association, under the auspices of Unesco, the International Social Science Council, and similar agencies. Thus the internal momentum of sociological work and study in each country, along with increasing international contact, created a new, more closely interrelated international community.

The Major Patterns of Institutionalization: The United States, Western Europe, the Third World, the Communist Societies

3.   Important differences among the national sociological communities could also be discerned. As in earlier periods, the most important differences were in the scope and pattern of institutionalization of sociology, and in its major intellectual trends and orientations. These trends and orientations were not static: they changed within each sociological community, and these changes, as we shall see, strongly influenced the direction of sociological work.

Such differences could be discerned first within the Western countries. Sociological communities in Western nations differed in the scope of institutionalization,[13] as measured by acceptance in academic institutions and attainment of independent academic status; scope of research and undergraduate and graduate teaching; the establishment of research bureaus; and the number of research and advisory positions in government and business. Generally, the scope of such institutionalization was broadest in the United States, then in the Netherlands and Japan, and somewhat narrower in Britain, Scandinavia, and Israel. Occasionally, as in the older universities of England, Italy, Switzerland, and Spain, sociology still had to fight for recognition, although older, established positions in these universities could serve as springboards for the establishment of special chairs, departments, and institutes of sociology in different faculties. However, these usually had a much less diversified base than in the United States.

Of equal interest are the differences in the over-all institutionalization of the sociologist's role and in the relative importance of different aspects of sociological activity. Such differences crystallized in the 1940s and 1950s into certain patterns which later changed in several directions.

In the United States, the academic component predominated in both teaching and research, with less emphasis placed on practical policy and much less on the critical or broader intellectual orientations of sociology.[14] Different centers of sociology varied in the relative weight given these orientations. Separate communities developed around different components of academic sociological activities, but were not institutionally segregated. Most found a place within the universities, and while different departments tended to emphasize different activities—theory, research methods, institutional analysis, social psychology, and the like—there were few in which other components were totally excluded.

It was in the United States that some of the major theoretical developments of the period took place. The structural-functional school became the central focus of theoretical discussion in sociology,[15] while both symbolic interactionism and new ecological approaches continued to exert their influence, even if their predominance varied. At the same time, many partial explicative paradigms were developed—the culture and personality school, studies of national character, and various applications of learning theory to social life which later spilled over to operant psychology.[16] Major fields of sociological research became systematized—community study, the reformulation of political sociology, stratification, and studies of modernization and development.[17] In all these fields there was a growing tendency to use analytic middle-range theories which cut across different areas of research, such as theories of primary group relations and relative deprivation. Most studies were undertaken within the contemporary institutional setting. These were rarely examined in the critical or historical fashion of the European tradition of Durkheim and Weber, although many concrete hypotheses and approaches were derived from their works and those of the American Founding Fathers. In fact, the orientation to their work became more and more prominent in American sociology during this period.[18] Interestingly, this tendency was, at least at first, closely connected with the heavy "positivist" translation or "domestication" of some major concepts of sociological analysis, such as bureaucracy or class, which were shorn of the critical implications of their original formulations by Weber and other Founding Fathers.[19]

At first, this evolving sociological analysis had few ties to the tradition of political analysis or to the more "radical" orientations in sociology. Similarly, one of the weakest aspects of American sociology at this period, as

Raymond Aron has pointed out,was the lack of historical and comparative institutional analysis.[20]

Yet even in the early postwar period, beginnings of all these trends were apparent. In the works of Seymour Martin Lipset, David Riesman, Daniel Bell, and, later on, Morris Janowitz and Alvin Gouldner, the evaluation of the broader institutional setting, based on a combination of the older tradition of political criticism with new more systematic middle-range theories developed.[21] At the same time the tradition of direct participant observation, which had had journalistic overtones in the Chicago school, became more systematized and analytic.[22]

The radical tradition, with strong emphasis on institutional analysis, was represented above all in the work of C. Wright Mills, and was later taken up by Irving Louis Horowitz, Alvin Gouldner, Norman Birnbaum, and in England and Canada, Tom Bottomore.[23]

Comparative institutional analysis was represented by Talcott Parsons' essays and those of his students, including Marion Levy. Later on such analysis became prominent in conjunction with studies of modernization and development.[24] All these trends—the critical analysis of institutions, comparative macrosocietal analysis, and above all the "radical" trend, which were marginal at the beginning of the postwar period, gained momentum from the late 1950s on.

4.   A similar pattern of intellectual and professional orientation, still centered in universities, but with a much stronger emphasis on practical professional activity, developed in the Netherlands and Japan.[25] Both countries produced eclectic but systematic and wide-ranging work in all major fields of sociological research, though much of it was oriented to the major centers of research in the United States and England.

In Scandinavia,[26] a strong tradition of systematic empirical research developed, influenced by some of the behavioristic schools of sociology and the positivism of George Lundberg, later by operant psychology and exchange theory. A more reflective trend was represented in Scandinavia by Torgny Segerstedt, whose "main concern has been with how symbols and symbolic manipulations make up man's social reality, and in his studies he has particularly systematized the concept of social norms and the sociological theory of social norms."

More comparative and institutional analysis is being undertaken in Norway by scholars like Vilhelm Aubert and Stein Rokkan, and a strong tradition of social research, initiated by Erik Rinde, has been established at the Institute of Social Research.

In Finland a more variegated tradition has crystallized, building on the earlier stage of sociology. Under the influence of Erik Allardt, macrosociological studies of the development of Finnish industrial society, sociopolitical cleavages, class relations, and similar subjects have been stressed.

Most Scandinavian countries have engaged in widespread applied research, but in general the practical and applied aspects of the sociological role, as well as the broader intellectual or critical orientation, have been weak.

In English universities,[27] there has been much stronger emphasis on sociology as a part of general intellectual education, though there has also been a strong practical orientation, associated with social work, planning, and policy. However, little university research has been done undertaken in connection with undergraduate and graduate teaching. With very few exceptions, of which Liverpool is probably the most outstanding, research by the academic staffs has been conducted apart from university teaching, either on a private basis or in separate units or institutions. At the same time, however, new traditions of empirical research, mostly demographic surveys and studies of social mobility, have been built on earlier trends in "social biology."

The major theoretical orientations of the postwar period were still greatly influenced by the traditions of Leonard Hobhouse and Morris Ginsberg who, with all their positive orientations to research in principle, did not really encourage it or find adequate ways of relating their macrosocietal and sociophilosophical interests with the new research concerns of the time. The important contemporary trend of historical-institutional analysis, building on the perspective of comparative institutions, was represented in the work of T. H. Marshall.[28] Also influential were the developments of the analytic functionalist framework of British social anthropology, which became highly institutionalized and began to extend into many fields beyond "tribal" societies.[29]

In Germany and France the picture was different. There was much greater over-all segregation of teaching and research, with teaching confined largely to the more traditionally organized universities, and research carried in separate institutes, though these were often grounded in some part of the academic system, as for example the École Pratique in France. In some of the German universities,[30] principally in Cologne and in the reestablished Frankfurt Institute, there was some tendency to combine teaching and research activities more closely, but it was not strong. There was still a sharp rift between the philosophical, speculative, often critical approach and the scholarly scientific attitude—between what René König later called the "theory of society and sociological theory." Thus the Frankfurt school produced a strong critique of positivistic sociology but did little original research; whatever they did carry out did not differ greatly from other kinds of research. The major thrust of research, represented by König, Renate Mayntz, and Erwing Scheuch, followed the "positivist" American pattern. Other German sociologists like Helmut Schelsky and Arnold Gehlen wavered between speculative sociology and philosophical anthropology, and the analysis of concrete problems pertaining to youth and industrial society.[31] Again, there was little relationship between these concerns and continuing research in academic settings—hence a split between historical, institutional, philosophical, and possibly political, analysis and newer techniques of empirical research.

In France,[32] a similar bifurcation between the intellectual and professional orientations of sociology developed, although its organizational bases differed from those in Germany. As we have seen, several centers and nuclei of research groups were established, but these were institutionally segregated from the major centers of teaching in the universities, where a much greater emphasis on theory and speculation prevailed. Although many university teachers participated in these centers, sometimes directing them, often taking part in joint symposia, the two types of activity were not jointly available to students and did not provide joint career paths.

Intellectually there was a certain dispersion of effort. The important work of Aron, focused intensively on problems of industrial society, progress, democracy, and totalitarianism, and based on the tradition of Montesquieu, Tocqueville, and to some degree Weber, was not concerned with abstract theoretical questions and, initially at least, had little influence on research. The influence of Georges Gurvitch continued, despite his efforts to the contrary, to be confined to the speculative tradition, having little impact on research,[33] while the various centers of research developed independently of these major analytic efforts. At the Centre des Études Sociologiques, research on the sociology of labor was greatly inspired by the works of Friedmann and the studies of lifestyles and urban ecology by P. H. Chombart de Lauwe.[34] In anthropology, the work of Claude Lévi-Strauss was to prove a major focus of new theoretical development, as was the more institutional macrosocietal anthropological work of scholars like Georges Balandier.[35]

5.   Educational and research institutions in Africa and Asia were largely extensions of institutions in the major European and later U.S.

centers.[36] In Latin America, as R. Lagos and R. Stavenhagen pointed out,[37] the social sciences failed to develop, largely because of the obstacles of the Hispanic cultural tradition, the narrow legalistic approaches dominating university studies, and the image of the sociologist as "intellectual" which predominated in these cultures. Nevertheless, several important bases of scientific research were established: in Buenos Aires under the guidance of Gino Germani; in Sao Paulo under the guidance of Florestan Fernandez; in the Inter-American School of Social Sciences (Flacso) in Santiago. From the start, these centers emphasized the combination of empirical and macrosocietal-historical or contemporary research, focused above all on studies of modernization.

In countries in Asia and Africa (with the notable exception of Japan), small nuclei of sociological activities developed in the form of university institutes and research bureaus, oriented largely to the work in Europe and North America. As C.F. Alger and Gene Lyons had put it,

> These historical movements left transnational social science highly asymmetrical, and this asymmetry led to dependency relations between social scientists in developing countries and those in the developed nations. Dependency relations derive from the dominant theories and methodologies in developed countries that are world-wide reference points for research and teaching, from the resources that are available in developed countries for advancing knowledge, the availability of means for publishing and distributing research findings, and the existence of major university centers in Europe and the United States that continue to attract, and often retain, first rate social scientists from all parts of the world.[38]

Only in the 1960s did this picture change.

6.   The development of sociology in the Communist bloc nations was much more hesitant than in the West, and it took a different path.[39] In the Soviet Union itself, the thriving centers of historical, empirical, and sociological research and teaching that had existed in several universities before and immediately after the 1917 Revolution were almost entirely wiped out under Stalinism. This contributed to the deterioration of the sociological tradition in Russia and the total loss of whatever distinctiveness it had attained. Historical and ethnographic work was conducted without reference to sociology, while theoretical considerations were absorbed into the official discussions of Marxism. A similar fate, albeit in different degrees and for different periods of time, overtook sociology in the Communist countries of Eastern Europe. The thriving traditions of

sociological research associated with the names of Florian Znaniecki, Jozef Chalasinki, and Stanislaw Ossowski in Poland, Dimitri Gusti in Roumania, and Arnost Blaha in Czechoslovakia, had in a sense to go "underground"—to be conducted not in teaching institutions or even academies, but often in the homes of the scholars.

Thus, in the Soviet bloc, at the beginning of the 1950s, the various institutional and intellectual components of sociology were decomposed, suppressed, or driven into marginal positions. Its more general theoretical considerations were seen as properly belonging to the domain of Marxist philosophy, and its empirical research was suspect as being "bourgeois"; history and ethnology were severed from sociology, and no orientation to contemporary institutional analysis was permitted.

Only a few very small nuclei and such scholars as Ossowski survived, in isolated, poorly recognized positions, but they proved to be of crucial importance in the revival of sociology in the late 1950s—a revival whose continuity was also at the mercy of political trends and vagaries. The members of these nuclei then emerged to lead the upsurge in sociology. Based on new institutional developments, this renewal made possible some receptivity to aspects of Western sociology. This openness was confined at first to technical-methodological issues—the level of research methods and survey analyses—and it was this which was initially acknowledged as the legitimate scope of sociology. Eventually, theoretical, semi-ideological, debate took place, especially in Russia and East Germany, focussing on Parsons' sociology but not involving other components of sociological analysis, particularly research or contemporary institutional and critical analysis.

Gradually, however, some practical attempts to redefine the scope of sociology and the role of sociologists were made. These attempts were based on a relatively high level of institutionalization of sociology in universities and academies, but they had to cope constantly with a totalitarian-political system which had developed its own official ideology. This ideology often claimed for itself a monopoly on part of the intellectual orientation which characterized the distinctiveness of sociology. Obviously, tensions could develop between this ideology and the attempts of sociology to legitimate itself. These tensions and ambivalences were strongest with respect to the very attempts at unifying the various components of sociological work, especially its critical and broader intellectual orientations, with continuing research. The central focus of such tensions was the relationship of sociology to Marxist philosophy, to various fields of contemporary and historical research, and to the critical evaluation of social reality. In some cases these attempts were closely related to the efforts at "opening" Marxism that were taking place in these countries, though some sociologists in Communist bloc countries avoided this dangerous ground.

Several ways of solving the problem of the definition of sociology and the relationships among its parts evolved in the Eastern bloc countries. One pattern, which emerged first in the Soviet Union, was characterized by very restricted institutionalization of the sociological role; by separation, except for declaratory statements, of research and theoretical-philosophical orientations; and by the almost complete denial of historical, comparative, and critical institutional analysis (as distinct from surveys) as part of sociologists' concerns. The sociologist's role was confined, in short, to the conduct of certain types of research to the exclusion of both the critical and the intellectual implications or components of this role.

In East Germany an entirely different pattern developed. It was characterized by advanced technical research and applied sociology in many fields: industry, the army, organizations, and the like, and by high levels of competence and broader analytic orientations, but confinement to a rigid framework of relatively sophisticated Marxist ideology which left the broader implications of sociological analysis entirely to official ideologists. In the other East European countries, different combinations of philosophical orientation and participation in Marxist debate developed along with a gradual broadening of research activity and a minimization of the critical role. But any combination at any given time was subject to the vagaries of political trends which could easily disrupt, and sometimes destroy, whatever had been attained.

Patterns of Sociologists' Roles and Intellectual Orientations

7. These patterns of institutionalization in different centers were closely related to varying orientations and concerns about components of the sociologist's role and the professional image and identity of sociology. Most activities were imbued with optimism about the intellectual relevance and practical potential of sociology, above all insofar as it could free itself from direct political or ideological involvement. Efforts to depoliticize and deideologize the role of the sociologist thus stressed the potential contribution of sociology to public service in what later seemed to be technocratic overtones.[40]

The foremost concern of the sociological communities which achieved high degrees of institutionalization—that is, the United States, England,

and the Netherlands—was at this stage the struggle for a secure base for such institutionalization, mainly in academic life and in professional scientific associations. In the emerging role-complexes, sociologists avoided direct involvement in political or ideological movements while maintaining some orientation to public service.

In countries with weak academic components and lacking diversified institutional grounding—France, Germany, Italy, and to some degree Latin America—the ideological or critical component of the sociologists' role was retained or developed, but not among the emerging nuclei of professional or practical sociologists.[41] This posture remained, rather, in the older academic community.

However great the differences may have been in different countries, nowhere was it possible to stress any single role component to the exclusion of others. The great variety of intellectual and role orientations, of mixes of components of sociological analysis, developed within a framework of stronger national and international contacts, within an emerging, if unevenly distributed, international scholarly community with new channels of mutual influence. These conditions made possible far-reaching changes in the initial national orientations which have been described above.

Thus, the more intellectual, philosophical and ideological orientations were continuously confronted with the tendency to greater institutionalization and professionalization and with the emphasis on scholarship and on professional and practical involvement, as reflected in the Italian discussion of "Sociologists and Centers of Power" and similar discussions in some Latin American countries.[42]

The stronger emphasis on scholarly and professional activities did not necessarily obliterate speculative and critical orientations, just as the emphasis on empirical research did not necessarily eclipse macrosocietal and historical-comparative analysis. However neglected these components may have been in the initial pattern of institutionalization in the major centers in the United States, England, Holland, they persisted in other countries, although they were segregated from other types of research.[43] Given increasing international contacts among sociological communities on the one hand, and the internal momentum of institutionalization in the major centers on the other, these perspectives could, and indeed did, provide new starting points for the critical evaluation of that very institutional reality.

Some of the institutional and intellectual developments that crystallized during the 1950s in the various sociological communities—both more and less central—will be commented on in the following chapters.

The major trends were a general growth in the number of organizations engaged in different kinds of sociological work and, from about the 1960s, steady growth in the number of students of sociology. This quantitative growth, which took place in most countries, did not, at least until the middle and late 1960s, greatly change the basic institutional pattern of sociological activity in each country. However, the confrontation between these institutional patterns and quantitative growth provided the setting for many developments in the sociological communities.

To understand these changes, however, we must first consider developments in sociological theory, analysis, and research.

Convergences in Sociological Analysis and Research; Trends in Codification

8.   The initial postwar period was characterized by several important trends in sociological analysis and research, most of them originating in the United States. As they spread to other sociological communities, they created a new framework of scholarly activity.

First was the continuing growth and diversification in almost all major fields of sociological research, more analytically and technically sophisticated research, and the extension of sociological research into new fields. Examples of this spread include the study of organizations; the study of professions; comparative macrosociological research, best illustrated in studies of development and modernization; and research on diverse aspects of social stratification, such as mobility, class life style, political behavior, and images of society.

Second, intensive effort was made to codify each sphere of analysis, to locate "middle-range" problems in different areas of sociological research; and relate these problems to the central concerns of sociological theory.[44]

Perhaps for the first time in the history of sociology, though following the direction of the Founding Fathers, serious attempts were made to define the analytic relationships of various subfields or areas of social life—institutions, groups, social problems, patterns of social behavior—to a macrosocietal framework. Virtually all fields of study—deviance, stratification, urban and political sociology, sociology of organizations —engaged in the codification and systematization of their major findings enhancing the continuity of their internal *Problemstellungen.*

The systematization of particular areas was accompanied by efforts to relate these fields to central problems in sociological theory. Many attempts at codification converged in the study of "qualitative" problems of social life, particularly modern social life: mass society, bureaucratization, the possibilities of maintaining primary and primordial attachments in different settings, or different types of political regimes. These analysis entailed a reorientation to the broader problems of sociological theory, and to the classics of sociology, although such efforts were only nominal in many cases.

The effort to relate specific areas of research to broader problems was reflected in the demand in the late 1940s to give up "grand theory" and to concentrate on middle-range theories.[45] But this very demand, heard on both sides of the Atlantic, was indicative of the concern with theoretical systematization and integration of work in different substantive fields. Thus various middle-range theories and comparative institutional analyses were incorporated into the central sociological tradition. In the early 1950s, this trend was associated with the revival of macrosociological and comparative study in anthropology, studies of "developing" societies, and other comparative historical studies.[46]

As macrosociological and other broad sociological problems were related to problems in different fields of research, and to methodological problems in the conduct of research, the examples of Durkheim and Weber were revived. The use of classic models in contexts that permitted greater systematization of data and methodological sophistication promised to close the gap between the problematics of general theory and substantive research, permitting also the analytic formulation[47] of research problems. However, these developments were often hesitant and the orientations to "theory" perfunctory. Often, as Peter Worlsey[48] has put it, they paid lip service to theory without relating theory to the concrete problems of specific research. Moreover, there was great variation in the theoretical approaches and research programs that were chosen.

Thus, the orientations and hopes of finding a common analytic or theoretical framework and of synthesizing various areas of research did not produce the desired unification or common framework. But they did enhance awareness in the sociological community of the importance of such relationships.

In line with these developments a shift took place in the self-perception and definition of sociology's relationship to other social sciences. The problems of the limits and subject matter of sociology and the *Methodenstreit* were transformed in this period into the search for common theories and problems,[49] such as theories of the development of culture and personality, or for common analytic frameworks, like the "theory of action" or system approach, which in principle might transcend any single discipline.

9.   The rapprochement of research and basic theory was related to the patterns of institutionalization of sociological inquiry, especially in the United States and Western Europe. It stemmed partly from institutionalization in academic life and the establishment of curricula which created common cores for different areas of specialization which were replicated in professional bodies and maintained through internal and international academic contacts. The trend was encouraged, too, by the increasing interest of educated publics in social attitudes and sociological thinking, and its applicability to practical affairs. The relationship between these institutional developments and tendencies to codification is reflected in the new textbooks and readers for undergraduate and graduate courses—both general textbooks and works in specialized fields. John Bennett and Melvin M. Tumin's *Social Life*, Kingsley Davis' *Human Society*, Logan Wilson and William Kolb's *Sociological Analysis* in the United States, and works in Holland, Scandinavia and other countries,[50] attest to the new types of orientation.

At the same time, research methodology advanced and was codified in specialized textbooks. These treated statistical methods appropriate to the social sciences and more analytic mathematical approaches to sociology.[51]

10.   The convergence and synthesis into one framework of the various trends in sociological analysis went through several phases. These can perhaps, best be traced by comparing the patterns of codification which emerged at the end of the preceding period—the late 1930s—with the postwar patterns of the 1940s and then of the 1950s.

The pattern of codification in the works analyzed in the preceding chapter—the *Handwörterbuch der Soziologie*, Richard Thurnwald's Symposium, the English *Study of Society* and above all the *Encyclopedia of the Social Sciences*[52]—started to give way to a new one. The differences are apparent in such works as *Twentieth Century Sociology, Modern Sociological Theory in Continuity and Change, Sociology Today*, and the counterpart review compendia published abroad, as well as the new *International Encyclopedia of the Social Sciences*.

A first significant shift in this pattern of codification is reflected in the collection of articles on *Twentieth Century Sociology* published in 1945 in the United States at the end of World War II. Edited by Georges Gurvitch and Wilbert Moore,[53] it also testified to the emerging mood of international cooperation fostered to no small degree by the many European scholars who had emigrated to the United States.

One part of this volume is a critical examination of the fields of sociology: research methods, theory, social change, social psychology, criminology, social control, sociology of law, knowledge, religion, economic organization, and so on. These chapters present broad surveys of the fields. The second section consists of studies by various sociologists of the state of the discipline in their respective countries: Lévy-Strauss on France, Albert Salomon on Germany, John Rumney on England, Robert E. L. Faris on the United States, and others on Eastern Europe and Latin America. The over-all picture in these surveys is that of greater emphasis on systems of thought, rather than on the tradition of research or on systematic relationships between the two. The United States is the only, and partial, exception, with a longer tradition of research in several fields—urban sociology, race relations, social psychology, some in which middle-range theories were developed.

Later codifying ventures concentrated on different areas of research and analyzed them more systematically. Thus *Modern Sociological Theory in Continuity and Change*, edited by Howard Becker and Alvin Boskoff,[54] discusses a broad span of topics: the state of sociology since World War I in some European countries and Japan; developments of research techniques and methodological controversies in America, theoretical developments in American sociology; criticisms of the functionalist approach; and so on. In this case, however, greater emphasis is placed on various fields of specialization, such as small groups, social stratification, religion, and the arts. The reviews give a fairly comprehensive enumeration of the diverse theoretical approaches and subjects studied in each field. They do not, however, assess the work critically from the point of view of possible theoretical syntheses of the analytic frameworks and research data.

A rather significant shift in the mode of codification is found in *Sociology Today*, the series of surveys published under the auspices of the American Sociological Association, initiated and planned by Robert K. Merton, then ASA president.[55] Unlike the earlier works, which brought together various areas of sociological analysis and different works within any single area, this collection presents a more analytic appraisal of each field in terms of some common theoretical framework.

To a large degree, these essays followed Merton's own earlier indications about the proper mode of codification in sociology. In these surveys an even wider range of specialized fields in sociology is reviewed, but the theoretical orientation and its relationship to research is far more highly accentuated, even if it does not reveal a unitary form. In some fields, as for example political sociology, an attempt is made to synthesize different theoretical approaches and to point out the new problems of research that follow from such a rapprochement. In other fields, such as the study of personality, or the study of disorganization and deviant behavior, the authors propose theoretical reorientations which may link previously unconnected topics of research in a more comprehensive framework and even go beyond this by indicating the relationship of these fields to the functioning of the wider social system. Finally, other reviews—for example, the chapter on the sociology of religion—deplore the neglect of theory and research in the field, or, as in the analysis of small groups, stress the need for a theoretical framework which will link diversified and unrelated studies.

In Europe, the attempts of codification undertaken in this period generally shift between the patterns of earlier attempts and that of *Sociology Today*. Perhaps the most comprehensive attempt at codification that appeared in the 1950s were the Dutch *Het Sociale Leven in Al Zün Facetten*, the French *Traité de Sociologie* edited by Gurvitch, and the various compendia edited by König in Germany. Most of these attempts, with the partial exception of the English efforts, brought into a common literary framework the research conducted in different specialized areas and the discussion of sociological theory, but did not bring the two areas together.[56] The codification of each subfield was presented primarily in terms of survey—that is, summaries of research—or of theoretical approaches, rather than in terms of critical analysis. There were few attempts to create a synthesis between data and theory, although the beginning of an effort could already be discerned. The special chapters on the history of sociology and on research methods were even less fully integrated with the other parts. In contrast to *Sociology Today*, the French and Dutch compendia tended to emphasize orientation to macrosocietal and comparative historical concerns. The French also stressed philosophical aspects of sociology, while the Dutch stressed its practical applications.

Attempts at codification were also expressed in a series of readers, the most influential of which probably were those published in the 1950s and 1960s by the Free Press[57]; in such fully or partly institutionalized periodical publications as *Current Sociology*, published since the early 1950s; and in various textbooks.

It was probably at this stage of codification that the image of sociology as a relatively coherent field working to attain a common framework emerged. This view was temporarily reinforced by a shift in the pattern of codification from about the mid-1960s—that is, to a pattern that stressed not only surveying the fields but developing further *Problemstellungen*, and looking within each field for central analytic problems.[58] It was also characterized by greater internal analytic specification of specific middle-range theories or models, some of which, like the theories of relative deprivation, primary groups, and reference groups, cut across research areas, producing specialized theories as well as integration with broader analytic paradigms.[59]

The attempts to codify the history of sociology now took the form not only of listing various schools and scholars, as Sorokin had done in the late 1920s in *Contemporary Sociological Theories,* but of analyzing the development of the analytic *Problemstellungen* of sociology. The two outstanding examples of this type of codification were *Theories of Society,* edited by Talcott Parsons, Edward Shils, Kaspar Naegele, and Jesse Pitts, in which the major sociological *Problemstellungen* were traced from their remote classical ancestry up to and beyond the earlier formulations of the structural-functional model; and Aron's *Main Currents in Sociological Thought,* in which the development of the more analytic *Problemstellungen* of sociology was related to specific questions about the nature and problems of modern society.[60]

At the same time, Merton began to develop a special approach to the analysis of the development of sociology. The framework employed took a largely institutional approach to the sociology of knowledge.[61]

This stage of codification found its apogee in the new *International Encyclopedia of the Social Sciences,* planned in the late 1950s and early 1960s and published in 1968. By then, however, new trends in codification had become apparent which challenged optimistic vision of a coherent discipline. These trends presented a more complex pattern—a pattern of stronger internal development in many fields; of growing analytic and methodological sophistication, coupled with great diversity in analytic orientation; of controversies about paradigmatic models; of increasing distance between the "middle range" and analytic developments in each area and the broader paradigms; and of greater dissociation between different approaches—for example, the "mathematical" microsociological and institutional approaches. Ironically, all these patterns had emerged somehow, in conjunction with the aspiration to unity.

11.   These movements and attempts at codification were also manifest in the changing patterns and activities of the international sociological community and in its international institutionalization. They were reflected in meetings and conferences, institutionalized especially in congresses and seminars of the International Sociological Association.

At first these meetings[62] were characterized by the presentation of "national" reports on the state of sociology in each country, along with reports on concrete research areas. Gradually a stronger emphasis developed on attempts at comparative codification both of research fields, such as social stratification, mobility, social change, and of research methods, as well as of national trends in the professionalization and application of sociology.

A shift also took place to more analytic *Problemstellungen* and, eventually, broader consideration of theory, analysis, and paradigms. By the time of the 1970 ISA Congress in Varna, however, and the 1974 Congress in Toronto, a split had emerged between those concerned with the continuous examination of different fields of sociological analysis and those involved in an ideological confrontation about the so-called "crisis of sociology." This will be discussed in detail in later chapters.

Notes

1. On trends in the institutionalization of sociological activities after World War II, see A. J. Reiss, "Sociology: the field," *International Encyclopedia of the Social Sciences,* Vol. 15 (New York: Macmillan, 1968), pp. 1–23; E. Shils, "The trend of sociological research," paper read at the 8th World Congress of Sociology, Evian, 1966; E. Shils, "Tradition, ecology, and institution in the history of sociology,"*Daedalus,* Vol. 99, No. 4 (Fall 1970), pp. 760–825.

2. S. A. Stouffer et al. *The American Soldier* (Princeton: Princeton University Press, 1949), 2 vols; T. W. Adorno et al, *The Authoritarian Personality* (New York: Harper, 1950); R. K. Merton, *Mass Persuation: the Social Psychology of a War Bond Drive* (New York: Harper, 1946); P. F. Lazarsfeld, *Radio and the Printed Page* (New York: Duell, Sloan and Pearce, 1940); P. F. Lazarsfeld and P. M. Kendall, *Radio listening in America* (New York: Prentice-Hall, 1948); Daniel Lerner (ed.), *Propaganda in War and Crisis* (New York: George W. Stewart, 1951); P. Lazarsfeld, B. Berelson, and H. Gaudet, *The People's Choice* (New York: Duell, Sloan and Pearce, 1944); P. F. Lazarsfeld and F. N. Stanton (eds.), *Communication Research, 1948–9* (New York: Harper, 1949).

3. E. Shils, "Tradition, ecology, and institution in the history of sociology," *op. cit.*

4. For developments in the major European sociological centers, see the general survey in H. Becker and H. E. Barnes, *Social Thought from Lore to Science,* Vol. 3 (New York: Dover, 1961), pp. xxxv–cii.

5. On Germany see W. E. Mühlmann, "Sociology in Germany: shift in alignment," in H. Becker and A. Boskoff (eds.), *Modern Sociological Theory in Continuity and Change* (New York: Dryden Press, 1957), especially pp. 682–694.

6. On France see J. Stoetzel, "Sociology in France: an empiricist view," in H. Becker and A. Boskoff (eds.), *Modern Sociological Theory in Continuity and Change, op. cit.,* especially pp. 643–657.

7. On Britain see W. J. H. Sprott, "Sociology in Britain: preoccupations," in H. Becker and A. Boskoff (eds.), *Modern Sociological Theory in Continuity and Change, op. cit.,* pp. 607–622.

8. On Scandinavia and the Netherlands see "Recent sociological research in Denmark,"

and A. N. J. Hollander and J. P. Kruijt," A survey of development of sociology in the Netherland," in *Transactions of the Second World Congress of Sociology*, Vol. 1 (International Sociological Association, 1954), pp. 6–10, 44–46; K. Bruun, "Sociological teaching in Finland," and J. P. Kruijt, "The university teaching of sociology in the Netherlands," in *Transactions of the Third World Congress of Sociology*, Vol. 7 (International Sociological Association, 1956), pp. 23–24, 25–31; E. Allardt, "Scandinavian sociology and Swedish sociology," *International Journal of Sociology*, Vol. 3 No. 2 (Fall–Winter 1973–74), pp. 9–71; J. A. A. van Doorn, "The development of sociology and social research in the Netherlands,"*Mens en Maatschappij*, Vol. 31, No. 4 (July–August 1956), pp. 189–264.

On Japan see K. Odaka, "Sociology in Japan; accommodation of Western orientations," in H. Becker and A. Boskoff (eds.), *Modern Sociological Theory in Continuity and Change, op. cit.*, especially pp. 720–730.

9. On Italy see C. Pellizzi, "Notes on the professional activities of sociologists in Italy . . .," in *Transactions of the Second World Congress of Sociology, op. cit.*, pp. 162–164; L. Gallino and E. Salvadori Saccomani, "Two generations of sociology in Italy," *Social Science Information*, Vol. 10, No. 3 (June 1971), pp. 133–150.

On Austria see L. Rosenmayr, "Teaching and professional activities in sociology in Austria," in *Transactions of the Third World Congress of Sociology, op. cit.*, pp. 5–6.

On Switzerland see R. Girod, "Switzerland," in J. S. Roucek (ed.), *Contemporary Sociology* (London: Peter Owen, 1958), pp. 847–850.

On Spain see E. G. Arboleya, "Spain," *ibid.*, pp. 824–839. For a much fuller and detailed analysis, though referring mostly to a later period, see Amando de Miguel, *Homo Sociologicus Hispanicus* (Barcelona: Barral Editores, 1973); A. de Miguel, *Sociologia O Subversion* (Barcelona: Plaza & Janes, 1975), especially Ch. 2.

10. On Japan see note 8 of this chapter.

On India see M. N. Srinivas, M. N. Panini, "The development of sociology and social anthropology in India," *Sociological Bulletin*, Vol. 22, No. 2 (September 1973), pp. 179–215; Santosh Kumar Nandy, "Aspects of development of sociology in India; a study in the sociology of sociology," in E. A. Tiryakian (ed.), *The Phenomenon of Sociology* (New York: Appleton-Century-Crofts, 1971), pp. 121–145.

For Latin America see G. Germani, "The development and present state of sociology in Latin America," in E. A. Tiryakian (ed.), *ibid.* pp. 99–120; for greater detail see G. Germani, *La Sociologia en la America Latina: Problemas y Perspectivas*. (Udeba, Buenos Aires, 1964). For some of the controversies that were raging in Latin American sociology in the early forties and that were very similar to both the earlier European Methodenstreit and the later ideological controversies, with the difference that it was the "conservative" philosophers that were the major critics of "empirical sociology," see G. Germani, *La Sociologia Cientifica, Apuntes para su Fundamentacion* (Mexico: Universidad Autonoma de Mexico, 1962) especially pp. i, iii, and G. Germani. "Una decada de discussiones metodologicas en la sociologia Latino-Americana," *Boletin del Inotituto de Sociologia Buenos Aires*, Vol. 10, No. 6 (1952), 87–105.

For an overall summary see A. Solari, R. Franco, and J. Jutkowitz (eds.), *Teoria y Accion Social: Interpretaciones Sociologicas del Desarrollo Latinoamericano* (Santiago de Chile: Latin American Institute for Social Studies, 1975).

On the early developments of sociology in Israel see S. N. Eisenstadt, "Sociology in Israel: 1948–1953," in *Transactions of the Second World Congress of Sociology, op. cit.*, pp. 26–31; S. N. Eisenstadt, "Recent trends of development in sociological research in Israel," in *Transactions of the Third World Congress of Sociology, op. cit.*, pp. 106–111.

For somewhat later developments see A. B. Cherns (ed.), *Social Science Organization and Policy*, First Series, Belgium, Chile, Egypt, Hungary, Nigeria, Srilanka (Paris: Unesco, 1974).

An interesting case study, that of French Canada, is analyzed in M. Fournier, "L'institutionalisation des sciences sociales en Québec," *Sociologie et Sociétés*, Vol. 5, No. 1 (1973), pp. 27–59.

11. P. Lengyel, "Phases and processes in the internationalisation of social sciences," paper read at an international seminar held at Bellagio, Italy, July 16–21, 1973, to be published in *International Social Science Journal*.

12. E. Shils, "The trend of sociological research," *op. cit.*

13. On the United States see A. J. Reiss, "Sociology: the field," *op. cit.;* E. Shils, "Tradition, ecology, and institution in the history of sociology," *op. cit.*

     On the other countries mentioned below see the respective quotations in notes 7–10 of this chapter.

14. On this see M. Janowitz, "Professionalization of sociology," *American Journal of Sociology*, Vol. 78, No. 1 (July 1972) pp. 105–135; R. W. Friedrichs, *A Sociology of Sociology* (New York: Free Press [1970], 1972), especially Ch. 4.

15. On this see Ch. 7, 8, and the bibliography quoted there.

16. For concise surveys of the fields of "culture and personality" and "national character," see M. E. Spiro, "Culture and personality," in *International Encyclopedia of the Social Sciences, op. cit.*, Vol. 3, pp. 558–563; G. A. De Vos, "National character," *ibid.*, Vol. 11, pp. 14–18.

     For the application of learning theory, see J. Dollard and N. E. Miller, *Personality and Psychotherapy* (New York: McGraw-Hill, 1950); J. Dollard, N. E. Miller, et. al., *Frustration and Aggression* (London: Kegan Paul, Trench, Trubner, 1944); J. Dollard and N. E. Miller, *Social Learning and Imitation* (London: Kegan Paul, Trench, Trubner, 1945).

     For the application of operant psychology see G. C. Homans, *Social Behavior: its Elementary Forms* (New York: Harcourt, Brace & World, 1961).

17. On community studies, see among others W. Spinrad, "Power in local communities," in R. Bendix and S. M. Lipset (eds.), *Class, Status and Power* (New York: Free Press, 1966), pp. 218–231.

     On political sociology see among others R. Bendix and S. M. Lipset, "Political sociology," *Current Sociology*, Vol. 6, No. 2 (1957); S. M. Lipset, "Political sociology," in R. K. Merton, et al. (eds.), *Sociology Today* (New York: Basic Books, 1959), pp. 81–114.

     For the area of stratification see for example D. G. MacRae, "Social stratification," *Current Sociology*, Vol. 2, No. 1 (1953–1954); S. M. Miller, "Comparative social mobility," *Current Sociology*, Vol. 9, No. 1 (1960); R. Bendix and S. M. Lipset (eds.), *Class, Status, Power, op. cit.*, 1953, 1966 editions.

     Studies of modernization and development of this period are well analyzed in Chong-Do-Hah and J. Schneider, "A critique of current studies of political development and modernization," *Social Research*, Vol. 35 (1968), pp. 130–158; S. N. Eisenstadt, *Tradition, Change and Modernity* (New York: John Wiley, 1973), Part 1.

18. See, for example, T. Parsons, *Essays in Sociological Theory* rev. ed. (Glencoe, Ill.: Free Press, 1963); and his earlier classic exposition in *The Structure of Social Action* (New York: McGraw-Hill, 1937); R. K. Merton, *Social Theory and Social Structure* (Glencoe, Ill.: Free Press, 1949), especially Chs. 2, 4, 8, 9, 11, 14; E. Shils, "Charisma, order, and status," *American Sociological Review*, Vol. 30, No. 2 (1965), pp. 199–213.

     See also Shils' earlier complaint about the lack of such orientation in his *The Present*

State of American Sociology (Glencoe, Ill.: Free Press, 1948); and his evaluation of the changes since then in his "The trend of sociological research," *op. cit.*

19. On this, see for example, the criticism against Warner's analysis of social class and Parsons' analysis of organizations in S. M. Lipset and R. Bendix, "Social status and social structure: a reexamination of data and interpretations," *British Journal of Sociology*, Vol. 2 (1951), Part 1, pp. 150–168, Part 2, pp. 230–254; H. A. Landsberger, "Parsons' theory of organizations," in M. Black (ed.), *The Social Theories of Talcott Parsons* (Englewood Cliffs, N.J.: Prentice-Hall, [1961], 1964), pp. 214–249.

   See also D. W. Rossides, "The legacy of Max Weber: a nonmetaphysical politics," *Sociological Inquiry*, Vol. 42, Nos. 3–4 (1972), pp. 183–210.

20. R. Aron, "Modern society and sociology," in E. A. Tiryakian (ed.), *The Phenomenon of Sociology, op. cit.*, pp. 158–170.

21. S. M. Lipset, *Agrarian Socialism* (Glencoe, Ill.: Free Press, 1950); D. Riesman, *The Lonely Crowd* (New Haven, Conn.: Yale University Press, 1950); D. Bell, *The End of Ideology* (Glencoe, Ill.: Free Press, 1960); D. Bell (ed.), *The New Radical Right* (New York: Doubleday, 1955), and an expanded new edition, *The Radical Right* (New York: Doubleday, 1963); M. Janowitz, *The Community Press in an Urban Setting* (Glencoe, Ill.: Free Press, 1952); M. Janowitz, *The Professional Soldier* (Glencoe, Ill.: Free Press, 1960); A. Gouldner (ed.), *Studies in Leadership* (New York: Harper, 1950); A. Gouldner, *Patterns of Industrial Bureaucracy* (New York: Free Press, 1954); A. Gouldner, *Wildcat Strike* (Yellow Springs, Ohio: Antioch Press, 1954).

22. See, for example, E. Goffman, *Asylums* (Garden City, N.Y.: Doubleday Anchor Books, 1961); E. C. Hughes, *French Canada in Transition* (London: Kegan Paul, Trench, Trubner, 1946); M. Janowitz, *The Community Press in an Urban Setting, op. cit.*

23. C. Wright Mills, *The Sociological Imagination* (New York: Oxford University Press, 1959); C. Wright Mills, *The Power Elite* (New York: Oxford University Press, 1959); I. L. Horowitz, *Foundations of Political Sociology* (New York: Harper & Row, 1972); I. L. Horowitz, *Professing Sociology: Studies in the Life Cycle of Social Science* (Chicago: Aldine, 1968); A. Gouldner, *The Coming Crisis of Western Sociology* (New York: Basic Books, 1970); A. Gouldner, "The sociologist as partisan: sociology and the welfare state," *The American Sociologist*, Vol. 3 (May 1968), pp. 103–116; N. Birnbaum, *The Crisis of Industrial Society* (New York: Oxford University Press, 1969); N. Birnbaum, *Toward a Critical Sociology* (New York: Oxford University Press, 1971); T. B. Bottomore, *Critics of Society: Radical Thought in North America* (London: G. Allen & Unwin, 1967); T. B. Bottomore, *Sociology as Social Criticism* (London: George Allen & Unwin, 1974); T. B. Bottomore, *Political Sociology* (London: Hutchison, 1972).

24. T. Parsons, *Essays in Sociological Theory, op. cit.*, especially Chs. 6, 13; M. J. Levy, "Contrasting factors in the modernization of China and and Japan," in S. Kuznets et al. (eds.), *Economic Growth: Brazil, India, Japan* (Durham, N.C.: Duke University Press, 1955), pp. 496–536.

   The studies of modernization are too numerous to enumerate here. For a concise survey see, for example, Chong-Do-Hah and J. Schneider, "A critique of current studies of political development and modernization," *op. cit.*

25. On the Netherlands and Japan see note 8.

   On the Netherlands see also J. E. Ellemers, G. J. A. Riesthnis, and J. H. J. Vermeulen, "Selected bibliography of social science publications on Netherlands' society published in foreign languages," *Sociologia Neerlandica*, Vol. 10, No. 1 (1974), pp. 99–113; Joachim Matthes, *Soziologie und Gesellschaft in den Niederlanden*, (Neuwied:

Luchterhand, 1965), especially Ch. 1 on development of sociology in the Netherlands, as well as all the materials brought there; J. A. A. van Doorn, *Beeld en Bekennis van de Nederlandse Sociologie* (Utrecht: Bijleveld, 1964).

26. On the Scandinavian countries see E. Allardt, "Scandinavian sociology and Swedish sociology," *op. cit.;* E. Allardt, G, Therbom, G. Aspelin, et al., "Svensk Sociologi," *Sociologisk Forskning,* Vol. 10, No. 2 (1973), pp. 5–63.

    The quotation on T. Segerstedt is taken from p. 26 of Allardt's "Scandinavian Sociology," *ibid.*

    For further details on development in Finnish sociology, see H. S. Lamminen et al., "Bibliography of Finnish sociology, 1960–1969," *Transactions of the Westermarck Society,* Vol. 19 (1973). See also, in greater detail, but in Finnish R. Alapuro et al. (eds.), *Suomalaisen Sosiologian Juuvet* (Helsinki: Werner Söderstom, 1973).

27. On Britain see note 7, and also E. Krausz, *Sociology in Britain: a Survey of Research* (London: Batsford, 1969).

    On earlier trends in social biology see P. Abrams, *The Origins of British Sociology, 1834–1914* (Chicago: University of Chicago Press, 1968), pp. 8–153.

    On the traditions of Hobhouse and Ginsberg see details in Chs. 2, 5, and J. Rex, *Discovering Sociology* (London: Routledge & Kegan Paul, 1973), especially Chs. 5, 20.

28. See, for example, T. H. Marshall, *Citizenship and Social Class* (Cambridge: Cambridge University Press, 1950); T. H. Marshall, *Social Policy in the Twentieth Century* (London: Hutchinson University Library, 1965).

29. For a concise survey of these developments see S. N. Eisenstadt, "Anthropological studies of complex societies," in S. N. Eisenstadt, *Essays in Comparative Institutions* (New York: J. Wiley, 1965), pp. 77–106.

30. On Germany see the reference in note 5 and M. Jay, *The Dialectical Imagination: a History of the Frankfurt School and the Institute of Social Research, 1923–1950* (Boston: Little, Brown, 1973), pp. 281–299.

    On the work of the Frankfurt school in Germany see the *Frankfurte Beiträge zur Soziologie,* published continuously by the Europeishe verlags-austalt since the early 1950s. Some of these works were brought together in *Soziologische Exkusen* in 1956, and translated as *Aspects of Sociology,* by the Frankfurt Institute for Social Research, with a preface by Max Horkheimer and Theodor W. Adorno (Beacon Press, 1972). Some of the implications of these different approaches are discussed in R. Klima, "Theoretical pluralism, methodological dissension, and the role of the sociologist: the West German case," *Social Science Information,* Vol. 11, Nos. 3–4 (1972), pp. 69–108. R König's elaboration of the distinction between theory of society and sociological theory can be found among others in R. König (ed.), *Soziologie* (Frankfurt: Fischer, 1958), p. 10.

31. For good illustrations of these trends in German sociology see, for example, R. König (ed.), *Das Interview: Formen, Technik, Answerlung* (Cologne: Verlag für Politik und Wirtschaft, 1957); R. König (ed.), *Beobachtung und Experiment in der Sozialforschung* (Cologne: Verlag für Politik und Wirtschaft, 1956); R. König (ed.), *Handbuch der Empirischen Sozialforschung* (Stuttgart: F. Enke, 1962, 1969), 2 vols.

    For illustration of other German sociological works in the empirical tradition that appeared in this period see, for instance, R. Mayntz, *Sociale Schichtung und Sozialer Wandel in einer Industrie-Gemeinde* (Stuttgart: F. Enke, 1958); Viggo Graff Blücher, *Freizeit in der Industriellen Gesellschaft* (Stuttgart: Ferdinand Enke, 1966); K. M. Bolte, *Sozialer Aufstieg und Abstieg* (Stuttgart: Ferdinand Enke, 1959). For a somewhat different trend, combining empirical data with macrosociological overtones, see:

H. Schelsky, "Gesellschaftlicher wandel," *Offene Welt*, No. 41 (1956); H. Schelsky, "Die jugend der industriellen gesellschaft und die arbeitslosigkeit," *Arbeitslosigkeit und Berufsnot der Jugend*, Vol. 2 (Cologne: 1952); H. Schelsky, "Berechtigung und anmassung in der managerherrschaft," in H. D. Ortlieb (ed.), *Wirtschaftsordnung und Wirtschaftspolitik ohne Dogma* (Hamburg: 1954); H. Schelsky, *Ortsbestimmung der Deutschen Soziologie* (Düsseldorf, Köln: E. Diederichs, 1959); H. Schelsky, *Auf der Suche nach Wirtlichkeit* (Düsseldorf, Köln: E. Diederichs, 1965); A. Gehlen and H. Schelsky (eds.), *Soziologie* (Düsseldorf, Köln: E. Diedrichs, 1955); A. Gehlen, *Der Mensch, seine Natur und seine Stellung in der Welt* (Bonn: Athenäum-verlag, 1950); A. Gehlen, *Studien zur Anthropologie und Soziologie* (Neuwied am Rhein: Luchterhand, 1963).

32.   On France see the reference in note no. 6; and Association Française de Sociologie, *La Sociologie en France*, submitted to the Sixth World Congress of Sociology, Evian, 1966.

33.   R. Aron, *L'opium des Intellectuels* (Paris: Calmann-Lévy, 1955), translated as *The Opium of the Intellectuals* (London: Secker & Warburg, 1957); R. Aron, *Dix-huit Leçons sur la Société Industrielle* (Paris: Gallimard, 1962), translated as *Eighteen Lectures on Industrial Society* (London: Weidenfeld & Nicolson, 1968); R. Aron, *La Lutte des Classes* (Paris: Gallimard, 1964); R. Aron, *Démocratie et Totalitarisme* (Paris: Gallimard, 1965), translated as *Democracy and Totalitarianism* (London: Weidenfeld & Nicolson, 1968); R. Aron, *La Société Industrielle et la Guerre* (Paris: Plon, 1959), translated as *War and Industrial Society* (London: Oxford University Press, 1958); G. Gurvitch, *Dialectique et Sociologie* (Paris: Flammarion, 1962); G. Gurvitch, *Déterminismes Sociaux et Liberté Humaine* (Paris: Presses Universitaires de France, 1955); G. Gurvitch, *Morale Théorique et Science des Moeurs: leurs Possibilités, leurs Conditions* (Paris: Presses Universitaires de France, 1948); G. Gurvitch, *The Social Frameworks of Knowledge* (Oxford: B. Blackwell, 1971); G. Gurvitch, *Sociology of Law* (London: Kegan Paul, Trench, Trubner, 1947).

34.   G. Friedmann, *Où Va le Travail Humain?* (Paris: Gallimard, 1959); G. Friedmann, *The Anatomy of Work, Labor, Leisure, and the Implications of Automation* (New York: Free Press, 1961); G. Friedmann, *Industrial Society: the Emergence of the Human Problems of Automation* (Glencoe, Ill.: Free Press, 1955); G. Friedmann, *Problèmes Humains du Machinisme Industriel* (Paris: Gallimard, 1946); G. Friedmann, *Traité de Sociologie du Travail* (Paris: A. Collins, 1964); P. H. Chombart de Lauwe, *Famille et Habitation* (Paris: Centre National de la Recherche Scientifique, 1959); P. H. Chombart de Lauwe, *Des Hommes et des Villes* (Paris: Payot, 1965); P. H. Chombart de Lauwe, *Paris et l'Agglomération Parisienne* (Paris: Presses Universitaires de France, 1952), 2 vols.; P. H. Chombart de Lauwe, *La Vie Quotidienne des Familles Ouvrières* (Paris: Centre Nationele de Recherche Scientifique, 1956).

35.   On Lévi-Strauss see details in Ch. 8. On other trends in social anthropology in France see G. Balandier, *Sociologie Actuelle de l' Afrique Noire* (Paris: Presses Universitaires de France, 1955), translated as *The Sociology of Black Africa* (London: Deutsch, 1970); G. Balandier, *Afrique Ambiguë* (Paris: Plon, 1957); G. Balandier, *Daily Life in the Kingdom of the Kongo from the Sixteenth to the Eighteenth Century* (New York: Pantheon Books, 1968); G. Balandier, *Political Anthropology* (London: Penguin, 1970).

36.   P. Lengyel, "Phases and processes in the internationalization of social sciences," *op. cit.*

37.   In papers for the seminar held at Bellagio, July 1973, to be published in the *International Social Science Journal;* P. Lengyel's paper, quoted in note 11 of this chapter, is the introduction.

38.   On Japan see note 8 of this chapter. See also C. F. Alger, G. M. Lyons, "Social science as a transnational system," report of their seminar at Bellagio, published in *International*

Social Science Journal, Vol. 26, No. 1 (1974), pp. 137–149. For the quotation see p. 138.

39. On the early developments of Russian sociology see M. M. Laserson, "Russian sociology," in G. Gurvitch and W. E. Moore (eds.), *Twentieth Century Sociology* (New York: Philosophical Library, 1945), pp. 671–702.

On present trends in Soviet sociology, discussed below, see G. Fischer, "Current Soviet work in sociology," in E. A. Tiryakian (ed.), *The Phenomenon of Sociology, op. cit.,* pp. 146–157; International Social Science Council, *Social Sciences in the U.S.S.R.* (Paris: Mouton; New York: Basic Books, 1965); R. Ahlberg (ed.), *Soziologie in der Sowyetunion* (Freiburg: Rombach, 1969); S. M. Lipset and R. B. Dobson, "Social stratification and sociology in the Soviet Union," *Survey,* Vol. 3 No. 88 (Summer 1973), pp. 114–185; E. A. Weinberg, *The Development of Sociology in the Soviet Union* (London: Routledge & Kegan Paul, 1973).

On the development of sociology, from its start to the present in other countries of the Communist Bloc, see J. J. Wiatr (ed.), *The State of Sociology in Eastern Europe Today* (Carbondale & Edwardsville, Ill.: Southern Illinois University Press, 1971).

On Hungary see also *Sociology in Hungary: Recent Issues and Trends,* (Budapest: Akadémia Kiado, 1974); B. Balla (ed.), *Soziologie und Gesellschaft in Ungari* (Stuttgart: Ferdinand Enke Verlag, 1974).

On Poland see also M. Hirszowicz, "Marxism, revisionism, and academic sociology in Poland," *International Journal of Contemporary Sociology,* Vol. 10, No. 1 (January 1973), pp. 40–52; S. Chodak, "How was political sociology possible in Poland?" *ibid.,* pp. 53–65.

On East Germany, see the two volumes edited by P. Ch. Ludz (ed.), *Soziologie und Marxismus in der Deutsche Demokratische Republik* (Neuwied: Luchterhand, 1972).

40. On this trend in the United States see R. W. Friedrichs, *A Sociology of Sociology, op. cit.,* especially Ch. 4.

In Britain, W. J. H. Sprott, "Sociology in Britain: preoccupations," *op. cit.*

In the Netherlands, J. A. A. von Doorn, "The development of sociology and social research in the Netherlands," *op. cit.;* J. A. A. van Doorn, *Beelden Bekennis van de Nederlandse Sociologie, op. cit.*

41. For Germany see M. Jay, *The Dialectical Imagination, op. cit.,* pp. 281–299; R. Klima, "Theoretical pluralism, methodological dissension, and the role of the sociologist: the West German case," *op. cit.*

For Latin America see G. Germani, "The development and present state of sociology in Latin America," *op. cit.*

On Italy see the materials in R. Treves, "Sociologi e centri di potere in Italia," in *Sociologi e Centri di Potere in Italia* (Bari: Lateza, 1962).

On France see Association Française de Sociologie, *La Sociologie en France,* submitted to the Sixth World Congress of Sociology, Evian, 1966.

42. On Latin America see the quotation in the preceding note.

On Italy see R. Treves, "Sociologi e centri di potere in Italia," *op. cit.;* L. Gallino and E. Salvadori Saccomani, "Two generations of sociology in Italy," *op. cit.*

43. This is for example the case in Germany, for which see the references in note 41.

44. On this and the trends discussed below, see E. Shils, "The trend of sociological research," *op. cit.*

45. On this see R. K. Merton, *Social Theory and Social Structure, op. cit.,* rev. ed. (1963), pp. 5–6; T. H. Marshall, "Sociology at the crossroads," inaugural lecture at the London School of Economics, 1946, reprinted as Ch. 1 of T. H. Marshall, *Class, Citizenship and*

Social Development (New York: Doubleday, 1964; published in England under the title *Sociology at the Crossroads*).

46. A good example of the incorporation of middle-range theories into the sociological tradition is the theory of reference group; for this see R. K. Merton, *Social Theory and Social Structure, op. cit.*, 1963 ed. especially Chs. 8 and 9; and the materials collected in H. H. Hyman and E. Singer,*Reference Group Theory and Research* (New York: Free Press, 1968); W. G. Runciman, *Relative Deprivation and Social Justice* (London: Routledge & Kegan Paul, 1966); E. Katz and P. F. Lazarsfeld,*Personal Influence* (Glencoe, Ill.: Free Press, 1955); E. Katz, "The two-step flow of communication: an up-to-date report on an hypothesis," *Public Opinion Quarterly*, Vol. 21, No. 1, (Spring 1957), pp. 61–78.

For surveys of the comparative studies revived in this period, see S. N. Eisenstadt, "Social institutions: comparative study," in *International Encyclopedia of the Social Sciences, op. cit.*, Vol. 14, pp. 421–428; S. N. Eisenstadt, "Antropological studies of complex societies," *op. cit.*

For studies of modernization see S. N. Eisenstadt,*Tradition, Change and Modernity, op. cit.*, especially Chs. 1 and 5.

47. See on this problem the discussion by E. Shils, "The trend of sociological research," *op. cit.*

48. P. M. Worsley," The state of theory and the status of theory," *Sociology*, Vol. 8, No. 1 (January 1974), pp. 1–17.

49. A. J. Reiss, "Sociology: the field," *op. cit.*

50. Among such textbooks and readers published during this period in the United States are J. W. Bennett and M. M. Tumin, *Social Life, Structure and Function: an Introductory Sociology* (New York: Knopf, 1948); K. Davis, *Human Society* (New York: Macmillan, 1949); L. Wilson and W. Kolb,*Sociological Analysis* (New York: Harcourt, Brace, 1949).

A good example of such a textbook in Holland is J. A. A. van Doorn and C. J. Lammers, *Moderne Sociologie: Systematick Analyse* (Utrecht/Antwerpen, Het Spectrum, 1959).

51. See for example C. Selltiz, M. Jahoda, M. Deutsch, et al. *Research Methods in Social Relations* (New York: Holt, 1959); S. Siegel, *Nonparametric Statistics for the Behavioral Sciences* (New York: McGraw-Hill, 1956); P. F. Lazarsfeld and M. Rosenberg (eds.),*The Language of Social Research* (New York: Free Press, 1955); F. E. Croxton, et al.,*Applied General Statistics* (London: I. Pitman, 1951); P. F. Lazarsfeld (ed.),*Mathematical Thinking in the Social Sciences*, (Glencoe, Ill.: Free Press, 1954); J. S. Coleman, *Introduction to Mathematical Sociology* (New York: Free Press, 1964).

52. A. Vierkandt (ed.),*Handwörterbuch der Soziologie* (Stuttgart: F. Enke, 1931); R. Thurnwald (ed.), *Soziologie von Heute* (Leipzig: C. L. Hirschfeld, 1932); F. Bartlett, M. Ginsberg, et al. (eds.),*The Study of Society: Methods and Problems* (London: Routledge & Kegan Paul [1939], 1949); E. R. A. Seligman and A. Johnson (eds.),*Encyclopedia of the Social Sciences* (New York: Macmillan, 1930–1935), 15 vols.

53. G. Gurvitch and W. E. Moore (eds.), *Twentieth Century Sociology, op. cit.*

54. H. Becker and A. Boskoff (eds.),*Modern Sociological Theory in Continuity and Change, op. cit.*

55. R. K. Merton, L. Broom, et al. (eds.), *Sociology Today, op. cit.*

56. S. J. Groenman et al. (eds.), *Het Sociale Leven in al Zijn Facetten* (Assen: Van Gorcum, 1958); G. Gurvitch (ed.), *Traité de Sociologie* (Paris: Presses Universitaires de France, 1958–1960), 2 vols.; R. König (ed.), *Soziologie op. cit.;* R. König (ed.), *Das Interview:*

Formen, Technik Answerlung, op. cit.; R. König (ed.), *Beobachtung und Experiment in der Sozialforschung, op. cit.;* R. König (ed.), *Handbuch der Empirischen Sozialforschung, op. cit.* For attempts at codification in England, see, for example, T. R. Fyvel (ed.), *The Frontiers of Sociology* (London: Cohen & West, 1964).

57. See for example the following readers, all published by the Free Press: R. Bendix and S. M. Lipset (eds.), *Class, Status, Power, op. cit.,* 1953 and 1966 editions; P. F. Lazarsfeld and M. Rosenberg (eds.), *The Language of Social Research, op. cit.:* R. K. Merton et al, (eds.), *Reader in Bureaucracy* (Glencoe, Ill.: Free Press, 1952); B. Berelson and M. Janowitz (eds.), *Reader in Public Opinion and Communication* (Glencoe, Ill.: Free Press, 1950; 2nd ed., 1966); E. G. Jaco (ed.), *Patients, Physicians and Illness* (Glencoe, Ill.: Free Press, 1958); W. J. Cahnman (ed.), *Sociology and History* (New York: Free Press, 1964); A. Halsey, J. Floud and C. A. Anderson, *Education, Economy and Society* (New York: Free Press, 1961); Paul K. Hatt and A. J. Reiss (eds.), *Reader in Urban Sociology* (Glencoe, Ill.: Free Press, 1957); B. H. Stoodley, (ed.), *Society and Self* (New York: Free Press, 1962); H. D. Stein and R. A. Cloward (eds.), *Social Perspectives on Behavior* (Glencoe, Ill.: Free Press, 1958); S. N. Eisenstadt, *Comparative Social Problems* (N.Y.: Free Press, 1964); B. Rosenberg and M. White (eds.), *Mass Culture* (Glencoe, Ill.: Free Press, 1960); N. W. Bell and E. F. Vogel (eds.), *A Modern Introduction to the Family,* (Glencoe, Ill.: Free Press, 1960); H. Eckstein and David E. Apter (eds.), *Comparative Politics* (New York: Free Press, 1963).

For similar types of readers, see also, for example, D. Katz, D. Cartwright, et al. (eds.), *Public Opinion and Propaganda* (New York: Dryden Press, 1954); W. Schramm (ed.), *Mass Communication* (Urbana, Ill.: University of Illinois Press, 1949); and also, of course, the various editions of E. E. Maccoby, T. M. Newcomb, and E. L. Hartley (eds.), *Readings in Social Psychology* (New York: Holt, starting in 1947).

58. For a good illustration of this trend see, for example, the works edited by J. A. Jackson and published by the Cambridge University Press; until now the following have been published: *On Social Stratification* (1968); *On Migration* (1969); *On Professions and Professionalization* (1970); *On Role* (1972).

59. For good illustrations of this trend, see, for example, R. Christie and M. Jahoda (eds.), *Studies in the Scope and Method of "The Authoritarian Personality,"* (Glencoe, Ill.: Free Press, 1954); R. K. Merton and P. F. Lazarsfeld (eds.), *Studies in the Scope and Method of "The American Soldier,"* (Glencoe, Ill.: Free Press, 1956); and the various readers mentioned in note 57.

60. P. A. Sorokin, *Contemporary Sociological Theories* (New York: Harper & Row, 1928); T. Parsons, E. Shils, et al. (eds.), *Theories of Society* (New York: Free Press, 1961), 2 vols.; R. Aron, *Main Currents in Sociological Thought* (London: Penguin, 1968, 1970), 2 vols.

61. R. K. Merton, *The Sociology of Science* (Chicago: University of Chicago Press, 1973); and J. Ben-David's review in *The New York Times Book Review,* November 11, 1973.

62. The congresses were held at the following times and places: the first congress, in Zürich, 1949; the second, in Liège, 1953; the third, in Amsterdam, 1956; the fourth, in Milan and Stressa, 1959; the fifth, in Washington, 1962; the sixth, in Evian-les-Bains, 1966; the seventh, in Varna, 1970; the eighth, in Toronto, 1974.

The proceedings of each meeting are published under the title *Transactions of the World Congress of Sociology* by the International Sociological Association.

7

The Emergence of the Structural-Functional Model as the Focus of Theoretical Discussion

Analytic Characteristics of the Structural-Functional Model

1. These gradual processes of intellectual and institutional development began in the 1940s, feeding on the great success of sociology during World War II, especially in America, where many European refugees —men like Paul Lazarsfeld, Hans Speier, Herbert Marcuse, Theodor Adorno, and Max Horkheimer—had participated in its development.[1] These processes, and the growing demand for teaching and services in sociology, gathered momentum in the 1950s and 1960s.

From virtually the first stages of this expansion, the structural-functional model—or the model of functional analysis, as represented in the works of Talcott Parsons, Robert K. Merton, Edward Shils, Kingsley Davis and others, became predominant in sociological theory.[2] This model, however, was not, as has often been claimed, the only reigning paradigm; rather it was the major focus of theoretical concerns and controversies within the sociological community, and it continued to serve as such a focus until the development of the most recent controversies.[3]

One cannot present here a detailed exposition of the functional-structural school and its varied development in the work of the above-mentioned scholars and many others. For the purposes of our analysis it is sufficient to present a summary statement of its basic tenets. Such a summary, as given recently by Bob Jessop, conveys the general perception of its premises in the sociological community.

Every social system is confronted with four functional problems. These problems are those of pattern maintenance, integration, goal attainment, and adaptation. Pattern maintenance refers to the need to maintain and reinforce the basic values of the social system and to resolve tensions that emerge from continuing commitment to these values. Integration refers to the allocation of rights and obligations, rewards and facilities, to ensure the harmony of relations between members of the social system. Goal attainment involves the necessity of mobilizing actors and resources in organised ways for the attainment of specific goals. And adaptation refers to the need for the production or acquisition of generalised facilities or resources that can be employed in the attainment of various specific goals. Social systems tend to differentiate about these problems so as to increase the functional capabilities of the system. Such differentiation—whether through the tem-·poral specialisation of a structurally undifferentiated unit or through the emergence of two or more structurally distinct units from one undifferen-tiated unit—is held to constitute a major verification of the fourfold func-tionalist schema. It also provides the framework within which are examined the plural interchanges that occur between structurally differentiated units to provide them with the inputs they require in the performance of their functions and to enable them to dispose of the outputs they produce.

Social order depends on the continuing fulfilment of the four functional problems and also on the maintenance of balanced relations between the social system, the other systems of action, and the physical environment. Failure to meet these requirements will lead to disturbances in the operation of social institutions and in the absence of successful resolution of these disturbances so as to ensure continuing conformity to institutionalised role expectations, to social change. Social change is always change in the norma-tive culture of the social system and can vary in degree from structural differentiation within an otherwise stable system to the dissolution of the system as such or its complete change through charismatic innovation. The extent of these disturbances and the degree of social change are contingent on a wide variety of factors and are to a considerable degree theoretically indeterminate.[4]

While a full analysis of the reasons for this model's predominance and effect would be premature, some indications may be suggested here. It is first necessary to stress, however—and this is also important for understanding the model's predominance, that despite many claims to the contrary, especially by opponents, the structural-functional school was neither uniform nor unchanging.

Parsons' own work evinced several significant changes of emphasis, from the voluntaristic emphasis in *The Structure of Social Action*, through the more systematic-classificatory and systemic emphasis in *Toward a General Theory of Action* and *The Social System* in the early 1950s, up to his more recent macrosocietal concerns with their heavy neoevolutionary emphasis and increasing interest in the analysis of the generalized media of exchange.[5] Throughout all these phases, Parsons also made extensive efforts to apply his general approaches to various concrete fields—family, kinship, stratification, education, and political sociology—with a strong cross-cutting interest in the analysis of modern societies, particularly American society.[6]

Second, different emphases developed within this broad model, notably the macrosociological and general theoretical interests associated with Parsons, and the middle-range or concrete, historical, institutional concerns associated with the names of Merton, Davis, Robin Williams, Jr., the earlier Marion J. Levy, Neil Smelser, Robert N. Bellah, and many others.[7] Within this school, many internal controversies, disputes and "openings" also emerged, which will be discussed in detail below.

The sustained development and internal heterogeneity of the structural-functional school have doubltless contributed to its centrality in theoretical controversy in sociology. But its predominance is due even more to certain inherent intellectual characteristics of this model, and to the implications of this model for sociological research and the organization of sociological work as it had developed at this stage.

Open-System Elements and Internal Closures in the
Structural-Functional Model

2.   On the analytic level, the strength of this approach lay in its development of a new and powerful explicative paradigm of society. This was the first explicative model, with the exception of the not-too-successful attempts of Mannheim and others in the 1930s,[8] that had been formulated since the work of the Founding Fathers. As such, it had great potential for synthesizing many aspects of sociological analysis and research within a common framework.

This model was very much in the tradition of the great sociological theories, consciously orienting itself to them and continually developing them. In his early *Structure of Social Action,* Parsons pointed out the possible philosophical and methodological convergences of the major traditions of sociological thought, especially those of Weber and Durkheim, and attempted to establish a unified framework of sociological analysis, rooted in these past traditions, but going beyond them. On the analytic level, this framework was closely related to the almost sole sociological paradigm to emerge from the debris of classical evolutionism, the British functional school of social anthropology associated with the names of A. R. Radcliffe-Brown and Bronislaw Malinowski.[9]

The suggestiveness of the structural-functional approach for theoretical and empirical extension was implicit in its conceptual apparatus. First, it developed and applied many classifications of social action and organization and of cultural symbols—for example, the pattern variables, the functional prerequisites, and the components of the system of action, in terms of which social and cultural systems were classified. Moreover, not only were these classifications systematically articulated; they were set into broad analytic frameworks with specific theoretical orientations and research derivations. For example, such classifying concepts as "pattern variables" and "social differentiation" were redefined in reference to the overall characteristics and functioning of social structure and personality, above all in reference to the mechanisms by which these systems worked.[10] In this way, the structural-functional model provided an analytic map of the components of social action and of social systems, analyzing each component in depth. It also based itself on developments in psychology, cultural anthropology, and system theory which it attempted to develop further.

Like the classic paradigmatic models, structural-functionalism combined a certain vision of the nature of society with the formulation of an analytic conception of social order. In principle, moreover, it also exhibited some major characteristics of open-system models.

It addressed itself explicitly to the problem of social order in terms of the basic sociological *Problemstellung.* That is, how could order be attained in social life, given both the multiplicity of goals, and the interdependence, of individuals; and how did the organization of such order—what sociological analysis now calls the institutional framework—deal with these two basic problems of social life?[11]

In principle, in answering these questions, the structural-functional model featured some of the main characteristics of open-system models analyzed above.[12] Specifically: It recognized all elements, or constituents, of social order as continuous and yet variable components of each other. It distinguished forcefully between these components as concrete entities and as analytic constructs. It attempted to formulate the interrelationships among the components of social order, and among the bases of its acceptance, in terms of systemic interdependence—that is, in such a way that each element, while seen as analytically separable, hence independent to some degree, was also a basic systemic component or referent of the other elements. It also emphasized the analysis of the internal systemic dynamics, interrelationships, and constant feedback among these components as the critical focus of sociological analysis.

Thus, although it certainly used a strong societal starting point, it included, from the beginning, major openings to the other starting points, particularly the individual and cultural. Parsons' own works attest to this openness. Not only in his earlier works, like *The Structure of Social Action,* were voluntaristic aspects heavily emphasized. In the later studies, too, one finds, despite the heavy societal systemic emphasis, assumptions about the structural autonomy and distinctions of the components and subsystems of social action—personality, society, and culture, as well as continuing efforts to articulate the mechanisms of their interrelationships.[13] Moreover, even the heavy systemic emphasis was conceived largely in terms, however vague or imprecise, of specifying the mechanisms through which broader systemic properties of social action in general, and of social systems in particular, were maintained and related to specific institutions, organizations, and patterns of individual behavior.[14] Last, the emphasis on values, as against power and economic inducements, as bases for acceptance of the social order, was seen in terms of cybernetic mechanisms of regulation of social action, rather than in terms of an absolute metaphysical "priority" of one aspect over the others.

In other words, values were not seen as separate metaphysical entities out of which social organization and patterns of individual behavior emanated, but as that element, or aspect, of human action around which the mechanisms regulating social activity tended to focus.

Moreover, this paradigm distinguished forcefully between individuals, societies, and cultural orders as concrete entities and as analytic constructs. The clarity and consistency of this distinction enabled Parsons and his students to explore, in a way that other contemporary open-system schemes like Sorokin's could not, the mechanisms that linked the major aspects or components of systems of action: personality, social system, and culture.[15] They achieved this, above all, because they could start from the general analysis of the basic orientation of social actors, defined in terms of pattern variables, moving to the analysis of roles, role-sets, and status-sets; then to social systems and their exigencies; up to the analysis of generalized media of exchange and the relationships among institutional spheres.[16]

Nevertheless, the structural-functional model was perceived as a closed-system paradigm in the sociological community, and not without justification. In its strong systemic emphasis, its societal starting point, and its tendency to stress the integrative function of values, it resembled closed-system models.[17] Yet, while structural-functionalism, like British functional anthropology, displayed "preferences" for particular bases or components of social order (e.g., cultural values), whatever closure it exhibited was not of the semimetaphysical type that had characterized the earlier closed systems. It derived, rather, from the assumption of relatively fixed relationships between the components of the paradigm —such as values, norms, institutions, and the like, and of the possible cybernetic centrality of one component, values or culture.

The Structural-Functional Model: Macrosocietal Analysis and Middle-Range Theories

3. Like many classic open-system approaches, and those of Sorokin and Mannheim,[18] the structural-functional approach was very much oriented to macrosociological study or a macrosociological approach. Much more than the others, however, it was receptive to developments in new fields and methods of research, and its proponents consistently attempted to specify its analytic research implications.

The various reasons for the great influence of the structural-functional model have been summarized in a critical assessment by Martin Landau, in which he indicates that the major value of this approach was in performing the "heuristic function of directing us toward theoretically fruitful fields of inquiry." Landau states:

> Items of the 'theory' embedded in it . . . can be taken as interesting hypotheses. These may be recast in the form of middle-range partial-system interrogatories, depending upon how we choose to use them in inquiry. . . . Parson's work constitutes something analogous to a unified field theory in social science. . . . It reflects a 'systems' view, and hence such attendant hypotheses as self-regulation and functional interdependence. . . . The postulate of functional requisites may lead us to ask, and perhaps help us discover, what does actually appear to be necessary to a system, or a subsystem, or a class of them. It can lead to questions about what apparently 'must be maintained', and how and by what types of institutions (structures) this is done.

Landau also points out that with all its deficiencies, "the essential premises of this model offer some working rules of inquiry," and that "it is also in one very limited sense at least possible to partially 'test' some of the fruits of this theory—i.e., to essay and assess its use as an ordering and explaining mechanism for studies that are empirically grounded."[19]

These analytic and research potentialities of the structural-functional model were enhanced through its restructuring of certain concepts which were already widely accepted in sociology. Many concepts like role, status, and institutions, which had been used before in sociological and anthropological research largely in a classificatory or descriptive way, underwent far-reaching analytic transformations from their earlier usage. These concepts became starting points for the specification of mechanisms through which various systems of action and microsociological settings were related to each other and to broader macrosocietal settings.[20]

In the work of sociologists like Merton, many of these concepts, such as role and status, became powerful tools for the analysis of the mechanisms which combined patterns of behavior and micro- and macrosocietal settings. The operation of these mechanisms was often explained in terms of restricted analytic middle-range theories, like that of relative deprivation.[21]

Another conceptual and analytic transformation was effected by Shils and others with respect to the concept of the primary group. This concept, which had had a rather narrow classificatory meaning in earlier studies, was now related to one basic element, the primordial element of social action, thus transforming the scope and intensity of the primary relationship into one basic, yet variable, element of the mechanism through which social cohesion was maintained. Similarly, concepts like prestige, power, solidarity, and instrumental relationships, derived from the tradition of "formal sociology," became in a sense "dynamized" and "generalized" as they were redefined as the major types of resources, rewards, and media of exchange in institutional life. Thus they attained broad explanatory use and power, applicable both to macrosocietal, general systemic analysis, and to analysis of interpersonal and other types of "micro" situations.[22]

Thus the adherents of this model, by virtue of combining the analytic transformation of concepts with broad, albeit vague, conceptions of the working of the social system, provided both an important framework for a macrosocietal approach and, perhaps paradoxically, some of the most important analytic starting points and concepts around which middle-range theories of different levels could converge.

To give just a few illustrations: From the late 1940s and early 1950s on, the possibilities of this model for dealing with middle-range problems were illustrated in Parsons' essays on different institutional aspects of modern societies and in Merton's works, which were more consciously oriented to the codification of middle-range theories. In the same period, Davis developed an entire series of middle-range hypotheses about institutional aspects of family, kinship, and youth structures, especially in modern structures. Levy applied some aspects of the structural-functional approach to the analysis of the Chinese family and its response to modernization, and to a more general comparative analysis of the modernization of China and Japan, while Williams applied a variation of the approach to the analysis of American society, combining functional analysis with analysis of change.[23]

Later, the impact of the broad structural-functional paradigm and its analytic concepts and orientations impinged on many areas of research. Hardly an area of research remained unaffected by these developments. In almost all fields of sociology, the structural-functional approach not only provided a general view, image, or map of the social system, but gave hints about more analytic specifications that could become foci of research. In such areas of research as stratification, political organization, educational sociology, and the study of deviance, many specific paradigms and research programs were related to or derived from the structural-functional framework.[24] In other substantive fields, as in studies of public opinion and voting behavior, which had developed strong concentrations on middle-range theories, not only were the concepts those that had been developed in the structural-functional model. This model also provided the basis for a broader analytic orientation.[25]

The influence of this model spread also to other disciplines. In political science, mainly through the works of Gabriel Almond and David Easton, it shaped, among other areas, the emerging fields of economic development and modernization as these researches became important.[26]

These influences of the structural-functional model do not imply that the specific theories, assumptions, or concrete elaboration of specific or general problems by Parsons or his students were well formulated or that they were validated by research. Nor do they necessarily invalidate the frequent criticism that the theories were conceptually and analytically vague, and that the relationship between concrete theories and the broader analytic orientations of the model was often very tenuous.[27] It should not be forgotten, however, that many of these criticisms were made in the context of a higher level of intellectual aspiration produced by the very development of this model.

This model also proved to be a very convenient framework for incorporating various closed- and open-system approaches that were directly or indirectly relevant to the structural-functional orientation. One of the most interesting was the attempt by Parsons and some of his followers to incorporate psychoanalytic assumptions into their schemes.[28] Later, we will see additional openings of this kind. In principle, the model was open to analytic developments in the various social sciences.

This openness of the structural-functional model also helped change the relationship of sociology to other social science disciplines, as the examples above indicate, in the direction of a search for common problems and common analytic frameworks, while the concerns about the proper subject matter and boundaries of sociology as a single delimited discipline became less central.

The Structural-Functional Model and the Institutional and Intellectual Development of Sociology in the Postwar Period

4.   The intellectual potential of the model was reinforced by the widespread institutionalization of sociological activity that characterized that period. Above all it was reinforced by anchorage in an expanding academic system and by the unification and codification of research which developed through the academic activities of sociologists.[29]

In the United States, this model emerged at a time of dissolution of older paradigms (like that of the Chicago School) and of reorientation to broader explicative models and macrosocietal analysis.[30] The structural-functional model thus met a number of emerging needs in the sociological community, in several ways. First, it provided continuity with former "master theories" and paradigms of social order. Second, it served as a focus for bringing together various areas of investigation into common analytic frameworks. Third, it revived the macrosociological orientation by opening up its problems to empirical research through the provision of broad orientating frameworks and—despite the claims of critics—powerful explanatory concepts which covered a wide range of fields and areas of social life.

Institutionally, the attraction of the structural-functional model was enhanced by the prestige of Harvard University, and by the great impact of the first generation of Parsons' students. These younger scholars, placed in the centers of American academic life, also greatly influenced the development of sociology in this time of expansion. Institutionally also, the close personal relationships and occasional collaboration between Parsons and Samuel Stouffer, between Merton and Lazarsfeld, and many others reflected the potential of alliance between structural-functional theory and research.[31]

Given the combination of these characteristics, influences, and circumstances, a unique situation appeared on the sociological scene in connection with this model. For the first time, both the intellectual and the institutional conditions existed that were necessary for the realization of the potential inherent in open-system approaches, and for the development of sustained, self-correcting, scholarly endeavor focused on cumulative development of the basic sociological problematics. The developing institutional frameworks permitted the formation of a relatively autonomous academic and professional sociological community, enabling sociologists to prove their commitment both to the pursuit of their discipline and to broad civic interests while freeing their work from direct political pressures or commitments.

Out of the combination of internal analytic and institutional tendencies and a receptive external intellectual climate, an image of sociology and of the structural-functional school emerged which became, from the 1950s on, the butt of major criticisms—such as those of C. Wright Mills and the Frankfurt school.[32] Related to this image was what Alvin Gouldner calls a prevailing "classicist" orientation: an orientation based on a doctrine of human nature which tended to emphasize the situation-transcending potency of human reason, reinforced, in Robert Friedrichs' terms, by a "priestly" as against a "prophetic" mode, and a weakening of the critical stance.[33] All these gave rise to the often exaggerated image of sociology's conservatism.

Yet in spite of the strong institutional standing of the structural-functional model, the structural-functional school did not become *the* predominant paradigm or model in the sociological community. In the United States, several other theoretical traditions attained prominence in the earlier 1920s: the interactionist perspective stemming from George Herbert Mead and Charles Cooley, and later developed by Arnold Rose; the ecological, as represented both in the Chicago school and later by the more formal demographic-ecological analysis of Amos Hawley in sociology and Julian Steward in anthropology; and the implicit behaviorist model developed by George Lundberg and others.[34] Some of these trends persisted later on.

In Europe, the structural-functional school was never fully accepted, though it had some influence indirectly through the great impact of the emerging American academic tradition on European studies. In many countries the model was viewed negatively, as the epitome of American sociology, and by the late 1950s and early 1960s there arose, from within European sociology, a cry against its ahistorical tendencies. The Frankfurt school had doomed it even earlier as part of "positivistic" noncritical sociology.[35]

Yet however widespread this dissent, there was for a long period of time no other broad sociological paradigm that could compete with it in terms of the specific analytic contributions it had made. None of the other approaches or models could satisfy in the same way the new intellectual interest of the sociological community: to relate different areas of research to a common framework, major traditions of sociological thought, and the reemerging macrosociological concerns. With the partial exception of the Frankfurt school, the major theoretical trends in Europe were either purely philosophic and speculative or, as in the work of Raymond Aron, concerned at first largely with the analysis of concrete institutional problems of modern society,[36] with only tenuous relations to either the emerging areas of research or to broader frameworks.

The only paradigmatic scheme developed in Europe in this period was, as we have seen in Chapter 6, the modified positivist model in Scandinavia, elaborated principally in Sweden under the influence of Lundberg.[37] At first, however, it lacked many of the broader theoretic orientations. Only much later was such an orientation developed within it as part of the confrontation with the structural functional model. The only sociological tradition which had maintained these macrosociological concerns after the breakdown of the great evolutionary schools—that is, the Marxist tradition—continued to be stagnant, even petrified, in this period. Positivist orientations had not yet recovered from that early breakdown, except for the very strong stimulus-response school in psychology, which as early as the late 1930s had exerted some influence on sociological research.[38] Its potential influence was obviously limited, however, in the light of sociological interest in broader system and macrosocietal issues.

This lack of alternatives did not mean that the various schools accepted structural-functionalism or that they lost their own momentum. Almost invariably, however, insofar as these models produced new theoretical or analytic orientations, and above all confrontations with more systematic research, they tended often to contend with the structural-functional model, and it was out of such confrontations that the most fruitful developments emerged.

Notes

1. The impact of the European refugees on the development of American sociology is discussed by M. Jay, *The Dialectical Imagination: a History of the Frankfurt School and the Institute of Social Research, 1923–1950* (Boston: Little, Brown, 1973), especially Ch. 6, 7. See also the fascinating autobiographical survey by Paul F. Lazarsfeld, "An episode in the history of social research: a memoir," in D. Fleming and Bernard Bailyn (eds.), *The Intellectual Migration, Europe and America, 1930–60* (Cambridge, Mass.: Harvard University Press, Belknap Press, 1969), pp. 270–338; and T. W. Adorno, "Scientific experiences of an European scholar in America," *ibid.*, pp. 338–371.

2. T. Parsons and E. Shils (eds.), *Toward a General Theory of Action* (Cambridge, Mass.: Harvard University Press, 1951); T. Parsons, *The Social System* (New York: Free Press, [1951], 1964); T. Parsons and N. J. Smelser, *Economy and Society* (New York: Free Press [1956], 1965); R. K. Merton, *Social Theory and Social Structure*, rev. ed. (New York: Free Press of Glencoe, 1963); K. Davis and W. E. Moore, "Some principles of stratification," *American Sociological Review*, Vol. 10 (April 1945), pp. 242–247; K. Davis, *Human Society*, (New York: Macmillan, 1949).

3. The influence of the structural-functional school and the controversies about it are discussed in greater detail in the next chapters.

4. B. Jessop *Social Order, Reform, and Revolution* (London: Macmillan, 1972), pp. 16–18. By permission of Macmillan London and Basingstoke.

5. The major stages of Parsons' work are best illustrated in the following order:

   The first stage: T. Parsons, *The Structure of Social Action* (Glencoe, Ill.: Free Press, 1949), 2 vols.

   The second stage: T. Parsons and E. Shils (eds.), *Toward a General Theory of Action, op. cit.*; T. Parsons, *The Social System, op. cit.*

   Parsons' macrosocietal neoevolutionary emphasis is developed in T. Parsons, *Societies: Evolutionary and Comparative Perspectives* (Englewood Cliffs, N. J.: Prentice-Hall, 1966).

   Parsons' analysis of generalized media of exchange is developed in T. Parsons, "On the concept of political power," in R. Bendix and S. M. Lipset (eds.), *Class, Status, and Power* (London: Routledge & Kegan Paul, 1967) pp. 240–265; T. Parsons, "On the concept of influence," *Public Opinion Quarterly*, Vol. 27 (spring 1963), pp. 37–62. One of the latest expositions is found in T. Parsons and G. M. Platt, *The American University* (Cambridge, Mass.: Harvard University Press, 1975), especially the Technical Appendix, pp. 425–451.

   One of the most valuable summaries and analyses of Parsons' work and its place in American sociology is to be found in G. Rocher, *Talcott Parsons and American Sociology* (London: Nelson, 1974), with an introduction by Stephan Mennell; its appendices include a useful bibliography of Parsons' writings as well as selected books and articles about him.

   A useful short survey of the development of Parsons' work can be found in N. C. Mullins and C. J. Mullins, *Theories and Theory Group in Contemporary American Sociology* (New York: Harper & Row, 1973), pp. 53–59.

6. These aspects of Parsons' work are illustrated in T. Parsons, *Essays in Sociological Theory* rev. ed. (New York: Free Press [1949], 1963).

7. These different emphases are analyzed in greater detail in the following discussion.

8. These earlier developments have been discussed in Ch. 5.

9. On this model see, among others, A. R. Radcliffe-Brown, *Structure and Function in Primitive Society* (London: Cohen and West, 1952); A. R. Radcliffe-Brown and D. Forde (eds.), *African Systems of Kinship and Marriage* (London: Oxford University Press, 1950); B. Malinowski, "Culture," in *Encyclopedia of the Social Sciences*, Vol. 4 (New York: Macmillan, 1931), pp. 621–645; E. E. Evans-Pritchard, *The Nuer* (Oxford: Clarendon Press, 1940); E. E. Evans-Pritchard, *Social Anthropology* (London: Cohen and West, 1951); E. E. Evans-Pritchard (ed.), *Institutions of Primitive Society* (Oxford: Basil Blackwell, 1954);M. Fortes, *The Dynamics of Kinship among the Tallensi* (London: Oxford University Press, 1945); M. Fortes and E. E. Evans-Pritchard (eds.), *African Political Systems* (London: Oxford University Press, 1940).

    For a general exposition see: A. Kuper,*Anthropologists and Anthropology, 1922–1972* (London: Allan Lane, 1972) Ch. 2–6.

10. On the concept of "pattern variables," see T. Parsons and E. Shils, (eds.), *Toward a General Theory of Action, op. cit.,* pp. 52–233; see also the review of G. Swanson, "The approach to a general theory of action by Parsons and Shils," *American Sociological Review,* Vol. 18 (1953), pp. 125–134.

    On the concept of "social differentiation" and its application, see T. Parsons, *Societies: Evolutionary and Comparative Perspectives, op. cit.,* (pp. 22–25 for definition of the concept); T. Parsons, "Some considerations on the theory of social change," *Rural Sociology* Vol. 26 (September 1961), pp. 219–239.

11. This is the statement of the problems given in J. Alexander, *The Logic of Paradigm Conflict in Sociological Theory,* unpublished doctoral dissertation, University of California, Berkeley, 1974; to be published by the University of California Press.

12. The analytic characteristics of the open-system models have been detailed in Ch. 4.

13. T. Parsons and E. Shils (eds.), *Toward a General Theory of Action, op. cit.,* pp. 52–233.

14. On this see, for example, T. Parsons, *The Social System, op. cit.;* T. Parsons and N. J. Smelser, *Economy and Society, op. cit.*

15. Among Sorokin's works see P. A. Sorokin, *Social and Cultural Dynamics,* (New York: American Book 1937–1941), 4 vols., and the one volume edition published in 1957 in Boston by Porter Sargent; P. A. Sorokin, *Society, Culture and Personality,* (New York: Harper & Row, 1947).

    Compare these with T. Parsons and E. Shils (eds.), *Toward a General Theory of Action, op. cit.;* T. Parsons,*The Social System, op. cit.;* T. Parsons, "A revised analytical approach to the theory of social stratification," in*Essays in Sociological Theory, op. cit.,* pp. 386–439.

16. On these aspects of structural-functional analysis see T. Parsons and E. Shils (eds.), *Toward a General Theory of Action, op. cit.;* T. Parsons and N. J. Smelser, *Economy and Society, op. cit.;* R. K. Merton, *Social Theory and Social Structure, op. cit.,* especially pp. 368–384; T. Parsons, "On the concept of political power," *op. cit.*

17. Many of the criticisms of the structural-functional model are discussed in greater detail in Ch. 8. A useful collection of such criticisms can be found in N. J. Demerath III and Richard A. Peterson (eds.), *System, Change and Conflict* (New York: Free Press, 1967).

18. On classic open-system approaches see Ch. 4; see also P. A. Sorokin, *Social and Cultural Dynamics, op. cit;* P. A. Sorokin, *Society, Culture, and Personality, op. cit;* K. Mannheim, *Man and Society in an Age of Reconstruction* (London: Kegan Paul, Trench, Trubner, 1940).

19. Statements taken from Martin Landau, "The use of functional analysis in American political science," *Social Research,* Vol. 35 (Spring 1968), pp. 48–75 *passim.*

20. For illustrations of the early uses of concepts like "role," "institutions," and the like, see, for example, the items quoted in note 9 of this chapter.

    For the contribution of the structural-functional model see T. Parsons and E. Shils (eds.), *Toward a General Theory of Action, op. cit.;* T. Parsons and N. J. Smelser, *Economy and Society, op. cit.;* K. Davis, *Human Society, op. cit.;* N. Gross, W. Mason and A. McEachern, *Explorations in Role Analysis* (New York: J. Wiley, 1958); S. A. Stouffer and J. Toby, "Role conflict and personality," *American Journal of Sociology,* Vol. 56, No. 5 (1951), pp. 395–406; B. J. Biddle and E. J. Thomas (eds.), *Role Theory* (New York: Wiley, 1966).

21. R. K. Merton, *Social Theory and Social Structure, op. cit.,* especially Ch. 8 and 9.

22. On earlier approaches, especially the tradition of "formal sociology," see details in Ch. 2, 4, and 5.

    On Shils' analysis and contribution on the primordial element in social action see E. Shils, "Primordial, personal, sacred, and civic ties," *British Journal of Sociology,* Vol. 8 (June 1957), pp. 37–52.

    On the "dynamization and generalization" of the concepts of power, prestige, and the like, see for example T. Parsons, "A revised analytical approach to the theory of social stratification," *op. cit.;* T. Parsons, "On the concept of political power," *op. cit.;* T. Parsons, "On the concept of influence," *op. cit.;* T. Parsons and N. J. Smelser, *Economy and Society, op. cit.;* T. Parsons and G. Platt, *The American University, op. cit.*

23. T. Parsons, *Essays in Sociological Theory, op. cit.,* especially Ch. 2, 3, 5–9, 12–14, 19; T. Parsons, *Structure and Process in Modern Societies* (Glencoe, Ill.: Free Press, 1960).

    For some of the most important of Merton's middle-range theories, and his attempts at their codification, see R. K. Merton, *Social Theory and Social Structure, op. cit.;* R. K. Merton, et al (eds.), *Sociology Today* (New York: Basic Books, 1959); K. Davis, et al., *Modern American Society: Readings in the Problems of Order and Change* (New York: Rinehart, 1949), the various papers of Davis collected in Part 9; M. J. Levy, *The Family Revolution in Modern China* (Cambridge, Mass.: Harvard University Press, 1949); M. J. Levy, "Contrasting factors in the modernization of China and Japan," in S. Kuznets, et al. (eds.), *Economic Growth: Brazil, India, Japan* (Durham, N.C.: Duke University Press, 1955), pp. 496–536; R. M. Williams, *American Society: a Sociological Interpretation,* 2nd ed. (New York: Knopf, 1960).

24. On the influence of the structural-functional approach on studies of stratification, see T. Parsons, "A revised analytical approach to the theory of social stratification," *op. cit.;* K. Davis and W. E. Moore, "Some principles of stratification," *op. cit.,* and also the analytical and research controversies provoked by the functional theory of stratification, the most outstanding of which are collected in R. Bendix and S. M. Lipset (eds.), *Class, Status and Power, op. cit.,* pp. 47–72.

    For a concise review of analytic approaches to political science which are based on or related to the functional-structural model, see: M. Landau, "The use of functional analysis in American political science," *Social Research,* Vol. 35 (1968), pp. 48–75; G. Bergeron, "Structure des fonctionnalismes en science politique," *Canadian Journal of Political Science,* Vol. 3, No. 2 (June 1970), pp. 205–240.

    On educational sociology, see the review of the functional approach and some of its criticism in M. A. Coulson, "Role: a redundant concept in sociology? some educational considerations," in J. A. Jackson (ed.), *Role* (Cambridge: Cambridge University Press, 1972), pp. 107–128.

On deviance, see T. Parsons, *The Social System, op. cit.*, especially Ch. 7; R. K. Merton, *Social Theory and Social Structure, op. cit.*, Ch. 4 and 5; M. B. Clinard, "The theoretical implications of anomie and deviant behavior," in M. B. Clinard (ed.), *Anomie and Deviant Behavior* (New York: Free Press, 1964), pp. 1–56.

25. On this see, for example, R. K. Merton et al., *Mass Persuasion* (New York: Harper, 1946); R. K. Merton, *Social Theory and Social Structure, op. cit.*, Part 3; S. N. Eisenstadt, "Communications and reference group behavior," in S. N. Eisenstadt, *Essays on Comparative Institutions* (New York: Wiley, 1965), pp. 309–343.

26. G. A. Almond, "A functional approach to comparative politics," in G. A. Almond and J. S. Coleman (eds.), *The Politics of Developing Areas*, (Princeton, N.J.: Princeton University Press, 1960); D. Easton, *A Systems Analysis of Political Life* (New York: Wiley, 1965).
    For some critical appraisals see Chong-Do Hah and J. Schneider, "A critique of current studies of political development and modernization," *Social Research*, Vol. 35 (1968), pp. 130–158; S. N. Eisenstadt, *Tradition, Change and Modernity* (New York: Wiley, 1973), Ch. 1 and 5.

27. On this see, for example, R. M. Williams, "The sociological theory of Talcott Parsons," and M. Black, "Some questions about Parsons' theories," in M. Black (ed.), *The Social Theories of Talcott Parsons*, (Englewood Cliffs, N.J.: Prentice-Hall, 1964), pp. 64–99, 268–288; and the earlier review by G. E. Swanson, "The approach to a general theory of action by Parsons and Shils," *op. cit.*

28. Most of Parsons' major works which integrate psychoanalytical contributions are in T. Parsons, *Social Structure and Personality* (New York: Free Press, 1964).
    For good analyses of this aspect of Parsons' work, as well as critical evaluation, see A. L. Baldwin, "The Parsonian theory of personality," and U. Bronfenbrenner, "Parsons' theory of identification," in M. Black (ed.), *The Social Theories of Talcott Parsons, op. cit.*, pp. 153–190, 191–213; D. Wrong, "The oversocialized conception of man in modern sociology," *American Sociological Review*, Vol. 26 (1961), pp. 183–193; for a later formulation of this problem see F. Weinstein and G. M. Platt, *Psychoanalytical Sociology* (Baltimore, Md.: Johns Hopkins University Press, 1973); and R. S Wallenstein and N. J. Smelser, "Psychoanalysis and sociology: articulation and applications," *International Journal of Psychoanalysis*, Vol. 50 (1969), pp. 694 ff.

29. On these aspects of the development of sociology see details in Ch. 6.

30. H. Kuklick, "A scientific revolution: sociological theory in the United States, 1930–1945," *Sociological Inquiry*, Vol. 43, No. 1 (1973), pp. 3–22.

31. See, on these problems, in greater detail, E. Shils, "Tradition, ecology, and institution in the history of sociology," *Daedalus*, Vol. 99, No. 4 (Fall 1970) pp. 794–796.

32. C. Wright Mills, *The Sociological Imagination* (New York: Oxford University Press, 1959), especially Ch. 2, 3, 4.
    The works of the members of the Frankfurt school which are critical of "traditional" sociological theory are too numerous to mention here. For good surveys see M. Jay, "Some recent developments in critical theory," *Berkeley Journal of Sociology*, Vol. 28 (1973–1974), pp. 27–44; D. Frisby, "The Frankfurt School: critical theory and positivism," in J. Rex (ed.), *Approaches to Sociology: an Introduction to Major Trends in British Sociology* (London: Routledge & Kegan Paul, 1974), pp. 205–229.

33. A. Gouldner, "Romanticism and Classicism—deep structures in social science," in A. Gouldner, *For Sociology* (London: Allan Lane, 1973), pp. 323–369; R. W. Friedrichs, *A Sociology of Sociology* (New York: Free Press, 1972), especially Ch. 3, 4, 5.

34. G. H. Mead, *Mind, Self and Society* (Chicago: University of Chicago Press, 1934); C. H.

Cooley, *Human Nature and the Social Order* (New York: Charles Scribner's Sons, 1902); C. H. Cooley, *Social Organization,* (New York: Charles Scribner's Sons, 1909); A. Rose, "A systematic summary of symbolic interaction theory," in A. Rose (ed.), *Human Behavior and Social Processes* (Boston, Mass: Houghton Mifflin, 1962), pp. 3–19.

On the ecological tradition of the Chicago school see R. E. L. Faris, *Chicago Sociology: 1920–1932* (San Francisco, Cal.: Chandler, 1967), especially Ch. 4, 5; A. H. Hawley, *Human Ecology: a Theory of Community Structure* (New York: Ronald Press, 1950); J. Steward, *Theory of Culture Change: the Methodology of Multilinear Evolution* (Urbana, Ill.: University of Illinois Press, 1955); G. Lundberg, *Foundations of Sociology* (New York: Macmillan, 1939); G. Lundberg, *Social Research, a Study in Methods of Gathering Data* (New York: Longmans, Green, 1942).

35. On the Frankfurt school's criticism of the structural-functional school see M. Jay, "Some recent developments in critical theory," *op. cit.;* D. Frisby, "The Frankfurt school: critical theory and positivism," *op. cit.*

For other European criticisms, especially those concerned with ahistorical tendencies, see R. Dahrendorf, "Out of Utopia: toward a reorientation of sociological analysis," *American Journal of Sociology,* Vol. 64 (1958), pp. 115–127; R. Aron, *Main Currents in Sociological Thought,* Vol. 2 (London: Penguin, 1970), pp. 250–252; R. Aron, "Modern society and sociology," in E. A. Tiryakian (ed.), *The Phenomenon of Sociology* (New York: Appleton-Century-Crofts, 1971), pp. 158–170.

36. On the theoretical contributions of the Frankfurt school see the quotations in note 35 and also M. Jay, *The Dialectical Imagination, op. cit.*

For illustrations of European theoretical approaches with a philosophical and speculative emphasis see, for example, the works of G. Gurvitch quoted in notes 33 and 56, of Ch. 6, and the works of A. Gehlen quoted in note 31 of Ch. 6.

The works of R. Aron concerned with the analysis of modern society are quoted in note 33 of Ch. 6.

37. On the positivist influence on Scandinavian sociology, see E. Allardt, "Scandinavian sociology and Swedish sociology," *International Journal of Sociology,* Vol. 3 (Fall-Winter 1973–1974), pp. 50–71.

38. J. Dollard and N. E. Miller, *Personality and Psychotherapy* (New York: McGraw-Hill, 1950); J. Dollard and N. E. Miller, et al., *Frustration and Aggression* (London: Kegan Paul, Trench, Trubner, 1944); J. Dollard and N. E. Miller, *Social Learning and Imitation* (London: Kegan Paul, Trench, Trubner, 1945).

8

The Major Analytic Controversies About the Structural-Functional Model;
the Main "CounterModels"

The Major "CounterModels" and Main Points of Criticism of the Structural-Functional Model

1.   Given the factors discussed in the preceding chapter, it is not surprising that the structural-functional model became, first, the center of renewed interest in sociological theory and, later, a focus for disputes and controversies about the nature and problems of sociological theory and the image of sociology. These discussions parallelled and later converged with debates about the functional model in social anthropology.

Beginning in the mid-1950s, these discussions tended to criticize the overall development of American sociology, which was often portrayed as combining a widespread positivist-empirical concern with research methodology and the predominance of the structural-functional model. An early expression of such criticism can be found in the writings of C. Wright Mills, who claimed that structural-functional theory, by stressing the centrality of values in attaining social consensus, had made social order and its legitimation unproblematic, that it disregarded conflict and social change and had removed the historical perspective from sociological analysis. Mills also claimed that because of the emphases on "scientism" (i.e. quantification) and the pressure to solve problems defined by those who financed research, research had become fragmented, untheoretical, and uncritical. Moreover, he claimed, that as a result of these pressures, empirical social research disregarded the analysis of substantive problems and the effect of social structure on the phenomena investigated. Finally, he charged that social science had shifted from its earlier reform-oriented critical liberalism to conservatism, and was helping those in the centers of power to further their interests and manipulate people.[1]

At the same time, Theodor Adorno and Max Horkheimer, and later, Jürgen Habermas and others, criticized functionalism in broader philosophical terms as being positivistic. They endorsed, by contrast, a critical, dialectic-hermeneutic approach.[2]

Criticisms of structural-functionalism opposed mainly its assumptions in critical areas of sociological theory: the vision of man and society it presumably implies; its paradigmatic model of social order; and its more concrete analytic paradigms, and research hypotheses.[3] Thus the most general criticism of this model produced alternative explanatory models, or "countermodels," of society whose basic assumptions differed from the supposed assumptions of functionalism.

Some of these were new models; others derived from older sociological traditions. The most important countermodels which were developed or sharpened in the controversy were:

1.   The "conflict" model vs. the "consensus" model, and the "power and conflict" model as against the "value-normative" one;

2.   The "individual-rational" model, often propounded in terms of some exchange model, vs. the systemic or functional one;

3.   The "group interest" model as against the "social system" or division of labor model;

4.   The "symbolic interactionist" model with its various derivations and individual meaning;

5.   The "symbolic-structuralist" (Claude Lévi-Strauss' model), which initially criticized the structural-functional model as applied to the British area of social anthropology, but later took up other problems in sociological analysis; and

6.   The "historical-systemic" model as against those emphasizing the general systemic qualities of societies, a type represented most fully, but not uniquely, in the various neo-Marxist models.[4]

Some of these countermodels, such as the interactionist, were directly related to some of the "secondary" streams and trends analyzed briefly above in Chapters 4, 5, and 6. Others, like the exchange model of George C. Homans and others, were closely related to paradigms derived from other disciplines, such as psychology or economics.[5] Closely related to the exchange model has been the approach developed by Elizabeth Bott, Jeremy Boissevain, Frederic Bailey, and more systematically by Frederic Barth. It stresses the importance of individual interaction in coalitions and networks, as against the "group" or "social system" emphasis of the classic functional model of British social anthropology.[6]

Many of the countermodels have tended to proclaim their ancestry in the classics of sociology. For example, the conflict model has related itself to various aspects of the several Marxist traditions, while the structuralist (Lévi-Strauss) model has often been presented as the principal legitimate heir to Durkheim and Marcel Mauss.[7] Although the development of these models was often combined with generational changes and the development of new clusters and nuclei of scholars, we will confine ourselves here to the analytic aspects of these controversies.

2.   Most criticisms voiced of the structural-functional model, which the countermodels claimed to overcome, focused on several different though related arguments. First, this model was seen as unable to explain social conflict and the processes of social change. The reasons for this failure were seen as several: its assumption of a basic social consensus on central societal values and goals; its emphasis on boundary-maintaining mechanisms of social control; and its implicit minimization of power and coercion as a means of social integration and change.[8]

A second criticism was its inability to explain the great range of historical institutional variability of social systems. This was seen as due to the generality of the concept of societal needs, or functional prerequisites, as defined in this framework. It was often argued that even if the existence of such needs in every social setting was accepted, the most that could be explained by them was the basic institutional differentiation which emerges in any society. They could not explain the variability in content, and in structural characteristics, of the institutions that fulfilled the same need in different societies. According to these critics, such variability was not explained in the structural-functional model but was taken as given.[9]

Closely related to these criticisms was the charge that the structural-functional model was necessarily ahistorical. Within this framework, the explanation of any concrete historical situation or phenomenon in terms of past influence and processes was relinquished in favor of a "static" or "circular" explanatory theory, based on the conception of social phenomena as being funtionally adjusted to one another through their contribution to societal needs, and on the assumption of the existence of equilibrating mechanisms in the social system which counteracted any of tendencies to functional maladjustment or inconsistency.[10]

Last were the claims that, given the strong systemic emphasis of the structural-functional school, the very autonomy of the individual—in his orientations to the social situation, which was stressed in *The Structure of Social Action,* had been neglected. He was reduced thereby to a "socialized" role performer acting according to the presumed needs of the social system.[11]

The Conflict and Power Model and the Individualistic Rational-Exchange and Game-Theoretical Models

3. The various countermodels were developed in different directions, depending on the real or assumed flaws of the structural-functional model that were chosen as the focus of criticism. These foci were the starting points for the construction of alternative paradigms.

Proponents of the "conflict" model and the closely related, often identical, "power" model criticized what they saw as a major tenet of the functional-structural model: the idea that the functioning of a social group or system depends on consensus of its participants on common goals and values related to the basic needs of the society. Such consensus, presumably, was a basic prerequisite for the functioning and continuity of the social system or order.

Against this assumption, scholars like Ralf Dahrendorf, John Rex, and to some extent C. Wright Mills presented the following arguments:

First, in any society, the dominant social goals and values are never accepted by all its members. In fact, they reflect and serve the interests of groups which are powerful enough to make their will dominant. Thus, it is the control of resources and power, not the presumed consensus on common values, that constitutes the core of the institutional setting of any society and the major mechanism of its continuity. Moreover, they claimed that it was wrong to postulate the existence of general universal needs of any social system. Whatever concrete needs developed in any concrete social system were determined by the specific goals of the system. And these, in turn, were set up largely through coercion and manipulation by the ruling elites.[12]

The second major juxtaposition of assumptions inheres in what John C. Harsanyi calls the "rational (individual) behavior" model as against the "conformist-functionalist" model. According to Harsanyi, the first model explains the development and variability of individual behavior in terms of the rational behavior of individuals and exchange among them. This is in contrast to the second model, which presumably explains such patterns of behavior and most institutionalized aspects of social life in terms of their presumed—but never proved—contribution to societal needs.[13]

This theme was taken up, with a somewhat different emphasis, by Homans and later modified by Peter M. Blau. Homans initially developed this theme in his and David M. Schneider's criticism of Lévi-Strauss' approach to the analysis of marriage norms. In this criticism they argued that norms regulating patterns of marriage were best explained by "efficient causes"—that is, by individual sentiments and choices, rather than in terms of "final causes"—or their presumed functional contribution to society as a whole.[14] Later this argument was expanded by Homans in a more general critique of the functional-structural approach. Here he elaborated the counterthesis that the roots of social behavior and order were given in the goals and interests of individuals. Homans further argued that social and institutional behavior emerged from exchange processes among individuals in which a combination of economic rationality and Skinnerian operant psychology provided the basic motivational forces and rules of interaction.

On the basis of these premises, Homans developed a set of assumptions and propositions with largely closed-system characteristics, and some derivative research programs. The most important of these assumptions was that every interaction between two or more individuals would continue as long as each participant: 1) received reinforcement from his partners in interaction that was congruent with his learned expectations and present mode of satisfaction and 2) when the interaction was profitable for him—that is, when the rewards received were greater than the costs incurred.[15]

The work of Homans was parallelled by earlier works in social psychology, such as those of John W. Thibaut and Harold H. Kelley, which attempted to explain such concepts as role, status, norms, and group goals by the exigencies of interaction between individuals and by their particular interests.[16]

Homans' and Blau's, and especially Harsanyi's, models share many assumptions about the rational bases of human behavior with game theory, like that of Thomas Schelling. The most recent developments and applications of these approaches can be found in James C. Coleman's work on collective decisions and William A. Gamson's on coalition theories.[17] The emphasis in anthropology on coalitions and networks[18] is also closely related to the rational model.

> *Symbolic Interactionist and Ethnomethodological Models, and Related Approaches*

4. Individualistic themes were also developed in a different direction of criticism of structural-functionalism which emerged from one of the most continuous and self-sustaining intellectual streams, symbolic interactionism. The roots of this model are in the work of Alfred Schutz and George Herbert Mead; they were expanded in the 1940s and 1950s in the work of Herbert Blumer and, to some extent, Arnold Rose, and later by Erving Goffman.[19] The focus of their criticism of the structural-functional model was its presumed presentation of man as a "role player," of the assumption that his human and social essence was exhausted by his performance of his social roles, and that the organizational, systemic aspect of social life was the constitutive element of social reality.

As against this view, they claimed that the individual's social essence lays in the process of individual interaction and in continual personal and interpersonal definitions of the social situation, in which elements of "objective givens" and "consciousness" are continually interwoven. This process is clearest on the level of daily interaction and encounters which are dissociated from the formal organizational role structure but which constitute the real core of the institutional structure of society.

The fundamental conceptions of symbolic interactionism were later stated by Jerome Manis and Bernard Meltzer:

1. Mind, self, and society are most usefully viewed as processes of human and interhuman conduct;
2. Language is the mechanism for the rise of mind and self;
3. Mind is an importation of the social process—that is, of interaction within the individual;
4. Human beings construct their behavior in the course of its execution, rather than responding mechanically to either external stimuli or such internal "forces" as drives, needs, or motives.[20]

These premises were restated in a later work in this form:

1. Human beings act toward things on the basis of the meanings that things have for them;

2. Meaning derives from social interaction;
3. Meanings are modified by their interpretations, as used by persons in actual situations.[21]

In some ways these criticisms are reminiscent of such earlier individualistic criticisms of structural-functionalism as Dennis Wrong's essay on the "over-socialized conception of man."[22] Wrong criticized the one-sided meaning which the structural-functional model seemed to give to the socialization process. In this model, socialization was seen as the basic mechanism that linked the individual to the social order by ensuring, through the learning process, the performance of his normatively defined social roles. Wrong did not deny that socialization fulfilled such a function. However, using concepts from Freud, who he felt was misinterpreted by functionalists, Wrong argued that the importance of socialization lays in its endowing man with a human-social identity, and with a general need and ability to live in a social-cultural order. However, Wrong asserted that this ability enables man to evaluate his own concrete social order critically, and to take an autonomous stand toward the concrete social roles he is required to perform in such an order.

Dahrendorf, in an earlier article on the concept of "role,"[23] also argued that man's personality, character, or identity is not the mere sum of the roles he learned to fulfill in society; there remains a zone of freedom and of moral choice which cannot be understood through the study of his roles. Consequently, according to Dahrendorf, although the concept of "role" remains one of the most important sociological tools for explaining how links emerge between the individual and society, this concept can capture only part of that totality which is the individual. Moreover, the over-emphasis on man as a mere player of roles defined for him *a priori* by an external social agent might have far reaching negative consequences for the understanding and definition of society and the individual.

In a recent, more systematic, individualistic critique of structural-functionalism, Eugene Weinstein and J. Tanur have stressed that this model relies too heavily on the assumption of mutuality of norms and on the degree of compatibility of normatively based role expectations as well as shared meanings; that it fails to analyze the process of interaction and its cognitive aspects, or to recognize that it is these cognitive processes that provide the social construction of reality and hence create or define, the nature of the individuals being aggregated into social structure; and that structural-functional theory is preoccupied with the needs of society, not with the purposes of people.[24]

The basic tenets of the individualist critique have been developed in many directions, the most systematic of which is ethnomethodology, associated with the names of Harold Garfinkel, Aron Cicourel, and others.[25]

> Ethnomethodologists questioned how actors know what is expected of them and which roles of the many that are possible are being evoked by different situations. The regularity of human behavior is sufficiently great that some systematic process clearly exists. Ethnomethodology's question is: How does it proceed? Ethnomethodology's answer requires studying the accounting and describing procedures for each member of a social order. Social order, then, is precarious, having no existence at all apart from those accounting and describing procedures. The focus is not on activity but rather on the process by which members manage *to produce and sustain a sense of social structure.* The attempt to understand these accounting procedures by members of a social order constituted ethnomethodology's radical break from standard American sociology.[26]

This radical break is found for example, in Cicourel's cognitive sociology, in which he attempts to find "how language and meaning are constitutive of the way in which everyday interaction is assembled and represented."

Much of the ethnomethodological criticism was based upon a radical philosophical critique of the assumptions of accepted research methods in sociology. The details of this trend will be discussed in a later chapter.

The very popular work of Peter Berger and his frequent associate, Thomas Luckmann, has also been deeply influenced by this approach. Although not explicitly critical of the structural-functional model, their writings have stressed individual interpretations and definitions of social situations as the major mechanisms of construction of social reality and of the working of institutions. The work of Berger and Luckmann in the sociology of religion has further developed this approach, strongly emphasizing the autonomy of the symbolic field, the indivi'dual's interpretation and definition of social situations, and the independence of that interpretation from the structural-organizational realm.[27]

Group Interest, Secondary Cybernetic, and Historical-Systemic
(Neo-Marxist) Models

5.   Another set of countermodels centered criticism on the strong systemic emphasis or assumptions of the structural-functional school. This emphasis assumes that societies are best conceived as "systems," characterized by systemic needs, boundaries, and boundary-maintaining

mechanisms, and that every society has functional prerequisites which must be fulfilled if such a society is to continue to exist. These prerequisites are met through the institutionalized division of labor, which assures that each part is functional to the working of the other parts and to the continuity of society as a whole, which according to this view, is often seen as analogous to a living organism.

The major "antisystemic" countermodels developed through these controversies were, first, what may be called the "ecological group" model, with a strong emphasis on conflict; second, the "historical-systemic" model; and finally, although rather indirectly, the "symbolic-structuralist." Some of the interactionist models have also contained very important antisystemic elements.

The "ecological group" model has been most fully developed in the works of Reinhard Bendix, who attributes his approach to Weber, and of his student, Randall Collins. Their studies have been paralleled by English social anthropologists like Emerys Peters and Jack Goody.[28] In varying degrees, they see society as a field of groups, each struggling to further its political, ideal, or economic interests. The result of these struggles depends on the groups' relative power and the extent of their success in legitimating these interests. To quote Collins:

> The main points of the historical sociology approach to politics are: *1.* The basic unit of analysis is the group or organization, viewed in relation to other organizations and groups with which it has contact. . . . The organizations existing at any particular time may include those formed in the entirely different context of an earlier historical period; there is no necessary trend toward uniformity of type among institutions in any particular area. This unit of analysis contrasts with the functionalist system of interdependent parts.
>
> *2 and 3.* The basic process that takes place in and among these units is the struggle of individuals and organizations to further their material and ideal interest. The emphasis is on the action of human beings; ideals and organizational forms are to be interpreted as the creations of human actors, as individuals try out various strategies to gain collaboration or the subordination of others. This process may be contrasted with the functionalist emphasis on behavior and institutions as performing functions in the division of labor within a system.
>
> *4.* The bases of stable coordination of human activities are constellations of interests, especially in solidary groups, and the dominance of certain groups. This explanation of social integration contrasts with the functionalist emphasis of the individual internalization of a society's wide set of values.

5. Political change is explained by the struggle for political advantage . . . made continual by the instabilities and dilemmas of legitimizing principles and of arrangements of domination. This explanation of change may be contrasted with the functionalist emphasis on system strains, cultural changes, and system evolution.[29]

Criticism of the systemic emphasis in structural-functionalism has taken a different direction in the work of the exponents of the "systems" or "secondary cybernetic" approach to the analysis of social systems, especially Walter Buckley, Magoroh Maruyama, and Karl Deutsch.[30] All these approaches take issue with the strong structural-functional emphasis on the equilibrating or homeostatic, as against the expanding or morphogenetic, aspects of social systems.

6. Closely related to the group interest and cybernetic models, yet containing many opposed assumptions, are a number of "historical-systemic" countermodels, most related in one way or another to Marxism. The most influential have been several neo-Marxist versions. Originating from the Frankfurt school represented by Habermas, they have been developed by several French Marxists and explicated in the work of Alain Touraine.[31]

All these models criticize severely the attempt of the structural-functional model to identify general abstract categories of social systems common to all societies, and stress the importance of the specific systemic characteristics of different historical situations which are determined by historically unique characteristics of the "forces of production," or of systems of domination prevailing in a given situation.

Touraine has taken up a somewhat similar position with regard to the historical specificity of social systems. However, his definition of the "forces" which determine the nature of each such specific situation, includes not only relations of production and class structure, but broader symbolic forces or trends akin to those emphasized by the structuralist school of anthropology, to be analyzed in the next section. Most important, these models, like the structuralist model, have stressed the importance of several hidden or "deep" dimensions of social organization—as well as those of conflict and contradictions and of historical transformations of society—as against the supposed structural-functional emphasis on value consensus and the integrative aspects of social systems. In this way they are closely related to other power and conflictual approaches, as well as some structuralist models.[32]

The Symbolic Structuralist Model

7. An almost opposite trend of criticism developed in various schools with strong culturalist assumptions which stressed the autonomy of the cultural symbolic dimension of human life. The most important and extreme representative of this trend has been Lévi-Strauss.[33] The point of departure for many of these scholars is the denial of the frequent functionalist assumption that the symbolic realm, as manifested, for example, in myth and ritual, is a function or reflection of the organizational integrative needs of the social system.

Lévi-Strauss' own emphasis on the autonomous characteristics of the symbolic sphere, and on its internal structure, stemmed largely from dissatisfaction with the direction that Durkheim's influence had taken in social anthropology. In this derivation, the structural-organizational and symbolic aspects were fully interwoven and the symbolic sphere was often explained in terms of its contribution to the working of the social system.[34] Lévi-Strauss stressed, rather, the high degree of autonomy and internal systemic structure of the symbolic realm and presented it as the most important dimension in understanding human nature, culture, and the social order.

Structuralism as developed by Lévi-Strauss, however, goes beyond mere emphasis on the autonomy, importance, or even predominance of the symbolic dimension in the construction of culture and society. It combines such emphasis with more specific assumptions about the structure and working of the symbolic sphere and its relationship to human behavior and social organization.

As Donald Macrae has put it, the basic premises of this approach are that "1) appearance in human conduct and affairs is not reality; 2) reality is structured; and 3) this structure is code-like."[35]

Or, to quote Eugene A. Hammel:

The reality sought by structural analysis, then, is not empirical reality but reality at the level of abstract pattern, in terms of certain diagnostic features of empirical phenomena. We seek in the observed phenomena evidence of a regularity that interests at some other level. In examining a machine-loomed fabric we look not for description at the number of alternating stripes of different colors but rather at the number of successive passes of shuttles bearing different threads. This concept of reality at a different level is not peculiar to structural analysis but is part and parcel of all scientific generalization. What distinguishes structural analysis is that its empirical phenomena are the stuff of human behavior and interaction, and that the abstract models built up to account for the empirical data are presumed to be at the level of mental phenomena.[36]

In greater detail, the crux of the structuralist claim is:

1. first, that there exists in any society or culture some "hidden structure" which is more real and pervasive than the overt social organization or behavioral patterns.
2. The rules which govern such structure are not concrete rules of organization, and are not derived from organizational or institutional needs or problems, but are crystallized as codes in the rules of the human mind.
3. It is these rules that are the essential constitutive elements of culture and society, providing deeper ordering principles of the social and cultural realms.
4. The most important of these rules (according, at least, to Lévi-Strauss and his followers) are the rules of binary opposition—contradictions which are inherent "givens" in all perceptions of the world, and the rules of transformation, which govern the ways in which these contradictions, supposedly inherent in the working of human minds, are resolved.
5. These principles of contradiction and transformation constitute the real models of the society—that is, the models according to which society is structured. These models need not be identical with the conscious models represented in the minds of its participants, or symbolized in various concrete situations and representations such as myths, although it is only or largely through a structural analysis of these representations that such rules can be derived.

Despite very contrasting points of departure, the structuralist and Marxist and neo-Marxist models share the emphasis on principles of "hidden structure" in explaining the organization and dynamics of societies, as against the "needs" or organizational principles presumably stressed by the structural-functional model. This similarity will be explored in greater detail below.

These models or countermodels, and, more important, their confrontation with the structural-functional model, were the focus of theoretical discussion and debate from the mid-1950s on.[37] Internal and external factors were closely interwoven in the development of these controversies, and we will now turn to the analysis of some of these developments.

Notes

1. C. Wright Mills, *The Sociological Imagination* (New York: Oxford University Press, 1959) especially Ch. 2, 3, 4.

2. H. Maus and F. Fürstenberg (eds.), *Der Positivismusstreit in der Deutschen Soziologie* (Neuwied und Berlin: H. Luchterhand Verlag, 1969).

For more comprehensive surveys of the critical-hermeneutic approach as developed by various scholars, especially those connected with the Frankfurt school, see M. Jay, *The Dialectical Imagination* (Boston: Little, Brown, 1973); M. Jay, "Some recent developments in critical theory," *Berkeley Journal of Sociology*, Vol. 18 (1973–1974), pp. 27–44; D. Frisby, "The Frankfurt school: critical theory and positivism," in J. Rex (ed.), *Approaches to Sociology: an Introduction to Major Trends in British Sociology* (London: Routledge & Kegan Paul, 1974), pp. 205–229.

3. The core assumptions of the structural-functional model are found, among others, in the following works: T. Parsons and E. Shils (eds.), *Toward a General Theory of Action,* (Cambridge, Mass.: Harvard University Press, 1951); T. Parsons, *The Social System* (New York: Free Press [1951], 1964); T. Parsons and N. J. Smelser, *Economy and Society* (New York: Free Press [1956], 1965); R. K. Merton, *Social Theory and Social Structure,* rev. ed. (New York: Free Press, 1963).

4. For the "conflict and power" model, see R. Dahrendorf, *Class and Class Conflict in Industrial Society* (Stanford, Cal.: Stanford University Press, 1959); J. Rex, *Key Problems in Sociological Theory* (London: Routledge and Kegan Paul, 1961).

For the "individual-rational" model, see G. C. Homans, *Social Behavior: its Elementary Forms* (New York: Harcourt, Brace & World, 1961).

For an evaluation of Homans' work, see the various papers collected in H. Turk and R. L. Simpson (eds.), *Institutions and Social Exchange: the Sociologies of T. Parsons and G. C. Homans* (Indianapolis and New York: Bobbs-Merrill, 1971); P. Ekeh, *Social Exchange Theory* (London: Heinemann, 1974), especially Ch. 5, 6.

For the further elaboration of the "individual-rational" model, see also P. Blau, *Exchange and Power in Social Life* (New York: J. Wiley, 1964); J. S. Coleman, "Individual interests and collective action," *Papers on Nonmarket Decision-Making,* Vol. 1 (Summer 1966), pp. 49–62; J. C. Harsanyi, "Rational-choice models of political behavior *vs.* functionalist and conformist theories," *World Politics,* Vol. 21, No. 4 (July 1969), pp. 513–538; J. C. Harsanyi, "Explanation and comparative dynamics in social science," *Behavioral Science,* Vol. 5, No. 2 (April 1966), pp. 136–145.

For the "group-interest" model, see R. Collins, "A comparative approach to political sociology," in R. Bendix (ed.), *State and Society* (Boston: Little, Brown, 1968), pp. 42–67; E. Peters, "Some structural aspects of the feud among the camel-herding Beduim of Cyrenaica," *Africa,* Vol. 37, No. 3 (1967), pp. 261–282.

On the "symbolic interactionist" model, see, for its early history, R. E. L. Faris, *Chicago Sociology: 1920–1932* (San Francisco, Cal.: Chandler, 1967), Ch. 6. For more recent developments, H. Blumer, *Symbolic Interactionism: Perspective and Method* (Englewood Cliffs, N.J.: Prentice-Hall, 1969); papers by P. M. Hall and R. M. Kanter in *Sociological Inquiry,* Vol. 42, No. 3–4 (1972), pp. 35–99.

For Lévi-Strauss' symbolic structuralism, see C. Lévi-Strauss, *Structural Anthropology* (New York: Basic Books, 1963); C. Lévi-Strauss, *Totemism* (Boston: Beacon Press, 1967); C. Lévi-Strauss, *The Savage Mind* (London: Weidenfeld and Nicolson, 1966); C. Lévi-Strauss, *The Elementary Structures of Kinship* (Boston: Beacon Press, 1969); C. Lévi-Strauss, *Mythologiques: The Raw and the Cooked* (New York: Harper and Row, 1969); C. Lévi-Strauss, *Mythologiques: du Miel aux Cendres* (Paris: Plon, 1967); C. Lévi-Strauss, *Mythologiques: L'origine des Manières de Table* (Paris: Plon, 1968); C. Lévi-Strauss, *Mythologiques: L'homme Nu* (Paris: Plon, 1971).

Of the many works which provide interpretations and criticisms of Lévi-Strauss, the following are very instructive: E. Leach, *Lévi-Strauss* (London: Fontana/Collins, 1970); P. Ekeh, *Social Exchange Theory, op. cit.,* especially Ch. 3, 4; M. Glucksman, *Structuralist Analysis in Contemporary Social Thought* (London: Routledge & Kegan Paul, 1974), Ch. 1–3; I. Rossi (ed.), *The Unconscious in Culture: the Structuralism of Claude Lévi-Strauss in Perspective* (New York: E. P. Dutton, 1974).

    For the "historical-systemic" model see for example, A. Touraine, *Production de la Société* (Paris: Seuil, 1973); and the various neo-Marxist approaches listed in note 31.

5. See the references in note 4 of this chapter for the "individual-rational" model.

6. On this see E. Bott, *Family and Social Network* (London: Tavistock, 1957); J. Boissevain (ed.), *Network Analysis: Studies in Human Interaction* (The Hague: Mouton, 1973); J. Boissevain, *Friends of Friends; Networks, Manipulators, and Coalitions,* (Oxford: Basil Blackwell, 1974); F. G. Bailey, *Stratagems and Spoils: a Social Anthropology of Politics* (Oxford: Basil Blackwell, 1970); F. Barth, "Models of social organization," occasional paper no. 23, Royal Anthropological Institute of Great Britain and Ireland, 1966.

7. For some of these references to the classics, see for example R. Dahrendorf, *Class and Class Conflict in Industrial Society, op. cit.:* C. Lévi-Strauss, "French sociology," in G. Gurvitch and W. E. Moore (eds.), *Twentieth Century Sociology* (New York: Philosophical Library, 1945), pp. 503–537; C. Lévi-Strauss, "Introduction à l'oeuvre de Marcel Mauss," in M. Mauss, *Sociologie et Anthropologie* (Paris: Presses Universitaires de France, 1950), pp. ix–lii; M. Glucksman, *Structuralist Analysis in Contemporary Social Thought, op. cit.,* Ch. 2 and 3.

8. These points are stressed, among others, by J. Rex, *Key Problems in Sociological Theory, op. cit.,* Ch. 6, 7; R. Collins, "A comparative approach to political sociology," *op. cit.;* J. C. Harsanyi, "Rational choice models of political behavior v. functionalist and conformist theories," *op. cit.*

9. These points are stressed, among others, by C. Morse, "The functional imperatives," in M. Black (ed.), *The Social Theories of Talcott Parsons* (Englewood Cliffs, N.J.: Prentice-Hall, 1961), pp. 100–152; J. C. Harsanyi, "Rational choice models of political behavior," *op. cit.*

10. On these points see, for example, R. Dahrendorf, "Out of Utopia: toward a reorientation of sociological analysis," *American Journal of Sociology,* Vol. 64 (1958) pp. 115–127; J. C. Harsanyi, "Explanation and comparative dynamics in social science," *op. cit.*

11. Parsons' earlier formulation can be found in T. Parsons, *The Structure of Social Action* (New York: Free Press [1937], 1968), especially Vol. 2, Ch. 18 and 19.

    For the major arguments on this point, see J. Rex, *Key Problems in Sociological Theory, op. cit.,* Ch. 6; D. Wrong, "The oversocialized conception of man in modern sociology," *American Sociological Review,* Vol. 26, No. 2 (1961), pp. 183–193; P. M. Hall, "A symbolic interactionist analysis of politics," *Sociological Inquiry,* Vol. 42, Nos. 3–4 (1972), pp. 35–75.

12. See R. Dahrendorf, *Class and Class Conflict in Industrial Society, op. cit.,* especially Ch. 5 and 6; J. Rex, *Key Problems in Sociological Theory, op. cit.,* especially Ch. 6 and 7; C. W. Mills, *The Sociological Imagination, op. cit.,* Ch. 2.

13. J. C. Harsanyi, "Rational choice models of political behavior *vs.* functionalist and conformist theories," *op. cit.*

14. G. C. Homans and D. M. Schneider, *Marriage, Authority, and Final Causes,* (Glencoe, Ill.: Free Press, 1955); P. Blau, *Exchange and Power in Social Life, op. cit.;* P. Blau, "Justice in social exchange," *Sociological Inquiry* (Spring 1964), pp. 193–206.

15. These assumptions can be found in G. C. Homans, *Social Behavior: its Elementary Forms*, *op. cit.*, especially Ch. 4 and 18.

For a critical appraisal of these assumptions, especially from the point of view of their ability to explain macro processes of institutionalization, see S. N. Eisenstadt, *Essays on Comparative Institutions* (New York: Wiley, 1965), Ch. 1; H. Turk and R. Simpson (eds.), *Institutions and Social Exchange*, *op. cit.*, especially S. N. Eisenstadt, "Societal goals, systemic needs, social interaction, and individual behavior: some tentative explorations," pp. 36–55.

16. J. W. Thibaut and H. H. Kelley, *The Social Psychology of Groups* (New York: Wiley 1959).

17. T. C. Schelling, *Strategy of Conflict* (New York: Oxford University Press, Galaxy Books, 1963); J. Coleman, "Foundations for a theory of collective decisions," *American Journal of Sociology*, Vol. 71, No. 6 (1966), pp. 615–627; W. A. Gamson, *Power and Discontent* (Homewood, Ill.: Dorsey Press, 1968); W. A. Gamson and A. Modigliani, *Untangling the Cold War: a Strategy for Testing Rival Theories* (Boston: Little, Brown, 1971).

18. On this, see the relevant works cited in note 6 of this chapter.

19. See, for example, G. H. Mead, *Mind, Self and Society* (Chicago: University of Chicago Press, 1934); A. Strauss (ed.), *G. H. Mead on Social Psychology* (Chicago: University of Chicago Press, 1964); A. Schutz, *On Phenomenology and Social Relations*, edited and with an introduction by H. R. Wagner (Chicago: University of Chicago Press, 1970); H. Blumer, *Symbolic Interactionism: Perspective and Method*, *op. cit.*; A. Rose, "A systematic summary of symbolic interaction theory," in A. Rose (ed.), *Human Behavior and Social Processes* (Boston: Haughton Mifflin, 1962), pp. 3–19, and others in this collection; E. Goffman, *The Presentation of Self in Everyday Life* (Garden City, N.Y.: Doubleday, 1959); E. Goffman, *Encounters* (Indianapolis, Ind.: Bobbs-Merrill, 1961); E. Goffman, *Asylums*, (Garden City, N.Y.: Doubleday Anchor, 1961); E. Goffman, *Stigma* (Englewood Cliffs, N.J.: Prentice-Hall, 1963); E. Goffman, *Behavior in Public Places* (New York: Free Press, 1963); E. Goffman, *Interaction Ritual* (Garden City, N.Y.: Doubleday Anchor, 1967).

For a collection of earlier and later expositions, see also C. P. Stone and H. A. Farberman (eds.), *Social Psychology through Symbolic Interaction* (Waltham, Mass.: Toronto, Xerox College Publishing, 1970).

20. J. G. Manis and B. Meltzer (eds.), *Symbolic Interaction: a Reader in Social Psychology* (Boston: Allyn & Bacon, 1967), p. 495.

21. H. Blumer, *Symbolic Interactionism: Perspective and Method*, *op. cit.*, p. 2.

22. D. Wrong, "The oversocialized conception of man in modern sociology," *op. cit.*

23. R. Dahrendorf, "Homo Sociologicus," in R. Dahrendorf, *Essays in the Theory of Society* (London: Routledge & Kegan Paul, 1968), pp. 19–87.

24. E. Weinstein and J. Tanur, "The nature of social interaction," unpublished manuscript, pp. 7–18.

25. H. Garfinkel, *Studies in Ethnomethodology* (Englewood Cliffs, N.J.: Prentice-Hall, 1967); A. Cicourel, *Method and Measurement in Sociology* (New York: Free Press, 1964); A. Cicourel, *Cognitive Sociology* (Harmondsworth, Penguin, 1973).

For interpretations and fuller surveys of this approach, see P. Filmer, "On Harold Garfinkel's ethnomethodology," in P. Filmer et al., *New Directions in Sociological Theory* (London: Collier-Macmillan, 1972), pp. 203–234; J. Douglas (ed.), *Understanding Everyday Life* (London: Routledge & Kegan Paul, 1971); J. Goldthorpe, "Review article: a revolution in sociology?", *Sociology*, Vol. 7, No. 3 (September 1973), pp. 449–462.

26. N. C. Mullins and C. J. Mullins, *Theories and Theory Groups in Contemporary American Sociology* (New York: Harper & Row, 1973), p. 195.

27. P. Berger and T. Luckmann, *The Social Construction of Reality* (London: Penguin, 1967). For their works in the sociology of religion, see for example P. Berger, *A Rumor of Angels* (Garden City, N.Y.: Doubleday, 1970); T. Luckmann, *The Invisible Religion* (London: Macmillan, 1967).
     For an attempt to combine this approach with institutional analyses, see P. L. Berger and B. Berger, *Sociology: a Biographical Approach* (New York: Basic Books, 1972).

28. R. Bendix and G. Roth, *Scholarship and Partisanship: Essays on Max Weber* (Berkeley, Cal.: University of California Press, 1971), especially Ch. 11; R. Collins, "A comparative approach to political sociology," *op. cit.;* E. Peters, "Some structural aspects of the feud among the camel-herding Beduim of Cyrenaica," *op. cit.;* J. Goody, *Comparative Studies in Kinship* (London: Routledge & Kegan Paul, 1969), pp. 120–141.

29. R. Collins, "A comparative approach to political sociology," *op. cit.,* p. 67.

30. W. Buckley, *Sociology and Modern Systems Theory* (Englewood Cliffs, N.J.: Prentice-Hall, 1967); W. Buckley (ed.), *Modern Systems Research for the Behavioral Scientist* (Chicago: Aldine, 1968); Magoroh Maruyama, "The second cybernetics: deviation-amplifying mutual causal processes," in W. Buckley (ed.), *Modern Systems Research for the Behavioral Scientist, op. cit.,* pp. 304–313; K. Deutsch, *The Nerves of Government* (New York: Free Press, 1963).

31. J. Habermas, *Strukturwandel der Offentlichkeit* (Neuwied & Berlin: Luchterhand Verlag, 1962, 1965, 1968, 1969); J. Habermas, *Theorie und Praxis: Sozialphilosophische Studien* (Neuwied: Luchterhand, 1963); J. Habermas, *Technik und Wissenschaft als Ideologie* (Frankfurt: Suhrkamp, 1968); J. Habermas et al. (eds.), *Hermeneutik und Ideologiekritik* (Frankfurt: Suhrkamp, 1971); J. Habermas, *Knowledge and Human Interests,* (Boston: Beacon Press, 1971); J. Habermas, *Legitimationsprobleme im Spätkapitalismus* (Frankfurt am Main: Suhrkamp, 1973); A. Touraine, *Production de la Société, op. cit.*
     This approach has also, of course, been developed by many neo-Marxist scholars and combined Structuralist-Marxists. As illustrations of such work, see L. Sebag, *Structuralisme et Marxisme* (Paris: Petite Bibliothèque Payot, 1964); M. Godelier, *Horizons, Trajets Marxistes en Anthropologie* (Paris: Maspero, 1973); C. Meillassou, *L'Anthropologie Economique des Guoro de Côte d'Ivoire* (Paris: Mouton, 1974); and many of the essays in the journal *Economy and Society.*
     The Marxist discussions on the Asian mode of production, as well as other developments in the Marxist school to be discussed in Ch. 10 are also relevant here; so are many of the discussions about studies of modernization. See, for example, S. Bodenheimer, "The ideology of developmentalism: American political science's paradigm-surrogate for Latin American studies," *Berkeley Journal of Sociology,* Vol. 15 (1970), pp. 95–137; G. Omvedt, "Modernization theories: the ideology of Empires?" in A. R. Desai (ed.), *Essays on Modernization of Underdeveloped Societies,* Vol. 1 (Bombay: Thacker, 1971), pp. 119–137.
     For the analysis of these studies, see S. N. Eisenstadt, *Tradition, Change, and Modernity* (New York: Wiley, 1973), Part 1.
     One of the latest illustrations of such an historical analysis is I. Wallerstein, *The Modern World System: Capitalist Agriculture and the Origins of the European World Economy in the Sixteenth Century* (New York: Academic Press, 1974).

32. On the conflict and power and the symbolic structuralist models, see note 4 of this chapter.

33. On Lévi-Strauss and the main assumptions of his approach, discussed below, see note 4 of this chapter.

For other approaches akin to that of Lévi-Strauss, see for instance L. Dumont, *Homo Hierarchicus* (London: Weidenfeld & Nicolson, 1970).

For similar approaches in linguistics and the study of folklore, see M. Glucksman, *Structuralist Analysis in Contemporary Social Thought, op. cit.,* Ch. 2 and 3; I. Rossi, (ed.), *The Unconscious in Culture, op. cit.;* M. Lane (ed.), *Structuralism: A Reader* (London: Jonathan Cape, 1970).

34. Durkheim's analysis of the interrelationship between the symbolic and structural aspects are developed in E. Durkheim, *The Division of Labor in Society* (New York: Free Press, 1964); E. Durkheim, *The Elementary Forms of Religious Life* (New York: Macmillan, 1915).

For this interrelationship as developed in social anthropology, see G. C. Homans, "Anxiety and ritual: the theories of Malinowski and Radcliffe-Brown," *American Anthropologist,* Vol. 43 (1941), pp. 164–172; V. Turner, "Myth and symbol," *International Encyclopedia of the Social Sciences,* Vol. 10 (New York: Macmillan, 1968), pp. 576–582.

35. D. MacRae, "Introduction" to R. Boudon, *The Uses of Structuralism,* (London: Heinemann, 1971), p. ix.

36. E. A. Hammel, *The Myth of Structural Analysis* (Reading: Mass: Addison-Wellesley, 1972), p. 3.

37. Some of the earlier criticisms of the structural functional school were collected in N. J. Demerath and R. A. Peterson (eds.), *System, Change and Conflict* (New York: Free Press, 1967). A later collection, focusing on the systemic approach to social life and criticising it from a Marxist viewpoint, is K. H. Tjaden (ed.), *Sozial Systeme* (Neuwied und Berlin: Luchterhand, 1971).

9

The Major Metascientific Controversies

1.   The theoretical and analytic developments analyzed above, grounded increasingly in research, attest to the potential of constructive breakthroughs in sociology. Recent developments in sociological analysis are more complicated, however, than the scholarly controversies over various "countermodels" indicate.

Along with these constructive developments, and often in close conjunction with them, there also developed in sociological communities, an outcry about the "crisis" in sociology, and a strong tendency to deny the distinctiveness of sociological analysis. To understand these developments, we must turn from the "internal" controversies to the "external," metascientific and metaanalytic debates of this period.

As in other historical situations of intense controversy—such as the first attempts to establish sociology as an autonomous discipline, and in the debates after the débacle of early positivist evolutionary sociology,[1] "internal" or substantive controversies were, or became, related to what may be called "external" disputes. These controversies often revived problems of the relationship between sociology and other closely related intellectual traditions—philosophical and ideological (especially critical) trends and orientations; neighboring academic and scientific disciplines. These disputes tended more than those in previous periods to converge with debates on the problems attending the increasing density and complexity of institutionalization of sociology. The constant extension of the range of issues debated produced a comprehensive and critical self-examination of the sociological endeavor.

211

2.   The apparently extraneous problems entailing other intellectual traditions blended with the controversies about various models. Thus, discussions of "symbolic structuralism" were related to the controversies in France between phenomenologists and existentialists. The Marxists tended to combine more substantive sociological discussion with theories of knowledge as well as of metaphysical and ontological premises and suppositions, those in the Frankfurt school being particularly concerned with the general relationships of "critical philosophy" to the social sciences. The discussions of "symbolic interactionism" later became closely related to discussions of phenomenology.[2]

These controversies were also, of course, related to various ideological trends. Some earlier representatives of the conflict model, especially C. Wright Mills, Barrington Moore, and Irving Louis Horowitz, exhibited markedly radical semi-Marxist, semi-Populist orientations; so have Tom Bottomore and Norman Birnbaum, major recent figures in the radical Marxist tradition in sociology.[3] In Germany, the merging of sociological with philosophical and ideological debates had already developed in the mid-1950s in the Frankfurt school, shortly after the return of Theodor Adorno and Max Horkheimer to Germany. In the 1960s, the revival of many Marxist trends in a majority of Western countries intensified the concurrent discussion of sociological and ideological components.[4] The Marxist ideological stance also became a very important element in the reaction, in many Third World countries, against the pattern of institutionalization of sociology, especially sociological research, that has been established in them—patterns, as we have seen, that were based to a large degree on American or English prototypes. The Marxist orientation in these countries was especially important in the criticism of various models of modernization and development.[5] The radical posture was later incorporated into other models—for example, in some versions of structuralism, through their relation to Marxism. Some symbolic interactionists were associated with certain radical ideological stances by virtue of their rejection of the institutional world.[6]

In some cases, discussions of countermodels were related to paradigmatic developments in other disciplines. Thus the exchange model, as we have seen, was closely related to developments in learning theory. The development of psychoanalysis also had a very powerful influence on the development of such areas of research as "culture and personality," although it was not directly involved with any of the "countermodels," and cut across many of them. An increasing sensitivity to history arose in connection with the work of various ecological-group and system theorists, and with the resurrection of comparative study, particularly of modernization.[7] Above all, as several examples have illustrated in previous chapters, developments and discussions in sociology were intimately related to those in anthropology,[8] often identical with, or cross-cutting, them.

3. These renewed openings produced a revival or reformulation of issues which had developed out of earlier tensions or encounters between sociology and closely related intellectual traditions. One debate involved the philosophic aspects of the methodological presuppositions of the social sciences, and especially of social research. Thus many methodological examinations were made of problems in sociological research and theory construction. Unlike the situation in earlier periods, however, these studies were based on much more sophisticated research traditions and methods. Thus in contrast to the past, discussions of the possibility of scientific analysis of human affairs became much more marginal, erupting only, as we will see, in rather extreme situations associated with the so-called "crisis" of sociology. In most of these discussions, epistomological questions were combined with the analysis of research and methodology and the examination of research areas.

Thus, general contemporary debates, like those associated with the names of Karl Popper, Peter Winch, Ernest Gellner, Joseph Agassi, and Ian C. Jarvie, tended both to take up concrete problems in the conduct of research, and to break new ground in philosophical-analytic areas in the methodology of the social sciences.[9] Many of these discussions highlighted the methodological weakness and shaky foundations of many sociological theories, the lack of specification of variables and testable hypotheses within them, the lack of clear relationships between theories and concepts, and the weaknesses of their operationalization.[10]

These discussions often converged with the works of methodologists operating within sociological research tradition: Paul Lazarsfeld, Raymond Boudon, Hubert Blalock, and Arthur Stinchcombe.[11] As in previous debates of this kind, one central, perennial issue was the philosophical and methodological problem entailed by the fact that the investigator is part of the object—social life—that he investigates, and that, consciously and (more important) unconsciously, he imposes his own categories on the objects and methods of research. This time however, discussion was closely related to the extensive development of research methodology, and involved actual examination of important methodological problems.

One such problem was the limit imposed upon "objective" study of

society by the usual methods of survey, questionnaires, participant observation, and other "establishment"-oriented methods. Undertaken in
many works that studied established research methods in detail, and in
discussions in the United States, Germany, France, and Italy,[12] these
examinations analyzed the hidden assumptions of these research
methods and the type of social reality they portrayed or assumed. Established methods, they charged, missed, neglected, or misinterpreted other
levels or aspects of social reality: the less official and verbal aspects, the
more fleeting, the more critical and symbolic, and the more physically
expressive, which were less dependent on reactions to the verbal intru-
sions of research.

As in earlier methodological debates of this type, these discussions, too,
raised the issue of the possibility of reducing social phenomena to "individualistic" (as against emergent, "collectivistic") factors. These debates,
naturally, led to the revival and elaboration of the problem of the type of
explanation most suited to sociology. Again, the presumably contradictory relationships were stressed between causal and apparently deterministic analyses, and those based on *Verstehen* and the imputation of
meaning to people's activities; and between causal, comparative generalizations and explanations in terms of unique historical situations.

Some of the prominent countermodels, the symbolic interactionist and
ethnomethodologist,[13] combined substantive and methodological claims.
As John Goldthorpe has summarized their argument:

> In its essentials, the argument in question is the following. The ways in
> which conventional sociologists define their problem areas ("race relations,"
> "formal organization," "juvenile delinquency," etc.) collect their data (by
> interviews, use of records, official statistics, etc.) and seek to explain "what
> happens" (through hypotheses and theories) all necessarily involve them, if
> only through their use of language, in drawing on a vast array of everyday
> common-sense meanings and understandings. These meanings and under-
> standings, they assume, are ones which they largely share with others—their
> respondents, informants, collaborators, readers or whoever; and such an
> assumption is obviously fundamental to their entire enterprise—the crucial
> resource for the social activity which is "doing sociology." Yet this resource
> remains quite unexplicated; it is simply "taken for granted." Thus, the
> ironic situation arises that the conventional sociologist proceeds with, as it
> were, a most remarkable and fascinating social construction beneath his feet
> which alone sustains him yet which he does not notice or at least leaves
> unexamined. The consequence is, then, that conventional sociology fails to
> attain any significantly higher level of theoretical awareness than that pos-
> sessed by the lay members of society themselves. While topic and resource

remain so confounded, sociology can never be more than an eminently "folk" discipline.[14]

These debates could also, though to a far lesser degree than before, give rise to discussions about the definition or scope of sociology, a question tied to the problem of the nature of sociological laws or explanations, as against those employed by psychology or by other social sciences. The problem of the nature of sociology's laws was taken up in a series of discussions. These included elaboration of the claim, by George C. Homans and proponents of the various countermodels most closely connected with the exchange model, that the true sociological explanations were psychological ones. But the first problem, that of the "true" scope of sociology, was rarely taken up; the only serious attempt at such analysis has been W. Runciman's recent *Sociology in Its Place*.[15] This work came out of an academic milieu, "Oxbridge," in which sociology was not yet fully established, a fact not without significance.

4.   Along with these more "restricted" or technical problems of methodological analysis, the broader epistemological and metaphysical assumptions of social sciences became a subject of discussion in conjunction with the assessment of "countermodels." Especially from the mid-1960s on, attempts were made to analyze these issues—to confront the prevailing sociological models with countermodels, on the basis not only of their analytic or theoretical presuppositions, but of their epistemological and philosophical (i.e., substantive and general world view) assumptions.[16] The historical development of all these debates cannot be detailed here: in Germany, the work of the Frankfurt school, culminating in the famous debate on positivism in German sociology; in France, George Gurvitch's attempts to construct a "dialectical sociology," and the later discussions based on the structuralist model; the more recent Marxist debates, which since the late 1960s have spread from France and Germany to other countries, especially England, Scandinavia, Holland, and Italy.[17] However, a brief summary of the debates in Germany can capture the flavor of these discussions[18] and the problems around which they centered.

W. Zapf has recapitulated the major points of the German debate:

> In present-day German sociology the question of the predication of general laws has sparked off a new controversy about methods, perhaps the only sharp difference of opinion there has been since 1945. The leading representatives of the discipline took part in the debate. Adorno took the view

that sociology must retain "social totality" as its central category. The conditions for the reproduction of a society cannot be sufficiently understood by means of empirical research. According to its own set of rules, empirical research must keep to facts, that is, in the final analysis, to the status quo. On the other hand, it must be remembered that the process of research itself is nothing but a factor in social totality. For Adorno and others (Horkheimer, Marcuse, Habermas, Goldmann) empirical procedures are necessary for the perception of "conditions," but factual reality is temporary and subject to change and must be assessed according to the "critical theory of society" to find out how much better it could be under different forms of organization. . . .

It is remarkable how little bearing this methodological controversy has on practical research. This has been stressed in the views expressed by Helmut Schelsky and Ralf Dahrendorf on the subject. Schelsky regards sociology, at least the practical research sociology undertakes, as "the descriptive history of contemporary society," which has no alternative but to make "anticipatory guesses" in an attempt to understand that society. As a theory, its task is that of "continuous reflection" on the conditions required for man's freedom from social constraint. It is a "comforting prospect" rather than prophecy. Dahrendorf sees experience as the ultimate criterion of science. He sets limits to the radius of action of experience, however, and tries thereby to leave room for man's freedom and obligation to take moral decisions. Science must be based on experience and must make general statements. Its results are subject to moral evaluation. Similarly, the process of research must, of necessity, use metascientific guidelines. It is as such guidelines that the "critical theory of society" and the *verstehende*, "anticipatory" type of analysis are of irreplaceable significance. There are more ways than one of achieving knowledge.[19]

René König rejected this concept in particularly lapidary terms. He calls the theory of society a "social reflection, not perception, but an impulse to action and an expression of contemporary forces at one and the same time." As against this, sociology should be a "specialized empirical science" dealing with "nothing but sociology." The debate was continued in 1961 between Adorno and Popper and flared up again between Jürgen Habermas and Hans Albert in 1964. In support of the "critical theory of society," Habermas claims that its analysis is aimed at "more than a postulation of the interdependence of historically neutral variables; and is an endeavor to unmask the objective context which helps to determine historical development." Habermas does not accept Popper's criticism of historicism. It is not general theories but epochal correlations which must be sought for. Instead of reopening the conflict between "understanding" and "explaining," the two approaches should be reconciled, insofar as theory measures and criticizes the subjective meaning of so-called facts against their temporary reality.[20]

Controversies Stemming from the Institutionalization of Sociology: the
Nature and Problems of Sociologists' Involvement in Society;
Articulation of the Dilemmas of Sociologists' Roles

5.   Alongside the debates about the methodological, philosophical, and metaphysical problems of sociology, a second series of intensive controversies developed over problems stemming from the institutionalization of sociology in academic life;[21] the spread of sociological research throughout private and governmental institutions closer to centers of power; involvement of social scientists in research and discussion of public policy, and in planning and executing of public policies; and their increasing involvement in political activities. The change in the organization of sociological work, from individuals or small groups working in relative isolation, or on the margin of academic and intellectual communities, to strong academic and professional sociological communities intensified the kinds of activities in which sociologists were engaged and the bases, components, and reference orientations of their roles. Each type of activity or of role-component could entail participation in, or orientation to, different organizational settings, publics, clienteles, and partners, exposing the sociological community to a greater number of pressures from varying publics and centers.[22]

The professionalization and diversification of sociologists' roles, activities, role-components, and relationships with various nonacademic publics and factions produced problems which provoked a wide range of serious discussions.[23] Among the more important issues were: first, those involving the ethics of social research. The most central problem was the "use" of human beings in such research. Second, there were problems related to invasion of privacy. This could take place through questioning or observation; more seriously, through the development of experimentation in which the subjects were often "manipulated" as mere "objects"; and, ominously, through the gathering of data, or "private" information, about individuals which could be accumulated and put at the disposal of various public and private agencies. Third were problems attendant upon the sponsorship of research by governmental and business offices and foundations. These problems, most fully and dramatically epitomized in the discussions of Project Camelot, ranged from the influence of sponsorship on problem selection and formulation to the classification of research results and the possible use of results by research sponsors for manipulative purposes. Finally, there was the question of possible influence by sponsors on the autonomy and professional orientation of participating sociologists.

Another set of issues for intensive discussion developed around the problem of the suitability of sociological knowledge for policymaking and the disposition of sociologists to engage in practical policy or enclose themselves in academic work. These issues emerged in the context of the area of the study of "social problems." This was a long-standing concern, especially in the United States, where it was closely related to the tradition of social reform. In the early 1950s, this concern found its expression in the establishment of the Society for the Study of Social Problems, which developed a long tradition of discussion and analysis of social problems.

During the late 1950s and in the 1960s, however, this area underwent a double process of "upgrading." First, it was transformed from a fringe specialization in research and theory into a central research concern, and its problems were reformulated in terms of macrosocietal analysis. Second, this movement of the study of social problems into the center of academic concern was further quickened by increasing public interest and controversy over the various "social problem" areas: ghettos, minorities, delinquency, housing, and so on.

With the transformation of this field, the possibility of sociologists' participation in policy planning and in broader fields became more salient. Thus, a series of intensive debates highlighted the problems attending the increased participation of sociologists as consultants, practitioners, or agitators, and the possible repercussions of such engagement on their scholarly activities.

One problem involved the tension between the tendency to engage in practical affairs and to abstain from them. Abstention could be justified on pure academic grounds or on a total "radical" negation of any involvement with centers of power. It is in this context that the problem arose of the suitability and adequacy of sociological knowledge as a base for policy recommendation. Many sociologists felt that they should put their resources at the disposal of policymaking processes, others had apprehensions about the immaturity of sociological knowledge and the danger of playing the role of practical magician, a role sociologists might only too willingly but naively accept.

A second complex problem stemmed from the dilemmas of the sociologist's role once he engaged in applied research and policy planning,—above all, between the critical and scholarly, on the one hand and the "technical" and engineering, on the other.

Thus, the possibility raised as early as 1943 by C. Wright Mills, in his analysis of the "Professional Ideology of Social Pathologists,"[24] reemerged as a focus of concern. Mills had asserted that sociologists might accept the definition of social problems that were provided by power groups or agencies, reinforcing a static or technocratic view of society and its problems. Now it was suggested that sociologists might, in defining social problems, support one particular view—whether conservative, reform, or revolutionary, and thus abdicate the exploration of alternatives to existing assessments of problems. Whether social research expanded the perceived alternatives or "froze" any given situation and its definition became an acute dilemma.[25]

6. The urgency of these issues increased with the rapid, though uneven, institutionalization and diversification of the sociologists' role. Here a double process took place. First, the broad considerations of the nature of sociologists' activities, which in earlier stages had been conceived largely in purely intellectual terms, became more and more concrete and were specified in institutional and organizational terms. Second, professional issues like the applicability of social theory and research to practical matters, or the role of sociologists in public or private enterprises, which had at first been presented as "technical" or organizational problems, were transformed into matters of general principle. Both impinged more and more on the central areas of sociological endeavor.

Out of these cross-cutting processes—the institutionalization of sociologists' activities and the discussion of professional issues analyzed above, several orientations became more fully articulated and activated.[26] First, tension mounted between the "critical" component of the sociologists' role, involving participation in ideological, political, and broad intellectual communities or publics, and that of "objective" research or the scholarly orientation, with its roots in academic institutions and publics. Within the critical component itself, tension developed between the view of sociology as a secular substitute for religion and the more detached nonutopian or nonpolitical stance. Other tensions included that between the practical, or applied, or professional components and the research or critical aspects of roles, and, in the applied orientation itself, the tension between "critical-utopian" or "enlightenment" and "engineering" orientations. The academic orientation itself embodied conflicts between the "humanist" and "scientific" models.

The particular tensions that provoked discussion were of course closely related to the specific problems raised by different aspects of institutionalization. Thus, problems connected with the sponsorship of research by different official agencies activated tensions between the "engineering" and "enlightenment" models—or, to use different language, between the relative predominance of the technocratic as against the critical components or orientations of sociologists. Similarly, the professional involvement of sociologists in nonacademic institutions, or as consultants to such institutions, activated the tension between the "scholarly" and "applied" orientations.

The various discussions involved a wide range of issues, both "internal" problems of sociological theory and research, and "external" methodological, philosophical, ideological, and professional issues. These internal and external issues converged on three areas, to be analyzed below: first, the possibility of a value-free sociology; second, the sociological enterprise itself, seen in sociology of knowledge perspectives; third, the critical-methodological analysis of some central concepts in sociological explanation. The tone of discussion in these areas constituted, as we shall see, an important indication of the impact of these controversies on the pursuit of sociological research and analysis.

Patterns of Segregation and Mutual Impingement; Different Types of Controversy

7. The issues in sociological controversy tended to coalesce in various constellations, which differed, in the degree to which the "internal" or "substantive," and "external"—philosophical, methodological, and ideological—aspects were present; and in the degree to which each aspect was pursued in its own framework or combined with the other. The constellations differed also in their impact on the continuity and development of research as well as in the concrete topics they incorporated.

The development of these constellations after the late 1940s showed several general trends: first, a gradual extension of specialized internal topics into broader considerations; second, increasing impingement, or overlapping of the topics of discussion; third, the convergence of many discussions on the analysis of basic assumptions of sociology, a broader conception of sociology, the intellectual identity of sociology, and the role of sociologists. Of the many concrete constellations that appeared within the framework of these general trends, only a few predominant types in different periods of the development of these controversies will be analyzed here.

8. One ideal type of debate, most closely approximated in the United States, and to some degree in Holland, Scandinavia, and Japan, in the late 1940s and early 1950s, was characterized by segregation of the internal

and external issues of controversy. In this type, or at this particular stage of its development, the relationship between the broader "paradigmatic" discussions and the analysis of research areas and systematic middle-range theories was relatively tenuous, although in principle the desire to establish such relationships grew with the tendency toward codification and its influence on research areas, middle-range theories, and research paradigms or programs.[27] This type was characterized by the fact that various external controversies—philosophical, methodological, ideological, and professional—were discussed as specialized issues without full or explicit consideration of their relationship to paradigms or research areas, and only rarely impinging on the internal momentum of these fields.

Methodological discussions were undertaken as a highly technical specialty; the results were summarized in special manuals or in compedia on research methods which abounded in that period. The more philosophical discussions, or those on the methodology of social sciences, such as those undertaken in the two symposia by Llewellyn Gross on sociological theory, and Don Martindale's analysis of different types of theories, were presented as marginal addenda to the more substantive theoretical or research activities within sociology without really impinging on them. Similarly, Kurt Wolff's analysis of several aspects of the sociological endeavor in terms of the sociology of knowledge, and Irving Louis Horowitz's analysis of different types of sociologists, were out of the mainstream of sociological work.[28]

The study of social problems was also perceived as a segregated specialty, defined in terms of social deviance and disorganization and pursued largely within the framework of the Society for the Study of Social Problems. To some extent this segregation helped keep the internal intellectual and analytic dynamics of this field segregated from the major stream of sociological analysis.[29] Within the framework of these developments, the radical criticisms of sociology by C. Wright Mills, Horowitz and, later, Barrington Moore, Morris Stein, and Arthur Vidich,[30] were a sort of specialization of their own. In this respect they were a regression from the central place which Robert Lynd's *Knowledge for What?*[31] had attained in the 1940s, although they shared with Lynd's work the critical examination of the possible impact of political involvement or apathy on the choice or neglect of research problems, the possibility of bias in their formulation, and the implications of these problems for the sociologist's involvement in policymaking.

Thus it was the "specialized," technical, organizational emphasis that predominated in professional debates until the late 1950s in the United States, England, and Holland. The major questions dealt with were teaching and research, curricula and organization of departments, the definition of sociologists' roles in various nonacademic settings, and the like.[32]

More general criticisms of sociology in philosophical or ideological terms were found in this period mostly in France, Germany, and to some degree Italy. In France, the major trend of such analysis was the work of Gurvitch and the attempts he inspired, such as those presented to the French Sociological Association to examine the social bases and conditions of the development of sociology. The discussions in Germany in the Frankfurt school combined from the start the ideological and philosophical aspects of sociological analysis with an emphasis on research.[33] In both France and Germany, however, weak institutionalization of sociology, particularly social research that was combined with teaching and applied work, and the divorce between centers of research and various philosophical approaches, made these debates remote and abstract specializations that were even more peripheral than the older *Methodenstreit*,[34] with little impact on the conduct of research.

Only later, when research was more fully institutionalized in German universities, did the confrontations between different "camps" focus on a combination of principled and concrete problems of sociological analysis. It was then, for example, that König, as indicated above, stressed the disjunction between critical theory and sociological theory, which he termed "theory of society" and "sociological theory." In Italy, a very intense discussion took place during this period of the relationships of sociologists to different centers of power, especially in terms of possible influence on policymaking. In Eastern European countries, the segregation between technical research and other parts of sociological analysis, which was reinforced by the political situation, limited discussion of internal or external sociological problems to lip service to Marxist generalizations.[35]

*The Weakening of Segregation: Mutual Impingement of
Developments in Research*

9. Segregation of the different topics of controversy was of course never complete. As early as the mid- or late 1940s, constellations of topics began to appear, especially in the United States, and internal and external theoretical disputes became linked to discussion of substantive developments in research areas and of professional problems.

Compared with earlier periods in the development of sociological theory, these controversies were more closely related to research. They took place alongside a phenomenal growth in research in all major fields of sociology and the systematization and codification of fields such as stratification, social change and modernization, theory of organizations, political sociology, and deviance and criminology. Until about the mid-1950s, developments in research and in theoretical work were characterized, as we have seen, by two tendencies. On the one hand, there was a tendency toward self-enclosure of a series of subfields, however methodologically or analytically weak, and of would-be middle-range theories. This trend was reflected in such middle-range theories as deferred gratification or differential association in criminology and deviance; convergence theory in studies of industrial societies; inner and other-directed personality in relation to mass society; social conditions of democracy and authoritarianship; primary relationships and groups in complex organizations; reference groups; the study of mobility and stratification theories; professions; and the theory of the "two-step" flow of communication.[36]

On the other hand, most of these substantive fields developed orientations to broader analytic frameworks, examination of assumptions of .analysis, ad hoc themes, and theories. Moreover, the internal momentum of research produced the recognition that the more fruitful of these middle-range theories—of primary groups, reference groups and orientations, differences between solidary, instrumental, and coercive elements in various social settings, and the like—contained many common analytic orientations and assumptions. These fields consequently converged to some degree on more general analytic frameworks.[37]

Thus, while the relationship between theoretical developments and the internal momentum of particular research areas was often sporadic, most of them developed general orientations to broad analytic problems or paradigms. This does not mean that the rapidly developing empirical research was concerned with analytic controversies, either for their own interest or for their bearing on research. It means simply that some orientation to broader problems became prevalent within the sociological community.

Closely related to this trend was also the incorporation into the broader trend of sociological analysis of works which were rooted in the earlier tradition of political analysis. Outstanding among these were David Riesman's *The Lonely Crowd;* Seymour Martin Lipset's *Agrarian Socialism, Union Democracy,* and *Political Man;* Morris Janowitz's *Professional Soldier;* and various studies of modernization and development.[38]

It was during this stage, or in the context of this type of controversy and attempt at codification that the structural-functional model became central in theoretical discussion.

The Weakening of Segregation: Impingement of External
Philosophical, Methodological, and Internal Controversies; The
Reexamination of Premises of Sociological Analysis

10.   From the middle or late 1950s on, a marked change took place in the pattern of segregation of discussions and the pattern of codification in sociology. The latter was characterized, as we have seen, by concern with examining different research areas in terms of common theoretical frameworks and common analytic concepts and theorems. At the same time, the segregated internal and external discussions in sociology began to be combined.

These two trends produced a marked change in the tenor of discussion in and of sociology. First, there was more examination of paradigmatic models and specific research programs and areas, such as ritual, modernization, stratification, and organization.[39] At the same time, though the trend was more marked in the early 1960s, internal and external issues in sociology began to be related.

Internal issues branched out by trying to incorporate the philosophical and ideological discussions of the various countermodels and use them in the restatement and reexamination of areas of research and of middle-range theories. Finally, studies of methodology and the philosophy of science were related to discussions of research methodology and were later examined for their general relevance to different research programs.[40]

11.   As these separate sociological discussions were related to each other and to discussions of the various countermodels, a hitherto latent and peripheral component became more active and central in discussion: the critical examination of epistomological and philosophical assumptions guiding the various basic approaches in sociology and related fields. This involved study of the ways in which philosophical assumptions influenced the development of the basic concepts and presuppositions of paradigmatic models and research in different areas, and a critical analysis of major sociological concepts—"institutions" and "institutionalization," "role," "political development"—and especially the tendency to

normative reification, or, to use Ingleby's definition, the turning of "hypothesized concepts" into "ideal terms from which deviations are not merely wrong but incorrect."[41]

It was natural that such examination should develop first in groups, like the Frankfurt school or various centers in France, in which these philosophical orientations had been continuously maintained. In the middle and late 1960s, such examination also took place, and in closer relationship to ongoing research, in research centers in Scandinavia where a strong tradition of empirical research had taken root. A quotation from Erik Allardt's recent analysis of some assumptions of Swedish sociology describes out the nature of such criticism:

> The overwhelming majority of Swedish sociological analyses of society are written with the assumption that social problems are something that a well meaning state can rectify. Problems are seen more or less as disturbances in interactions. There are mechanisms for ostracism, barriers to fine culture, inequalities of power, structural injustices, isolation of immigrants, etc., but in writing about these phenomena authors have had more or less expressly addressed themselves to the authorities.
>
> An investigation into the basic assumptions concerning man and society that are implicit in Swedish social welfare and welfare policy would certainly be a fascinating topic for study. A document recently published by the Welfare Board is perhaps symptomatic. Its title is "Social Goals, Structural Changes and Solving Problems of Relating in their Contexts Makes for an Integrated Society." There is no doubt that this approach is humanist. Human beings are not to be coerced: difficulties are to be confronted by structural changes and by solving problems of relating. But the goal is also clear: an integrated society. The self-evidentness with which the Welfare Board believes that all should be helped to have more or less the same goals is conspicuous.[42]

Another crucial element which entered into these discussions was, as mentioned, the reexamination of major analytic concepts, especially in terms of their possible normative reification. Of special interest are the reexaminations (more fully analysed in Chapter 10) of central concepts in sociological analysis, such as that of role. In addition to the purely analytic developments discussed above, many studies, especially in Germany, critically examined the origin and limitation of the concept of "role," indicating its constraining effects on the understanding of concrete aspects of social life and the possibilities of human creativity.[43] Similarly, with respect to the concept of "institutions," several studies—for example, René Lourau's *Analyse Institutionelle* and, to some degree, certain Italian studies and Turaine's and Willener's "action sociology"—pointed out that the accepted usage of "institutionalization" implies a constricted view of social life. They suggested a more critical analysis of the process of institutionalization which might open up new possibilities of new orientation to action.[44]

As these philosophical and ideological discussions examined the different models and countermodels, and the assumptions of sociological research, they brought about a renewed interest in philosophical assumptions about the nature of man and society which were associated with the major sociological paradigms. They involved the possible scope of man's creativity, the place and possibility of reason in man's construction of social and cultural reality, and the nature of the historicity of man's experience. Most discussions claimed that the predominant sociological schools entertained a passive conception of man, minimizing the possible scope of his creativity. They stressed the autonomous role of reason as against systemic exigencies and called for a review of these restrictive assumptions.

One of the most interesting attempts at such examination was the critical analysis of philosophical presuppositions in social psychology, undertaken by a group of European scholars. The epistemological and philosophical assumptions of the purely experimental approach of the predominant schools of social psychology were examined not only internally but also for their limiting impact on the formulations of research problems and because of their mechanistic, deterministic conception of man.[45]

Such critical examination could, of course, be related to the philosophical criticisms of explicative paradigms analyzed above and to various ideological stances, like "radical" sociology. In this process, it could produce or reinforce attempts at a general reappraisal of sociology and its place in the intellectual community.

Discussions of the Institutional Premises of Sociology; Critical Analysis of Sociological Concepts and Research, and of the Problems of a Value-Free Sociology

12. The broader examination of the place of sociology in the intellectual community was reinforced by the parallel broadening of discussion and controversy over the organizational and professional problems of sociological analysis. These trends were exhibited in the changing topics of discussions in *The American Sociologist*[46] and other international

sociological journals. From an overwhelming concern with problems of teaching and research and the organizational and professional affiliation of sociologists, they moved to problems of ethics of research, of engagement in policy and to different sociological activities and roles.

From the beginning, almost all these discussions focused on the problem of maintaining the autonomy of the sociologist's role and the value and institutional bases of such autonomy. However, significant changes occurred in the conception of the bases of this autonomy.

Considerations of autonomy went beyond such organizational or technical problems as professional organization. "Wider" or "deeper" roots of such autonomy were sought in terms of the place of sociology in the intellectual, scientific, and political universe. These discussions were thus brought closer to the broad criticisms based on the philosophical and ideological concerns.

This tendency to broader critical examination of sociology was reinforced by the institutionalization of sociological activity, which spurred the sociological community and the general public to examine critically the claims of sociology that it could contribute to a better society. Such criticism was later intensified by broader sociopolitical upheavals, particularly those related to race problems and the Vietnam war.

As a result of these, an awareness gradually developed of the complex ethical, social and political implications of sociological research. It was seen that many activities of sociologists had broad societal repercussions, could influence intellectual discussion and public opinion, and impinge upon critical debate of such controversial problems as poverty, race, class relations, and student rebellion. All these developments indicated the need for reexamination of the conception of professional autonomy that had developed in the late 1940s and early 1950s,[47] which had assumed that sociologists stood at a distance from direct political involvement, and which had stressed their purely "technical" and academic professional roles.

13. The trend toward reexamination of sociological activity was expressed in the growth of the study of social problems; discussions of the possibility and limits of a value-free sociology; closely related attempts to analyze aspects of sociological research from the perspective of the sociology of knowledge; a new exploration of the relationship between sociological analysis and social practice; and criticism of the structural-functional school and debates between the countermodels. The study of social problems, moving from its status as a marginal specialization into a central

place in the analytic framework of sociology, came to assume particular importance in terms of public interest.

Attention to the problems of a value-free sociology and a sociology of knowledge was displayed not just in frequency of these discussions but in their shift from the technical and academic philosophical discussions of Gurvitch, Wolff, and the Frankfurt school, who fought on two fronts, against the "positivists" and against orthodox Marxism, to more direct confrontations of these problems with concrete sociological analysis.[48] Some of the critical issues in a value-free sociology were raised, in the earlier stages of these debates, in Howard Becker's discussion with Alvin Gouldner at the 1966 meeting of the Society for the Study of Social Problems. Against Becker's claim for the necessity, in any social research, to consider the viewpoints of all sides,—of the "top dog" and the "underdog"—Gouldner affirmed the importance of transcending any given social situation, any existing social structure, in terms of broader values which could serve as a basic vantage point for a critical examination of this reality.[49] At first these debates stressed full self-examination of open and hidden values in any sociological research and of the limitations imposed by such values. Gradually, however, these discussions took a more principled stand which, in a blend of Marxist and early Mannheimian orientations, questioned, or at least posed the problem of, the very possibility of an objective scholarly enterprise in sociology.[50]

This trend developed in close connection with the self-examination of sociology in terms of the sociology of knowledge. At first it consisted in general, not too serious, examination of the presumed hidden assumptions of "bourgeois" sociology. In the 1960s, however, more probing examinations were made of the influence of hidden presuppositions of sociologists on the conduct and results of research. Critical analysis focused on the influence of the usually implicit assumptions of many sociological theories, especially the structural-functional model; on the presumed conservative stance of many sociologists in the choice and formulation of research problems; and on the "thematic" perception of social life presented in research.[51]

Another trend, especially in Europe, used the approach of Mannheim's early works, to analyze different national patterns of sociological endeavor and research. Many of these analyses were general diatribes against American or American-style research as inhumanistic or unphilosophical. More serious attempts, however, were of the kind best illustrated by Raymond Aron's analysis of the broad differences between American and European sociology, in which he stressed the lack of preoccupation in American sociology with the historical dimension of social life and with comparative macrosocietal study.[52]

With the broadening scope of discussion, a far-reaching transformation took place of these debates and analyses of social and intellectual frameworks and conditions of sociological research, and of the possibility of a value-free sociology. Among the best known illustrations of this trend in the late 1960s were Gouldner's *The Coming Crisis of Western Sociology*, Robert Friedrichs' *Sociology of Sociology*, and the many discussions which paralleled and followed the publication of these works in the United States and throughout Europe.[53] Both works tried to analyze the impact of external factors on the pursuit of sociological analysis, and the presuppositions of the structural-functional school and certain countermodels. These aspects, however, were, on the whole, overshadowed by the denial of the possibility of a value-free sociology, and by what can be seen as a total relativization of all possible approaches, increasing doubts about the possibility of objective scholarly research in sociology.

These changing patterns of discussion stand out most clearly if we compare them to the list of problems which Robert K. Merton, in the late 1950s, had singled out as the most important problems of sociological contention. These were: "the alleged cleavage between substantive sociology and methodology"; "the lone scholar and the research team"; "the microscopic and the macroscopic"; "experiment and natural history in sociology"; "reference groups of sociologists"; and "sociology versus social psychology."[54]

Changing Modes of Criticism of the Structural-Functional Model

14.   The changing patterns of discussion were reflected in the modes of discussion of the various models and countermodels and in the criticism of structural-functionalism. During the stage of more segregated discussion, this criticism was either "external"—undertaken in terms of methodology or the philosophy of science. This type of approach is found in the symposia edited by Gross and in the work of Martindale. Or the criticism could be largely methodological and analytic as illustrated by Max Black's symposium; the vigorous development of internal sociological countermodels, especially the conflict countermodel of Dahrendorf and the beginnings of the exchange model; and the continuity of the interactionist paradigm more as a parallel than as a direct challenge to the structural-functional model.[55]

Originally, most discussions of the countermodels were also segregated from involvement in particular research areas—stratification, deviance, industrial and organizational sociology, and the like, usually using only illustrations from different fields to make their theoretical points. The only exceptions, themselves almost theoretical, were the Davis-Moore-Tumin debate on stratification, and, to a lesser degree, several analyses of small groups made in connection with the exchange model.[56]

With the increasing "density" of sociological debate, criticisms of the structural-functional model moved beyond purely substantive criticism. They centered on charges of conservatism in the tone and orientation of this model, because of its presumed emphasis on value-free sociology, and consensus, and its concern with stability of the social systems. Earlier examples of these approaches were the Stein and Vidich critical survey of community studies and Barrington Moore's general critique, which combined his own emphasis on power in social life with a detailed criticism of the effect of conservative assumptions in the "positivist" and functional school on the conduct of research in various areas and in reinforcing the status quo.[57]

To these criticisms claims were gradually added that the analytic orientations and ideological deficiencies of the model also influenced the selection of crucial problems of research. Neglected problematics were those dealing with power relationships, the class struggle, the potential claims of the "underdog," social change, and the autonomous creative potential of individuals. Instead, social organizations were seen from the perspective of the "topdog" and in terms of self-maintaining mechanisms. To take a few illustrations: Some interactionists, like Everett C. Hughes who worked in the Chicago tradition, claimed that studies of socialization into role behavior as undertaken by Merton and William J. Goode stressed the "official," normative aspects of such roles, and not the power or exploitative aspects. These could be seen and felt, it was claimed, far better, from "beneath," by those who entered the system and even failed within it.[58] Similarly, many accusations were made that studies of hospitals, business firms, schools, deviance, had developed a conservative bias in the selection of topics for research, a bias emphasizing the official view of the "establishment" of these institutions. Thus the managerial model tended to be predominant in organizational theory, and the viewpoint of official control agencies in the studies of deviance.[59]

With greater mutual impingement of issues of discussion, the various aspects of criticism of the structural-functional model came increasingly to be related to each other. This interrelationship was facilitated by the increasing momentum of research; codification of different fields, the development of research beyond the earlier stages of codification; and the unification of many research fields into common frameworks, which made them more susceptible to broader critical examination. The development, cross cutting, and mutual reinforcement of various closed- and open-system paradigms and research programs enhanced the possibility and desire for such examination.

As a result, more attempts were made to review entire areas of research, such as stratification and modernization, assess the positive and negative impact of the structural-functional model on them, and suggest ways of overcoming the negative impact by recourse to countermodels.[60] In conjunction with these trends an even more general, total criticism of the structural-functional model emerged—a criticism that can be found in the works by Gouldner, Friedrichs, and Dick Atkinson, as well as in many discussions throughout the world. This criticism focused not only on the specific theoretical or analytic aspects which were points of departure for various countermodels, but assumed, as we will see in Chapter 11, much broader analytic, philosophical, and ideological dimensions.[61]

Critical Self-Examination in Other Social Sciences: A Brief Note

15.   The several types of "self-criticism" were not limited to sociology, but developed in other social sciences. Closest to those in sociology were probably those in psychology, anthropology, and political sciences. Here the major lines of criticism, although far from identical in content, intensity of discussion, and centrality to issues in sociology, were not dissimilar. In social psychology, and to some degree in psychology, a somewhat unique examination was undertaken of the basic presuppositions of major approaches, and of the ethical problems of involvement of psychologists in applied research.[62] In anthropology, especially in the United States, the most acute problems and discussions were those related to the involvement of anthropologists in political and security settings —for example, counterinsurgency activities—and to implications of possible white ethnocentrism for the conduct, structure, and meaning of anthropological inquiry. The more theoretical discussions centered on the structuralist approach, and the problem of "meaning" in anthropology, especially the possibility of understanding alien cultures and modes of thought.[63] In political science, major areas of dispute were the prevalence of the behavioral model and functional analysis, with their reification of the status quo and existing power relations; the neglect of the question

of values; the neglect of political philosophy; and the prevalence of developmental as against "ethical" models and approaches.[64]

To some degree such controversies also developed in economics, taking several directions but almost all focused on the need for "political economy" rather than prevailing technical, econometric modes of analysis. Various attempts were made to analyze the assumptions of existing orthodoxies and their trend to "mystification and reification of social reality." The more technical of these discussions centered on problems of welfare economics and stressed the importance of discussing such political issues as capital distribution and the role of the state in "monopoly capitalism."[65]

The Changing Tenor of Contemporary Sociology; Contradictory Trends in Sociological Analysis

16.   The above developments were linked to far-reaching changes in the tenor of contemporary sociology. First, there developed a renewed critical orientation which emphasized distance from existing social structures, attempting to evaluate existing social reality more critically. This development revived the tensions which had been so prominent for the Founding Fathers, between trends in existing situations and the orientation of protest which tried to transcend these trends in seeking, sometimes naively, sometimes seriously and self-critically, institutional alternatives.[66]

As the research by Lipset and Ladd, and by Rachel Javetz has shown, the critical orientation was strongest among the more established and productive sociologists. This in turn prompted the reexamination of the given concepts and concrete *Problemstellungen* in terms of some of the orientations of protest which had predominated in earlier phases of sociology.[67] The result was a situation in which the tension between the "classical" and "romantic" approaches to sociology[68] became almost a constant element in sociological debate, and in which sensitivity to the problem of the range of human creativity in social life, and to the place of reason within it, was again awakened.

Notes

1. On the controversies of these earlier periods, see details in Ch. 2, 3, 5, above.

2. On the relationship of symbolic structuralism to the controversies between phenomenologists and existentialists see, among the many works, O. Ducrot et al.,

Qu'est-ce que le Structuralisme (Paris: Editions du Seuil, 1968); J. Pavain-Viel, *Analyses Structurales et Idéologies Structuralistes* (Toulouse: Edouard Privat, 1969); (Various authors) *Structuralisme et Marxisme* (Paris: Union Générale d'Editions, 1970); I. Rossi (ed.), *The Unconscious in Culture* (New York: Dutton, 1974); G. Schiwy, *Der Französiche Strukturalismus* (Reinbeik: Rowohlt, 1969).

Some of the debates on Marxism are illustrated in L. Sebag, *Marxisme et Structuralisme* (Paris: Payot, 1964), and in the *International Journal of Sociology*, Vol. 2, No. 2–3 (1972). This issue, devoted to the disputes between Marxists and structuralists, contains articles published earlier in the French quarterly *Pensées*.

For concise surveys of the discussions in the Frankfurt school see M. Jay, "Some recent developments in critical theory," *Berkeley Journal of Sociology*, Vol. 18 (1973–1974), pp. 27–44; D. Frisby, "The Frankfurt school: critical theory and positivism," in J. Rex (ed.), *Approaches to Sociology* (London: Routledge & Kegan Paul, 1974), pp. 205–229.

On the relationship of symbolic interactionism to discussions in phenomenology, see for example M. Phillipson, "Phenomenological philosophy and sociology," in P. Filmer, et. al., *New Directions in Sociological Theory* (London: Collier-Macmillan, 1972) pp. 119–163.

3. C. Wright Mills, *The Sociological Imagination* (New York: Oxford University Press, 1959); C. Wright Mills, *The Power Elite* (New York: Oxford University Press, 1959); B. Moore, *Political Power and Social Theory* (New York: Harper & Row, 1962); R. P. Wolff, B. Moore, and H. Marcuse, *A Critique of Pure Tolerance* (Boston: Beacon Press, 1969). I.L. Horowitz, *Foundations of Political Sociology,* (New York: Harper & Row, 1972); I. L. Horowitz, *Professing Sociology: Studies in the Life Cycle of Social Science* (Chicago: Aldine Publishing Company, 1968); T. B. Bottomore, *Political Sociology* (London: Hutchison, 1972); T. B. Bottomore, *Sociology as Social Criticism* (London: G. Allen & Unwin, 1974); N. Birnbaum, *The Crisis of Industrial Society* (New York: Oxford University Press, 1969; N. Birnbaum, *Toward a Critical Sociology,* (New York: Oxford University Press, 1971).

4. M. Jay, "Some recent developments in critical theory," *op. cit.;* D. Frisby, "The Frankfurt school: critical theory and positivism," *op. cit.;* R. Klima, "Theoretical pluralism, methodological dissension, and the role of the sociologist; the West German case," *Social Science Information,* Vol. 11, No. 3–4 (1972), pp. 69–108.

5. For illustrations of Marxist or radical criticisms of studies of modernization, see G. Omvedt, "Modernization theories: the ideology of empire?" in A. R. Desai (ed.), *Essays on the Modernization of Underdeveloped Societies,* Vol. 1 (Bombay: Thacker, 1971), pp. 119–137; A. R. Desai, "Need for reevaluation of the concept," in A. R. Desai (ed.), *op. cit.,* pp. 458–474; W. Wertheim, *Evolution and Revolution* (Harmondsworth: Penguin Books, 1974); G. Frank, *Capitalism and Underdevelopment in Latin America: Historical Studies of Chile and Brazil* (New York: Monthly Review Press, 1969); G. Frank, *Latin America: Underdevelopment or Revolution* (New York: Monthly Review Press, 1969); G. Frank, *Lumpenbourgeoisie; Lumpendevelopment; Dependence, Class & Politics in Latin America* (New York: Monthly Review Press, 1972); L. Martins (ed.), *Amerique Latine, Crise et Dépendence* (Paris: Anthropos, 1972); R. Stavenhagen, *Les Classes Sociales dans les Sociétés Agraires* (Paris: Anthropos, 1969); H. F. Cardoso and F. Weltford (eds.), *America Latina, Ensayos de Interpretacion Sociologica Politica* (Santiago de Chile: Editorial Universitaria, 1970).

6. On Structuralism & Marxism see for example L. Althuser et al., *Lire le Capital* (Paris:

Maspero, 1965); L. Althuser, *For Marx* (London: Penguin, 1969); A. Touraine, *Production de la Société* (Paris, Seuil, 1973); M. Godelier, *Horizons, Trajets Marxistes en Anthropologie* (Paris: Maspero, 1973); L. Sebag, *Marxisme et Structuralisme, op. cit.* For a radical stance of symbolic interactionism, see for instance P. M. Hall, "A symbolic interactionist analysis of politics," *Sociological Inquiry*, Vol. 42, No. 3–4 (1972), pp. 35–75; J. Urry, *Reference Groups and the Theory of Revolution* (London: Routledge & Kegan Paul, 1973); D. Atkinson, *Orthodox Consensus and Radical Alternative* (London: Heinemann, 1971); D. Silverman, *The Theory of Organizations* (London: Heinemann, 1970).

7. On the relationship between the exchange model and learning theory, see for example P. Ekeh, *Social Exchange Theory* (London: Heinemann, 1974), especially Ch. 5, 6.

    For a good survey of developments in the "culture and personality" school see G. A. de Vos and A. A. Hippler, "Cultural psychology," in G. Lindzey and E. Aronson (eds), *Handbook of Social Psychology*, Vol. 4 (Reading, Mass.: Addison-Wesley, 1969), pp. 323–417; A. Inkeles and D. J. Levinson, "National character: the study of modal personality and sociocultural systems," in G. Lindzey and E. Aronson (eds.), *op. cit.*, pp. 418–506.

    On the sensitivity to history which arose from various theories and models, see for example R. Collins, "A comparative approach to political sociology," in R. Bendix (ed.), *State and Society* (Boston: Little, Brown, 1968), pp. 42–67; A. Touraine, *Production de la Société, op. cit.;* S. N. Eisenstadt, *Tradition, Change and Modernity* (New York: Wiley, 1973), Ch. 1 and 5; A. R. Desai (ed.), *Essays on Modernization of Underdeveloped Societies,* (Bombay: Thacker, 1971), 2 vols; Walter L. Bühl, *Evolution und Revolution, Kritik der Symmetrischen Soziologie* (München: W. Goldman Verlag, 1970); the special issue on Soziologie und Sozialgeschichte of the *Kölner Zeitschrift für Soziologie und Sozialpsychologie*, No. 16 (1972); W. L. Bühl, ed., *Funktion und Struktur—Soziologie oder Geschichte* (München: Nymphenburger Verlagshandlung, 1975).

8. On this relationship see details especially in Ch. 7 and 8.

9. K. Popper, *The Poverty of Historicism* (London: Routledge & Kegan Paul, 1957); K. Popper, *Objective Knowledge* (London: Oxford University Press, 1972).

    For debates with Popper's theses, mainly by scholars associated with the Frankfurt school, see H. Maus and F. Fürstenberg (eds), *Der Positivismusstreit in der Deutschen Soziologie* (Neuwied und Berlin: Luchterhand, 1969); P. Winch, *The Idea of Social Science* (London: Routledge & Kagan Paul, 1958); E. Gellner, "The new idealism—cause and meaning in the social sciences," in A. Giddens (ed.), *Positivism and Sociology* (London: Heinemann, 1974), pp. 129–156; I. C. Jarvie, *Concepts and Society* (London: Routledge & Kegan Paul, 1972); I. C. Jarvie and J. Agassi, "The problem of rationality of magic," *The British Journal of Sociology*, Vol. 18, No. 1 (March 1967), pp. 55–75.

    For similar debates conducted in earlier periods in the history of sociology see details in Ch. 2 and 5, above, and also W. Hirsch, *Philosophie und Sozialwissenchaften* (Stuttgart: F. Enke, 1974).

10. G. C. Homans, *The Nature of Social Science,* (New York: Harcourt, Brace & World, 1967), pp. 14ff.; M. Black, "Some questions about Parsons' thories," in M. Black (ed.), *The Social Theories of Talcott Parsons* (Englewood Cliffs, N.J.: Prentice-Hall, 1961), pp. 268–288; R. Borger and F. Cioffi (eds.), *Explanation in the Behavioral Sciences* (Cambridge: Cambridge University Press, 1970).

11. For the most important illustrations of this approach see R. Boudon and P. F. Lazarsfeld, *Le Vocabulaire des Sciences Sociales, Concepts et Indices* (Mouton: Paris, 1965); R. Boudon and P. F. Lazarsfeld, *L'Analyse Empirique de la Causalité* (Paris: Mouton, 1966); H. M. Blalock, *Causal Inferences in Nonexperimental Research* (Chapel Hill, N.C.: Univer-

sity of North Carolina Press, 1964); H. M. Blalock, *Theory Construction* (Englewood Cliffs, N.J.: Prentice-Hall, 1969); H. M. Blalock and A. B. Blalock (eds.), *Methodology in Social Research* (New York: McGraw-Hill, 1968); A. Stinchcombe, *Constructing Social Theories* (New York: Harcourt, Brace & World, 1968).

12. On the foci of these more recent discussions, which are mentioned below, see the following summaries in P. Rossi (ed.), *Ricerca Sociologica e Ruolo del Sociologo* (Bologna: Il Mulino, 1972): A. Martinelli, "Il dibattito metodologico negli Stati Uniti," pp. 177–215; B. Becalli, "Il dibattito metodologico in Inghilterra," pp. 215–233; R. Scarterrini, "Il dibattito metodologico in Francia," pp. 233–259; G. E. Rusconi, "Il dibattito metodologico nella Germania Federale," pp. 259–285.

    See also G. A. Gilli, *Come Si Fa Ricerca* (Milano: Arnoldo Mandadori, 1971); M. Truzzi (ed.), *Verstehen: Subjective Understanding in the Social Sciences* (Reading, Mass.: Addison-Wesley, 1974), Parts 2 and 3; J. Habermas, *Zur Logik der Sozialwissenschaften* (Frankfurt: Suhrkamp, 1971); B. Schäfers (ed.), *Thesen zur Kritik der Soziologie* (Frankfurt: Suhrkamp, 1969); D. Phillips, *Knowledge from What?* (Chicago: Rand McNally, 1971); D. Phillips, *Abandoning Method* (San Francisco: Jossey-Bass, 1973); D. Phillips, "Paradigm and incommensurability," *Theory and Society* Vol. 2, No. 1 (Spring 1975), pp. 37–63; K. D. Opp, *Methodologie der Sozialwissenschaften* (Reinbeik: Rowohlt, 1970).

13. H. Blumer, *Symbolic Interactionism: Perspective and Method* (Englewood Cliffs, N.J.: Prentice-Hall, 1969); B. N. Meltzer, J. W. Petras, and L. T. Reynolds, *Symbolic Interactionism: Genesis, Varieties and Criticism* (London: Routledge & Kegan Paul, 1975); H. Garfinkel, *Studies in Ethnomethodology* (Englewood Cliffs, N.J.: Prentice-Hall, 1967); R. Turner (ed.), *Ethnomethodology* (Harmondsworth: Penguin, 1974); A. Cicourel, *Method and Measurement in Sociology* (New York: Free Press, 1964); A. Cicourel, *Cognitive Sociology* (Harmondsworth: Penguin, 1973); P. Filmer et al., *New Directions in Sociological Theory, op. cit.*

14. J. H. Goldthorpe, "A revolution in sociology?" (review article), *Sociology*, Vol. 7, No. 3 (1973), p. 451. © Oxford University Press, 1973. "By permission of the Oxford University Press."

15. W. G. Runciman, *Sociology and its Place and Other Essays* (Cambridge: Cambridge University Press, 1970); G. C. Homans, *The Nature of Social Science, op. cit.*

16. For a general analysis of different models and countermodels from this point of view, see A. Gouldner, *The Coming Crisis of Western Sociology* (New York: Basic Books, 1970); For an analysis of Homans' exchange theory see P. Ekeh, *Social Exchange Theory, op. cit.* especially Ch. 6.

    For the analysis of the premises of Marxist structuralism and symbolic structuralism see M. Glucksman, *Structuralist Analysis in Contemporary Social Thought* (London: Routledge & Kegan Paul, 1974); I. Rossi (ed.), *The Unconscious in Culture, op. cit.;* and the items in notes 12 and 13 above, especially the analyses in P. Rossi (ed.), *Ricerca Sociologica e Ruolo del Sociologo, op. cit.*

17. On the debate on positivism in Germany see H. Maus and F. Fürstenberg (eds.), *Der Positivismusstreit in der Deutschen Soziologie, op. cit.;* G. Gurvitch, *Dialectique et Sociologie* (Paris: Flammarion, 1962).

    On the discussions of the structuralist model see the relevant items quoted in note 2, above and also note 18 below.

    For illustrations of the discussions conducted in England see J. Rex (ed.), *Approaches to Sociology: an Introduction to Major Trends in British Sociology, op. cit.*

    On Scandinavia see E. Allardt, "Scandinavian sociology and Swedish sociology," *International Journal of Sociology*, Vol. 3 (fall-winter 1973–1974), especially pp. 32–36; E. Allardt et al., "Svensk Sociologi," *Sociologisk Forsking*, Vol. 10 (1972–1973).

On Holland see H. Wallenburg, "Onbehagen en Kritische sociologie," *Mens en Maatschappij* (Maart-April, 1969) Vol. 44, pp. 101–113; R. Sierksma, "Naar een nieuwe sociologie," and P. Ten Have, "Emancipation and culture," in *Mens en Maatschappij* (Juli-Augustus 1970), Vol. 45, pp. 233–246, 246–266; H. Wallenburg, "Ideeën voor een Kritische makrosociologie," J. Gadourek, "Apologia pro sociologia sua," in *Mens en Maatschappij*, Vol. 46, No. 1–2 (1971), pp. 147–166; 166–197; D. L. Phillips, "Some cautionary notes on sociological research," J. Gadourek, "D. L. Phillips' research to end the research," J. Goudsblom, "Ideologie en wetenschap: A. Gouldner over de crisis in de sociologie," in *Mens en Maatschappij*, Vol. 47, No. 2 (1972), pp. 101–119, 119–129, 129–141; H. Hoefnagels, "Over de mogelijkheid en de wenselijkheid van een kristische sociologie," *Mens en Maatschappij*, Vol. 47, No. 3–4 (1972), pp. 236–253.

On Italy see P. Rossi (ed.), *Ricerca Sociologica e Ruolo del Sociologo, op. cit.*

18. The discussions evoked by structuralism and some of its philosophical suppositions are summarized by I. Rossi, "Intellectual antecedents of Lévi-Strauss' notion of unconscious," in I. Rossi (ed.), *The Unconscious in Culture, op. cit.*, pp. 7–31.

19. W. Zapf, *Complex Societies and Social Change: Problems of Macro-Sociology in the Social Sciences; Problems and Orientations,* (Paris: Mouton [Unesco], 1968), pp. 256–257. By permission of Mouton Publishers. © Unesco, 1968.

20. *Ibid.*

21. On the trend of growing institutionalization, see details in Ch. 6.

22. For an early analysis of the variety of orientations in the sociologist's role and of the dilemmas and pressures to which they give rise, see R. K. Merton, "Social conflict over styles of sociological work," *Transactions of the Fourth World Congress of Sociology,* (International Sociological Association, 1961), pp. 21–44.

For more recent statements, see, for example, C. J. Lammers, "Mono- and polyparadigmatic developments in natural and social sciences," (University of Leyden: Institute of Sociology, 1973); R. Klima, "Einige widersprüche in rollen-set der soziologen," in B. Schäfers (ed.), *Thesen zur Kritik der Soziologie, op. cit.,* pp. 80–96; Yngvar Lochen, *Sociologens Dilemma* (Oslo: Gyldendal Norskverlag, 1970); A. Pagani, *Responsabilita del Sociologo* (Milano: Edizioni di Communita, 1964); L. Gallino, "Crisi della sociologia, ricerca sociologica, ruolo del sociologo," in P. Rossi (ed.), *Ricerca Sociologica, op. cit.,* pp. 309–327; P. Bourdieu, J. C. Passeron, and J. C. Chamboredon, *Le Métier du Sociologue,* Livre I (Paris: Mouton, 1968); A. de Miguel, *Sociologia o Subversion* (Barcelona: Plaza Janes, 1975), especially Ch. 1, 2, 3, 6, 7.

23. On the main foci of these debates see R. Bendix, "Sociology and ideology," in E. A. Tiryakian (ed.), *The Phenomenon of Sociology* (New York: Appleton-Century Crofts, 1971), pp. 173–187; H. S. Becker, "Whose side are we on?" *Social Problems,* Vol. 14 (winter 1967), pp. 239–247; A. W. Gouldner, "The sociologist as a partisan: sociology and the welfare-state," *The American Sociologist,* Vol. 3 (May 1968), pp. 103–116; H. J. Gans, "Social science for social policy," in I. L. Horowitz (ed.), *The Use and Abuse of Social Science* (New Brunswick, N.J.: Transaction Books, 1971), pp. 13–34; J. D. Douglas (ed.), *The Impact of Sociology* (New York: Appleton-Century-Crofts, 1970); J. D. Douglas (ed.), *The Relevance of Sociology* (New York: Appleton-Century-Crofts, 1970); I. L. Horowitz, *Professing Sociology; Studies in the Life Cycle of Social Science* (Chicago: Aldine, 1968), especially Parts 2 and 3; I. L. Horowitz, *Foundations of Political Sociology* (New York: Harper & Row, 1972), especially Ch. 16–20, 25; G. Sjoberg (ed.), *Ethics, Politics, and Social Research* (London: Routledge & Kegan Paul, 1967); *American Sociologist,* Vol. 6, supplementary issue (June 1971).

These debates did not bypass anthropology. On this see G. Engel-Lang, "Professionalism under attack: the case of the anthropologists," *Social Science Information*, Vol. 10, No. 3 (1971), pp. 117–132.

For the debates in sociology, see also R. Klima, "Einige widersprüche im rollen-set der soziologen," *op. cit.;* Y. Lochen, *Sosiologens Dilemma, op. cit.;* J. Goudsblom, *Belansvan de Sociologie* (Utrecht: Het Spectrum, 1974).

24. C. W. Mills, "The professional ideology of social pathologists," *American Journal of Sociology*, Vol. 49 (September 1943), pp. 165–180.

25. The discussions on all these problems are by now too numerous to be listed except in specialized bibliographies. Some of the earlier discussions are to be found in A. W. Gouldner and S. M. Miller (eds.), *Applied Sociology: Opportunities and Problems* (New York: Free Press, 1965), especially Ch. 6.

   Some of the later discussions can be found in J. D. Douglas, "The relevance of sociology," in J. D. Douglas (ed.), *The Relevance of Sociology, op. cit.,* pp. 185–233; C. J. Lammers, "Mono- and polyparadigmatic developments in natural and social sciences," *op. cit.*

   One of the most rigorous discussions of the possible technocratization of sociological theory has been conducted in Germany between N. Luhmann and J. Habermas; see J. Habermas and N. Luhmann, *Theorie der Gesellschaft oder Sozialtechnologie* (Frankfurt: Suhrkamp, 1971); W. D. Narr, D. H. Runze, et al., *Theorie der Gesellschaft oder Sozialtechnologie; Neue Berträge zur Habermas-Luhmann Diskussion* (Frankfurt: Suhrkamp, 1974); H. J. Siegel, *System und Krise-Beitrag zur Habermas-Luhmann Diskussion* (Frankfurt: Suhrkamp, 1974);

   For other works on technocratization of theory see B. Schäfers (ed.), *Thesen zur Kritik der Soziologie, op. cit.;* C. Koch and D. Senghaas, *Texte zur Technokratie Diskussion* (Frankfurt: Europeischen Verlagsanstalt, 1971).

   For Italy, A. Pagani, *Responsibilita del Sociologo, op. cit.;* F. Ferraroti, *Una Sociologia Alternativa* (Bari: De Donato, 1972).

26. For concise analyses of the main orientations and poles in the sociologist's role, discussed below, see R. K. Merton, "Social conflict over styles of sociological work," *op. cit.;* R. W. Friedrichs, *A Sociology of Sociology* (New York: Free Press, 1970), especially Ch. 3–6; E. Shils, "The calling of sociology," in T. Parsons et al. (eds.), *Theories of Society*, Vol. 2 (New York: Free Press, 1961), pp. 1405–1448; I. L. Horowitz, "Mainliners and marginals: the human shape of sociological theory," in L. Gross (ed.), *Sociological Theory: Inquiries and Paradigms* (New York: Harper & Row, 1963), pp. 358–383; M. Janowitz, "Professionalization of sociology," *American Journal of Sociology*, Vol. 78, No. 1 (July 1972), pp. 105–135; R. Klima, "Einige widersprüch im rollen-Set der soziologen," *op. cit.;* A. Pagani, *Responsabilita del Sociologo, op. cit.;* Y. Lochen, *Sosiologens Dilemma, op. cit.;* P. Bourdieu, J. C. Passeron and J. C. Chamboredon, *Le Métier du Sociologue, op. cit.;* J. D. Colfax and J. L. Roach (eds.), *Radical Sociology* (New York: Basic Books, 1971).

27. On this see the analysis in Ch. 6, above.

28. On codification in the methodological field, see details in Ch. 6 above. See also L. Gross (ed.), *Sociological Theory: Inquiries and Paradigms, op. cit.;* L. Gross (ed.), *Symposium on Sociological Theory* (New York: Row, Peterson, 1959); D. Martindale, *The Nature and Types of Sociological Theory* (Boston: Houghton Mifflin, 1960).

   Wolff's analysis is to be found in K. Wolff, "The sociology of knowledge and sociological theory," in L. Gross (ed.), *Symposium on Sociological Theory, op. cit.,* Ch. 18.

For Horowitz's analysis see I. L. Horowitz, "Mainliners and marginals: the human shape of sociological theory," op. cit.

29. R. W. Friedrichs, A Sociology of Sociology, op. cit., Ch. 4, especially pp. 85–86. For one of the first shifts towards the integration of the study of social problems with the mainstream of sociology, see A. Gouldner and S. M. Miller (eds.), Applied Sociology, op. cit.; also S. N. Eisenstadt (ed.), Comparative Social Problems (New York: Free Press, 1964); R. K. Merton and R. Nisbet (eds.), Contemporary Social Problems (New York: Harcourt Brace, 1961), which since its first publication in 1961 has appeared in three revised and enlarged editions.

30. C. W. Mills, The Sociological Imagination, op. cit., especially Ch. 2–4; C. W. Mills, "The professional ideology of social pathologists," op. cit.; I. L. Horowitz, Professing Sociology: Studies in the Life Cycle of Social Science, op. cit.; I. L. Horowitz, Foundations of Political Sociology, op. cit.; B. Moore, Political Power and Social Theory, op. cit.; R. P. Wolff, B. Moore and H. Marcuse, A Critique of Pure Tolerance, op. cit.; M. Stein and A. Vidich (eds.), Sociology on Trial (Englewood Cliffs, N.J.: Prentice-Hall, 1963); M. Stein, The Eclipse of Community: an Interpretation of American Studies (Princeton, N.J.: Princeton University Press, 1960).

31. R. Lynd, Knowledge for What? (Princeton, N.J.: Princeton University Press, 1939).

32. Some of these debates appeared in handbooks published in that period, such as Sj. Groenman et al. (eds.), Het Sociale Leven in Al Zijn Facetten (Assen: Van Gorcum, 1958); T. R. Fyvel (ed.), The Frontiers of Sociology (London: C. A. West, 1964); R. König (ed.), Das Interview: Formen, Technik, Answertung (Cologne: Verlag fur Politik und Wirtschaft, 1957); R. König (ed.), Beobachtung und Experiment in der Sozialforschung (Cologne: Verlag fur Politik und Wirtschaft, 1956); R. König (ed.), Handbuch der Empirischen Sozialforschung (Stuttgart: F. Enke, 1962, 1969), 2 vols.

33. G. Gurvitch, Dialectique et Sociologie, op. cit.
      For the analysis of the social bases and conditions of sociology by the French Sociological Association see the entire issue of Cahiers Internationaux de Sociologie, Vol. 26 (1959).
      For good surveys of the discussions in the Frankfurt school see M. Jay, "Some recent developments in critical theory," op. cit. D. Frisby, "The Frankfurt school: critical theory and positivism," op. cit.

34. On the Methodenstreit, see the analysis in Ch. 2 and 5, above.

35. On König and other scholars involved in these discussions, see the quotation of Zapf in section 4 of this chapter.
      On Italy see Sociologi e Centri de Potere in Italia (Bari: Laterza, 1962).
      For these problems in the development of sociology in Eastern European countries see, for example, J. J. Wiatr (ed.), The State of Sociology in Eastern Europe Today (Carbondale & Edwardsville, Ill.: Southern Illinois University Press, 1971); N. Birnbaum, "The crisis in Marxist sociology," in J. D. Colfax and J. L. Roach (eds.), Radical Sociology, op. cit., pp. 108–131; P. Berger (ed.), Marxism and Sociology—Views From Eastern Europe (New York: Appleton-Century-Crofts, 1969).

36. On criminology and deviance see E. H. Sutherland and D. R. Cressey, Principles of Criminology, 6th ed. (Chicago: Lippincott, 1960); D. R. Cressey, Delinquency, Crime, and Differential Association (The Hague: Martinus Nijhoff, 1964); W. G. Runciman, Relative Deprivation and Social Justice (London: Routledge & Kegan Paul, 1966).
      For a review of theories of convergence of industrial societies see S. N. Eisenstadt, Tradition, Change and Modernity, op. cit., especially Ch. 1.

On inner- and other-directed personalities in relation to mass society see D. Riesman, *The Lonely Crowd* (New York: Doubleday Anchor, 1953).

On conditions of democracy and authoritarianship see for example: S. M. Lipset, *Political Man* (New York: Dobuleday, 1960).

Some of the studies of the importance of primary relations and groups in complex organizations are summarized and analyzed in the following works: G. C. Homans, *The Human Group* (New York: Harcourt Brace, 1950); P. M. Blau and W. R. Scott, *Formal Organizations* (San Francisco: Chandler, 1962).

For reference groups see R. K. Merton, *Social Theory and Social Structure,* rev. ed. (New York: Free Press, Glencoe, 1963), especially Ch. 8 and 9.

For stratification see R. Bendix and S. M. Lipset (eds.), *Class, Status and Power, op. cit.,* 1953 and 1966 editions.

For professions see T. Parsons, "The professions and social structure," in T. Parsons, *Essays in Sociological Theory* (New York: Free Press, 1963), pp. 34–49; H. M. Vollmer and D. L. Mills (eds.), *Professionalization* (Englewood Cliffs, N.J.: Prentice-Hall, 1966); H. Jamous and B. Peloille, "Changes in the French university-hospital system," in J. A. Jackson (ed.), *Professions and Professionalization* (Cambridge: Cambridge University Press, 1970), pp. 111–152.

For the theory of "two-step flow of communication" see H. Menzel and E. Katz, "Social relations and innovation in the medical profession: the epidemiology of a new drug," in E. E. Maccoby et al. (eds.), *Readings in Social Psychology* (New York: Holt, Rinehart, and Winston, 1958), pp. 532–545; E. Katz, "The two-step flow of communication: an up-to-date report on an hypothesis," *Public Opinion Quarterly,* Vol. 21, No. 1 (spring 1957), pp. 61–78.

37. See illustrations of these tendencies in the various readers of that period, cited in Ch. 6, above.

38. D. Riesman, *The Lonely Crowd, op. cit.;* S. M. Lipset, *Agrarian Socialism* (Glencoe, Ill.: Free Press, 1950); S. M. Lipset et al., *Union Democracy* (Glencoe, Ill.: Free Press, 1956); S. M. Lipset, *Political Man, op. cit.;* M. Janowitz, *The Professional Soldier* (Glencoe, Ill.: Free Press, 1960).

On studies of modernization see S. N. Eisenstadt, *Tradition, Change and Modernity, op. cit.,* Ch. 1 and 5; Chong-Do-Hah and J. Schneider, "A critique of current studies of political development and modernization," *Social Research,* Vol. 35 (1968), pp. 130–158.

39. On the examination of the functional-structural model see details in Ch. 8.

On the further examination of this model and the major "countermodels," see details in Ch. 10.

40. For these various trends see the materials quoted in notes 2–6, 9–11, 13 respectively.

41. On the examination of models in terms of their epistemological and philosophical assumptions, see illustrative materials in note 16 of this chapter.

For the critical analysis of the concepts "role," "institutions," and so on, see details in Ch. 8 and in Ch. 10.

For a survey of studies which refer to the critical examination of the concept of "political development" in particular and of "modernization" more generally, see S. N. Eisenstadt, *Tradition, Change and Modernity, op. cit.,* Ch. 1 and 5, and the literature quoted there in extenso; and above all C. Leys (ed.), *Politics and Change in Developing Countries* (Cambridge: Cambridge University Press, 1969); R. A. Packenham, "Approaches to the study of political development," *World Politics,* Vol. 17 (1964), pp.

108–120; A. R. Desai (ed.), *Essays on Modernization of Underdeveloped Societies, op. cit.* For the quotation, see D. Ingleby, "Ideology and the human sciences: some comments on the role of reification in psychology and psychiatry," *The Human Context,* Vol. 2, No. 2 (July 1970), p. 169.

42. E. Allardt, "Scandinavian sociology and Swedish sociology," *op. cit.,* pp. 66, 69.

43. R. Dahrendorf, "Homo Sociologicus: on the history, significance, and the limits of the category of social role," in R. Dahrendorf, *Essays in the Theory of Society* (London: Routledge & Kegan Paul, 1968), pp. 19–87.

For a broader and more diversified critical examination of the concept "role," see also J. A. Jackson (ed.), *Role* (Cambridge: Cambridge University Press, 1972); F. Haug, *Kritik der Rollentheorie und ihrer Anwendung in der Bürgerlichen Deutschen Soziologie* (Frankfurt: Fischer/Verlag, 1972).

44. R. Lourau, *L'Analyse Institutionelle* (Paris: Les Editions de Minuit, 1970); F. Basaglia, *L'Instituzione Negata: Rapporto da un Ospedale Psichiatrico* (Torino: Giulio Einaudi, 1968); A. Touraine, *Sociologie de l'Action* (Paris: Seuil, 1965); A. Willener, *The Action-Image of Society* (London: Tavistock, 1970).

45. J. Israel and H. Tajfel (eds.), *The Context of Social Psychology: a Critical Assessment* (London, New York: Academic Press, 1972); N. Armistead (ed.), *Reconstructing Social Psychology* (Harmondsworth: Penguin, 1974).

46. See, for example, *American Sociologist,* Vol. 6, supplementary issue (June 1971).

47. For materials illustrative of this trend as well as of the various related issues discussed here, see note 23 of this chapter.

See also the materials collected in J. D. Colfax and J. L. Roach (eds.), *Radical Sociology, op. cit.;* L. T. Reynolds and J. M. Reynolds (eds.), *The Sociology of Sociology* (New York: David McKay, 1970); J. D. Douglas (ed.), *The Relevance of Sociology, op. cit.;* J. D. Douglas (ed.), *The Impact of Sociology, op. cit.*

48. G. Gurvitch, *The Social Frameworks of Knowledge* (Oxford: B. Blackwell, 1971); K. Wolff, "The sociology of knowledge and sociological theory," in L. Gross (ed.), *Symposium on Sociological Theory, op. cit.*

On the Frankfurt school see M. Jay, "Some recent developments in critical theory," *op. cit.;* D. Frisby, "The Frankfurt school: critical theory and positivism," *op. cit.*

For a broader analysis of the relationship of the Frankfurt school to orthodox Marxism, see M. Jay, *The Dialectical Imagination: a History of the Frankfurt School and the Institute of Social Research, 1923–1950,* (Boston: Little, Brown, 1973); L. T. Reynolds and J. M. Reynolds (eds.), *The Sociology of Sociology, op. cit.* Parts 1 and 3.

49. H. S. Becker, "Whose side are we on?," *op. cit.;* A. W. Gouldner, "The sociologist as partisan: sociology and the welfare state," *op. cit.*

For a useful general analysis see also U. Beck, *Objektivität und Normativität: die Theorie—Praxis Debatte in der Modernen Deutsche und Amerikanische Soziologie* (Hamburg: Rowohlt, 1974), especially Part 3.

50. Illustrations of somewhat milder approaches can be found, for example, in A. W. Gouldner, "The sociologist as partisan: sociology and the welfare state," *op. cit.;* S. J. Bodenheimer, "The ideology of developmentalism: American political science's paradigm—surrogate for Latin American studies," *Berkeley Journal of Sociology,* Vol. 15 (1970), pp. 95–137.

The more extreme approaches are represented, for example, in such texts as are quoted in note 51, as well as the essays collected and edited by P. Rossi (ed.), *Ricerca Sociologica e Ruolo del Sociologo, op. cit.*

Gouldner's own rather ambivalent position can be found both in his *The Coming Crisis of Western Sociology, op. cit.;* and above all in his collection of essays *For Sociology* (New York: Basic Books, 1974). See also L. Coser's review of *For Sociology* in the *American Journal of Sociology*, Vol. 80, No. 4 (January 1975), pp. 1009–1011.

51.   For illustrations see, for example, D. Cohn-Bendit et al., "Why sociologists?" and J. Horton, "The fetishism of sociology," in J. D. Colfax and J. L. Roach (eds.), *Radical Sociology, op. cit.,* pp. 61–66, 171–193.

52.   R. Aron, "Modern society and sociology," in E. A. Tiryakian (ed.), *The Phenomenon of Sociology, op. cit.,* pp. 158–170.

Some of the scholarly works on the development of sociology in different settings which follow this trend are collected in E. A. Tiryakian (ed.), *The Phenomenon of Sociology, op. cit.,* especially Part 1.

See also P. Abrams, *The Origins of British Sociology, 1834–1914,* (Chicago: University of Chicago Press, 1968); T. N. Clark, *Prophets and Patrons: The French University and the Emergence of the Social Sciences* (Cambridge, Mass.: Harvard University Press, 1973); A. Oberschall, "The institutionalization of American sociology," in A. Oberschall (ed.) *The Establishment of Empirical Sociology: Studies in Continuity, Discontinuity and Institutionalization* (New York: Harper & Row, 1972), pp. 187–251; A. B. Cherns (ed.), *Social Science: Organization and Policy,* First Series: Belgium, Chile, Egypt, Hungary, Nigeria, Sri Lanka (Paris: Unesco, 1974).

For an illuminating analysis of the impact of changing social situations on social research see E. K. Scheuch, "Sozialer wandel und sozialforschung: über die beziehungen zwischen gesellschaft und empirischer sozialforschung," *Kölner Zeitschrift für Soziologie und Sozialpsychologie* (Köln und Opladen: Westdeutscher Verlag GmbH, 1965), pp. 1–48.

53.   A. W. Gouldner, *The Coming Crisis of Western Sociology, op. cit.;* R. Friedrichs, *A Sociology of Sociology, op. cit.*

For a critical review of these works see J. Ben-David, "The state of sociological theory and the sociological community: a review article," *Comparative Studies in Society and History*, Vol. 15, No. 4 (October 1973), pp. 448–472; *Rassegna Italiana di Sociologia*, Vol. 13, No. 4 (October-December 1972), entire issue, especially the articles by G. E. Swanson, R. A. Peterson and John O'Neill.

For an illustration of radical analysis of the history of sociology see H. Schwendinger and J. R. Schwendinger, *The Sociologists of the Chair: a Radical Analysis of the Formative Years of North American Sociology, 1883–1922* (New York: Basic Books, 1974).

See also the discussions reported in P. Rossi (ed.), *Ricerca Sociologica e Ruolo del Sociologo, op. cit.;* W. Hochkeppel (ed.), *Soziologie zwischen Theorie und Empirie* (München: Nymphenburger, 1970), especially pp. 135–153.

54.   R. K. Merton, "Social conflict over styles of sociological work," *op. cit.*

55.   L. Gross (ed.), *Symposium on Sociological Theory, op. cit.,* Ch. 9; D. Martindale, *The Nature and Types of Sociological Theory, op. cit.,* Chs. 17–19; M. Black (ed.), *The Social Theories of Talcott Parsons, op. cit.;* R. Dahrendorf, *Class and Class Conflict in Industrial Society* (Stanford, Cal.: Stanford University Press, 1959).

56.   K. Davis and W. E. Moore, "Some principles of stratification," *American Sociological Review*, Vol. 10, No. 2 (1945), pp. 242–249; M. M. Tumin, "Some principles of stratification: a critical analysis," *American Sociological Review*, Vol. 18 (August 1953), pp. 387–393.

For analysis of small groups made in connection with the exchange model's criticism of functionalism, see, for example, G. C. Homans, *Social Behavior: its Elementary Forms* (New York: Harcourt, Brace and World, 1961).

57. A. J. Vidich and M. Stein (eds.), *Reflections on Community Studies* (New York: Wiley, 1964), essays by Stein and Vidich, Ch. 6, 11, which stress the problems stemming from the emphasis on value-free sociology and the bureaucratization of research; B. Moore, *Political Power and Social Theory, op. cit.*, especially Chs. 3, 4.

58. E. C. Hughes, *The Sociological Eye* (Chicago and New York: Aldine, Atherton, 1971), Chs. 13, 14, 28, 33, 34, 43.

59. For organizational theory see, for example, D. Silverman, *The Theory of Organizations: a Sociological Framework, op. cit.*, especially Chs. 2, 3, 6, 7, 10.

For deviance see, for example, J. D. Douglas (ed.), *Deviance and Respectability* (New York: Basic Books, 1970); I. Taylor, P. Walton, and J. Young, *The New Criminology: for a Social Theory of Deviance* (London: Routledge & Kegan Paul, 1973); L. Taylor and I. Taylor (eds.), *Politics and Deviance* (Harmondsworth: Penguin, 1973); K. D. Opp, *Kriminalität und Gesellschaftstruktur* (Neuwied: Luchterhand, 1968); K. D. Opp, *Abweichendes Verbalden und Gesellschaftstruktur* (Neuwied: Luchterhand, 1974).

For an interesting critical approach see also D. Chapman, *Sociology and the Stereotype of the Criminal* (London: Tavistock, 1968).

A good collection of debates which combine analysis of a particular field with different paradigmatic approaches can be found in A. Effrat (ed.), *Perspectives in Political Sociology* (New York: Indianapolis: Bobbs Merrill, 1972).

For such evaluation of the anthropological field see C. J. J. Vermuelen and A. de Ruijter, "Dominant epistemological presuppositions in the use of the cross-cultural survey method," *Current Anthropology*, Vol. 16, No. 1 (March 1975), pp. 29–52.

60. For such a review of stratification see, for example, S. N. Eisenstadt, "Prestige, participation, and strata formation," in J. A. Jackson (ed.), *Social Stratification* (Cambridge: Cambridge University Press, 1968), pp. 62–103.

For such reviews as they relate to modernization see, for example, S. N. Eisenstadt, *Tradition, Change and Modernity, op. cit.*, Chs. 1 and 5; A. R. Desai (ed.), *Essays on Modernization of Underdeveloped Societies, op. cit.*, 2 vols.

For illustrations of such reviews from a narrower perspective see J. H. Goldthorpe, "Theories of industrial society: reflections on the recrudescence of historicism and the future of futurology," *Archives Européennes de Sociologie*, Vol. 12, No. 2 (1971), pp. 263–288; S. J. Bodenheimer, "The ideology of developmentalism," *op. cit.*

For general criticisms of the structural-functional model, above all as applied to macrosocietal research in general and to studies of modernization in particular, see also W. L. Bühl, *Evolution und Revolution: Kritik der Symmetrischen Soziologie, op. cit.*; K. H. Tjaden, *Soziale System und Sozialer Wandel* (Stuttgart: F. Enke, 1969); A. D. Smith, *The Concept of Social Change: a Critique of the Functionalist Theory of Social Change* (London and Boston: Routledge & Kegan Paul, 1973).

61. A. W. Gouldner, *The Coming Crisis of Western Sociology, op. cit.*; R. Friedrichs, *A Sociology of Sociology, op. cit.*; D. Atkinson, *Orthodox Consensus and Radical Alternative, op. cit.*, especially Chs. 5, 7, 8.

See also the reports on the debates in various countries reported in P. Rossi (ed.), *Ricerca Sociologica e Ruolo del Sociologo, op. cit.*; and the materials quoted in note 4 of this chapter, which relate to the criticism of "traditional" sociology as developed in Germany. For Germany and other European countries see also the materials quoted in note 17 of this chapter.

62. On this see for example D. Ingleby, "Ideology and the human sciences: some comments on the role of reification in psychology and psychiatry," *op. cit.* S. Koch, "Reflections on the state of psychology," *Social Research,* Vol. 38, No. 4, (1971), pp. 669–710; J. Israel and H. Tajfel (eds.), *The Context of Social Psychology: a Critical Assessment, op. cit.;* L. Hudson, *The Cult of the Fact* (New York: Harper, 1973).
    A more extreme radical approach can be found in P. Brown (ed.), *Radical Psychology* (London: Tavistock, 1973); J. Gabel, *La Fausse Conscience: Essai sur la Reification* (Paris: Edition de Minuit, 1962).

63. On the aspects of criticism in anthropology see G. Engel-Lang, "Professionalism under attack: the case of the anthropologists," *op. cit.;* B. Scholte, "Discontents in anthropology," *Social Research,* Vol. 38, No. 4 (1971), pp. 777–807; "The state of anthropology," *Times Literary Supplement* (July 6, 1973); "The state of anthropology," M. Gluckman's reply," in *Times Literary Supplement* (July 20, 1973); D. Hymes (ed.), *Reinventing Anthropology* (New York: Random House, 1972); I. C. Jarvie, "Epistle to the anthropologists," *American Anthropologist,* Vol. 77, No. 2 (June 1975), pp. 253–266.
    For crucial problems involved in the discussions on structuralism in anthropology, see for example: D. Goddard, "Conceptions of 'structure' in Lévi-Strauss and in British anthropology," *Social Research,* Vol. 32, No. 4, (1965), pp. 403–427; M. Glucksman, *Structuralist Analysis in Contemporary Social Thought, op. cit.,* especially Ch. 2.

64. The dissatisfactions in political science are well represented, in G. J. Graham and G. W. Carey (eds.), *The Post-Behavioral Era* (New York: McKay, 1972); H. P. Dreitzel (ed.), *Recent Sociology,* No. 1, *On the Social Basis of Politics* (New York: Collier-Macmillan, 1969); and in the several new journals in the field, as, for example, *Politics & Society.*

65. On the controversies in economics, see J. O'Connor, *The Fiscal Crisis of the State* (New York: St. Martin's Press, 1973); M. Olson, C. K. Clague, "Dissent in economics: the convergence in extremes," *Social Research,* Vol. 38, No. 4 (1971), pp. 751–776; A. Lindbeck, *The Political Economy of the New Left* (New York: Harper, 1971) and the introduction by Paul A. Samuelson; E. K. Hunt and J. G. Schwartz (eds.), *A Critique of Economic Theory* (Harmondsworth: Penguin Books, 1972).

66. For the renewed critical orientation to social reality, see, for example, T. B. Bottomore, *Sociology as Social Criticism, op. cit.;* S. M. Lipset, R. B. Dobson, "Social stratification and sociology in the Soviet Union," *Survey,* Vol. 88, No. 3 (summer 1973), pp. 114–185, especially pp. 114–115; B. Fay, *Social Theory and Political Practice* (London: George Allen & Unwin, 1975); C. Fletcher, *Beneath the Surface: An Account of Three Styles of Sociological Research* (London: Routledge & Kegan Paul, 1974) Part 3; E. C. Hughes, *The Sociological Eye, op. cit.,* especially Part 4; the special issue of the *American Journal of Sociology,* Vol. 78, No. 1 (July 1972), published as *Varieties of Political Expression in Sociology* (Chicago: University of Chicago Press, 1972); A. Effrat (ed.), *Perspectives in Political Sociology, op. cit.;* L. Gallino, "Crisi della sociologia, ricerca sociologica, . . ." in P. Rossi (ed.), *Ricerca Sociologica, op. cit.;* F. Ferrarotti, *Una Sociologia Alternativa, op. cit.;* A. de Miguel, *Sociologia o Subversion, op. cit.;* P. Bourdieu, J. C. Chamboredon, J. C. Passeron, *Le Métier du Sociologue, op. cit.*
    For orientations of this type in Dutch sociology, see the relevant materials quoted in note 17 above.
    For Scandinavian sociology, see above all Vols. 8, 9, 10, 11 of *Sociologisk Forsking;* Y. Lochen, *Sosiologens Dilemma, op. cit.*
    See also: A. Touraine, *Pour la Sociologie* (Paris: Editions du Seuil, 1974), especially Chs. 1 and 6; A. Solari, R. Franco, J. Jutkowitz, (eds), *Teoría y Accion Social: Inter-*

pretaciones Sociológicas del Desarrollo Latinoamericano, (Santiago de Chile: Latin American Institute for Social Studies, 1975).

The more extremist manifestation of such radical orientations can be found in journals like the *Berkeley Journal of Sociology,* and notably the *Insurgent Sociologist.*

67. S. M. Lipset and E. C. Ladd, "The politics of American sociologists," *American Journal of Sociology,* Vol. 78, No. 1 (July 1972), pp. 67–104; R. Jawetz, "American Sociology: a Study in the Sociology of Sociology," unpublished doctoral dissertation, Harvard University, Cambridge, Mass., 1972, Chs. 2 and 4; A. Touraine, *Pour la Sociologie, op. cit.*

For the orientations of protest in the earlier phases of sociology, see Chs. 2 and 3 above.

68. On the meaning of the "classical" and "romantic" approaches to sociology, see A. W. Gouldner, *The Coming Crisis of Western Sociology, op. cit.,* pp. 115–116; and A. W. Gouldner, *For Sociology, op. cit.,* Ch. 11.

For illustrations of these tensions, as well as those between the critical and scholarly orientations of sociologists, see the following debates: A. Effrat (ed.), *Perspectives in Political Sociology, op. cit.;* F. Ferrarotti, *Una Sociologia Alternativa, op. cit.;* A. de Miguel, *Sociologia o Subversion, op. cit.;* A. Touraine, *Pour la Sociologie, op. cit.;* A. Solari, R. Franco, J. Jutkowitz, (eds), *Theoría y Accion Social, op. cit.*

10

Major Analytic Developments and Openings

1. What, then, was the impact of these changing modes of discussion—the weakening of "segregated" discussion and the reexamination of the premises of sociological analysis—on the pursuit of sociological work? The impact was rather contradictory, for the various modes of discussion tended to develop analytically in two distinct directions.

On the one hand, debate encouraged the broadening of the sociological tradition and the deepening of its analytic framework.

Along with these potentially constructive developments, however, the convergence of different aspects of sociological discussion raised the possibility of abdication of the distinctiveness, autonomy, and progress of sociological analysis.

In this chapter we will analyze the constructive aspects of these developments. The following chapter will cover their negative consequences.

The Trend Toward Analytic Openings

2. The most constructive aspect of theoretical debate lay in this fact: Although, the countermodels were often presented as self-contained explicative paradigms, totally different from the structural-functional model and from each other, they in fact contained potential openings with important and constructive theoretical implications. To analyze the nature of these mutual openings, we must return to criticisms of the

structural-functional model. The most natural starting points for such an examination are those aspects of criticism that touched on the central core of sociological analysis—that is, on the components of the model of social order which had presumably been developed by the structural-functional school.[1]

The structural-functional model contained three important components: a strong emphasis on values and consensus as major mechanisms for the acceptance of social order; a sociologistic or social-structural point of analytic departure; and a strong systemic, presumably ahistorical, conception of society. Given these central characteristics, one would expect that all antithetical models would display a combination of several emphases—on power and interests, conflict and change, and a nonsystemic approach. However, even a preliminary look at most recent controversies indicates that this was not the case. Rather, within most of these countermodels, many different cross-cuttings developed on the basis of combinations of components of this paradigm.

To give only a few illustrations: It has already been emphasized, even by extreme critics of Talcott Parsons, that the classic Marxist approach contains most of the basic ingredients of a very strong functionalist-systemic approach, even though it combines them with a strong emphasis on conflict and on change. On the other hand, in spite of the fact that Parsons' work on the whole has often been criticized as "static" and nonhistorical, his own more recent work emphasizes an evolutionary and historical perspective.[2] Similarly, Ralf Dahrendorf has combined an emphasis on conflict and power with a strong systemic view of society. Randall Collins, and to some degree Reinhard Bendix, by contrast, have tended to combine such emphasis on conflict and power relations with an anti-systemic approach.[3]

Among those who uphold the interactionist point of view, some, like Dick Atkinson, combine an interactionist view with very strong antisystemic orientations, while others, like John Rex, combine a strong emphasis on meaningful definitions of situations by individuals with a strong emphasis on power and systemic aspects of social structures.[4]

The emphasis on the symbolic dimension may take a strong "structuralist" orientation, as in the work of Claude Lévi-Strauss, which disregards both the dimensions of power and of organizational needs of society. Or it may be associated with a strong predilection to analyze systemic exigencies, focused on power and conflict, as is the case with French Marxists who have combined Lévi-Strauss' structuralism with the "traditional" Marxist approach.[5]

A varied combination of elements can also be found in the controversy about the historical specificity of societies as against their systemic dimensions and presumed evolutionary tendencies. Most neo-Marxists accuse structural-functionalism of lacking historical specificity and for stressing values as an autonomous force in society, combining their definition of such specificity with a heavy emphasis on power and conflict. Yet they nevertheless define such specificity in very strong systemic terms. Moreover, many of them fully recognize that Marx and many of his followers combined their insistence on the historical specificity of societies not only with a strong systemic orientation but with an evolutionary perspective.[6] Others who stress the historical specificity of social life, such as Bendix and Collins, deny the validity of both an evolutionary perspective and the unqualified emphasis on systemic qualities of social organization.[7]

Such varied cross-cuttings have developed not only in general discussion, but in controversies in substantive research areas: social change and modernization, social stratification, deviance, and the theory of organization.[8]

These cross-cuttings have important analytic consequences. First, the components which seem to converge in the structural-functional model need not necessarily go together; hence the criticisms of this model need not necessarily give rise to completely different, closed, and exclusive paradigms. A great variety of paradigms are possible, each with its own combination of these analytic components. Even more important for our analysis, however, is the fact that these frequent cross-cuttings among aspects of the various models indicate an opening up of all these approaches. These openings are, in principle, identical to those we encountered in our discussion of the earlier stages of development of sociological theory, above all in the transition from the closed- to open-system approaches and within the various open systems.[9]

Openings with Respect to the Symbolic Dimension of Human Behavior

3.   We will begin by analyzing these openings and their analytic consequences with respect to the relationship between models stressing the symbolic or cultural bases of social order and those stressing other components of social order, such as "social" and "individual" bases. The first set of controversies will be those between the structural-functional model and the structuralist approaches on the place of the symbolic dimen-

sion in the construction of social life and the relationship of this dimension to the organizational aspects and working of social groups and systems.

In sociology and social anthropology, this controversy developed in the late 1950s as part of the more general criticism of the structural-functional reductionist view, which saw the symbolic dimension mainly as a reflection of the social organization, of society. This controversy provided significant openings with respect to the autonomy and internal systemic properties of the symbolic realm, and to the possibility of "direct" relationships between this realm and individual activities, social capacities, and patterns of interaction—relationships which could not be seen only as a reflection of the systemic needs of social organization.

The study of ritual provides a good illustration of these trends in approaching the symbolic field. In the interwar period, the two main social science interpretations of ritual were closely related to two major closed-system paradigms, the psychoanalytic and the "sociologistic." According to the first approach, religious ritual is given an "individualistic" interpretation. Ritual and its symbols are conceived as the expression of and means of coping with unresolved basic human conflicts, conflicts which have their roots in a prehistorical event of primordial, exemplary significance for the human condition—such as the murder of the leader of the tribe by his sons.[10]

This psychological orientation was developed in greater detail and specification in American anthropology, especially in the so-called "culture-and-personality" school. According to this approach, most of the central rituals, such as various *rites de passage,* are culturally devised means of coping with basic problems which emerge in the course of personality development, as for example the Oediphus complex. The function of the rites in this and similar cases is to resolve these problems at the level of personality and to avoid the negative consequences that unresolved personality disturbances might have for the individual and for the larger social context alike.[11]

The basic "sociologistic" analysis of ritual was given full impetus by the English anthropologists, especially by A. R. Radcliffe-Brown, who was followed by his direct and indirect disciples, Meyer Fortes and Max Gluckman; this analysis was influenced by Émile Durkheim and the earlier work of William Robertson-Smith.[12] In this tradition, ritual is presented as fulfilling a universal function of social integration. In Durkheim's analysis the function of ritual was seen as that of strengthening the commitment of members of society to its collective identity. The English anthropological school stressed a more cybernetic function of ritual: that of ensuring the adequate performance of social roles neces-sary for the functioning of society as a structural system.

A somewhat different, more "psychological," interpretation was given by Bronislaw Malinowski, who argued that the main function of ritual was to reduce individual anxiety arising on such occasions as death and natural disasters. The collective nature of the ritual, according to Malinowski, strengthened both the beliefs transmitted during its per-formance and the integration of society.[13]

Common to these approaches was the assumption that the content and symbols communicated in ritual were by and large secondary to its basic social function, or were derived from it, and that, given the existence of any ritual, the successful performance of its function was more or less assured.

Both closed-system approaches to the symbolic field, the psychological and the sociologistic, were challenged from the 1950s on in a series of approaches which in one way or another stressed the autonomy and possibly the predominance of the symbolic sphere in the construction of social and cultural reality. The most complete expression of this emphasis on the autonomy and primacy of the symbolic dimension, and on its constitutive role in the formation of human culture and society, is found, as was noted, in the work of Lévi-Strauss. His work exhibits very strong characteristics of a closed-system approach and, consequently, a possible reification of the symbolic sphere.

Unlike the British and American schools in anthropology, the struc-turalists concentrated more on the study of myth than of ritual and tried to analyze it in terms of general, presumably unconscious, rules of the human mind. These rules were oriented to basic oppositions or contradic-tions, such as those between nature and culture, which they reorganized in differing patterns so as to resolve them.[14] Thus, they constituted the core of the "hidden structure" of culture and society.

The extreme structuralist approach asserted not only the existence of certain autonomous properties and dynamics of the symbolic sphere —properties which could not be explained by their social and psychologi-cal functions, or by the rules and needs of societies or individuals. It maintained above all that it was the special properties of the symbolic sphere, the rules of the human mind, that determined the basic rules and characteristics of social reality.

4.   The closed-system analyses of the symbolic dimension in social life and organization began to be opened in the late 1950s. These attempts

stemmed from increasing dissatisfaction with the logical closure of Lévi-Strauss' system and the apparent closure of the structural-functional and culture-personality models, which reduced the symbolic dimension to its purely organizational or psychological function. The alternative models tried to "dynamize" and "open" the symbolic system in its relationship both to social structure and to individual behavior.

These openings did not deny the autonomous qualities of either the social or the psychological spheres, nor, obviously, of the symbolic spheres. Rather they tried to diversify the rules of the symbolic realm by relating them not only to the logical properties of human thought but to the existential problems of human life and to the organization of the social order. Second, they tried to probe more deeply the mechanisms through which these symbolic orientations became part of the working of groups and societies, and the differential effects of the cultural realm on such working.

These openings can also be illustrated by the study of ritual. In the early 1950s, Clyde Kluckhohn developed a more "open" psychological approach to the study of ritual in which the integrative social function of ritual, which had been taken for granted, was made a variable—a problem for research.[15]

Some of the most important developments in the analysis of the symbolic sphere were later made by Clifford Geertz. Geertz stressed the importance of the contents of culture that were transmitted in ritual and their relevance for the understanding of the social function of ritual. He also demonstrated that ritual did not always have integrative results, especially when its norms contradicted other cultural orientations to which its participants were committed. In more general terms, Geertz stressed both the respective autonomy of the cultural-religious and ideological systems and their continuous interpenetration with the "actual" social world.[16]

Geertz and other scholars like Victor Turner and Thomas O. Beidelman, have developed more differentiated approaches to the relations between the symbolic, social, and personal levels of social action. Their main thesis is that the fundamental attributes and contents of symbolic systems are related to man's basic existential nature, that it is in the symbolic sphere that the basic predicaments of human existence in its various aspects—biological, social, and cultural—are most fully defined and articulated. Thus the situations in which such symbolization takes place need not necessarily be a direct reflection of social organization, although they define some of the bases of social structure and its tensions.

Turner notes the tendency in many rituals and myths to emphasize the element of "communitas," as against the institutional division of labor, and claims that it is in such situations that the symbolization of the various predicaments of the human situations becomes most fully articulated. In general, such situations are seen as defining the more liminal zones in which "the indeterminate margins which surrounded discrete elements in a symbolic field become especially articulated and constitute these as special danger zones."[17] Similarly, Beidelman sees ambivalence and contradiction as inherent in any ritual, and as rooted not only in the conflicts of social organization, but in the very symbolic construction of social and cultural reality which becomes related to social organization.[18]

Turner and Beidelman, whose approach has roots in the Freudian tradition and in that of Lèvi-Strauss, do not reject the view that ritual may have integrative social functions. They argue, however, that the successful performance of such functions depends on emotional states aroused by specific symbols. Specifically: ritual symbolism, expressing a basic contradiction between "natural man" and society and culture, and rooted in the biopsychical nature of man, evokes strong emotions which are selectively channeled in socially constructive directions by some rituals, but tend to have more destructive consequences in other cases.

In a similar vein, Mary Douglas has developed a program of what may be called "anthropological phenomenology." She attempts to analyze the major types of natural symbols which develop in response to the basic predicaments of human biological and social situations, or "givens." These symbols, while cutting across concrete social organizations, are closely interwoven with them.[19]

The more differentiated approach to the internal characteristics of the symbolic sphere and its relationship to social organization raised again the problem of the mechanisms through which it was related to institutional life. Anthropologists close to the structuralist tradition sought to locate the institutional anchorages and implications of the major types of symbolic orientations, and several scholars attempted to extend the structuralist model beyond the study of primitive societies and kinship systems to more complex societies. Louis Dumont, who has done perhaps the most significant work in this area, tried to relate the symbolic structure of Indian civilization to the organizational aspects of Indian society, and to explain how the hierarchical conception of the world and of the social order had shaped the institutional dynamics of Indian civilization. Luc de Heush, in his investigation of African tribes,[20] attempted to specify some institutional meeting places between the symbolic sphere as a constitutive factor of social order and the social organizational aspects of the working of social systems.

Concern with the relationship between the symbolic pattern or order and the organizational aspects of social life has been prominent in the work of Edmund Leach, one of Lévi-Strauss' major critical followers among the senior group of British anthropologists. In his analysis of Old Testament stories about the succession of Solomon, Leach not only analyzed the common logical symbolic structure underlying these stories, but, going beyond Lévi-Strauss, showed that this common structure became meaningful only if it was related to the recurring problems of the political and cultural identity and the organization of power in the society in Israel of that time. In his work on Burma and Ceylon, Leach stressed the importance of such symbolic orientations in the definition of the boundaries of ethnic, religious, and political collectivities and the interrelationships between them.[21]

Under the influence and often the guidance of Leach, further attempts have been made in England to reexamine central areas of anthropological research, like myths and kinship, in the light of possible analytic and empirical confrontation between the structuralist and the organizational or institutional approaches. They have tried to indicate, first, how the symbolic orientations that define the major problems of human and social existence both symbolically and institutionally are related to various biological and ecological data, or "givens"; and, secondly, how such different orientations produce different institutional answers to these problems.[22] Also significant in this context has been David Schneider's effort to distinguish forcefully between symbolic orientations as against the behavioral and organizational aspects of kinship, particularly in the American kinship structure, and to point out some of the ways in which these symbolic orientations influence and possibly direct the latter.[23]

5. The openings from purely symbolic emphases to treatments of the social-organizational dimension of social order were reinforced by parallel openings toward the symbolic dimension which developed among both the structural-functionalists and conflict and exchange theorists. The opening to the symbolic dimension in the structural-functional school started in Parsons' own work and was most fully elaborated by Edward Shils. It developed from the refinement of the distinction between the different systems of social action—personality, culture, and social system—prominent in Parsons' work, a distinction based in part on Pitirim Sorokin's distinction between logico-meaning and functional integration of social systems.[24]

Parsons, unlike Sorokin, was aware from the beginning of the importance of identifying the systemic properties, characteristics, and boundaries of each of these, autonomous subsystems of action. But the distinction between these systems and the stress on their autonomy was to some degree analytically blurred in Parsons' exposition, first because of the assumption, often found in his work, that these systems are organized in a hierarchy, with the cultural-symbolic level exercising a central cybernetic function of control over the other two; and, second, because of the assumption of homology, or relatively close one-to-one relationships, between all these systems, the crucial connecting link being in this case the well-known "pattern variables."

Thus Parsons did not explore, as fully as his own program demanded, the various autonomous properties of the symbolic sphere, nor did he specify fully enough which of these properties were most relevant to the constitution of different aspects of institutional life, or which mechanisms—besides socialization—linked the symbolic to the institutional sphere.

Here Shils' analysis of the charismatic and its place in the social order provided a crucial advance. Following Durkheim and Weber, Shils reemphasized the centrality of the symbolic dimension in the life of the individual and in the construction of social reality, anchoring it in a basic quest for meaning and order. Relating this to Weber's conception of the charismatic, Shils pointed out that this orientation constituted one of the basic modes of social and cultural activity and of the ways in which individuals related themselves to society. Moreover, Shils attempted, more than did Weber himself, to locate the specific institutional anchorage of this charismatic dimension. He specified that different institutional positions possessed different importance in expressing such symbolic orders or meaning, and pointed to the societal center (or centers) as the apex of such institutional anchorage of the charismatic dimension.[25]

In this context one should note also the very interesting effort by Edward Tiryakian to combine the structural-symbolic with the structural-functional approach. Tiryakian designates the sphere of the sacred and symbolic as the crucial element in the construction of the boundaries and identity of a society, providing the "meaning," or normative and cognitive focus, through which the structuring of social organization takes place. Second, he identifies this normative focus with the Parsons-Shils-Bales "pattern-maintenance" phase of social interaction. He has also attempted to indicate various institutional and subinstitutional loci in which such symbolic orientation may be especially visible, and in which, above all, the self-portrayal of a society's "real," though often "unconscious," nature, as well as symbolic opposition to it, are articulated.[26] These loci may be fully ritualized situations, or less formalized but pervasive "esoteric" subterranean situations woven into the institutional nexus of society but separate from it and often opposed to its official symbols.

Significantly, some of Parsons' latest work, especially his reinterpretation of Durkheim, has also further differentiated the major aspects of the symbolic realm. Distinguishing the sacred, the moral, and the categorial (i.e., the *a priori* components of the cognitive systems), he has indicated their different contributions to the construction and working of societies.[27]

Some Marxists like Maurice Godelier and Lucien Sebag[28] have also attempted to specify the institutional loci of principles of a society's "hidden structure" in a combination of structuralist and Marxist ("mode of production") terms. This specification has often led them, through the confrontation of the two approaches and through the analysis of their data, to abandon the "simplifications" or "closures" of either camp—the rigid Marxist distinction between "base" and "superstructure," and the structuralist emphasis on general rules of the human mind without specification of their institutional anchorage. As a result, they have sought the mechanisms through which the symbolic realm becomes part of the working of social system and provides some of its principles.

These attempts, however limited, have already pinpointed two basic directions in which to look for some of the institutional derivatives of symbolic orientation. The first are broad principles or ground rules of social interaction, which seem to govern or influence the working of the central institutional spheres in a society. The second, is the representation and symbolization of such principles, and their concrete application in ritual or esoteric situations.

6.   A different range of openings toward the symbolic dimension developed within the conflict and exchange models. Despite the criticism of the emphasis on values and consensus in the functional-structural model, proponents of the conflict and interest approach—Dahrendorf and Rex, for example—did not deny the importance of values or symbols as references of social action. Rather, following Weber, they stressed the close relationship between specific group interests and values, and the tendency to legitimize such interests in terms of some values or images of the "good society" or the "rules of the game."[29]

Similarly, the purely individualistic exchange model, as represented by George C. Homans, John Harsanyi, and exponents of game theory, also opened up toward the symbolic dimension. This expansion took place, first, through changed views of the nature and scope of individual goals.

At first, exchange theorists stressed such goals as money, goods, services, power, and to some degree the satisfaction of psychological needs, such as love, social approval, and so on. Second, most of these goals were conceived as discrete, and specific to those concrete interactional situations and frameworks in which individuals happened to participate at a given moment.[30]

Gradually, however, a shift took place in the perception of the universe of individual goals, particularly through a recognition of the symbolic dimension in their references. Thus, Harsanyi admits that to explain variability in individual behavior it is necessary to include within the range of goals or rewards not only wealth and power but prestige and status. Moreover, Harsanyi defines the latter in a broader way than many earlier individualists, by stressing that prestige and status may be related to the quest for participation in a broader social or cultural setting or order, and that it may be bestowed on those who in part try to actualize or represent such order, regardless of immediate rewards or profits.[31]

Another aspect of the symbolic dimension—a wider normative order from the point of view of individual behavior—is illustrated by the centrality of the concept of "distributive justice" in Homans' exchange model. Working with an exchange model based on principles of the free market, Homans left this principal normative element unexplained, even though he fully recognized its importance. Thus, as Peter Blau has shown, this norm—which, according to Homans, regulates the rates of exchange between individuals—is not explained by the economic and psychological assumptions on which his model is based: it can only be understood as derived from wider general values and conceptions of justice, which transcend any immediate situation of interaction and exchange.[32]

To some extent, this is also true of the constitutional arrangements to which James Coleman alludes in his analysis of the way in which the interests of legislators affect the crystallization of collective decisions. And indeed Coleman, aware of the limitations of Homans' free-competitive exchange model, recognizes that without the assumption of prior individual acceptance of some social or institutional order, of rules of the game, the exclusive emphasis on individual interests and the rational calculus of profit may lead to a theoretical impasse and to an assumption that real life will be a continual Hobbesian war of all against all.[33]

Interestingly, the openings toward the symbolic dimension which developed out of individualistic approaches resembled the first openings between the symbolic and the structural-functional approaches in an important respect. The place of the symbolic dimension, for exchange theorists, in defining both the range of individuals' goals and the ground rules of social interaction, may in turn be related to the principles of "hidden structure" so often stressed by the symbolic structuralists.

Openings with Respect to the Systemic Nature of Social Order

7.   A broad range of parallel analytic openings, focused on the systemic qualities of social organization, also developed through the confrontations between functionalism and the conflict, exchange, and ecological "group" models, as well as the less intensive confrontation among the countermodels themselves. The common starting point of their criticism of functionalism was their strong emphasis on the "negotiability" of institutional arrangements, and of the great influence of elements of power in the process of such negotiations. This they held up against the structural-functional school's assumption of institutional arrangements as given, based on the systemic needs of any group or social system, and upheld by value consensus. Yet, despite the caveats about the systemic qualities of social life, systemic perspectives on institutional orders and interpersonal relations began to develop within these approaches, parallel to those developed on the symbolic dimension of social life.

This can be seen first in the individualist paradigms of exchange theorists. In Homans' earlier work, *The Human Group,* the systemic division of labor is taken for granted as a starting point in the analysis of face to face interaction between individuals, although it is also seen as continually influenced and changed by such interaction.[34] In his later, more rigorously individualistic approach, however, Homans tried to explain the development of institutional forms from elementary social behavior: from exchanges among individuals, from the rules that govern them, and from the individual rewarding values of these transactions—the "primary rewards":

> No doubt the origin of many institutions is of this sort. The behavior once reinforced for some people in one way, which I call primary, is maintained in a larger number of people by other sorts of reinforcement, in particular by such general reinforcers as social approval. Since the behavior does not come naturally to these others, they must be told how they are to behave —hence the norm. . . .
>
> The first point I should like to make about the relations between institutions and elementary social behavior is that institutions, as explicit rules

governing the behavior of many people, are obeyed because rewards other than the primary ones come to be gotten by obeying them, but that these other rewards cannot do the work alone. Sooner or later the primary rewards must be provided. Institutions do not keep on going forever of their own momentum.[35]

Even here Homans is aware, though in a less explicit way than in his earlier work, that the larger societal context, particularly the macrosocietal level, discloses certain systemic elements—that is, stable rules of transactions of general applicability. The following quotation attests to this recognition:

> The larger, finally, the number of persons concerned and the more complicated their interdependence, the less it is possible to leave their mutual adjustments to the rough and the tumble of the face-to-face contact. They must go by the rule, work by the book, which also means that institutional behavior tends to become impersonal. Although all recurrent behavior tends, sooner or later, to be described and consecrated in explicit norms, now the process is hastened. Indeed, one of the institutional innovations without which the others cannot get very far must be an organization that specializes in the sanctioning of norms, that is, a legal system.[36]

These theoretical orientations are based on several assumptions which on the one hand implicitly recognize the emergent systemic qualities and normative aspects of institutional frameworks, but on the other do not yet fully explicate the relationship between these qualities and "elementary" social interaction. Accordingly there arise several problems which are not fully explicated in the works of these scholars.

One problem not fully explicated is how generalized norms of behavior can be derived from specific individual interests, especially in situations in which these interests are not complementary.

The second problem is the assumption, again not fully explicated, of the homology both of the rules which govern interaction between two persons and in larger settings, and of the "media" of such interpersonal exchange—power, esteem, and so on, and those of institutional exchange—money, prestige, institutionalized power, and the like.

The third difficulty is that the systemic elements to which Homans himself alludes may create differentiations in power and in the bargaining positions of individuals or groups. Thus some processes of exchange may not fit the free market economic model on which Homans builds his main theoretical arguments.

Hence there arises here, as Homans fully recognizes, the problem of the adherence of such exchange to some rules of distributive justice. The construction and upholding of these rules, however, is beyond the scope of Homans' analysis.[37]

These difficulties suggest that the links between individual interests and their gratification by primary rewards, and the institutionalization and perpetuation of generalized norms and enduring institutional frameworks is more complex than is stated in Homans' explicit theoretical formulations on the problem. Indeed, Blau, who attempts a more elaborate explanation of the possible links between the macrosocietal order and the microsocial level of individual interaction, concludes that indirect, macrosocietal exchange has an emergent quality not entirely derivable from microsocial exchanges, and that is it characterized by systemic qualities regulated by well-defined norms. Moreover, Blau stresses that these mediating norms of the macrosocietal transactions are stabilized by various processes of institutionalization and legitimation, such as socialization, legitimation of differences of power between groups, and so on.[38]

These discussions attest to the increasing recognition within the "individualistic" camp, of several systemic aspects of social interaction, often through confrontation with concrete research problems, as for example the analysis of small groups or of processes of crystallization of status. Specifically, three systemic attributes were acknowledged by individualistic theorists.

First was the recognition that in most situations, special roles emerge whose incumbents define the collective goals of any group, represent or symbolize it, and take some care of its organizational (systemic) needs or problems.

Second was the acceptance, already seen in a preliminary way in Homans and Blau, of the ubiquity—and crucial importance—of such organizational and normative arrangements as resources, rewards, and media of exchange, which facilitate indirect interaction and exchange as basic components of the institutional order.

Third, and closely related, was the recognition of the importance of the setting up ground rules of interaction differing from routine social interaction.[39]

The antisystemic ecological-group approach also embodied a tentative recognition of systemic properties in social life and of stable elements in the division of labor. Thus, in the studies proposed by Emerys Peters as an alternative to the functional model in anthropology, the conflict relationships which evolve between groups struggling to further their interests are not entirely arbitrary, but are conceived as based on some rules (the emergence of which is not, however, elaborated). In Collins' work, indirect recognition of some systemic properties of societies can be seen in his emphasis, in the analysis of social change, on understanding the historical conditions of any given society.[40]

The concrete analysis presented in their work shows that out of any long-term interaction between various groups, some division of labor, or some kind of systemic interrelationship among them, develops, and that even a continual struggle over resources tends to become institutionalized in an organized fashion with systemic boundary-maintaining tendencies, through such institutional mechanisms as norms, roles, and institutional rules of interchange. Moreover, the very constitution of basic groups, be they family groups or strata, already assumes some basic division of labor, and some common, at least symbolic, interaction between them. In fact, their strong emphasis on the importance of groups assumes, as Peter Worsley and his collaborators have put it,[41] that each of these units does indeed evolve some consensus and systemic properties which are seemingly denied to the overall system.

Conflict theorists, while attacking assumptions of consensus and placing instead emphasis on struggle and its tendencies to disrupt boundary-maintaining efforts, also began to acknowledge relationships between tendencies to system maintenance and processes of conflict. Of special importance here was the recognition, inherent in the Marxists' analysis and in that of Dahrendorf, that the full understanding of conflict can be attained only through the analysis of its systemic bases and referents; that the outcome of any important conflict is the establishment of some new system, or the redefinition of the old; and that the very stress on the ubiquity of conflict in social systems implies—even if on grounds of expediency or submission to coercion—some norms of conflict regulation.[42]

8.   Within the structural-functional model itself, the picture of a closed system so often connected with this school began to change. As early as in the late 1940s, Robert K. Merton advanced the view that the kinds of functional relationships that existed between the various parts of a whole could not be presupposed *a priori*. They were to be determined by empirical research, which would also disclose both the functional and dysfunctional implications of any specific pattern of behavior or of social organization.[43]

This point was further elaborated, beyond the "strict" functionalist camp but very much within the structural-functional tradition, by Alvin Gouldner. Without abandoning the systemic view of society, Gouldner argued that it was not justifiable on either empirical and theoretical grounds to employ an organic model or analogy indiscriminately. He stressed the theoretical possibility that parts or subsystems of any society might have or aspire to functional autonomy—that is, the ability to define and provide for their own needs independently of other parts of the whole.[44]

Closely related to this "open" view of the systemic qualities of the social order was the increasing recognition that the functional autonomy of system elements could produce conflict and social change. This point, already apparent in Merton's distinction between functions and dysfunctions, was more fully elaborated in the late 1950's by Gouldner who stressed that: 1) some foci of social change might be related to the tendencies of groups or parts of a society to redefine a given situation to attain greater autonomy for themselves; and that 2) groups already possessing such functional autonomy, because of lesser dependence on the status quo, could be more prone to initiate and accept social change.[45]

One of the most important openings in this direction within the functional-structural school can be found in the work of William J. Goode. In his analysis of the concept of role, Goode argues, for example, that any individual in society may find himself under strains which originate in the process of fulfilling his social roles, because these roles may impose contrasting demands on the allocation of available resources for their fulfilment. The individual's response to these strains may be a more or less rational manipulation of his resources, in the course of which he may neglect some of his roles, or he may try to change the expectations that various persons in role-sets have toward him. These responses to role-generated strains show how problematic the strong systemic emphasis of Parsons' assumption of "complementarity of expectations" in social roles turns out to be. They also show that such strains, as Goode indicates, may be conducive to changes in role behavior, which in turn may have triggering effects on changes in the larger social system.[46]

In a similar vein, many studies of small groups and of organizational structure and behavior, also starting from structural systemic premises, have in a variety of ways rediscovered the autonomy of subsystems and of individual activity within organizations, an autonomy that may permit actors to redefine and change the contents of roles and reevaluate their required investments in the light of rewards attached to roles.[47]

New and far-reaching implications of the weakening of the closed-systemic view are found in studies of social change carried out in the functionalist tradition. Thus, the relationship between the equilibrium of the total system and the autonomy of its components is stressed in Neil Smelser's analysis of the Industrial Revolution, in which he shows how uneven are the changes which other institutional spheres (cultural, political, stratification) undergo following economic development. Although there is an assumption in his work that adaptation and integration will follow any such initial change, his analysis also implies that lags and disorganization in other loci of the social system are sometimes unavoidable.[48]

Robert Bellah's analysis of religious evolution contains another set of assumptions about the existence of autonomous, though closely interdependent, systems—of individuals (personality), culture, and society, each influenced by the others and open to them, but not fully predetermined by them, carrying its own momentum and directions of change. Bellah's analysis still retains some closed-system characteristics because of its assumption that in each state of evolution the various dimensions of the religious—symbolic, structural-organizational, and those rooted in personality development, change concomitantly and in a parallel direction and pattern. His concrete analyses, however, particularly of the development of Japanese society, indicate that this convergence is never full or assured.[49]

Interestingly, some of the major openings from the closed-system approach are given, at least potentially, in Parsons' own work on comparative and evolutionary perspective, which recognizes the pluralistic nature of the systemic boundaries of what was designated as "society." The most important implications of this type are found first in the distinction Parsons makes between the international (i.e., European) system and national communities, and between boundaries of cultural systems (e.g., Christianity) and political or social systems. Similarly, his distinction between "archaic" and "historic" societies, on the one hand, and "seed-societies" on the other, each with different systemic properties and impact on other societies, illustrates an awareness of the different dynamics of each system and the potential for open relationships between the boundaries of cultural and political systems. These studies not only illustrate an interesting shift in Parsons' own scientific interests, but bring out again a suggestive parallel with some problems in the Marxist analysis of change and its evolutionary assumptions.[50]

Openings with Respect to Historical and Systemic Dimensions of Social Systems

9.　Openings in the way the systemic qualities of the social system were analyzed can also be traced in the developments in Marxism and its confrontation with other models, above all the structural-functional and the structural-symbolic paradigms. The openings developed largely in comparative studies of different modes of production, particularly the "Asian mode of production" and in the analysis of the place of the state and political power in social systems.

The discussions of the Asian mode of production highlighted the difficulties in explaining all social systems in terms both of a predominant economic factor and of a uniform scheme of development for all societies. The main sources of this difficulty were, first, the recognition of potentially autonomous forces of kinship images and principles, and of ideology in general; and, second, of the autonomous place of the state in the construction of any specific mode of production. This last problem was fully explored by Antonio Gramsci, whose Italian experience probably sensitized him to this problem and its impact on the formation of different types of class consciousness.[51]

The most important opening on the part of the Marxists was the recognition that the internal structure of society was given not only in its relations of economic power but in the deeper structure which—even when defined as "mode of production"—could not be subsumed under any single institutional determinant, and which probably had multiple facets and principles.

These two openings in the Marxist approach converged in the works of scholars like Sebag and Godelier, who were closely related to the structuralist school and were interested in a genuine comparative analysis. The following quotation from Godelier brings out the tenor of this convergence quite clearly:

L'erreur de départ qui interdit toute solution est de considérer économie et parenté dans les societés primitives comme deux structures extérieures l'une à l'autre, comme l'infrastructure et la superstructure. En fait, l'économist distinguera facilement les forces productives de ces sociétés (chasse, agriculture, élevage, etc.) mais il ne pourra "isoler" des rapports de production "autonomes." Ou du moins, il les distinguera dans le fonctionement même des rapports de parenté. Ceux-ci déterminent les droits de l'individu sur le sol et ses produits, leurs obligations de recevoir, donner, coopérer. Ils déterminent également l'autorité de certains sur d'autres en matière politique, religieuse. Ils constituent enfin, comme le montre C. Lévi-Strauss, l'"armature sociologique" de la pensée "sauvage," un des schèmas organisant les représentations mythiques du rapport culturenature, homme-animaux-plantes.

Donc dans ce type de société, les rapports de parenté fonctionnent comme rapports de production, rapports politiques, schèma idéologique. Le parenté est donc ici à la fois infrastructure et superstructure. . . .

Expliquer l'évolution des sociétés primitives, c'est expliquer l'apparition de nouvelles fonctions incompatibles avec le maintien d'anciennes structures sociales. Le problème du passage aux sociétés de classes et à l'État se ramène donc en partie à celui de savoir dans quelles conditions les rapports de parenté cessent de jouer le rôle dominant, d'unifier toutes les fonctions de la vie sociale. . . .

L'étude scientifique de l'évolution des structures sociales (parenté, politique, religion, économie, etc.) n'est donc que l'étude des fonctions, des formes, de l'importance, de la place qu'occupe chacune de ces structures, selon les types de formation économique et sociale et de leurs transformations. On ce rapport de chaque structure sociale à toutes les autres constitue la structure même de la société. Il fonde la causalité propre de chacune de ses structures sociales et leur correspondance réciproque. Mais cette correspondance n'éxiste que dans certaines limites et celles-ci révèlent en définitive le contenu objectif et historique de chaque structure. . . .

Faire la théorie de l'évolution différenciée des sociétés, c'est donc faire en même temps la théorie scientifique de la parenté, de la politique, de l'idéologie. . . .

Pour qu'ils ne soient que "superstructure," pour que les rapports de parenté "se spécialisent," ne soient qu'un rapport social assurant la reproduction de l'espèce humaine et gardant un aspect économique sans intervenir directement dans la production, il faut des conditions historiques très particulières. . . .

Il en est de même pour que la religion ne soit plus qu'idéologie, affaire personnelle, conception non scientifique du monde. Il faut se refuser à projeter sur toute société ces catégories modernes correspondant à des rapports sociaux spécifiques. . . .

Il va sans dire que, seules, de telles analyses peuvent éclairer les difficultés que rencontre le développement économique et politique dans les sociétés où des rapports de parenté, la religion (Islam, Hindouisme, Bouddhisme), les formes du pouvoir (royauté, chef de tribes, etc.) ont un tout autre contenu que dans les sociétés occidentales capitalistes et socialistes. Les échecs de certaines entreprises de développement en Asie, en Afrique, en Amérique Latine sont là pour le rappeler et ils ne sont pas dus à l' "irrationalité" du comportement des "indigènes."[52]

Similar important openings to the recognition of the autonomy of the level of daily life, of the daily symbolic construction of reality, on the one hand, and of the field of cultural creativity, on the other, can be found in the work of Marxists like Henri Lefebvre or Lucien Goldmann.[53] Some of the debates between Marxists and upholders of the structural-functional or system approach, most of which took place in Germany, point up some convergences between these approaches, especially on the emphasis to be given to unique historicity of each society and the general systemic approach to societies. While many Marxists and some who saw themselves as Weberians often criticized the structural-functional approach for the generality and abstraction of its systemic definition of society, their own terminology—such as "mode of production" and "system of domination"—was not less general and abstract. The fact that these critics stressed the differential historical content of these general terms does not in principle negate the general, abstract, or the systemic view of the social system. It only indicates their increasing sensitivity to the importance of the general criteria by which different specific societies might be compared.[54] Of special interest here is the recent emphasis in Marxist or Marxist-inspired analyses on international systems in general, particularly the modern capitalist or imperialist system. These analyses use general systemic qualities of supranational entities to explain the dynamics of concrete societies.[55]

At the same time, however, other developments in comparative sociology stemming from the structural-functional school[56] illustrate greater recognition of the importance of the specific characteristics of different historical societies.

A closely related development alluded to above, particularly in the works of Parsons, Smelser, and Bellah, has been the recognition not only of the ubiquity and importance of conflict, in any social system, but also of systemic contradictions which generate different processes of societal change and hence different patterns of historical formations.

10.   One of the most important extensions or openings with respect to the systemic generalities of social systems has been the shift, among several scholars, from a closed-system to a dynamic, cybernetic, and open-system view of social systems. Using this approach, scholars like Walter Buckley, Karl Deutsch, to some extent Amitai Etzioni and lately Gerald Hage, have criticized the closed view of the social system which they attribute to the structural-functional model.[57] Above all they criticize the mechanistic conception of the relationship between the system and its environment, and the emphasis on homeostatic tendencies and the internal and external forces which may disrupt such homeostasis.

As against this view, proponents of the cybernetic or open systemic approach emphasize the constant tendencies of societies to expansion; "morphogenesis"; and the great importance of mechanisms of feedback and of "secondary cybernetics"—that is, "of all processes of mutual causal relationship that amplify an insignificant or accidental kick, build up deviation and diverge from the initial condition."[58]

Unlike the ecological group model, this approach, while accepting the struggle among groups as an important ingredient of social life, has placed much greater emphasis on the systemic qualities of social systems. While this approach had had few direct applications in research, some interesting beginnings can be indicated. Reuben Hill had made a provocative application of this approach to the field of the family, trying to synthesize many "old fashioned" studies of the family around an open-systemic approach. More recently, Gerald Hage has used this approach in analyzing theories of organization.[59]

Another combination of the "open-systemic" approach with strong macrosocietal analysis can be found in the work of Norbert Elias, which has been popular in parts of Europe especially Holland and Germany. Elias has extended his work of the late 1930s on the process of civilization in the direction both of more concrete historical study and a configurational approach to social systems which sees any society as a specific historical configuration of some basic elements of social and cultural life.[60]

Most openings with respect to the systemic qualities of social orders have also pointed to the importance of distinguishing different levels or aspects of social systems—systems and subsystems, different collectivities and orders, which might coalesce in different ways in different situations; and between the more "organizational" aspects of such systems and "deeper," "hidden" principles of their structures.

Openings with Respect to the Individual and Social Structure

11. A similar range of openings, problems and new directions evolved from developments within the symbolic interactionist model and its confrontations with the structural-functional model. These came up with respect to the relationship between the individual and organized social life. The symbolic interactionist approaches have contributed greatly to the understanding of the ways in which individuals, through seemingly autonomous activities, construct social reality, and have sharpened the entire perspective of the social order as a negotiated one—one in which formal goals and institutional arrangements in any situation are not simply given, but are attained through various processes of bargaining, struggle, negotiations, and a search for common ground.[61]

At the same time all these developments have sharpened the importance of exploring the elements of power relationships and the systemic structuring that develop in any situation of interaction, as well as the relationship between the interpersonal definition of situations and the organizational and systemic aspects of social order. Thus, Eugene Weinstein and J. Tanur see one of the major challenges for the interactionist approach as explaining how "structural connections between episodes of social interaction create the fabric of social life," while Aaron Cicourel, for example, attempts to identify how individual processes of cognition and linguistic interchange contribute to the emergence of social structure with its rules and norms.[62]

Openings in the structural-functional school have developed around the relationship between individual and social order under the influence of symbolic-interactionism. The importance of the interactionist element, of the definition of the situation, was of course heavily stressed in Parsons' earlier work, though later it was submerged in his systemic emphasis. Some of these orientations were taken up in Merton's writing on reference groups, and were parallelled by many works in social psychology.[63]

Interesting efforts to combine institutional analysis with the process of individual definitions of situations have also been made by Peter Berger and Thomas Luckmann.[64]

A parallel opening with respect to the individual as an autonomous agent within the social structure and its normatively regulated organizational components, was developed in functional (i.e., primarily British) social anthropology. An early statement by one of the main exponents of the British social anthropological school, Raymond Firth, focused on the difference between "social structure" and "social organization." Social structure was defined as patterns of behavior, "the qualities [of which] are primarily those of persistence, continuity, form, and pervasiveness. . . . There is an expectation of sameness or an obligation to sameness." Social organization was defined as "adaptation of behavior in respect of given ends, control of means in varying circumstances, which are set by changes in the external environment or by the necessity to resolve conflict between structural principles. If structure implies order, organization implies a working towards order—though not necessarily the same order."[65]

This line of exploration within the social-anthropological tradition was extended by the Norwegian anthropologist Fred Barth in two interesting directions. First, Barth emphasized the importance of the game-like interaction between individuals for the determination of structural principles of social organization. He analyzed the way interaction among individuals was usually carried out in normatively defined frameworks, but stressed that individuals might react to such normative or symbolic constraints in different ways. These different reactions could produce new normative definitions which might then take on some independent life of their own. Such normative elements were necessary elements in any stable interaction. However, because of the constraints they imposed on free interaction, their relationship to specific individual needs and wishes was not given or assurred, but tended to be problematic, and varied from situation to situation.

Second, Barth and his colleagues recognized the critical importance of institutional entrepreneurs in creating new normative and institutional frameworks. Of special interest was their expansion of the concept of entrepreneurship to refer exactly to those types of institutional activities that bridge the gap between previously unconnected social spheres, and between activities and goals of different individuals, through the crystallization of new normative and evaluative principles.[66]

Openings Involving Mechanisms of Acceptance of Social Order

12.   As was the case in earlier phases of the development of sociological theory, the various openings, though different in detail, led to the awareness that the analysis of social order centered on the systemic interrelationships among its components and on the dynamics of their interaction.[67] This entailed a shift in emphasis to the analysis of the mechanisms through which such interaction takes place, an emphasis that led, in turn, to another range of openings in the area of the bases of acceptance and legitimation of social order. Particularly, attention centered on defining to what degree social order was based on coercion (power), moral commitment to values, or inducements to self-interest, and to what degree society was characterized by conflict or consensus.

A crucial development in the more recent controversies was the transformation of these concepts from metaphysical or "natural" forces into analytic tools which defined mechanisms through which the relations among components of social systems and order were maintained. This transformation developed first in the work of the structural-functional school, particularly Parsons, who formulated these concepts to designate several aspects of social interaction: major types of resources used in social interaction; major types of institutionalized goals; major social rewards; and general media of exchange.[68]

Significantly, it was around these developments that one of the most interesting convergences between the functional-structural and the exchange model took place—Coleman's development of the concept of "political money," a concept foreshadowed in Blau's work on exchange and one which was very close to Parsons' and Smelser's analysis of the interchanges between institutional spheres in society.[69] This convergence suggested forcefully that the process by which resources and rewards were continually converted into general media of exchange and vice-versa was central to the analysis of social life.[70]

A further analytic advance was the recognition, implied both in structural-functional analysis and in many countermodels, and derived from the Founding Fathers, that these concepts also denoted the major types of symbolic orientations to the social system. An interesting illustration of this development has been Etzioni's analysis of different modes of compliance characterizing different social systems, and his attempt to specify the structural and organizational implications of the different bases of compliance.[71]

A second important aspect of these openings was the acknowledgement, within each approach (despite claims to the contrary) of multiple bases of acceptance of the social order. Within the functional-structural school, which presumably based social order on value consensus attained though socialization, Merton's distinction between functional and dysfunctional elements of institutions introduced power as an important element in the origin and maintenance of institutions.[72] Similarly, the conflict model, though it emphasized interests and power as bases of acceptance of social order, recognized the importance of values in shaping such acceptance.[73] Within the exchange model, Homans stressed the individual calculus of interests as the basis of acceptance of social order, but Coleman, Blau, and Harsanyi also stress power differences and the quest for order as bases for accepting any given institutional arrangement.[74]

Third was the recognition that the degrees of acceptance of social order, whatever the base, must be seen as variables, operative in every social setting but in different degrees in different social situations or structures.[75]

Fourth, many of the more recent works accepted the notion of interrelationships among the several bases of compliance—though this would have seemed paradoxical in terms of the conflicting models alone.

Thus several sociological researches became important meeting grounds for conflictual and symbolic approaches in both their structuralist and interactionist forms, producing a very interesting articulation of the close relationship between power and values: emphasis, on the one hand, on the importance of power in the construction of symbolic universes, and, on the other, of the importance of legitimation and definition of meaning for the institutionalization of power.[76] This came close to the insights that charisma and orientations to the sacred provided bases not only of consensus but of dissensus and struggle, and that any such struggle was organized institutionally.[77]

To give one illustration: some recent studies, strongly critical of the classic models of the professions, have indicated how professions tend to crystallize around areas in social life which seem to be perceived, or cause themselves to be perceived, as close to the sacred. By virtue of this image they possess or attract power and generate struggles the nature of which cannot be derived from either a "simple" functionalist view of professions as contributing to social integration, or as emerging from the more "routine" struggle of power and interests of different individuals or groups.[78]

These developments impinged also on the consensual and conflict-based views of society. Here, as with the bases of acceptance of social order, the concepts of "consensus" and "conflict" were transformed from metaphysical forces or total, general characterizations of social order into analytic variables. Moreover, interesting convergences appeared between analyses of the bases of acceptance of social order and the analyses of consensus and conflict as bases of social order. Instead of assuming that either value consensus, or conflict based on power and interests, was the sole basis of social order, totally explaining its functioning, theorists saw the crucial analytic problem as the analysis of different patterns and combinations of consensus and conflict; of their different bases as they developed in various societies or groups; and of their influence on the working of these societies. In other words, it became evident that the crucial problem is that of the calculus of consensus in a society: of the ways in which individuals evaluate different aspects of the social order, and in which such evaluation affects their acceptance of a particular order and its institutional framework and their own positions in it.[79]

Openings Among Analytic Approaches and the Broadening of the Sociological Tradition

13.   We could continue to illustrate the openings among different sociological schools and approaches—the very schools and approaches which claimed to be mutually exclusive. Even these few illustrations, however, enable us to indicate some of their wider implications for the development of sociological theory and analysis.

These openings had features resembling many major developments in the history of sociological theory, and like the openings in earlier periods, their implications pointed in two different yet complementary directions.[80] First, they involved a deeper understanding of the characteristics and autonomy of each component of social order—especially of the major systems of social action, personality, culture and social systems. Second, insofar as various tendencies to analytic closure were overcome within them, the schools based on any starting point, "individual," "social," or "cultural," came to see the phenomena belonging to other spheres as autonomous components of social order which influenced the crystallization, and particularly the variability, of the component considered "basic" in any given approach. They tended also to recognize the possibility of direct interrelationships among each pair of components, that were not mediated solely by the needs or problems of the "basic" component (e.g., the "social system" or "culture"). Similarly, the openings involving systemic qualities of social order, the relative importance of various bases of legitimation, and the consensual or conflict-ridden nature of social order, pointed out that all these were variables rather than absolute qualities of social systems.

Accordingly, all these analytic openings contributed to the awareness that the focus of the construction of social order and of the regularities of social life lay in the dynamics of interaction among its major components and the systemic interrelationships among them. This entailed, as in former periods of sociological analysis, continuous shifts of emphasis: first, to the analysis of the mechanisms through which the crystallization of such interaction took place; second, to the recognition that such mechanisms were found in the various interrelationships between the aspects or components of social life, not in vague, general, external metaphysical forces; and third, to attempts to relate these mechanisms to the analysis of the processes of social organization, institution building, and change and transformation of personality, and social and cultural systems, as well as the mechanisms of feedback among them.

This extension and deepening of the sociological *Problemstellung* took place through an interesting combination of certain convergences and constructive divergences among the paradigmatic models and approaches. The convergences among these different approaches in contemporary sociology were exhibited first in a growing conceptual similarity among most of them.

This similarity was closely related to trends in the codification of sociology,[81] trends which were apparent in most textbooks, among other sources, from the mid-1950s to the late 1960s. All approaches tended to use, though often in apparently different ways, similar ranges of concepts, such as roles, resources, and rewards, which denote aspects of individual behavior. They also tended to use similar terms defining various types of groups, both natural groups like family, community, and "artificial," specialized groups. Furthermore, they all tended to delineate common major types of institutions—political, economic, and familial institutions—to denote the basic nexus of the social division of labor and of social interaction.

This convergence was not merely semantic. It was rooted in the fact that the upholders of each approach admitted to some degree the existence of aspects of social order stressed by the other approaches, and above all the various emergent qualities of institutional life and social organization in their relationship to personality and cultural symbols.

In other words, most of these approaches seem to have accepted some basic assumptions of the other approaches as "evolutionary universals" of any human society.[82] The most important accepted "evolutionary universals" were the division of labor and the institutional organization of groups and societies and of role allocation; the pursuit by individuals of both "private" and institutionalized goals in social interaction; the importance of symbolic models and orientations, and the meaningful definition of the situation by participants in social interaction, in the patterning of such behavior and organization; and the importance and relative autonomy of ecosystemic arrangements.

Similarly, most of these approaches acknowledged the importance in social life of normative elements and sanctions, and of power and coercion in upholding such normative patterns. They probably also concurred that social life and activities evinced organizational and systemic tendencies, but that at the same time any systemic tendency might be countered by internal conflicts and contradictions, and the pressures of various external factors.

In greater detail: most of these approaches shared the view that the source of the social division of labor and of the institutional distribution of roles lies in the fact that people cannot achieve their goals except within the context of social life; that no single individual, or even single nuclear family, can be totally self-sufficient in attaining its goals or desiderata; that in order to reach these goals an individual or family must give up or exchange certain of its resources for those of other people or groups; and that concrete organizations and institutions, as well as the more informal yet pervasive and forceful interpersonal situations, are built up through the varied responses and interactions between different people or groups, who, in order to implement their varied goals, undertake processes of interaction or exchange with other people or groups.

Beyond this, most of these approaches tended to accept the view that individuals or groups who engage in such interaction are not randomly distributed in any society. Interaction and exchange take place between people in structurally different positions—that is, different cultural, political, family or economic positions. The resources at their disposal are also greatly determined by these institutional positions and vary according to the specific characteristics of the different institutional spheres. These concrete positions and the degree of their acceptance by their incumbents may be outcomes of former processes of institutional interaction and exchange and of the aspirations and goals of people occupying them.

Similarly, most of these approaches saw the central importance, in maintaining the institutional order, of generalized media of exchange—money, power, influence, and the like—which assure the society-wide production, conversion, and flow of resources.

The broadening of sociological analysis and the sharpening of its analytic tools through discussion was not, of course, confined to these conceptual and analytic convergences. Their importance lay, rather, in providing basis for further development. The focus of these developments was the distinction between the general properties of social life, which can be seen as evolutionary universals of human society, and the crystallization of any specific institutional pattern; and the consequent rejection of any organizational or institutional setting as "given" or explicable in purely systemic-functional terms.

Starting from this premise, the major theoretical discussions led first to the abandonment of assumptions of fixed relationships between the major components of social order. This in turn resulted in a much more diversified view of the social system through the reexamination of the levels of institutional order—i.e., roles, social needs, phases, institutions, norms, and the interrelationships among them; a deeper understanding of the autonomy and internal systemic characteristic of each component of the social order—i.e., the individual, social groups and subsystems, the symbolic domain, and the ecological system; and the recognition of the multiplicity of relationships between them, and of the differential impact of these relationships on the crystallization of different levels and aspects of institutional order.

As a result of these trends, many explanatory concepts which had often served as bases for the construction of typologies were decomposed into variables, the relations between which became problems of research, thus leading to the quest for new principles or laws which organize or structure the interrelationships between the components of social order. In this way, the reexamination and systematization of various middle-range theories and explanations of regularities in social and institutional behavior and organization was also facilitated. All these openings, then, did serve to broaden the scope of sociological theory, sharpen its analytic tools, and extend and enrich the sociological tradition.

The Reexamination of Major Concepts and Assumptions of Sociological Analysis: Institutional Order as Negotiated and the Search for "Deep Structure"

14. The more diversified view of social order gave rise to a far-reaching reexamination of many central concepts in sociological analysis, for example, "roles" and "institutions," and criticism of many central assumptions of sociological analysis.

As we indicated in the preceding chapter, the revision of the concept of role, developed through research and analysis in both the dominant structural-functional model and the counter models, which produced criticism notably in Germany, Italy, and France.[83] Against its widespread use in "positivist" sociological research, these revisions stressed the constraints of the concept of role on the understanding of many concrete aspects of social life, and of its more subterranean, informal, and potentially "anti-systemic" tendencies.

The upshot of these revisions was the recognition that "role" should not be taken as "given"—that is, as a pattern of behavior or as a normative definition of behavior that is fixed in the institutional structure of society and to which individuals adjust themselves through socialization and interaction with other people.[84] Rather, the very formation of any specific role—the articulation of its goals and the crystallization of its symbolic, organizational, and technical components—was an outcome of various social forces or mechanisms which created, from the potential of various institutional pressures and personal goals operating in any given society, the actual crystallizations of the different components of any specific role.[85] Different components of any role might thus be profitably studied for the different degree of institutionalization in each of them and the degree to whether any of them became institutionalized.

Similarly, the crystallization of different roles might, in its turn, influence the institutional structure of a society.[86] The processes of creation and crystallization of different roles took place constantly in all societies, even the most stable ones. Even if the basic definition of a role was more or less constant over long periods of time, the relative emphasis on its different components would vary according to different situations and forces which impinged on it, and among different individuals. Thus, the role-map of a society was to be seen, not as completely fixed and given, but as continually undergoing recrystallization. Moreover, this approach implied that individual role performance was not a static sum of attributes and the realization of fixed expectations and norms set by "society." It was rather, a much more differentiated process involving individual aspirations and perceptions in a variety of situations, emphasizing different aspects of normatively regulated behavior in each situation, and often producing different meanings of the same role. Indeed, it was this encounter between individuals and supposedly "given" roles that often created different constellations of the components of a role, different subroles, and even new roles.

A similar important shift, stemming from the discussion of models and countermodels as well as research, took place in the conceptual approach to the analysis of institutions. Acceptance of the institutional map of a society as given gave way to the analysis of the process of institutionalization and a tendency to see it as a process of constant crystallization of different types of norms, organizations, and frameworks which regulated the processes of exchange of different institutional commodities among social actors. Such institutionalization was not, random or purely accidental, of course, but neither was it fixed or unchanging. Thus, it became evident that, while the analysis of any concrete institutional pattern had to start from the existence of institutional arrangements as inherent in the very nature of human society, any concrete pattern was the result of interaction between people placed in different structural positions and between pressures of organizational and other environmental forces as they impinged on these activities.[87]

15.   The critical examination of the basic assumptions of sociological analysis permeated almost all areas of research: family, sex roles, stratification, health, deviance, political sociology, sociology of religion and ritual, the sociology of organization, macrosocietal historical comparative studies, studies of modernization.[88]

Out of it developed several new orientations guiding these areas of research. The importance of these orientations varied, of course, among fields, but in all these areas they produced extensive analyses of middle-range theories and the development of new research programs.

These orientations focused on two major analytic themes derived from criticisms of the perceived suppositions of the structural-functional school and controversies about the various models. First was the rejection of the "natural" givenness of any single institutional order in terms of its needs or prerequisites, a rejection which demanded explanation of all institutional arrangements in terms of a negotiated order. Second was the seemingly contrary emphasis on the search for principles of hidden or deep structure—as distinct from the organizational exigencies—of any interaction or institutional setting.

This perception of the negotiated nature of the institutional order was rooted in the fact that, implicitly or explicitly, almost all these approaches sharply underlined the difference between analysis of the general nature of social order and the more detailed analysis of specific societies, groups, or patterns of behavior. In other words, it was assumed that existence of the evolutionary universals of human society listed above did not explain the crystallization of any of their specific concrete types—of any specific social groups or organizations, any specific type of division of labor, symbolic pattern, interaction, or individual behavior.

Thus, as we have indicated, any given institutional arrangement—be it the formal structure of a factory or hospital, the division of labor in the family, the official definition of deviant behavior, the place of a ritual in a given social setting or the construction of a macrosocietal order—was no longer taken for granted, as given and derivable from its functional place in the social system. Accordingly, the patterns of behavior that developed in that institutional framework could no longer be examined primarily in terms of their contribution to, or deviance from, its functioning. The very establishment of such institutional arrangements was transposed from a "given" into a problem to be studied in terms of processes of negotiation among participants in these processes.

The explanation of the ways in which such a process developed was usually attempted on several levels, not all, of course, in the same studies. First, explanation was attempted in terms of types of power relationships, negotiations, struggles, and coalitions set up in such processes. Second, the coercive element, as well as the element of conflict and struggle, in any such process was stressed. Third, importance was placed on the manipulation of symbols in such processes, on attachment to symbols, and on the combinations of symbolic and power orientations and their coalescence into patterns of interaction and institutional frameworks. Fourth, the possibility that participants in interaction would attach different meanings and definitions to such situations was stressed, as was the possibility that these definitions were related to different perceptions of their roles by different incumbents. Fifth, strong emphasis was placed on the importance, in such processes, of the autonomy of any subset, subgroup, or subsystem, whose definitions of goals might differ from those of the broader organization or institutional set. Sixth, increasing emphasis developed on the environments within which any social setting operates, above all of the international system for the analysis of total societies or macrosocietal orders.

At the same time, many of these researches sought principles of "deep" or "hidden" structure which would explain the dynamics of any pattern of interaction or institutional setting in terms other than those of organizational or functional exigency and which would also provide the principles according to which meaningful definitions of concrete situations were constructed by individuals.

It was especially with respect to the setting up of the ground rules of such interaction, and of the legitimation of the boundaries and goals of any given collectivity, social system, or institutional arrangement, that the importance of the various symbolic orientations, in conjunction with the power element, was stressed.

The Contributions of the Different Models and Approaches and the Confrontation Among Them.

16. These orientations developed in the analyses of the processes of crystallization of concrete patterns of behavior, collectivities, institutional settings, and cultural traditions and symbols. They resulted from the combined impact of research in the different areas and the more theoretically rigorous confrontations of the various models and approaches. Thus, unlike the case in earlier periods of development, the broadening and diversification of sociological analysis was attained not just through discussion of models and countermodels but through the closer relationship of such discussion to research.

Of course, the controversies over each countermodel developed in different ways, in terms of deepening understanding of the components of social order, as well as their relationship to research. What follows is a brief discussion of these developments.

The structuralist-symbolic approach, by denying that the symbolic could be derived from the organizational dimension of social life, contributed greatly to the analysis of the autonomous construction of the symbolic dimension and the search for basic rules of some "hidden structure" which, beyond direct organizational principles, influenced the working of institutional complexes and societies. The structuralist symbolic approach had its first great impact in the areas of kinship and various types of symbolic creativity, such as mythology, folklore, and literature. Later it was also applied to broader macrosocietal fields: primitive societies at first, then more complex societies, particularly in the work of Louis Dumont and of Luc de Heusch.[89]

The conflict and exchange models, which questioned the givenness of any institutional system and stressed the negotiability of the social order, together with the developing structural-functional tradition, produced a reexamination of the place of power and of the mechanisms of its regulation. The ecological approach, in addition, created new interest in different types of collectivities and populations which might also cut across any specific macrosocietal order. The conflict approach, as represented by Ralf Dahrendorf, Lewis Coser, and Max Gluckman, developed a strong emphasis on the study of different types of political systems and the mechanisms of political allocation, while the group ecological approach was especially influential in the study of the boundaries of different parts of societies. The greatest impact of the exchange model was on the study of behavior and interaction in small groups and informal settings within more formal organizations, and of some processes of stratification, especially the crystallization of status systems and status congruence.[90]

The symbolic interactionist and ethnomethodological approaches provided a fuller understanding of the different dimensions of the construction of social reality through the seemingly autonomous activities of individuals. Their major contribution was in the exploration of different levels and types of "informal" and "subterranean" situations of human interaction which cut across formal arrangements and institutional settings. Here they laid bare the less fully organized dimensions of everyday life, their phenomenology and nature; the structure and rules of interaction that took place within them, as distinct from the formal institutional definition of goals; the mechanisms of interaction through which such situations were constructed and their perception on the part of participants; and their impact on different levels of formal social organization. They also identified some processes, such as "labelling" or "denoting," through which such situations were constructed and maintained. Thus they sharpened the perception of the ways in which the formal goals, institutional arrangements, and common norms in any given setting, rather than being assumed as "given", were attained through various processes of bargaining, struggle, interaction, and mutual evaluation.

The symbolic-interactionist approach was first applied, as in the work of Erving Goffman, to the study of face to face situations, informal daily encounters, and the informal aspects of other more formal institutionalized situations.[91] Later it was also applied to many organizational and institutional areas, as in organization studies intended to determine how the process of crystallization of institutions and role construction operated through the interaction of informal or other groups. In many ways these efforts extended the work of scholars like Everett Hughes, who had analyzed the working of an organization "from below," and Anselm Strauss and others, who had examined the negotiated informal order of various organizations, as against their formal goals.[92] The applicability of this analysis to major institutional fields has also been tested recently in the field of political sociology. Finally, some of the major tenets of symbolic interactionism have been taken up, especially but not exclusively in England, by such scholars as Dick Atkinson and David Silverman who made it the basis of a radical alternative to all the institutional-organizational models of classical sociology ranging from Marx through Durkheim and Weber to Parsons.[93]

The major analytic contribution of the more "open" Marxist approaches was their emphasis on the relationship between power elements and the systemic characteristics of social order; on the basic laws (resembling the structuralists' hidden structure) which regulate the structure of the system; on the systemic nature of conflict, in the sense of systemic contradiction in the dynamics of social systems; and on the historicity of such dynamics. Neo-Marxist approaches had their major impact on macrosocietal and comparative-institutional studies—studies of primitive and historical societies, of modernization and development, and of systems of power in modern societies.[94]

The contributions of the several theoretical approaches to different areas of research varied, of course, in significance. Many "applications" were no more than programmatic declarations and occasions for debate rather than direct contributions to research. Yet, to a large extent, it was through the combination of analytic considerations with research that the most significant theoretical openings developed, demonstrating the possibility of enlarging and enriching both paradigmatic models of social order and concrete research, as well as their synthesis.

Growing Converence, Constructive Divergence, and the Possibility of Broadening the Sociological Tradition.

19.   Disagreements and differences in emphasis and research programs in the models and countermodels hardly disappeared in the light of diversified approaches, convergences, and broadened frameworks of sociological analysis. One the contrary, it was the combination of the

broadening sociological tradition with the confrontation of analytic approaches and research areas that created these fruitful possibilities; the potentials of sociological development were most clearly discerned in the very points of divergence.

The fruitfulness of these implications lay in the fact that components of social order taken as given in one approach constituted basic problems to be explained in others. Furthermore, while the initial tendency of each approach was to explain any such "given" in terms of its own basic assumptions, this very tendency made the blind spots of each approach more obvious, thus pointing out crucial problems of sociological analysis still to be faced.

Thus, as we have seen, the "individualists" did not accept the givenness of any specific type of social organization or division of labor, or the explanation of norms and their institutionalization and perpetuation in terms of socialization as the sole mechanism. Rather, they attempted to explain the institutional order in terms of basic rules of individual interaction and exchange, or in terms of coercion, power, and influence. But in the attempt to do so, the limitations of their narrower assumptions became more apparent. As we have seen, George C. Homans, working with an exchange model based on principles of the free market, left unexplained one of the principal normative elements in this model, the criteria of distributive justice. Similarly, James Coleman left unexplained the constitutional arrangements according to which the formation of coalitions and of exchange of power—through which collective goals or symbols of collective identity are adopted—are regulated.[95]

Another problem was faced by the social system oriented schools. They refused to assume the emergence and institutionalization of social life from routine individual interaction, claiming that the former had to be explained in terms of special mechanisms stemming from the "needs" of social organization. Yet they in turn had to explain how these processes were related to individuals' goals, interaction, search for meaning, and cultural orientations; how, and in what kind of social situations, these orientations were activated;[96] and in what way the patterns of social interaction through which such "needs" were activated and institutionalized differed from other, more routine aspects of social interaction. They also had to identify the carriers of boundary-maintaining mechanisms of different types of social systems and collectivities, and the ways in which various systems coalesced through the activities of these carriers.

Those with an anti-systemic bias had to explain the emergent systemic and boundary-maintaining tendencies in groups and collectivities. Conversely, those who stressed the "needs" of social systems had to explain the mechanisms through which such needs were articulated and related to activities of individuals and to the institutionalization of collective goals and public goods.[97]

Those who insisted on the autonomy or primacy of the symbolic dimensions had to specify the nature of the exact institutional loci and mechanisms through which the symbolic dimensions of human activities impinged on institutional life and on the working of social systems.[98] All these factors were, in a sense, taken as unproblematic by the first wave of symbolic structuralists.

At the same time, the "individualists" and the "collectivists" alike had to explain both the unbiquity of the symbolic dimension and the ways in which different individuals or organizational settings selected or created different symbolic orientations.[99] They had also to specify the nature of those aspects of institutional structure and interpersonal relations which were shaped by such symbolic orientations; their relationship to other aspects of institutional structure; and the conditions and mechanisms of their institutionalization, maintenance, and change.

A similar situation developed in the discussion of the historicity of societies and the possibility of meaningful comparative analysis. Upholders of both views—that is, those who looked for general laws of society, and those who claimed that each society had to be studied in its historical specificity[100]—had to specify both the nature of the specific social forces which shaped any historical situation and the possibility of explaining these forces in general analytic terms. Similarly, those who, like the Marxists, stressed conflict and contradiction in the social system had to explain fully the tendencies to stability and continuity that marked different levels of social systems and various collectivities. Those who stressed stability and continuity were required to analyze, first, the ways in which conflict and contradiction were contained within different levels of social systems and, second, the difference in the influence of different types of conflict on continuity and change of these different levels.

18.   The many developments in sociological analysis bear out the assertion made at the beginning of this chapter that the contemporary situation in sociological theory is characterized by the opening up and potential transformation of the major explicative paradigms of sociological analysis and the sharpening of its analytic tools. These processes are similar, in principle, to those which characterized the first changes from major closed-system to open-system approaches and the opening of open-system approaches.

What distinguished the more recent analytic developments, however, is that they were based much more on the combination of theoretical analysis with research. They attested, moreover, to the fruitfulness and possibility of the transformation—however analytically or methodologically weak—of theoretical paradigms into "scientific" paradigmatic frameworks of research programs; of the continuous development of such programs; and of their revision by the internal momentum of analysis and research.

But this was only one possibility. Along with the constructive developments which permitted broader frameworks of sociological tradition and a more refined analytic apparatus, other developments in this period threatened the distinctiveness, autonomy, and progress of sociological analysis. In order to understand this contradictory development, we must proceed to the analysis of other aspects of controversy in and about sociology.

Notes

1. The core assumptions of the functional-structural paradigm in sociology can be found, as already indicated above, in T. Parsons and E. Shills, (ed.), *Toward a General Theory of Action* (Cambridge, Mass.: Harvard University Press, 1951); T. Parsons, *The Social System* (New York: Free Press, [1951]1964); T. Parsons and N. J. Smelser, *Economy and Society* (New York: Free Press [1956], 1965).

   For the classic statements of the functional approach in anthropology see A. R. Radcliffe-Brown, *Structure and Function in Primitive Society* (London: Cohen & West, 1952); B. Malinowski, "Culture," *Encyclopedia of the Social Sciences*, Vol. 4 (New York: Macmillan, 1931), pp. 621–645.

2. For claims of similarity between Parsons' and Marx's systemic approaches, see A. W. Gouldner, *The Coming Crisis of Western Sociology* (New York: Basic Books, 1970), pp. 226–231.

   For the criticism against Parsons' work as static and nonhistorical, see for example, R. Dahrendorf, "Out of Utopia," *American Journal of Sociology*, Vol. 64 (1958), pp. 115–127.

   For Parsons' evolutionary and historical perspectives see T. Parsons, *Societies: Evolutionary and Comparative Perspectives* (Englewood Cliffs, N.J.: Prentice-Hall, 1966).

3. On this see R. Dahrendorf, *Class and Class Conflict in Industrial Society* (Stanford, Cal.: Stanford University Press, 1959), especially Chs. 4, 5, 6; R. Collins, "A comparative approach to political sociology," in R. Bendix (ed.), *State and Society* (Boston: Little, Brown, 1968), pp. 42–67; R. Bendix and G. Roth, *Scholarship and Partisanship: Essays on Max Weber* (Berkeley: University of California Press, 1971), especially Ch. 11.

4. D. Atkinson, *Orthodox Consensus and Radical Alternative* (London: Heinemann, 1971), especially Chs. 7, 8; J. Rex, "Review essay," *American Sociological Review*, Vol. 36, No. 1 (1971), pp. 125–127; J. Rex, *Key Problems in Sociological Theory* (London: Routledge &

Kegan Paul, 1961), especially Chs. 6, 7; J. Rex, *Sociology and the Demystification of the Modern World* (London: Routledge & Kegan Paul, 1974).

5. For a full bibliography of Lévi-Strauss' works see note 26 of Ch. 4. For the specific aspect discussed here see for example: M. Glucksman, *Structuralist Analysis in Contemporary Social Thought* (London: Routledge & Kegan Paul, 1974).

6. A. Touraine, *Production de la Société* (Paris: Seuil, 1973); A. Touraine, *Pour la Sociologie* (Paris: Seuil, 1974), Ch. 2; M. Godelier, *Horizons, Trajets Marxistes en Anthropologie* (Paris: Maspero, 1973); L. Sebag, *Marxisme et Structuralisme* (Paris: Payot, 1964); K. Eder (ed.), *Die Entstekung von Klassengesellschaften* (Frankfurt am Main: Suhrkamp, 1973); C. Seyfarth and W. Sprondel (eds.), *Religion und Gesellschaftliche Entwicklung* (Frankfurt am Main: Suhrkamp, 1973).

7. See the relevant quotations in note 3 of this chapter.

8. On these various areas of research, from the point of view of this discussion, see S. N. Eisenstadt, *Tradition, Change and Modernity* (New York: Wiley, 1973), Chs. 1 and 5; E. de Kadt and G. Williams (eds.), *Sociology and Development* (London: Tavistock, 1974); S. N. Eisenstadt, "Prestige, participation, and strata formation," in J. A. Jackson (ed.), *Social Stratification* (Cambridge: Cambridge University Press, 1968), pp. 62–103.

     For stratification, especially the implied convergence between the exchange and functionalist approaches on the origins of inequality, see also P. Ekeh, *Social Exchange Theory* (London: Heinemann, 1974), Ch. 6.

     For deviance, see for instance Y. Young, "New directions in subcultural theory," in J. Rex (ed.), *Approaches to Sociology* (London: Routledge & Kegan Paul, 1974), pp. 160–186.

     For theories of organization see D. Silverman, *The Theory of Organisations* (London: Heinemann, 1970); A. M. Bowey, "Approaches to organisation theory," *Social Science Information*, Vol. 11, No. 6 (1972), pp. 109–128.

9. These transitions have been discussed in greater detail in Ch. 4, above.

10. S. Freud, "Totem and taboo," in N. Birnbaum and G. Lenzer (eds.), *Sociology and Religion: a Book of Readings* (Englewood Cliffs, N.J.: Prentice-Hall, 1969), pp. 58–66.

11. On this see for example J. W. M. Whiting et al. "The function of male initiation ceremonies at puberty," in E. E. Maccoby et al. (eds.), *Readings in Social Psychology*, (New York: Holt, Rinehart and Winston, 1958), pp. 359–370.

12. A. R. Radcliffe-Brown, *Structure and Function in Primitive Society, op. cit.*, Ch. 8; M. Fortes, "Ritual festivals and social cohesion in the hinterland of the Gold Coast," *American Anthropologist*, Vol. 38, No. 4 (1936); reprinted as Ch. 6 in M. Fortes, *Time and Social Structure* (London: Athlone, 1970), pp. 147–167; M. Fortes, *Oedipus and Job in West African Religion* (Cambridge: Cambridge University Press, 1959); M. Gluckman, *Rituals of Rebellion in South-East Africa,* The Frazer Lecture, 1952 (Manchester: Manchester University Press, 1954), republished in M. Gluckman, *Order and Rebellion in Tribal Africa* (Glencoe, Ill.,: Free Press, 1963).

     The earlier influences can be found in: E. Durkheim, *The Elementary Forms of Religious Life* (New York: Macmillan, 1915); William Robertson Smith, *The Religion of the Semites* (New York: Meridian [1889], 1956).

13. B. Malinowski, "The public and the individual character of religion," in N. Birnbaum and G. Lenzer (eds.), *Sociology and Religion: a Book of Readings, op. cit.*, pp. 144–158.

14. Lévi-Strauss' detailed analysis of myths is found in the series *Mythologiques,* quoted in note 26 of Ch. 4. For a more concise exposition see C. Lévi-Strauss, *Structural*

Anthropology (New York: Basic Books, 1963), Ch. 11; C. Lévi-Strauss, *The Savage Mind* (Chicago: University of Chicago Press, 1966).

15. C. Kluckhohn, *Navaho Witchcraft* (Boston: Beacon Press [1944] 1963).

16. On Geertz's interpretation of ritual see C. Geertz, "Ritual and social change: a Javanese example," in S. N. Eisenstadt (ed.), *Comparative Perspectives on Social Change* (Boston: Little, Brown, 1968), pp. 94–113; C. Geertz, "Religion as a cultural system," in M. Banton (ed.), *Anthropological Approaches to the Study of Religion* (London: Tavistock, 1966); pp. 1–46.

   For Geertz's interpretation of ideology as a symbolic sphere see C. Geertz, "Ideology as a cultural system," in D. Apter (ed.), *Ideology and Discontent* (New York: Free Press, 1964), pp. 47–76.

   Some of the newer approaches in ritual can be found in M. Gluckman (ed.), *Essays on the Ritual of Social Relations* (Manchester: Manchester University Press, 1962); J. S. La Fontaine (ed.), *The Interpretation of Ritual* (London: Tavistock, 1972); B. Meyerhoff (ed.), *Secular Rituals Considered* (forthcoming).

17. For Geertz's further development of the relationship between culture and social structure as here discussed, see C. Geertz, "Deep play: notes on the Balinese cockfight," *Daedalus* (Winter 1972), pp. 2–37.

   For Turner's analysis of the symbolic sphere and its relationship to basic existential problems and to social structure see V. Turner, *The Ritual Process: Structure and Anti-Structure* (Chicago: Aldine, 1969); V. Turner, "Forms of symbolic action," mimeo, 1967; V. Turner, "Myth and symbol," in *International Encyclopedia of the Social Sciences*, Vol. 10 (New York: Macmillan, 1968), pp. 576–582.

18. For all these aspects see T. O. Beidelman, "The Swazi royal ritual," *Africa*, Vol. 36 (1966), pp. 373–405; T. O. Beidelman, "Some sociological implications of culture," in J. McKinney and E. A. Tiryakian (eds.), *Theoretical Sociology: Perspectives and Developments* (New York: Appleton-Century-Crofts, 1970), pp. 499–527.

19. M. Douglas, *Natural Symbols* (Harmondsworth: Penguin, 1973); M. Douglas (ed.), *Rules and Meanings* (Harmondsworth: Penguin, 1973); R. Needham (ed.), *Right and Left: Essays on Dual Symbolic Classification* (Chicago: University of Chicago Press, 1973).

   Needham's work follows R. Hertz's and M. Mauss' classical analyses: R. Hertz, *Mélanges de Sociologie Religieuse et de Folklore* (Paris: F. Alcan, 1928); R. Hertz, *Death: and the Right Hand* (London: Cohen & West, 1960), first published in *L'Année Sociologique*, 1907; M. Mauss, "Les variations saisonniéres dans les sociétés Eskimo," *L'Année Sociologique*, Vol. 9 (1904–1905), pp. 39–132; M. Mauss, *The Gift* (Glencoe, Ill. Free Press, 1954); M. Mauss, "Une catégorie de l'esprit humain: celle de personne, . . ." *Journal of the Royal Anthropological Institute*, Vol. 68 (July–December, 1938).

20. L. Dumont, *Homo Hierarchicus* (London: Weidenfeld & Nicolson, 1970); L. de Heusch, *Pourquoi L'épouser* (Paris: Gallimard, 1971); L. de Heusch, *Essais sur le Symbolisme de L'Inceste Royal en Afrique* (Bruxelles: Université Libre de Bruxelles, 1958); L. de Heusch, *Le Rwanda et la Civilisation Interlacustre: Études d'Anthropologie Historique et Structurale* (Bruxelles: Université Libre de Bruxelles, 1966).

21. For Leach's analysis of the stories of the Old Testament see E. Leach, "The legitimacy of Solomon," *Archives Européennes de Sociologie*, Vol. 7, No. 1 (1966), pp. 58–101.

   For a criticism of this analysis see M. Pamment, "The succession of Solomon: a reply to E. Leach's essay "The legitimacy of Solomon,'" *Man*, Vol. 7, No. 4 (1972), pp. 635–643; A. Malamat, "Tribal societies: Biblical geneologies and African lineage systems," *Archives Européennes de Sociologie*, Vol. 14, No. 1 (1973), pp. 126–136.

For Leach's analysis of Burma and Ceylon see E. Leach, *Political Systems of Highland Burma* (London: London School of Economics, 1954); E. Leach, "The frontiers of Burma," *Comparative Studies in Society and History,* Vol. 3 (1960), pp. 49–68; E. Leach (ed.), *Aspects of Caste in South India, Ceylon, and North West Pakistan* (Cambridge: Cambridge University Press, 1960); E. Leach, *Pul Eliya: a Village in Ceylon: a Study of Land Tenure and Kinship* (Cambridge: Cambridge University Press, 1961).

22. E. Leach (ed.), *The Structural Study of Myth and Totemism* (London: Tavistock, 1967).

23. D. M. Schneider, *American Kinship: a Cultural Analysis* (Englewood Cliffs, N.J.: Prentice-Hall, 1968); D. M. Schneider and R. T. Smith, *Class Differences and Sex Roles in American Kinship and Family Structure* (Englewood Cliffs, N.J.: Prentice-Hall, 1973).

24. Sorokin's distinction between the logico-meaning and functional integration of social systems is found in P. Sorokin, *Society, Culture and Personality* (New York: Cooper Square, 1962); P. Sorokin, *Social and Cultural Dynamics* (New York: American Book Company, 1937).

    For Parsons' elaboration of the distinctiveness of the systems of personality, culture, and society, their modes of interrelationship and mechanisms, and the concept of "pattern-variables," see T. Parsons, E. Shils, (eds.), *Toward a General Theory of Action, op. cit.,* Part 2, Chs. 1–5.

25. For Shils' discussion of the symbolic and charismatic dimensions of social life and of their institutional anchorage see E. Shils, "Charisma, order and status," *American Sociological Review,* Vol. 30, No. 2 (1965), pp. 199–213; E. Shils, "Center and periphery," in *The Logic of Personal Knowledge: Essays Presented to M. Polanyi* (London: Routledge & Kegan Paul, 1961) pp. 117–131. These and other significant articles have been now collected in E. Shils, *Center and Periphery: Essays in Macrosociology* (Chicago: University of Chicago Press, 1975).

    For a further elaboration of these aspects see also S. N. Eisenstadt, *Social Differentiation and Stratification* (Glenview, Ill.: Scott, Foresman, 1971).

26. E. A. Tiryakian, "A model of societal change and its lead indicators," in S. Z. Klausner (ed.), *The Study of Total Societies* (New York: Anchor, 1967), pp. 69–98; E. A. Tiryakian, "Structural sociology," in J. C. McKinney and E. A. Tiryakian (eds.), *Theoretical Sociology: Perspectives and Developments, op. cit.,* pp. 112–135.

    For the concept of phases of the social system, including that of "pattern-maintenance," see T. Parsons, R. F. Bales, and E. Shils, *Working Papers in the Theory of Action* (Glencoe, Ill.: Free Press, 1953), especially Chs. 4 and 5.

27. T. Parsons, "Durkheim on religion revisited: another look at the *Elementary Forms of Religious Life,*" in C.Y. Glock and P.E. Hammond (eds.), *Beyond the Classics: Essays in the Scientific Study of Religion* (New York: Harper & Row, 1973), pp. 156–181.

28. M. Godelier, *Horizons, Trajets Marxistes en Anthropologie, op. cit.;* L. Sebag, *Structuralisme et Marxisme, op cit.;* P. Bourdieu, *Zur Soziologie der Symbolischen Formen* (Frankfurt am Main: Suhrkamp, 1970, 1974), especially Chs. 2 and 4.

29. For Dahrendorf's and Rex's emphases on the importance of values see R. Dahrendorf, "In praise of Thrasymachus," in R. Dahrendorf *Essays in the Theory of Society* (London: Routledge & Kegan Paul, 1968) pp. 129–150; J. Rex, *Key Problems in Sociological Theory, op. cit.,* especially Ch. 6.

    Weber's analysis of the relationship between values and interests is widely dispersed among his various works. A good and concise illustration, however, is his analysis of charisma. On this see *Max Weber on Charisma and Institution Building,* selected papers edited and with an introduction by S. N. Eisenstadt (Chicago: University of Chicago Press, 1968), pp. 48–65.

For Weber's approach to the problem of values and interests see also R. Collins, "A comparative approach to political sociology," *op. cit.*

30. For illustration of the discrete and situation-bound approach to individual goals, see for instance G. C. Homans, *Social Behavior: its Elementary Forms* (New York: Harcourt, Brace & World, 1961).

31. These points are to be found in J. C. Harsanyi, "A bargaining model for social status in informal groups and formal organizations," *Behavioral Science,* Vol. 11, No. 5 (September 1966), pp. 357–369.

32. For Homans' concept of "distributive justice," see G. C. Homans, *Social Behavior: Its Elementary Forms, op. cit.,* Chs. 4 and 12.

See also the discussion in P. Ekeh, *Social Exchange Theory, op. cit.,* especially Ch. 6.

For Blau's analysis and criticism of the concept of "distributive justice" as developed by Homans, see P. Blau, "Justice in social exchange," *Sociological Inquiry,* Vol. 34 (Spring 1964), pp. 193–206.

For an illustration of the "opening" of the exchange model toward symbolic and value dimensions transcending face-to-face interaction, see also J. Race, "Toward an exchange theory of revolution," in J. W. Lewis (ed.), *Peasant Rebellion and Communist Revolution in Asia* (Stanford, Cal.: Stanford University Press, 1974), pp. 169–204.

33. For these aspects stressed by Coleman see J. S. Coleman, "Foundations for a theory of collective decisions," *American Journal of Sociology,* Vol. 71, No. 6 (1966), pp. 615–627; J. S. Coleman, "Individual interests and collective action," *Papers on Nonmarket Decision Making* (summer 1966), pp. 49–62; J. S. Coleman, *Models of Change and Response to Uncertainty* (Englewood Cliffs, N.J.: Prentice-Hall, 1964); J. S. Coleman, "Game models of economic and political systems," in S. Z. Klausner (ed.), *The Study of Total Societies, op. cit.,* pp. 30–45.

34. For the criticisms by the various "counter-models" of the systemic emphasis of the structural-functional school, see details in Ch. 8, above.

For Homans' earlier systemic emphases see G. C. Homans, *The Human Group* (New York: Harcourt, Brace, 1950).

35. G. C. Homans, *Social Behavior: its Elementary Forms, op. cit.,* pp. 381, 382, 383. Copyright © 1961 by Harcourt Brace Jovanovich, Inc., and reprinted with their permission.

36. G. C. Homans, *Social Behavior: its Elementary Forms, op. cit.,* p. 388. Copyright © 1961 by Harcourt Brace Jovanovich, Inc., and reprinted with their permission.

37. The problematic aspects of Homans' approach as outlined here are further elaborated in the various papers in H. Turk and R. L. Simpson (eds.), *Institutions and Social Exchange* (New York and Indianapolis: Bobbs-Merrill, 1971), especially S. N. Eisenstadt, "Societal goals, systemic needs, social interaction, and individual behavior: some tentative explorations," pp. 36–55.

For similar criticisms of Homans' approach, especially those stressing the relationship between institutional positions and power differences, see especially Coleman's first two works, quoted in note 33 above, and also R. M. Emerson, "Operant psychology and exchange theory," in R. L. Burgess and D. Bushell (eds.), *Behavioral Sociology: the Experimental Analysis of Social Process* (New York: Columbia University Press, 1969), pp. 379–405.

38. For these points, stressed by Blau, see P. Blau, *Exchange and Power in Social Life* (New York: John Wiley, 1964), Introduction, Chs. 1 and 10; P. Blau, "Justice in social exchange," *op. cit.;* G. C. Homans, "The relevance of psychology to the explanation of social phenomena," P. Blau, "Comment," G. C. Homans, "Reply," in R. Borger and F.

Cioffi (eds.), *Explanation in the Behavioral Sciences* (Cambridge: Cambridge University Press, 1970), pp. 313–328, 329–339, 340–343, respectively.

39. The points stressed here are to a certain extent elaborated by scholars who belong to the "individualistic" school. For this see J. W. Thibaut and H. H. Kelley, *The Social Psychology of Groups* (New York: Wiley, 1959); F. Barth, "Models of social organization," Occasional Paper No. 23, Royal Anthropological Institute of Great Britain and Ireland, London, 1966.

    For a further theoretical elaboration of these points see also S. N. Eisenstadt, *Social Differentiation and Stratification, op. cit.*, especially Chs. 1–3.

40. E. Peters, "Some structural aspects of the feud among the camel-herding Beduim of Cyrenaica," *Africa*, Vol. 37, No. 3 (1967), pp. 261–282; R. Collins, "A comparative approach to political sociology," *op. cit.;* R. Collins, *Conflict Sociology: Toward an Explanatory Science* (New York: Academic Press, 1975).

41. P. M. Worsley et al., *Introducing Sociology* (Harmondsworth: Penguin, 1970), pp. 387–388.

42. For Dahrendorf's systemic emphases see R. Dahrendorf, *Class and Class Conflict in Industrial Society, op. cit.*

    For other similar Marxist emphases, see the works quoted in note 6 above and such recent neo-Marxist works as J. Friedman, "Tribes, states, and transformation," in M. Bloch (ed.), *Marxist Analysis in Social Anthropology* (London: Malaby, 1975), as well as the entire volume.

43. R. K. Merton, "Manifest and latent functions," in R. K. Merton, *Social Theory and Social Structure* (Glencoe, Ill.: Free Press, 1949 and subsequent editions).

44. For Gouldner's concept of "functional autonomy" and its analytic implications see A. W. Gouldner, "Reciprocity and autonomy in functional theory," in L. Gross (ed.), *Symposium on Sociological Theory* (New York: Harper & Row, 1959), pp. 241–271.

45. For Merton's analysis of functions and disfunctions and their implications for social change see R. K. Merton, "Manifest and latent functions," *op. cit.*

    For Gouldner's analysis of the implications of functional autonomy for social change see A. W. Gouldner, "Reciprocity and autonomy in functional theory," *op. cit.*

46. For Goode's analysis of role strains and their implications for role behavior and social change see W. J. Goode, "A theory of role strain," *American Sociological Review*, Vol. 25 (1960), pp. 483–496.

    For Parsons' analysis of complementarity of expectations in role behavior and the mechanisms which sustain it, see T. Parsons and E. Shils (eds.), *Toward a General Theory of Action, op. cit.*

47. For a more detailed statement of these aspects based on an analysis of some roles in Israeli society, see S. N. Eisenstadt, D. Weintraub, and N. Toren, *Analysis of Processes of Role Change* (Jerusalem: Israel University Press, 1967).

    The autonomy of individuals in their role behavior has also been recognized by scholars belonging to the functional school of anthropology; see for example R. Firth, "Some principles of social organization," in R. Firth, *Essays on Social Organization and Values* (London: Athlone, 1964), pp. 59–87.

48. N. J. Smelser, *Social Change in the Industrial Revolution: an Application of Theory to the British Cotton Industry* (Chicago: University of Chicago Press, 1959).

    For similar developments in anthropology—that is, open system assumptions in relation to social change, see for example M. Fortes, *Time and Social Structure, op. cit.;* M. Gluckman, *Order and Rebellion in Tribal Africa, op. cit.*, especially the introduction, pp. 1–50; M. Banton (ed.), *The Social Anthropology of Complex Societies* (London: Tavistock, 1966); I. M. Lewis (ed.),*History and Social Anthropology* (London: Tavistock, 1968); A. Kuper,*Anthropology and Anthropologists: The British School, 1922–1972* (London: A. Lane, 1973), especially Chs. 6–8.

49.   For Bellah's analysis of religious evolution see R. N. Bellah, "Religious evolution," in N. Birnbaum and G. Lenzer (eds.),*Sociology and Religion: a Book of Readings, op. cit.*, pp. 67–83.

For Bellah's analysis of the development of Japanese society see R. N. Bellah,*Values and Social Change in Japan*, Asian Cultural Studies (Tokyo: International Christian University, 1963), pp. 13–56.

50.   For the open systemic elements in Parsons' work as discussed here see T. Parsons, *Societies: Evolutionary and Comparative Perspectives, op. cit.*, especially Chs. 4–6.

On the parallelism between the problematic aspects of the evolutionary assumptions of Marx and of other classic scholars, and those of Parsons and other modern functionalists, see R. A. Nisbet, *Social Change and History* (New York: Oxford University Press, 1969), especially Chs. 5–8.

For interesting parallelisms between the Parsonian and Marxist approaches to social evolution see also K. Eder (ed.), *Die Entstekung von Klassengesellschaften, op. cit.:* C. Seyfarth and W. M. Sprondel (eds.), *Religion und Gesellschaftliche Eintwicklung, op. cit.;* R. Döbert,*System Theorie und die Eintwicklung Religiöser Deutungssysteme* (Frankfurt am Main: Suhrkamp, 1973).

51.   For a detailed bibliography on the discussions of the Asian mode of production, as well as Gramsci's works, see note 60 of Ch. 4.

52.   For the "open" elements in Sebag's work, see for example L. Sebag, *Marxisme et Structuralisme, op. cit.*

The quotation from Godelier is taken from M. Godelier,*Horizons, Trajets Marxistes en Anthropologie, op. cit.*, pp. 170–172. Reprinted with the permission of François Maspero, Éditeur. See also J. Friedman, "Tribes, states and transformation," *op. cit.*

53.   H. Lefebvre, *Everyday Life in the Modern World* (London: Allen Lane, 1971): L. Goldmann, *Sciences Humaines et Philosophie* (Paris: Gauthier, 1966); L. Goldmann, *Structures Mentales et Creation Culturelle* (Paris: Anthropos, 1970); L. Goldmann,*Pour une Sociologie du Roman* (Paris: Gallimard, 1964), and his classic*Le Dieu Caché: Étude de la Vision Tragique dans les Pensées de Pascal et dans le Thèatre de Racine* (Paris: Gallimard, 1956).

54.   On the debates between German Marxists and the functional-structural school on the historicity as against general system approach to the analysis of societies, see J. Habermas and N. Luhmann, *Theorie der Gesellschaft oder Sozialtechnologie* (Frankfurt: Suhrkamp, 1971); W. D. Narr, D. H. Runze, et al., *Theorie der Gesellschaft oder Sozialtechnologie–Neue Beiträge zur Habermas-Luhmann Diskussion* (Frankfurt: Suhrkamp, 1974); H. J. Siegel, *System und Krise—Beitrag zur Habermas-Luhmann Diskussion* (Frankfurt: Suhrkamp, 1974); K. Eder (ed.), *Die Entstekung von Klassengesellschaften, op. cit.*

For criticism in the Weberian tradition of the general system approach, see for example R. Collins, "A comparative approach to political sociology," *op. cit.;* R. Bendix and G. Roth, *Scholarship and Partisanship: Essays on Max Weber, op. cit.*, Ch. 11.

55.   S. J. Bodenheimer, "The ideology of developmentalism: American political science's paradigm–surrogate for Latin American studies,"*Berkeley Journal of Sociology*, Vol. 15 (1970), pp. 95–137; H. F. Cardoso and F. Weltfort (eds.), *America Latina: Ensayos de*

Interpretacion Sociologica Politica (Santiago de Chile: Editorial Universitaria, 1970); W. Wertheim, *Evolution and Revolution* (Harmondsworth: Penguin, 1974). For the fullest development of this approach see I. Wallerstein, *The Modern World System: Capitalist Agriculture and the Origins of the European World-Economy in the Sixteenth Century* (New York: Academic Press, 1974).

56. Developments in comparative sociology are surveyed in S. N. Eisenstadt, "Social institutions: comparative study," *International Encyclopedia of the Social Sciences*, Vol. 14 (New York: Macmillan, 1968), pp. 421–429; B. Moore, *Social Origins of Dictatorship and Democracy* (Boston: Beacon Press, 1966).

   For illustrations of some more recent developments see S. N. Eisenstadt (ed.), *Political Sociology* (New York: Basic Books, 1971); M. Jänicke (ed.), *Politische Systemkrisen* (Köln, Berlin: Kiepenheuer und Witsch, 1972); S. M. Lipset and S. Rokkan (eds.), *Party Systems and Voter Alignments: Cross-National Perspectives* (New York: Free Press, 1967); S. N. Eisenstadt and S. Rokkan (eds.), *Building States and Nations* (Beverly Hills, Cal.: Sage Publishers, 1973), 2 vols; W. Zapf (ed.), *Theorien des Sozialen Wandels* (Köln, Berlin: Kiepenheuer & Witsch, 1969); I. Vallier (ed.), *Comparative Method in Sociology* (Berkeley: University of California Press, 1971).

57. W. Buckley, *Sociology and Modern Systems Theory* (Englewood Cliffs, N.J.: Prentice-Hall, 1967); W. Buckley (ed.), *Modern Systems Research for the Behavioral Scientist* (Chicago: Aldine, 1968); K. Deutsch, *The Nerves of Government* (New York: Free Press, 1966); K. Azumi and J. Hage, *Organizational Systems: a Text-Reader in the Sociology of Organizations* (London: D. C. Heath, 1972); A. Etzioni, *The Active Society: a Theory of Societal and Political Processes* (New York: Free Press, 1968); A. Etzioni, "Toward a macrosociology," in J. C. McKinney and E. A. Tiryakian (eds.), *Theoretical Sociology, op. cit.*, pp. 69–97.

58. M. Maruyama, "The second cybernetics: deviation amplifying mutual causal processes," in W. Buckley (ed.), *Modern Systems Research for the Behavioral Scientist, op. cit.*, p. 304.

59. For Hill's application of the open systems approach to the study of the family see R. Hill, "Modern systems theory and the family: a confrontation," *Social Science Information*, Vol. 10, No. 5 (1971), pp. 7–26.

   For Hage's application of the open systems approach to theories of organization see K. Azumi and J. Hage, *Organizational Systems, op. cit.*

60. For Elias' earlier work see N. Elias, *Uber den Prozess der Zivilisation* (Basel: Verlag zum Falken, 1938), 2 vols. For his later work related to open systems approach, see for example N. Elias, *Die Höfische Gesellschaft* (Neuwied: Luchterhand, 1969); N. Elias, *Was ist Soziologie?* (München: Juventa, 1971).

61. For illustrations of the application of the symbolic interactionist approach, see for example H. Blumer, *Symbolic Interactionism: Perspective and Method* (Englewood Cliffs, N.J.: Prentice-Hall, 1969); E. Goffman, *The Presentation of Self in Everyday Life* (Garden City, N.Y.: Doubleday Anchor Books, 1959); E. Goffman, *Encounters* (Indianapolis: Bobbs-Merrill, 1961); E. Goffman, *Asylums* (Garden City, N.Y.: Doubleday Anchor Books, 1961); G. P. Stone and H. A. Farberman (eds.), *Social Psychology Through Symbolic Interaction* (Waltham, Mass.: Xerox College Publishing, 1970); D. Silverman, *The Theory of Organizations, op. cit.;*

62. For Weinstein's and Tanur's criticism of symbolic interactionism see E. Weinstein and J. Tanur, "Purposive interaction," to be published as a forthcoming issue of the Cornell Journal of Human Relations in memory of L. Reissman.

For Cicourel's approach see A. Cicourel, *Cognitive Sociology* (Harmondsworth: Penguin, 1972).

For the problematic aspects of symbolic interactionism concerning the explanation of the stable and systemic elements of social life, as well as of power differences, see also the discussion conducted by P. M. Hall and R. Moss-Kanter in *Sociological Inquiry*, Vol. 42, Nos. 3–4 (1972), pp. 35–99; P. Worsley, "The state of theory and the status of theory," *Sociology* Vol. 8, No. 1 (January 1974), pp. 1–17.

63. Parsons' earlier stress on the interactionist element in the definition of the situation is found in his analysis and synthesis of the classics of sociology. For this see T. Parsons, *The Structure of Social Action* (New York: McGraw-Hill, 1937).

For his later, more systemic emphases, see his works quoted in note 1 of this chapter.

For Merton's analysis of reference groups see R. K. Merton, *Social Theory and Social Structure*, (1963), *op. cit.*, especially Chs. 8, 9.

For works in social psychology which emphasize the individualistic element in social interaction, see, among earlier works, J. W. Thibault and H. H. Kelly, *The Social Psychology of Groups*, *op. cit.* Later works are best represented in G. P. Stone and H. A. Farberman (eds.), *Social Psychology Through Symbolic Interaction*, *op. cit.*

64. P. Berger and T. Luckmann, *The Social Construction of Reality* (London: Allen Lane, 1967).

Although the confrontation between psychoanalytic and "classical" sociological analysis is beyond our concern here—since the psychoanalytic approach has not developed, perhaps because of its own strong functionalist premises, into a counter-model in sociology—it may be worthwhile to mention here that a similar opening took place in the relationship between the two. It is probably just one of the many that have been taking place between different "closed system" approaches, irrespective of whether they portrayed themselves as full "countermodels."

The "opening" of sociology toward psychoanalytic elements was undertaken by many scholars, among them Parsons. For concise and critical surveys of his various works in this field see A. L. Baldwin, "The Parsonian theory of personality," and U. Bronfenbrenner, "Parsons' theory of identification," in M. Black (ed.), *The Social Theories of Talcott Parsons*, (Englewood Cliffs, N.J.: Prentice-Hall, 1964), pp. 153–190; 191–213.

For other illustrations of sociological orientations to psychoanalysis, see, for example, E. Erikson, *Young Man Luther: a Study in Psychoanalysis and History* (New York: W. W. Norton, 1958); E. Erikson, *Childhood and Society*, 2nd ed. (New York: Norton, 1963).

For a general analysis of this trend see F. Weinstein and G. M. Platt, *Psychoanalytical Sociology* (Baltimore, Md.: Johns Hopkins University Press, 1973).

65. R. Firth, "Some principles of social organization," *op. cit.*, p. 61.

66. For all the analytic contributions of Barth which are outlined here see F. Barth, "Models of social organization," *op. cit.*

67. For earlier developments in sociological theory on modes of interrelationship among components of social order, see the discussions in Chapter 4, above, on the transition from closed to open system approaches.

68. For Parsons' analysis of the concepts of resources, rewards, and media of exchange, see T. Parsons, "A revised analytical approach to the theory of social stratification," in T. Parsons, *Essays in Sociological Theory*, rev. ed. (New York: Free Press, 1963), pp.

386–439; T. Parsons, "On the concept of political power," in R. Bendix and S. M. Lipset (eds.), *Class, Status and Power* (New York: Free Press, 1966), pp. 240–265; T. Parsons, "On the concept of influence," *Public Opinion Quarterly*, Vol. 27 (Spring 1963), pp. 37–62.

The latest development of his approach to the analysis of the media of interchange is to be found in T. Parsons and G. Platt, *The American University* (Cambridge, Mass.: Harvard University Press, 1974), Technical Appendix.

69. For Coleman's concept of "political money," see J. S. Coleman, "Political money," *The American Political Science Review*, Vol. 64, No. 4 (December 1970), pp. 1074–1087.

For Blau's approach on this matter see P. Blau, *Exchange and Power in Social Life, op. cit.*

For the analysis by Parsons and Smelser of interchanges between different institutional spheres, see T. Parsons and N. J. Smelser, *Economy and Society, op. cit.*, especially Ch. 2.

70. For a further theoretical development of these aspects see S. N. Eisenstadt, *Social Differentiation and Stratification, op. cit.*, especially Chs. 1–3.

71. A. Etzioni, *A Comparative Analysis of Complex Organizations: On Power, Involvement and their Correlates* (Glencoe, Ill.: Free Press, 1961).

72. R. K. Merton, "Manifest and latent functions," *op. cit.*

73. For the stress on values and consensus in the conflict model see J. Rex, *Key Problems in Sociological Theory, op. cit.*, Chs. 6, 7; R. Dahrendorf, "In praise of Thrasymachus," *op. cit.*; R. Dahrendorf, *Class and Class Conflict in Industrial Society, op. cit.*, especially Chs. 5, 6, 7.

74. For Homans' assumption of individual calculus of interests as the basis of acceptance of social order, see G. C. Homans, *Social Behavior: its Elementary Forms, op. cit.*, especially Chs. 4, 18.

For Coleman's, Blau's, Harsanyi's stress on the importance of power differences and quest for order as bases of acceptance of social order, see J. S. Coleman, "Foundations of a theory of collective decisions," *op. cit.*; J. S. Coleman, "Individual interests and collective action," *op. cit.*; P. Blau, *Exchange and Power in Social Life, op. cit.*, especially Chs. 5, 9, 10; J. C. Harsanyi, "A bargaining model for social status in informal groups and formal organizations," *op. cit.*; J. C. Harsanyi, "Explanation and comparative dynamics in social science," *Behavioral Science*, Vol. 5, No. 2 (April 1966), pp. 136–145.

75. For the further elaboration of this point see S. N. Eisenstadt, "Societal goals, systemic needs, social interaction, . . ." *op. cit.*

76. For the development of the relationship between power and values in the symbolic interactionist tradition, see, for example, P. M. Hall, "A symbolic interactionist analysis of politics," *Sociological Inquiry*, Vol. 42, Nos. 3–4 (1972), pp. 35–75.

For the development of the relationship between power and values in the symbolic structuralist tradition, see, for example E. A. Tiryakian, "Structural sociology," *op. cit.*

For concrete research on these problems as related to professions, see, for example, H. Jamous and B. Peloille, "Changes in the French university-hospital system," in J. A. Jackson (ed.), *Professions and Professionalization* (Cambridge: Cambridge University Press, 1970), pp. 111–152; and as related to the concept of role, see the materials collected in J. A. Jackson (ed.), *Role* (Cambridge: Cambridge University Press, 1972).

77. For the modern analysis of charisma as source of dissensus and struggle, see E. Shils,

"Charisma, order, and status," *op. cit.;* E. Shils, "Center and periphery," *op. cit.*
For a fuller elaboration of the constructive and destructive tendencies of charisma,
see S. N. Eisenstadt (ed.), *Max Weber on Charisma and Institution Building, op. cit.,*
especially the introduction.

78. For the classic analysis of professions in the functionalist tradition see T. Parsons,
"The professions and social structure," in T. Parsons, *Essays in Sociological Theory, op.
cit.,* pp. 34–49.
For the analysis of professions in relation to elements of sacredness, power, and
struggle, see H. Jamous and B. Peloille, "Changes in the French university-hospital
system," in J. A. Jackson (ed.), *Professions and Professionalization, op. cit.*

79. For a more detailed analysis of the concept "calculus of consensus" as a variable
expressing different possible orientations of individuals to the social order, see S. N.
Eisenstadt, "Societal goals, systemic needs, social interaction, . . ." *op. cit.*
The point stressing that the consensual and conflictual images of society are not
necessarily exclusive concepts, but may be also complementary, is developed by R. W.
Friedrichs, "Dialectical sociology: toward a resolution of the current crisis in Western
sociology," *British Journal of Sociology,* Vol. 23, No. 3 (September 1972), pp. 263–274;
and E. Shils, *Center and Periphery: Essays in Macro-Sociology, op. cit.,* Introduction.

80. For details on the theoretical openings that occurred in earlier periods in the history
of sociology, see Ch. 4, above.

81. For details on the trends of codification in sociology, especially after World War II,
see Ch. 6, above.

82. Some of the "evolutionary universals" of human society have been analyzed by T.
Parsons. For this see T. Parsons, "Evolutionary universals in society," *American
Sociological Review,* Vol. 29, No. 3 (1964), pp. 339–357; S. N. Eisenstadt, *Social
Differentiation and Stratification, op. cit.,* Chs. 1–4.

83. For the criticism of the concept "role" from within the structural-functional model,
see for example W. J. Goode, "A theory of role strain," *op. cit.*
For the critical reexamination of this and related concepts in Germany, see for
example R. Dahrendorf, "Homo Sociologicus: on the history, significance, and limits
of the category of social role," in R. Dahrendorf, *Essays in the Theory of Society, op. cit.,*
pp. 19–87; D. Claessens, "Rollentheorie als bildungsbürgerliche verschleierung-
sideologie," in *Verhandlungen des 16 Deutschen Soziologentages,* April 1968, (Stuttgart:
F. Enke Verlag, 1969), pp. 270–281; F. Hang, *Kritik der Rollentheorie* (Frankfurt am
Main: Fisher Verlag, 1972).
For similar criticisms in Italy and France, see G. A. Gilli, *Come si fa Ricerca* (Milano:
Arnoldo Mondedori, 1971); R. Lourau, *L'Analyse Institutionelle* (Paris: Les Éditions de
Minuit, 1970).
For further commentary see J. A. Jackson (ed.), *Role, op. cit.*

84. For the criticism of socialization as a mechanism which can ensure normative, ex-
pected role-behavior, see among others D. Wrong, "The oversocialized conception of
man in modern sociology," *American Sociological Review,* Vol. 26, No. 2 (1961), pp.
183–193; and the various discussions of the concept of role cited in note 83 of this
chapter.

85. For brilliant analyses of the possibilities of individuals to manipulate the different
components of their roles in various situations, see E. Goffman, *The Presentation of Self
in Everyday Life, op. cit.;* E. Goffman, *Asylums, op. cit.;* E. Goffman, *Encounters, op. cit.;*
See also: K. Wolff, *Trying Sociology* (New York: Wiley, 1974).

For the analysis of the structural dynamics of different aspects of roles see S. N. Eisenstadt et al., *Analysis of Processes of Role Change, op. cit.*

86. This possibility has been recognized even by functionalist scholars; see for example W. J. Goode, "A theory of role strain," *op. cit.*

87. The shift from institutions as "given" to their conception as outcomes of processes of exchange and interaction among individuals is reviewed and analysed by S. N. Eisenstadt, *Social Differentiation and Stratification, op. cit.*, especially Chs. 1–3; S. N. Eisenstadt, "Social institutions," in *The International Encyclopedia of the Social Sciences, op. cit.*, Vol. 14, pp. 409–421.
     ¶In this connection see also R. Lourau, *L'Analyse Institutionelle, op. cit.*

88. The materials related to the trend of critical reexamination of various fields of research are too numerous to cite; the following illustrations, however, provide an instructive picture of the general trend:
     For family and sex roles, see H. P. Dreitzel (ed.), *Family, Marriage, and the Struggle of the Sexes*, Recent Sociology No. 4 (London: Collier-Macmillan, 1972); J. Bernard, "My four revolutions: an autobiographical history of the A.S.A.," in J. Huber (ed.), *Changing Women in a Changing Society* (Chicago: University of Chicago Press, 1973), pp. 11–29.
     For general theories of stratification, see S. N. Eisenstadt, *Social Differentiation and Stratification, op. cit.*; J. A. Jackson (ed.), *Social Stratification, op. cit.*
     For the theory of status incongruence, see S. Box and J. Ford, "Some questionable assumptions in the theory of status inconsistency," *Sociological Review*, Vol. 17, No. 2 (1969), pp. 187–201; E. E. Sampson, "Studies in status congruence," in *Advances in Experimental Social Psychology*, Vol. 4 (1969), pp. 225–270.
     For the convergence theory of stratification, see M. Scotford-Archer and S. Giner, "Social stratification in Europe," in M. Scotford-Archer and S. Giner (eds.), *Contemporary Europe: Class, Status and Power* (London: Weidenfeld & Nicolson, 1971), pp. 1–59; J. H. Goldthorpe, "Social stratification in industrial society," in R. Bendix and S. M. Lipset (eds.), *Class, Status and Power* (New York: Free Press, 1966), pp. 648–659.
     For the area of studies of health, see H. P. Dreitzel (ed.), *The Social Organization of Health*, Recent Sociology No. 3 (London: Collier-Macmillan, 1971).
     For deviance, see I. Taylor and L. Taylor (eds.), *Politics and Deviance* (Harmondsworth: Penguin Books, 1973); I. Taylor, P. Walton, and J. Young, *The New Criminology: for a Social Theory of Deviance* (London: Routledge & Kegan Paul, 1973); J. Young, "New directions in subcultural theory," *op. cit.*; H. S. Becker, "Whose side are we on?" *Social Problems*, Vol. 14, (winter 1967), pp. 239–247; A. W. Gouldner, "The sociologist as partisan: sociology and the welfare state," *American Sociologist*, Vol. 3 (May 1968), pp. 103–116; D. Chapman, *Sociology and the Stereotype of the Criminal* (London: Tavistock, 1968).
     For political sociology, see H. P. Dreitzel (ed.), *The Social Basis of Politics*, Recent Sociology No. 1 (London: Collier-Macmillan, 1969); *Sociological Inquiry*, Vol. 42, Nos. 3–4 (1972), entire issue; S. N. Eisenstadt (ed.), *Political Sociology, op. cit.*; R. Collins, "A comparative approach to political sociology," *op. cit.*
     For a critical reexamination of theories of ritual, see the materials quoted in notes 10–18 of this chapter.
     A good collection in which the major classical and modern theoretical perspectives in the sociology of religion are represented is N. Birnbaum and G. Lenzer (eds.), *Sociology and Religion: a Book of Readings, op. cit.*

For relatively recent critical reorientations in the field, see P. Berger, *A Rumor of Angels* (Garden City, N.Y.: Doubleday Anchor, 1970); T. Luckmann, *The Invisible Religion* (London: Macmillan, 1970).

For the sociology of organization, see, for example, D. Silverman, *The Theory of Organizations, op. cit.;* A. M. Bowey, "Approaches to organization theory," *op. cit.*

For comparative studies see, for example, S. N. Eisenstadt, "Social institutions: comparative study," *op. cit.;* R. Bendix and G. Roth, *Scholarship and Partisanship, op. cit.,* Ch. 11.

For studies of modernization and development, see Chong-Do-Hah and J. Schneider, "A critique of current studies of political development and modernization," *Social Research,* Vol. 35 (1968), pp. 130–158; A. R. Desai (ed.), *Essays on Modernization of Underdeveloped Societies* (Bombay: Thacker, 1971), 2 vols.; S. N. Eisenstadt, *Tradition, Change and Modernity, op. cit.,* especially Chs. 1 and 5; R. Nisbet, *Social Change and History, op. cit.;* E. de Kadt and G. Williams (eds.), *Sociology and Development, op. cit.*

89. For a detailed list of Lévi-Strauss' works on myths and kinship see note 26 of Ch. 4, above.

For other studies of kinship and myth influenced by symbolic-structuralism, see, for example, D. M. Schneider and R. T. Smith, *Class Differences and Sex Roles in American Kinship, op. cit.;* E. Leach (ed.), *The Structural Study of Myth and Totemism, op. cit.*

For a concise survey of works on folklore and literature carried on in the tradition of structuralism, see M. Glucksman, *Structuralist Analysis in Contemporary Social Thought, op. cit.,* especially Ch. 3.

For illustrations of studies of primitive and traditional societies carried on in the tradition of symbolic-structuralism, see the works of L. Dumont and L. de Heusch which are quoted in note 20 of this chapter.

A combination of Marxist and Structuralist approach is to be found in M. Godelier, *Horizons, Trajets Marxistes en Anthropologie, op. cit.;* L. Sebag, *Marxisme et Structuralisme, op. cit.*

90. For illustrations of the conflict approach mentioned here see R. Dahrendorf, *Class and Class Conflict in Industrial Society, op. cit.;* L. Coser, *The Functions of Social Conflict* (London: Collier-Macmillan [1956], 1964); M. Gluckman, *Rituals of Rebellion in South-East Africa, op. cit.;* R. Collins, *Conflict Sociology, op. cit.*

For the stress on the problematic aspect of boundary-maintenance by social systems in the ecological group approach see, for example, E. Peters, "Some structural aspects of the feud among the camel-herding Beduim of Cyrenaica," *op. cit.;* J. Goody, *Comparative Studies in Kinship* (London: Routledge & Kegan Paul, 1969), pp. 120–141.

For an extensive list of studies based on the exchange model or influenced by it, see A. Heath, "Review article: exchange theory," *British Journal of Political Science,* Vol. 1 (1971), especially pp. 116–119.

For Homans' theory of status congruence, see G. C. Homans, *Social Behavior: Its Elementary Forms, op. cit.,* especially Ch. 12.

For the application, development, and criticism of Homans' theory of status congruence, see, for example, E. E. Sampson, "Studies in status congruence," *op. cit.;* S. Box and J. Ford, "Some questionable assumptions in the theory of status inconsistency," *op. cit.;* W. G. Runciman, *Relative Deprivation and Social Justice* (London: Routledge & Kegan Paul, 1966).

91. For illustrations of these aspects of Goffman's work, see E. Goffman, *The Presentation of Self in Everyday Life, op. cit.;* E. Goffman, *Encounters, op. cit.;* E. Goffman, *Asylums, op. cit.*

See also G. Psathas (ed.), *Phenomenological Sociology* (New York: Wiley, 1973); R. E. Best, "New directions in sociological theory: a critical note on phenomenological sociology and its antecedents," *British Journal of Sociology,* Vol. 26, No. 2 (June 1975), pp. 133–143.

92. For the application of symbolic interactionism to the study of organizations see, for example, D. Silverman, *The Theory of Organizations, op. cit.*

For a critical examination of this work, see A. M. Bowey, "Approaches to organization theory," *op. cit.*

E. C. Hughes' studies have been collected in E. C. Hughes, *The Sociological Eye* (Chicago, New York: Aldine, Atherton, 1971), especially Parts 3 and 4.

For A. Strauss' work on the negotiated order of formal organizations, see, for example, A. Strauss et al., "The hospital and its negotiated order," in E. Friedson (ed.), *The Hospital in Modern Society* (New York: Free Press, 1963), pp. 147–169; A. Strauss, *Mirrors and Masks* (Glencoe, Ill.: Free Press, 1959).

A. Strauss, B. Glaser, *Status Passage* (Chicago: Aldine, Atherton, 1971).

93. For the application of symbolic interactionism to political sociology see, for example, the discussion between P. M. Hall and R. Moss Kanter in *Sociological Inquiry,* Vol. 42, Nos. 3–4 (1972), pp. 35–99.

For its influence on Atkinson's and Silverman's work see D. Atkinson, *Orthodox Consensus and Radical Alternative, op. cit.;* D. Silverman, *The Theory of Organizations, op. cit.;* P. Filmer, D. Silverman, et al., *New Directions in Sociological Theory* (London: Collier-Macmillan, 1972).

94. For illustrations of neo-Marxist approaches to the study of primitive and historical societies, see M. Godelier, *Horizons, Trajets Marxistes en Anthropologie, op. cit.;* L. Sebag, *Marxisme et Structuralisme, op. cit.;* P. Bourdieu, *Zur Soziologie der Symbolischen Formen, op. cit.;* B. Hindess and P. Q. Hirst, *Pre-Capitalist Modes of Production* (London: Routledge & Kegan Paul, 1975); C. Meillassoux, *Anthropologie Économique des Gouro de Côte d'Ivoire* (Paris: Mouton, 1964); C. Meillassoux, (ed.), *The Development of Indigenous Trade and Markets in West Africa* (London: Oxford University Press, 1971); C. Meillassoux, "From reproduction to production," in H. Bernstein and B. van Arkadie (eds.), *Development and Underdevelopment* (London: Allen & Unwin, 1972); J. Friedman, "System, structure and contradiction in the evolution of "Asiatic" social formations," Unpublished doctoral dissertation, Columbia University, New York, 1972; E. Terry, "L'Organisation Sociale des Dida de Côte d'Ivoire," *Annals de l'Université d' Abidjan* (1969).

Some of the broader implications of these analyses for comparative studies of ancient societies can be found in R. McAdams, "Anthropological perspectives on ancient trade," and comments, *Current Anthropology,* Vol. 15, No. 3 (September 1974), pp. 239–258.

For neo-Marxist approaches to the study of modernization and development see, for example, S. J. Bodenheimer, "The ideology of developmentalism, . . ." *op. cit.;* R. Owen and B. Sutcliffe (eds.), *Studies in the Theory of Imperialism* (London: Longman, 1972); B. J. Cohen, *The Question of Imperialism: the Political Economy of Dominance and Dependence* (New York: Basic Books, 1973); C. K. Wilber (ed.), *The Political Economy of Development and Underdevelopment* (New York: Random House, 1973); C. Palloix, *Problème de la Croissance en Économie Ouverte* (Paris: Maspero, 1972); R. Stavenhagen,

Sept Thèses Erronées sur l'Amérique Latine ou Comment Décoloniser les Sciences Humaines (Paris: Anthropos, 1973).

For neo-Marxist studies of systems of power in modern societies, see, for example, N. Birnbaum, *The Crisis of Industrial Society* (New York: Oxford University Press, 1969); R. Miliband, *The State in Capitalist Society* (London: Weidenfeld & Nicolson, 1969); R. Marris, *The Economic Theory of "Managerial" Capitalism* (New York: Basic Books, 1968); N. Poulantzas, *Les Classes Sociales dans le Capitalisme d'Aujourd'hui* (Paris: Seuil, 1974).

Major contributions to the study of modern society have also been made by scholars of the Frankfurt school. Their multifaceted analyses are too numerous to cite. For good surveys of these works, both earlier and more recent, see M. Jay, *The Dialectical Imagination* (Boston: Little, Brown, 1973); M. Jay, "Some recent developments in critical theory," *Berkeley Journal of Sociology*, Vol. 18 (1973–1974), pp. 27–44.

For an interesting attempt at a Marxist approach to geography and urban studies, see D. Harvey, *Social Justice and the City* (London: Edward Arnold, 1973).

95. For Homans' rule of "distributive justice," see G. C. Homans, *Social Behavior: its Elementary Forms, op. cit.*, Chs. 4 and 12.

For a criticism of Homans' inadequate explanation of the origins of this rule, see for example P. Blau, "Justice in social exchange," *op. cit.*

Coleman's inability to explain the rules which regulate the exchange processes developed by him is evident in J. S. Coleman, "Foundations for a theory of collective decisions," *op. cit.*

96. The inability of the structural-functional school to relate individual and group goals to systemic needs has been stressed, of course, by the exchange, conflict, and ecological countermodels, which have been quoted in this chapter and in Ch. 8, above.

For the criticism of the functional model for its minimal regard for divergent subjective meanings and cultural orientations, see for example J. Rex, "Social structure and humanistic sociology: the legacy of the classical European tradition," in J. Rex (ed.), *Approaches to Sociology, op. cit.*, pp. 187–204.

97. For criticism of the functional model's failure to analyze the processes of articulation and institutionalization of systemic needs, see for example C. Morse, "The functional imperatives," in M. Black (ed.), *The Social Theories of Talcott Parsons, op. cit.*, pp. 100–152; S. N. Eisenstadt, "Societal goals, systemic needs, social interaction, . . ." *op. cit.*

98. For a criticism of symbolic structuralism's failure to analyze the mechanisms which relate the symbolic dimension to the working of social systems, see M. Glucksman, *Structuralist Analysis in Contemporary Social Thought, op. cit.*, Ch. 3.

99. The neglect, or taking for granted, of the symbolic dimension, especially in Homans' exchange theory, has also been stressed and criticized by P. Ekeh. For this see P. Ekeh, *Social Exchange Theory, op. cit.*, especially Chs. 5, 6.

100. On the debates between the historically specific and general systemic approaches to societies, see the materials quoted in note 54 of this chapter.

11

The Broadening of the Sociological Tradition and the Outcry of Crisis in Sociology

The Contradictory Impact of the Controversies on the Development of Sociological Research and Analysis

1. The constructive openings analyzed above were not the only developments taking place. Other trends were toward the increasing convergence of different aspects of sociological discussions, and the possible abdication of the distinctiveness, autonomy, and progress of sociological analysis.

Such destructive tendencies can be explained by the simple fact that these developments, even in their most positive aspects, were still a far cry from comprehensive, systematic integration of research and theory and new and more widely accepted models. Indeed, constant reexamination of paradigms and fields of research, and the quest for paradigms, could also (given the slim success of these efforts compared with higher levels of aspiration) produce widespread dissatisfaction within the sociological community. By stressing weakness, fragmentation, and poor coordination of theory and research these debates created a general, if often latent, *malaise.*[1]

296

But just as the constructive development of the sociological tradition was not ensured by the mere occurrence of analytic advances, so, too, dissatisfaction with the state of the field was not in itself a surrender of the distinctiveness of sociological analysis. Contradictory possibilities inhered in the different modes of discussion that came to characterize the controversies analyzed in Chapters 9 and 10, and it is to an analysis of these modes that we now turn.

The Major Modes of Controversy in Contemporary Sociology

2.   As discussions continued, the mutual relevance and convergence of the "internal" and "external" issues, and the different modes of their combination, became increasingly apparent and structured. Each mode was usually a concrete constellation of three major components which took on different values. First was the degree to which the cognitive autonomy of each philosophical, methodological, and substantive component of the controversy was recognized, and the degree to which the central role of scholarly analysis and research in the pursuit of societal analysis was accepted. Second was the degree of acceptance of, and even commitment to, distinctive sociological tradition: concern with broader paradigmatic orientations; analytic and methodological interests; the sustained pursuit of scholarly analysis in various fields; and the hope of achieving high standards while criticizing actual performance. Third was the degree of perceived tension among the components of the sociologist's role, as against the desired subordination of most components under one major aspect, for example, the "technical professional" or the "critical."

These components were in principle and fact independent of each other and could coalesce into different constellations. But some constellations became more typical than others. Two broad modes of joining the issues of controversy can be distinguished. Each was composed of components which could, to some degree, vary independently of each other, and each tended to have different intellectual and institutional repercussions.

The first constellation, predominant in the debates of the late 1940s and 1950s, was characterized by the recognition of the intellectual autonomy of each component of controversy and by acceptance of the autonomy of scholarly analysis and the central role of research. This trait was generally accompanied by commitment to the role components of specifically sociological analysis: paradigmatic, analytic and methodological concerns, belief in scholarly analysis, and the hope of high intellectual accomplishment.

The disputes in which this mode of controversy was predominant were characterized by a willingness, for the most part, to live with the various tensions of the sociologist's role and subject. In different periods, one of these role orientations might be stressed at the expense of others. However, because of commitment to the broader sociological endeavor and to scholarly cognitive analysis, such restricted emphasis could not long be maintained.

The second, or abdicative, mode of discussion, contrasting sharply with the preceding one, was characterized by the denial of both the autonomy and the ultimate possibility of the cognitive scholarly endeavor in sociology; and by the subordination of this effort to other orientations, philosophical, ideological, or political. One type of submergence combined philosophical (structuralist, phenomenological, or Marxist) trends with internal analytic paradigms, each of which was proclaimed as a totally closed philosophical camp.

Ideological-political orientations could also be combined with analytic paradigms. This type of combination was associated in varying degrees with skepticism about the possibility of autonomous sociological analysis; denial of tension between critical and scholarly aspects of the sociologist's role; and endorsement of the merging of intellectual endeavor with direct political or activist effort. Thus it stressed immediacy and the destruction of boundaries between scholarly, practical, and political activities. This in a sense was the extreme development of Irving L. Horowitz's "anti-sociologist" role—that is, a role whose incumbent "owes a functional allegiance to a source of authority, or to a set of ideas, which is outside the control system of sociology." In its recent development, however, it also embodied new political activism, as well as strong antinomian and millenarian bents.[2]

Each of these modes, or ways of uniting internal and external controversy, had repercussions on the development of sociological analysis and research. These repercussions, in fact, were decisive in shaping the outcome of the convergence of internal and external problems in discussion, and thus the development of sociological analysis and work.

The "Constructive" Mode of Discussion

3.   The central characteristic of the "constructive" mode, its commitment to scholarly analysis and research, and belief in their possibility, can best be seen in the nature and dimensions of debate—particularly "radical" criticism—conducted in that tradition. For example: the Frankfurt

school and George Gurvitch made severe philosophical critiques of the methodological assumptions of sociology. Yet they never negated empirical or comparative institutional research as such, or the development of better and more sophisticated research methods. As we have seen, the Frankfurt school engaged in empirical research—in community studies and studies of mass media—which was seen as capable of representing their specific theoretical approach and in this way demonstrating its superiority to positivist empiricism. C. Wright Mills could decry the actual uses and application of research techniques, but he did not deny their potential utility, and he himself engaged in such detailed studies as those of Puerto Rico. Similarly, though somewhat later, Norman Birnbaum, while criticizing many aspects of contemporary research in sociology, still upheld the importance of research for the sociological enterprise, and decried the negation of research in the name of ideological tenets.[3]

Research-oriented theorists who engaged in these discussions did not, for their part, deny in principle the possibility of such philosophical or methodological discussions, even if most were usually skeptical of their utility for sociological research. Indeed, some of the more outstanding among them, for example Paul Lazarsfeld, Talcott Parsons, and Ralph Dahrendorf, participated in the discussions.[4] It was only natural, then, that many of the controversies among the "camps" accepting this mode of discussion were focused on mutual, though often general, evaluation of research topics, and tried to show the merits of their respective models through application to research areas. The best known of the earlier of such attempts, though itself not systematically oriented to research, was the Davis-Moore-Tumin controversy and its offshoots in the field of stratification. Similarly, to use a few almost random illustrations, Alvin Gouldner developed some of his analytic criticisms of the functional school, particularly of its presuppositions in the study of bureaucracy, both on a general analytic level and through concrete field studies. Mills' general polemics were closely related to attempts to refute, on the basis of concrete research, the accepted "consensual" view of the American system of power or stratification, the distribution of power in American society, and the class situation of the white collar. Birnbaum tried to illustrate his critical stance by examining Weber's Protestant Ethic thesis in relation to Zwinglianism in Zurich.[5]

Even in Germany, where from the beginning a much more uncompromising view of the differences between "positivist" and "hermeneutic" or "dialectic" approaches was taken, serious attempts were made to elucidate theoretical points with research. As we have seen, the Frankfurt school launched a series of research monographs on community studies, mass media, and the like, aimed at elaborating, through research, their specific conception of mass society, which was grounded in a combination of Marxism and phenomenological studies. The school attempted to compare its own type of research with parallel studies undertaken at that time in the United States.[6]

Another important focus of dispute was the comparative study of industrial societies: the degrees of convergence of these societies, and the impact of different political regimes (especially democratic as against totalitarian) on their operation. Indeed, at a meeting of the German Sociological Association devoted to "late capitalism or industrial society," an attempt was made to determine the respective validity of each theory by reference to common research problems. Later, the studies of development and modernization also provided such a focus.[7] Similarly, many controversies in anthropology which touched on basic analytic oppositions were focused on empirical studies of kinship orders and systems or on the study of ritual.[8]

The orientation of this mode of discussion was evident in the nature of controversy between the structural-functional school and various countermodels.[9] Scholars who criticized the structural-functional school in this particular mode often stressed that the various analytic weaknesses of the structural-functional or positivist model were closely related. But they did not deny a common ground of interest or the possibility of a common critical approach to these problems. Most important, they did not deny the possibility of discussing each aspect of the "dominant" sociological model—philosophical premises, paradigmatic assumptions about the nature of social order, derived theories, or research problems—on its own merits.

Even when the weaknesses of the structural-functional model were linked to the ideological bias of its proponents, it was implicitly and even explicitly assumed that they could be at least partially improved through scientific discourse and criticism. Some participants in these controversies may have assumed that there was a natural "package deal" between the different aspects of the model they opposed. On the whole, however, such a package deal was not seen as a "must," or at least was not upheld as an ideal situation.

Moreover, while many critics presented their views as countermodels to structural-functionalism, they did not necessarily see themselves as totally opposed to it. Indeed, many expressed hope of future convergence or synthesis.[10] In attempting to create such a synthesis, they tended also to reorient themselves to the classics of sociology, Marx, Weber, and Durkheim, thus implicitly stressing the continuity of the sociological endeavor. Furthermore, many participants directed their criticism not only against structural-functional or "positivistic" sociology, but also against aspects of other models, including, paradoxically enough, Marxism. Thus, Barrington Moore severely criticized the Soviet system and its ideological underpinnings, and Herbert Marcuse could, at that time, subject Soviet Marxism to severe critical analysis, while Birnbaum in his well-known analysis of Marxist sociology stressed that both Marxist and "bourgeois" sociologists (however defined) must face the need to analyze different, and to some degree complementary, aspects of the modern class structure which each had neglected. Presumably only through such a confrontation could a further understanding of the dynamics of class in different modern societies by arrived at.[11]

It was largely the more "closed orthodox" members of different camps, "positivists" and "structuralists," but especially Marxists, who opposed any attempt at finding common ground with other camps. In the orthodox Marxist camp, for example, severe criticism appeared of Maurice Godelier's attempts to open Marxism to structuralism and anthropological research, and of Jurgen Habermas' more open analysis of social reality and attempt to divorce such analysis from direct political engagement. Similarly, only the extreme structuralists denied the utility of scholarly intercourse with other anthropologists and kept all discussion exclusively within the philosophical camp.[12] These outcries were still made largely outside the sociological or anthropological communities, mostly by people who had never accepted the premises of an autonomous sociological analysis and scholarship.

4. The conceptions of the sociologists' role in the "constructive" mode of discussion present a rather more complicated picture, which changed as the tensions between components of this role were variously perceived. As we have seen, the initial tendency after World War II in the central sociological communities was implicitly to deny the importance of incorporating into the sociologists' role any problems wider than organizational issues grounded in academic and professional settings.

The predominance of this attitude was challenged increasingly by discussion of the ethical aspects of research and of problems and tensions stemming out of the sociologists' engagement in public policy. The accusation was made—but still in the mode of scholarly controversy analyzed above—that the sociological establishment was technocratic, entirely accepting the definition of its problems and of social reality as stated outside the profession by the "powers that be," or by the agencies which sponsored research. In the context of this mode of controversy the accusation could also be made that existing academic sociology, because of its tendency to schematic theories, its neglect of the problem of power in social life, and its lack of critical concern with contemporary society, did not live up to its pretension of explaining "real life," above all the nature of the contemporary historical reality.

Thus it came to be recognized by participants in this mode of controversy that the professionalization of sociology placed many demands beyond the purely academic or intellectual on sociologists, and that no easy way existed to overcome tensions inherent in the manifold components of the sociologist's role. At the same time, sensitivity to these tensions also produced still within this mode of discussion, a continual critical examination of different aspects of sociological analysis, with potentially enriching effects on the development of this analysis.[13]

The "Constructive" Mode and the Potential Broadening of the Sociological Tradition

5. The emphasis on scholarly analysis and its cognitive autonomy and the acknowledgement of tension among the components of the sociologist's role were accompanied by a recognition of the complicated relationship between external influences on sociology and the internal development of sociological analysis and research. Even scholars who were not swept along by extreme political ideologies were much more sensitive to the changing pattern of commitment to social problems and inquiries, to demands to relate their studies to actual social problems, and above all to the implications of sociological analysis for a critical examination of social reality. Thus Allen Barton, assessing himself as a liberal, pointed out how radical sociologists in different historical-political situations (e.g., in periods of political stagnation, political opportunity, and after a change-oriented movement) might act so as to extend both the scholarly sociological endeavor and its possible contribution to a radical evaluation of social reality. He suggested ways in which they could also use studies of social problems and situations that had been undertaken by "conservative" sociologists.[14]

Similarly, the discussions of the possibility of a value-free sociology, and the various attempts to analyze the sociological enterprise as sociology of knowledge, were conceived in these modes of discussion as investigations of the limits in validity of each approach or piece of research. The possibility of objective scholarship in sociology, however, was not denied.[15] Hence these scholars recognized, implicitly or explicitly, the importance of translating or transforming the "external" impacts into the framework of sociological analysis and *Problemstellung*. The more radical sectors of the sociological community were also committed to the pursuit of sociological scholarship, and attempted to broaden the scope of sociological analysis and incorporate many approaches critically into a broader macrosocietal analysis—even when they themselves did not distinguish between their political and ideological views and the critique of sociological analysis.

These combinations of a radical stance with constructive sociological analysis are illustrated, instructively, by two recent works, John Urry's *Reference Groups and the Theory of Revolution* and the analysis by Ian Taylor, Paul Walton, and Jock Young of major tendencies in criminology and deviance study. In the first, the author attempts to bring standard reference group theory into the context of a macrosocietal analysis, focusing on problems of social change and revolution. The second is an interesting, albeit still largely programmatic, attempt to relate major trends in the study of deviance to a macrosocietal analysis of social conflict in a Marxist vein.[16]

Another work of this kind is John Rex's *Sociology and the Demystification of the Modern World*.[17] However one may judge the validity of its analysis of major types of contemporary social systems—capitalist, socialist, and Third World, it is clearly a serious attempt to combine macrosociological analysis with a critical orientation that is nevertheless not identifiable with any single political or ideological approach.

One important indication of the consciousness of the primacy and autonomy of sociological analysis was belief in, and endorsement of, a multiplicity of views and approaches to major issues, particularly the possibility of cross-cutting positions on these issues. Such cross-cuttings did develop with respect to the relationship between ideological and analytic approaches, even among the most extreme exponents of such views. Thus, different radical trends took different conceptual or analytic aspects to demonstrate the supposed conservatism of established sociology. To illustrate: Gouldner, who criticized Parsons and others in the name of "reflexive sociology," concentrated in *The Coming Crisis of Western Sociology*[18] (insofar as he dealt with substantive analysis) on the closed-system approach of functionalism and charged it with failing to recognize the relative autonomy of the individual and of culture. He then upheld a mild open-system approach, together with a strong emphasis on the autonomy of the individual and on power relationships. Robert Friedrichs criticized both conflict and consensus models as ideological and analytically restrictive, and called for the development of a dialectical sociology to overcome these deficiencies. That dialectic was defined largely in terms of the relationship between the sociologist as scholar and as active citizen. Dick Atkinson pointed out the heavy structural-institutional and systemic emphasis, which he found in Marx, Weber, and Parsons alike, as the main source of conservatism, while the realm of freedom was found, according to him, in the emphasis on individual interaction, the search for meaning, and the individual's definition of the situation. As against this, many neo-Marxists focused their criticisms on the general level of abstraction and the nonhistorical emphasis of the structural-functional school, but not on its heavy structural or systemic emphasis, as the main source of its political and ideological conservatism.[19] Even more interesting were the similar cross-cuttings in discussions of the intellectual and practical issues entailed in the sociologist's participation in public policy in the *American Sociologist*[20] and other sources.

The existence and strength of such cross-cuttings was a very important indicator of the potential internal strength of the sociological tradition. The special characteristic of the "constructive" mode of sociological discussion was the acceptance of these cross-cuttings and the parallel recognition that most "models" and "countermodels" could be adopted by different political or philosophical approaches, and could be seen as "radical" by some and "conservative" by others.[21]

6.   Thus all the developments associated with the "positive" mode of discussion could, in principle, contribute to the broadening of the framework of sociological analysis; the deepening of the internal tradition of sociology through the rediscovery of the Forerunners and Founding Fathers; to bridges of long-term discontinuity between earlier traditions and contemporary research; and to constructive analytic openings and greater, if not perfect, integration with research and methodological criticism.

Such a broadening manifested itself in several ways which can be traced in the topics and areas of discussions in journals, curricula, and textbooks. First, there were serious efforts to incorporate many trends into a broader framework, principally the Marxist stream and various philosophical and sociophilosophical trends discussed above, which had remained outside or on the margin of this tradition. Similarly, such older traditions as the Chicago school with its emphasis on change, flux, and the informal aspects of social life, which also were marginal, were incorporated into the central sociological tradition through discussions of the various countermodels.[22] Such incorporation took place insofar as the dialogue between different camps developed in terms of common examination of problems of sociological analysis and research, rather than in dogmatic, segregated discussion.

Second, many attempts were made to evaluate the different possibilities of reformulating, broadening, and changing the paradigmatic frameworks of sociological analysis, incorporating different models or orientations in new ways. Some important illustrations of this tendency were Irving Zeitlin's effort to unite Marx, Mead, and Freud as bases of a new explicative paradigm of sociology; Jonathan Turner's exposition, among many others, of the common meeting points or frameworks of divergent trends in sociological theory, and Randall Collins' and Makowski's attempt to incorporate, on the level of textbook explication, the contributions of Simmel, Marx, Weber, and others into a common, if not necessarily homogeneous, framework.[23]

Third, these developments were often accompanied by increasing emphasis on aspects of social life which were seen as neglected by "mainstream" sociology. Thus power and force became important analytic factors, and several important dimensions of human life (e.g., the esoteric or "mystical," and the aesthetic) were rediscovered.

Fourth, new areas and topics of research were proposed, most derived from the emphasis on reactivating the critical stance of sociology. These topics included a reemphasis of the importance of power relations, reflected in the critical examination of the so-called industrial-military complex of multinational corporations, the impact of technology on social life, and, perhaps most important, problems related to equality.[24]

Fifth, and unlike the case in other periods of "crises," these developments were more closely, though unevenly, linked to the actual conduct of research, and attempted above all to examine the relationships between paradigmatic models and research areas and middle-range theories.[25]

Moreover, such examinations often involved the constructive confrontation of different approaches, confrontations which led to the synthesis of these approaches in a broader paradigmatic framework. Significant instances of such developments are found in several works published in Germany which brought together studies from structural-functional, Marxist and structuralist approaches in various substantive areas: macrosocietal analyses of the development of "archaic," stratified societies; studies of religion and societal evolution, of delinquency, and of the family. These works of synthesis examined the respective premises of these studies, the mutual implications of these premises, and tried to develop a common research program.[26]

Similarly, several new journals were established emphasizing Marxist and other radical perspectives, which undertook the scholarly and analytic examination of central problems in sociological analysis and research. At the same time, established journals broadened their interests to include a critical examination of the premises and research implications of many "newer" and "old-new" approaches.[27]

In this context one may also cite the efforts to develop a "sociology of the future." This orientation was based on a combination of "reflexive" examination of the premises of sociological analysis and study of social trends.[28]

The "positive" mode of discussion, then, reinforced the trends analyzed above: the examination of paradigmatic models; the development of specific research programs, areas of research , and new fields; and attempts to relate such studies to the philosophical and ideological presuppositions of the various countermodels. These discussions also took up studies of the methodology and philosophy of science, of research methodology, and, later, their implications for research programs.

The philosophical, methodological, and other "external" analyses conducted in this mode of discussion were seen either as contributions to a reformulation in sociological analysis and research, or as autonomous specializations within the framework of sociological activity. They were not seen, however, as substitutes for, or alternatives to, the mainstream of sociological analysis.

Above all, these developments had far-reaching implications for the analytic reexamination of different fields of research. As has been noted, the most important consequence was the renewed emphasis on macrosocietal analysis and the attempt to combine various kinds of theory —both explicative paradigms and middle-range theory—with research. These developments could not in themselves overcome the methodological weaknesses in sociological research, or bring greater systematic and analytic unity to different areas of sociological research. Yet, while these "constructive" trends did not directly contribute to such developments, they did so indirectly—by strengthening the autonomous intellectual and organizational bases of sociological research, and by sharpening the awareness of their possibilities.

The "Abdicative" Mode of Discussion and the Crisis in Sociology

7. The repercussions of the second mode of discussion were of course, entirely different. Denying the primacy of cognitive scientific objectivity in sociological discussion, and implying instead, aesthetic, philosophic,

ideological, and "experimental" criteria, its proponents expressed these postures most conspicuously in their attitudes to research; their patterns of mutual criticism in general and criticism of structural-functionalism in particular; and their formulations of the problem of a value-free sociology.

All these tendencies fed on the general latent dissatisfactions with the lack of unification of sociology alluded to above. Critics employing the "abdicative" mode, however, coped with these dissatisfactions in a special way. In a sense they made a virtue of necessity or would-be necessity, not merely magnifying the weaknesses of sociology but using them above all to justify the abdication of the distinctiveness and autonomy of sociological analysis.

Such abdication could manifest itself in several different, but related ways. First, it was apparent in the tendency to develop, along with the variety of new crossings between external and internal fields of discussions, a greater dissociation between such analysis and concrete research problems. Moreover, there was a tendency to substitute the proclamation of general "principled" stands on these problems for actual research. Often, these stands justifyied the impossibility of research in a manner that resembled the debates in the late nineteenth and early twentieth centuries, especially in Germany, between philosophical schools.[29] Very often, such developments were accompanied by an increasing preoccupation with the philosophical-metaphysical aspects of social research to the preclusion of the conduct of research itself, as the very possibility and desirability of research were denied in the name of particular philosophical or ideological beliefs and assumptions.

The effect of these attitudes, in their mildest form, was to move the center of sociological discourse from the pursuit of research into marginal, external fields—social philosophy, philosophical self-examination of sociology, and methodology—which, being catalysts in the core of sociological analysis, could "seize" the center of sociological endeavor. In principle, such emphasis could lead to the substitution of social philosophy, or the methodology of science for sociology, and reduce the continuity and integration of different aspects of sociological inquiry. The topics of many discussions—about the hidden dimensions of society, the philosophical or existential possibility of sociological research, and the existential, personal, and social bases of such pursuits—tended in such situations to change from marginal, even if often very important, liveners of sociological discourse into central problems of analysis, often serving as substitutes for the research whose possibility they denied. Moreover, these discussions could indeed easily develop into more prolonged fads and fashions to which certain sociologists succumbed as, combining dissatisfaction with the state of sociological analysis and research with a predisposition to this mode of discussion, they sought salvation for themselves and for sociology.

But the full impact of these tendencies could be discerned only in the structural consequences of this mode of discussion: the compartmentalization of "schools," each with its own paradigms and research programs, and above all the tendency to develop metaphysical, ideological and political closure. These tendencies developed in several directions. First was the formation of closed philosophical-paradigmatic camps. Such trends were most apparent in the case of the structuralists and the Marxists; the latter school, generally combined philosophical and ideological closure.[30] Such ideological closure could also be found among proponents of the interactionist and above all ethnomethodological schools, where it was combined with both a radical and a philosophical stance.[31] Even countermodels which had not adopted philosophical or ideological positions, such as the exchange model, could still present their claims in terms of a totally closed philosophical-analytic system.[32]

Second, these tendencies were especially intensified insofar as political and ideological elements were combined with scholarly and philosophical components. Such combinations had their sharpest repercussions on the mode of discussion of different models and countermodels, affecting first structural-functionalism, then spreading to the entire range of disputes about sociology.

Among many upholding a "sectarian" view, the specific criticisms of the functional-structural model, positivistic sociology, and the like, blended into a perspective which saw all the aspects of this model as logically, and existentially united in one closed philosophical-ideological system.[33] The presumed conservative ideological and philosophical bias of this model, together with its assumption of a value-free sociology and its positivist epistemological tenets, was seen as providing a closed metaphysical view of the nature of social life and even human destiny, and thus as implying a certain model or paradigm of social order. It was claimed that this model, setting down specific assumptions, concepts, and analytic tools for the analysis of basic major sociological problems, consequently influenced the selection of concrete problems for sociological research and the mode of their explanation, the choice and presentation of concrete theories in different fields of research, and the consequent formulation of concrete hypotheses. These hypotheses and choices of problems, because of their emphasis on the contribution of a given phenomenon—even deviance or conflict—to the maintenance of the particular system, and because of their emphasis on mechanisms of equilibrium and not change, were seen as favoring the status quo, accepting any existing social order and minimizing criticism of it.

According to these critics, the philosophical flaws, epistemological narrowness and analytic weaknesses of this paradigm produced sociological theories which were both morally wrong and empirically incorrect, necessarily resulting in the breakdown of their own analytic or research paradigms.

Given the inherent interrelatedness of the weaknesses in structural-functionalism, the only alternative, according to this view, was to construct various "totalistic" countermodels, "total" explanatory paradigms of society that would be part of an entirely new, ideological sociology. The proposed new sociology took several forms—the reflexive sociology ⌐ propounded by Gouldner, the dialectic sociology suggested by Friedrichs, various types of radical sociology and radical-Marxist approaches in France, Germany, England, and the United States.[34] The several proposals claimed, with varying intensity, that a sociology combining new epistemological, philosophical, ideological, and analytic orientations, and abandoning pretensions to value-free sociology, could by the very force of its premises develop a superior analytic framework and research program, overcoming the deficiencies of the prevailing functional and positivistic model.

Among these claims for a "new" sociology, one may distinguish several nuances which are of great importance in relating this view to the development of sociological tradition and analysis. Thus, some claims for a radical or reflexive sociology could be associated, as in the case of Gouldner, with efforts at scientific analysis of the historical and social roots of sociology; or, as in the case of Friedrichs and Atkinson, with analysis of the philosophical assumptions of several sociological theories. They might also be related, as with Birnbaum and Tom Bottomore, to attempts to develop the "new" sociology within the framework of a continuing tradition of critical sociological analysis.[35] In the work of such scholars, one discerns a strong ambivalence or tension between the proclaimed ideological commitment and denial of the possibility of a value-free sociology, on the one hand, and attempts to maintain some of the traditions of autonomous independent scholarship, on the other. This ambivalence left open the problem of the relationship between philosophical, ideological, political, and epistemological assumptions and sociological analysis, at least to some degree, thus permitting similar criticism of different concrete aspects of sociological analysis from different epistemological points of view.[36]

This tension or ambivalence is almost entirely absent among many other so-called "radical" sociologists, who wanted sociology to be subsumed, both intellectually and organizationally, under political, ideological, and would-be philosophical orientations and programs which would presumably indicate the direction for sociology. A quotation from such a recent exposition can illustrate some of the nature of this approach.

> The social theory of our radical age is thus drastically different from traditional social theory. It is different, first, in substance. Radical social theory liberates rather than represses. Radical social theory and traditional social theory are different, secondly, in their form. Rather than necessarily being systematically formulated and highly analytical, radical social theory tends to be less orderly, more descriptive, and highly critical. Third, the social theory in our radical age, in comparison to the theories inherited from former ages, differs considerably in its sources. Whereas the traditional social theories were, for the most part, formulated and presented by established philosophers, social scientists, and the like, radical social theory is suggested by anyone—and everyone. Radical social theory is not an elite theory, coming necessarily from the prominent intellectuals of the day. Instead, radical social theory is constantly being made by the people.
>
> And it is this fact that makes today's social theory so relevant: it is derived from our experiences and it, in turn, makes us act in the creation of new experiences. Never before has social theory been such an integral part of action. Theory and action are becoming one. As this happens we do not necessarily look to books for our social theory, but social theory is found in our everyday activities, in the way we live our lives. Radical social theory is in itself a revolutionary social theory.[37]

One of the most extreme manifestations of this extreme stand was the constant pressure on more serious scholars like Gouldner, who remained committed to the scholarly pursuit of sociology, to give up such autonomy in the name of acceptance of radical political premises and directives.[38]

The prevalence of this mode of discussion had extensive repercussions on the development of the sociological community and its work. The convergence of many trends in controversy with proclamations of the several types of radical sociology changed the tenor of all the arguments and criticisms analyzed earlier—transforming them, in fact, into extreme sectarian political attack and acrimony.

Tendencies to sectarianism could also be found, of course, in disputes between paradigms in a scholarly field. But in the extreme mode of discussion, these tendencies were strongly reinforced by the combination of philosophical (and epistemological) with analytic explicative paradigms into closed schools. Above all, it was the combination of these philosophical schools with political and ideological camps that created the strongest sectarianism. The consequence, as Merton has so brilliantly refined the distinction, was an emphasis on "insider-outsider" differences in the pursuit of sociological inquiry, and a claim that only those belonging to a certain ethnic or ideological group could understand any phenomenon involving such groups—or even social order itself.[39] In its more extreme form, the impact of these developments could easily produce a total balkanization of research, a disruption of its continuity, and a strong emphasis on continually starting anew. Such an emphasis was found even among many proclaimed Marxists, who often used Marxism as a symbol rather than a starting point for serious scholarly discussion.

The combination of these trends intensified the manifestations and consequences of the "abdicative" mode of discussion. It gave rise to the total negation of the possibility of many major components of sociological analysis; to the magnification of many of its methodological weaknesses and denial of the possibility or validity of any empirical research methods, which were in principle seen as tied to a distorted, partial, and "manipulated" view of reality; and to general proclamations, in the name of some sectarian vision, of a general "crisis" in sociology.[40] Other developments were the negation of the original sociological *Problemstellungen* and the denial of the importance of critical scholarly analysis of the mechanisms of social order and its variability. In lieu of such analysis, proclamations were made about the wickedness of a given social order—declarations, for example, that the social order was subject to the power of the military-industrial complex—rather than analytic discussions of that complex.[41]

Despite assertions of belief in reason and in human solidarity, these types of proclamation often gave rise to new simplicist deterministic conceptions of social life, and to skepticism about the extension of reason and reasoned critique to the study of human affairs. Thus the contribution of sociology to a broadening critical tradition in society was also relinquished as a hope.

As a result of these tendencies, sociology could be presented as consisting of completely closed, "totalistic" paradigms which differed not only in their analytic premises but also in their philosophical, ideological, and political assumptions, minimizing the possibility of scholarly discourse on problems of common interest.[42] Such a trend could easily lead, in turn, to the even worse bifurcation of sociological analysis between dogmatic metaphysical assertions about the nature of society and sociological inquiry, on the one hand, and the emphasis on purely technical aspects of sociological research to be used in administrative affairs, on the other.

It was the continuing spread of these developments that produced a widespread malaise in sociology; an acceptance of its being in a situation of crisis. This feeling was intensified by the fact that, probably for the first time in the history of sociology, these developments were world-wide and communication among different sociological communities intensive. Needless to say, these claims were not accepted by everybody in the sociological community. Nevertheless, they gave rise to a widespread acceptance of the validity of the outcry about the crisis of sociology.

Thus, indeed, sociology has arrived at a critical juncture, a point of both great promise and of possible disintegration. It may therefore be worthwhile at this point to bring together some threads of our analysis insofar as they bear on the reasons why such a combination of "constructive" and "destructive" developments is possible in sociology, and what the conditions are that may influence the outcomes of crisis in either direction.

Notes

1. For materials related to the debates about the state of theory and research in sociology, and the relationship between them, see notes 10 and 11 of Ch. 9, above.

2. Illustrations of the mode of discussion which endorses abdication of the autonomy of scholarship in the sociologist's role and in sociological analysis, are found, for example, in D. Cohn-Bendit et al., "Why sociologists?" and J. Horton, "The fetishism of sociology," in J. D. Colfax and J. L. Roach (eds.), *Radical Sociology*, (New York: Basic Books, 1971), pp. 61–66, 171–193, respectively; V. Capecchi, "Struttura e technice della ricerca," in P. Rossi (ed.), *Ricerca Sociologica e Ruolo del Sociologo* (Bologna: Il Mulino, 1972), pp. 23–121, and almost all the papers in *Sociological Inquiry*, Vol. 40, No. 1 (1970).

   For I. L. Horowitz's analysis, see I. L. Horowitz, "Mainliners and marginals: the human shape of sociological theory," in L. Gross (ed.), *Sociological Theory: Inquiries and Paradigms* (New York: Harper & Row, 1967), especially pp. 375–377.

3. For Gurvitch's philosophical criticism of sociology, see G. Gurvitch, *Dialectique et Sociologie* (Paris: Flammarion, 1962).

   For concise surveys of the critical stand of the Frankfurt school toward "traditional" sociology, see M. Jay, "Some recent developments in critical theory," *Berkeley Journal of Sociology*, Vol. 18 (1973–1974), pp. 27–44; D. Frisby, "The Frankfurt school: critical theory and positivism," in J. Rex (ed.), *Approaches to Sociology* (London: Routledge & Kegan Paul, 1974), pp. 205–229.

   For the empirical research conducted by the Frankfurt school, see the *Frankfurte Beiträge zur Soziologie*, published continuously by the Europeische Verlags Anstalt since the early 1950s. Some of these works were brought together in *Soziologische Exkursen*, in 1956, and translated as *Aspects of Sociology* (Boston: Beacon Press, 1972), by the Frankfurt Institute for Social Research, with a preface by M. Horkheimer and T. W. Adorno. The impression one receives of these researches is that while they did sometimes attempt to provide new perspectives, such as that of the impact of the broader society on the local community, these are not analytically distinct from the concepts or approaches of the community studies undertaken by positivists.

For Mills' criticism of the use and application of research techniques, see C. W. Mills, *The Sociological Imagination* (New York: Oxford University Press, 1959) especially Chs. 2–4.

For Mills' studies of Puerto Rico, see C. W. Mills et al., *The Puerto-Rican Journey: New York's Newest Migrants,* (New York: Harper, 1950).

For Birnbaum's arguments on the relationship between research and political and ideological stances, see N. Birnbaum, "On the sociology of current social research," in N. Birnbaum, *Toward a Critical Sociology* (New York: Oxford University Press, 1971), pp. 214–231.

4. For illustrations of such discussions in which the scholars mentioned here participated as well as others involving opposed sociological and philosophical "camps," see W. Hochkeppel (ed.), *Soziologie Zwischen Theorie und Empirie: Soziologische Grundprobleme* (München: Nymphenburger Verlagshandlung. 1970); E. Topitsch (ed.). *Logik der Sozialwissenschaften* (Köln: Kiepenheuer & Witsch, 1972). See also R. Boudon (ed.), *L'Analyse Empirique de la Causalité: choix de textes publié sou la direction de Raymond Boudon et Paul Lazarsfeld* (Paris, Mouton, 1966, 1969).

5. The Davis-Moore-Tumin controversy, as well as some of its influences on later discussions in the field of stratification, is found in R. Bendix and S. M. Lipset (eds.), *Class, Status and Power* (New York: Free Press, 1966), pp. 47–72.

For additional influences of this controversy, see W. Buckley, "Social stratification and the functional theory of social differentiation," *American Sociological Review,* Vol. 23 (1958), pp. 369–375; D. Wrong, "The functional theory of stratification: some neglected considerations," *American Sociological Review,* Vol. 24 (1959), pp. 772–782.

Gouldner's ideological and scientific criticism of functionalism at that period can be found in A. W. Gouldner, *For Sociology* (New York: Basic Books, 1974), especially Chs. 6, 7, 8.

For an earlier analytical criticism with more direct relevance to the study of bureaucracy, see A. Gouldner, "Reciprocity and autonomy in functional theory," in L. Gross (ed.), *Symposium on Sociological Theory* (New York: Harper & Row, 1959), pp. 241–271.

For an illustration of Gouldner's critical study of bureaucracy, see A. Gouldner, *Patterns of Industrial Bureaucracy* (New York: Free Press, 1954).

For Mills' critical studies of the system of power and stratification in general (in American society) and of the low white-collar worker's situation in particular, see C. W. Mills, *The Power Elite* (New York: Oxford University Press, 1959); C. W. Mills, "The middle classes in middle-sized cities," *American Sociological Review,* Vol. 11, No. 5 (1946), pp. 520–529; C. W. Mills, *White Collar: the American Middle Classes* (New York: Oxford University Press, 1951).

For Birnbaum's critical examination of the Protestant Ethic thesis in relation to Swinglianism, see N. Birnbaum, "The Zwinglian Reformation in Zurich," in N. Birnbaum, *Toward a Critical Sociology, op. cit.,* pp. 133–161.

6. For the studies of the Frankfurt school discussed here, see the relevant materials quoted in note 3 of this chapter.

7. The discussions on capitalism and industrial society at the meetings of the German Sociological Association were published as *Spätkapitalismus oder Industriegesselschaft?* Verhandlungen des 16 Deutschen Soziologentages (Stuttgart: F. Enke, 1969).

For the critical reexamination and confrontation of theories of modernization and development, see the relevant materials cited in note 88 of Ch. 10, above.

8. For illustrations of analytic controversies in anthropology about the study of kinship, see, for example, Homans' critical discussion of Levi-Strauss' studies; G. C. Homans and D. Schneider, *Marriage, Authority and Final Causes* (Glencoe, Ill.: Free Press, 1955); See also: J. Goody, *Comparative Studies in Kinship* (London: Routledge & Kegan Paul, 1969); R. Needham (ed.), *Rethinking Kinship and Marriage* (London: Tavistock, 1971); and for a good survey, H. W. Scheffler, "Kinship, descent, and alliance," in J. J. Honigmann (ed.), *Handbook of Social and Cultural Anthropology* (Chicago: Rand McNally, 1973), pp. 747–795.

   For the controversies about the study of ritual, see in detail the discussion in Ch. 10, above, as well as the materials quoted in notes 10 to 18 of that chapter.

9. The basic controversies between the functional-structural school and the various countermodels are discussed in detail in Chs. 8 and 10, above.

10. For arguments in favor of such a possible synthesis, see for example R. Dahrendorf, *Class and Class Conflict in Industrial Society* (Stanford, Cal.: Stanford University Press, 1959), especially Ch. 5.

    For later statements in this vein, see R. W. Friedrichs, "Dialectical sociology: toward a resolution of the current crisis in Western sociology," *British Journal of Sociology*, Vol. 23, No. 3 (September 1972), pp. 263–274; E. Weinstein and J. Tanur, "The nature of social interaction," unpublished manuscript.

11. For B. Moore's and H. Marcuse's criticism of the Soviet system, see B. Moore, *Soviet Politics* (Cambridge, Mass.: Harvard University Press, 1950); B. Moore, *Terror and Progress: U.S.S.R.,* (Cambridge, Mass.: Harvard University Press, 1954); H. Marcuse, *Soviet Marxism; a Critical Analysis* (New York: Columbia University Press, 1958).

    For N. Birnbaum's critical reexamination of some aspects of Marxist and "bourgeois" sociology, (especially in the field of stratification), see N. Birnbaum, "The crisis in Marxist sociology," in J. D. Colfax and J. L. Roach (eds.), *Radical Sociology, op. cit.,* pp. 108–131.

12. For the orthodox Marxist criticism of M. Godelier, see the special issue, on the debate between Structuralism and Marxism, of *International Journal of Sociology*, Vol. 2, Nos. 2–3 (1972).

    A good summary of the various criticisms of Habermas' open approach can be found in M. Jay, "Some recent developments in critical theory," *op. cit.*

    For the extreme position of the philosophically-oriented structuralists, see some of the materials and bibliography in I. Rossi (ed.), *The Unconscious in Culture* (New York: Dutton, 1974); in M. Lane (ed.), *Structuralism: a Reader* (London: Jonathan Cape 1970); J. Parain-Viel, *Analyses Structureles et Ideologies Structuralistes,* (Toulouse: E. Privat, 1969).

13. The increasing awareness of the sociological community of tensions inherent in the sociologist's role, and of the ethical problems of research, are fully discussed in Ch. 9, above. The relevant materials pertaining to these problems are cited in notes 22 and 23 of Chapter 9.

    For additional materials related to the problematic aspects of sociological research as discussed here, see also H. C. Kelman, *A Time to Speak: on Human Values and Social Research* (San Francisco: Jossey-Bass, 1968), a work primarily concerned with the problematics of research in social psychology; S. M. Miller, "Letter to the editor," *Social Policy* (November-December, 1974), pp. 44–47, which discusses mainly the research of minority groups.

    For trends in critical analytical reexamination of various fields, see the materials quoted in note 88 of Ch. 10 above.

14. A. Barton, "Empirical methods and radical sociology: a liberal critique," in J. D. Colfax and J. L. Roach (eds.), *Radical Sociology, op. cit.,* pp. 460–477.

    For illustration of the points discussed here see also D. Kubat (ed), *Paths of Sociological Imagination,* (New York: Gordon and Breach, 1971).

    For a more radical stand which nevertheless criticizes the separation of radical sociology from the mainstream of "traditional" sociological research and analysis, see N. Birnbaum, "Sociology: discontent present and perennial," *Social Research,* Vol. 38, No. 4 (1971), pp. 732–750, See also N. Birnbaum, "An end of sociology?" *Social Research,* Vol. 42, No. 3 (1975), pp. 933–967.

15. For an illustration of such a stand, see, for example, P. M. Hauser, "On actionism in the craft of sociology," in J. D. Colfax and J. L. Roach (eds.), *Radical Sociology, op. cit.,* pp. 425–439.

16. J. Urry, *Reference Groups and the Theory of Revolution* (London: Routledge & Kegan Paul, 1973); I. Taylor, P. Walton, and J. Young, *The New Criminology: for a Social Theory of Deviance* (London: Routledge & Kegan Paul, 1973).

17. J. Rex, *Sociology and the Demystification of the Modern World* (London: Routledge & Kegan Paul, 1974).

18. A. Gouldner, *The Coming Crisis of Western Sociology* (New York: Basic Books, 1970).

19. For Friedrichs' position, see R. Friedrichs, *A Sociology of Sociology* (New York: Free Press [1970], 1972), especially Ch. 12; R. Friedrichs, "Dialectical sociology, . . ." *op. cit.*

    For a view which is, to a certain extent, similar to that of Friedrichs, see D. L. Sallach, "Critical theory and critical sociology: the second synthesis," *Sociological Inquiry,* Vol. 43, No. 2 (1973), pp. 131–140.

    D. Atkinson's interpretation of Marx, Parsons, and others, as well as his interactionistic approach, is found in D. Atkinson, *Orthodox Consensus and Radical Alternative* (London: Heinemann, 1971), especially Chs. 3, 5, 7, 8.

    For illustrations of the neo-Marxist criticism of the generality and nonhistorical character of the structural-functional school, see the relevant materials cited in note 54 of Ch. 10, above.

20. On these discussions, see especially the *American Sociologist,* Vol. 6 (June 1971), supplementary issue.

    In connection to these discussions see also H. Gans, "The positive functions of poverty," *American Journal of Sociology,* Vol. 78 (September 1972), pp. 275–289; J. Hanson, "Comment on Gans' 'The positive functions of poverty,' " *American Journal of Sociology,* Vol. 79, No. 3 (November 1973), pp. 705–707, and Gans' reply, pp. 707–709.

21. As illustrations of the possibility of seeing such cross-cuttings, see:

    For Marxism and neo-Marxism—that is, for the emphasis on their conservative implications, D. Atkinson, *Orthodox Consensus and Radical Alternative, op. cit.*

    For the possible conservative or radical implications of symbolic interactionism, see the discussion between P. M. Hall and R. Moss Kanter in *Sociological Inquiry,* Vol. 42, Nos. 3–4 (1972), pp. 35–99.

    For the radical and conservative elements in exchange theory compare the points stressed by J. Race, "Toward an exchange theory of revolution," in J. W. Lewis (ed.), *Peasant Rebellion and Communist Revolution in Asia* (Stanford, Cal.: Stanford University Press, 1974), pp. 169–204, as against those of P. Ekeh, *Social Exchange Theory* (London: Heinemann, 1974), especially Chs. 5, 6.

22. One of the ways in which the Marxist tradition was incorporated into the main sociological tradition was through macrosocietal study of primitive, historical, and

modern societies, as well as studies of modernization and development. As illustrations of this trend, see note 94 of Ch. 10, above.

Another illustration of the incorporation of philosophical trends is the renewed interest in phenomenology and its relationship to sociological analysis. On this see, for example, P. Filmer et al., *New Directions in Sociological Theory* (London: Collier-MacMillan, 1972).

One of the schools which originates from the Chicago tradition is, of course, symbolic interactionism. For a fuller discussion of symbolic interactionism see Chs. 8 and 10, above, and the materials cited there.

For illustrations of renewed attempts to incorporate symbolic interactionism into the mainstream of the sociological tradition see, for instance, P. Filmer, *New Directions in Sociological Theory, op. cit.;* E. Weinstein and J. Tanur, "The nature of social interaction," *op. cit.;* the discussions between P. M. Hall and R. Moss Kanter, cited in note 21 of this chapter; D. Silverman, *The Theory of Organisations* (London: Heinemann, 1970).

Significant attempts to bring together various aspects of symbolic interactionism and general problems of social structure are found in the festschrift for Herbert Blumer by T. Shibutani (ed.), *Human Nature and Collective Behavior* (Englewood Cliffs, N.J.: Prentice-Hall, 1970).

The other important sector of the Chicago school is the combined ecological community study which has also undergone a very significant renewal and been set in a more systematic framework, largely under the guidance of Morris Janowitz. For illustrations of this trend, see G. D. Suttles, *The Social Order of the Slum* (Chicago: University of Chicago Press, 1968); G. D. Suttles, *The Social Construction of Communities* (Chicago: University of Chicago Press, 1972); A. Hunter, *Symbolic Communities* (Chicago: University of Chicago Press, 1974); W. Kornblum, *Blue Collar Community* (Chicago: University of Chicago Press, 1974).

Of great interest from this point of view is also the collection of E. C. Hughes' essays, see E. C. Hughes, *The Sociological Eye, Selected Papers* (Chicago and New York: Aldine, Atherton, 1971).

Of special interest in this context are the Heritage of Sociology series edited by Morris Janowitz and published by the University of Chicago Press, in which European classics of sociology, (Weber, Durkheim, Marx, Geiger, Tönnies), the British and other schools, and American classics, particularly the Chicago school (Thomas, Burgess, Ogburn, etc.) were published in a new "modern" framework emphasizing their sharing of a common broad framework.

23. M. Zeitlin, *Rethinking Sociology: a Critique of Contemporary Theory* (New York: Appleton-Century-Crofts, 1973); J. Turner, *The Structure of Sociological Theory* (Homewood, Ill.: Dorsey Press, 1974); R. Collins and M. Makowski, *The Discovery of Society* (New York: Random House, 1972).

For an interesting attempt at convergence between functionalism and Marxism from a Marxist point of view, see P. Sztompka, *System and Function* (New York: Academic Press, 1974).

For additional illustrations of the analysis of different paradigms from a broader theoretical point of view, see A. Boskoff, *Theory in American Sociology* (New York: T. Y. Crowell, 1970); the somewhat earlier reader by Walter L. Wallace (ed.), *Sociological Theory* (Chicago: Aldine, 1969); the more recent one on *Theories and Paradigms in Contemporary Sociology,* edited by R. S. Denisoff, O. Callahan, and M. H. Levine (Itasca, Ill.: F. E. Peacock, 1974); and G. Ritzer, *Sociology, a Multiple-Paradigm Science* (Boston: Allyn & Bacon, 1975).

24. As illustrations of the growing trend to critical examination of some of these problems, note their relative salience in the last years in older professional journals, as, for example, the *American Journal of Sociology.*

    For the topics related to the military-industrial complex see, for example, S. Lieberson, "An empirical study of military-industrial linkages," *American Journal of Sociology,* Vol. 76, No. 4 (January 1971), pp. 562–584; A. Szymanski, "Military spending and economic stagnation," *American Journal of Sociology,* Vol. 79, No. 1 (July 1973), pp. 1–14; and the related debate between A. Szymanski and P. Sweezy in *American Journal of Sociology,* Vol. 79, No. 3 (November 1973), pp. 709–711; as well as the discussions by various authors of the problems raised by Szymanski and Sweezy in *American Journal of Sociology,* Vol. 79, No. 6 (May 1974), pp. 1452–1477.

    For the problem of inequality see, for example, B. R. Schiller, "Stratified opportunities: the essence of the vicious circle," *American Journal of Sociology,* Vol. 76, No. 3 (November 1970), pp. 426–442; "American sociology and Black Americans," by various authors, *American Journal of Sociology,* Vol. 76, No. 4 (January 1971), pp. 627–742; I. Rosenwaike, "Interethnic comparisons of educational attainment," *American Journal of Sociology,* Vol. 79, No. 1 (July 1973), pp. 68–77; M. Zeitlin, "Corporate ownership and control; the large corporation and the capitalist class," *American Journal of Sociology,* Vol. 79, No. 5 (March 1974), pp. 1073–1119; B. Heyns, "Social selection and stratification within schools," *American Journal of Sociology,* Vol. 79, No. 6 (May 1974), pp. 1434–1451.

25. For illustrations of the trend to reexamine various paradigms in the light of various fields of research, see, for instance, the materials cited in note 88 of Ch. 10, above.

26. For illustrations of such works see, for example, K. Eder (ed.), *Seminar—Die Entstehung von Klassengesellschaften* (Frankfurt am Main: Suhrkamp, 1973); C. Seyfarth, W. Sprondel (eds.), *Seminar—Religion und Gesellschaftliche Entwicklung,* (Frankfurt am Main: Suhrkamp, 1973); and several other special issues of the "Seminar" in the paperback edition of Suhrkamp.

27. As illustrations of new journals with a radical bent see, for example, *Economy and Society* (London: Routledge & Kegan Paul); *Theory and Society* (Amsterdam: Elsevier)

    Among the older journals in which such shifts can be discerned in the last few years, see the *Berkeley Journal of Sociology; Sociological Inquiry; Social Research;* to some extent the *American Journal of Sociology.* In Europe, see above all, *Acta Sociologica; Sociology;* and *Mens en Maatschappij.*

28. For attempts to develop a sociology of the future see, for example, W. Bell, J. A. Mau (eds.), *The Sociology of the Future: Theory, Cases and Annotated Bibliography* (New York: Russell Sage, 1971).

29. The growing centrality of the topics discussed above among preoccupations of the sociological community is illustrated by the great output of works concerned with them; see for example H. Maus and F. Fürstenberg (eds.), *Der Positivismusstreit in der Deutschen Soziologie* (Neuwied und Berlin: Luchterhand, 1969); P. Rossi (ed.), *Ricerca Sociologica e Ruolo del Sociologo, op. cit.;*

    See also the materials quoted in note 23 of Ch. 9, above, as well as J. O'Neill, *Sociology as a Skin Trade* (London: Heinemann, 1972); R. Quinney, "From repression to liberation: social theory in a radical age," in R. A. Scott and J. D. Douglas (eds.), *Theoretical Perspectives on Deviance* (New York: Basic Books, 1972), pp. 317 ff.

    On the debates in Germany during the late nineteenth century and in the 1920s see the discussions and the relevant materials cited in Ch. 2, above, and also R. König,

Studien zur Soziologie (Frankfurt am Main: Hamburg, Fischer Bücherei, 1971), pp. 9–37.

30. For the tendency to philosophical and ideological closure in Marxism, see, for example, R. Klima, "Theoretical pluralism, methodological dissension, and the role of the sociologist: the West German case," *Social Science Information*, Vol. 11, Nos. 3–4 (1972), pp. 69–108.
     For a similar tendency among structuralists, see the respective materials cited in note 12 of this chapter, and the additional works cited in note 2 of Ch. 9.

31. For tendencies to radicalism and a philosophical stance in symbolic interactionism and in ethnomethodology see, for example, D. Atkinson, *Orthodox Consensus and Radical Alternative, op. cit.*; J. Urry, *Reference Groups and the Theory of Revolution, op. cit.*; H. Garfinkel, *Studies in Ethnomethodology* (Englewood Cliffs, N.J.: Prentice-Hall, 1967); A. Cicourel, *Method and Measurement in Sociology* (New York: Free Press, 1964); P. Filmer et al., *New Directions in Sociological Theory, op. cit.,* especially Part 2.

32. For illustrations of totalistic philosophical-analytic claims on the part of the exchange model see G. C. Homans, "Bringing men back in," *American Sociological Review*, Vol. 29, No. 6 (1964), pp. 809–818; G. C. Homans, "Prologue: the sociological relevance of behaviorism," in R. L. Burgess and D. Bushell (eds.), *Behavioral Sociology: the Experimental Analysis of Social Process* (New York: Columbia University Press, 1969), pp. 1–24.

33. For examples of the "totalistic" critical conception of structural-functionalism as presented below, see, for example, J. Horton, "The fetishism of sociology," *op. cit.*; J. Horton, "Order and conflict theories of social problems as competing ideologies," in *American Journal of Sociology*, Vol. 71 (1965), pp. 701–713.

34. A. Gouldner, *The Coming Crisis of Western Sociology, op. cit.*; R. Friedrichs, *A Sociology of Sociology, op. cit.*
     For illustrations of other radical approaches in the United States, consult the following for the outlook which emerges from most of the collected papers: J. D. Colfax and J. L. Roach (eds.), *Radical Sociology, op. cit.*; *Sociological Inquiry*, Vol. 40, No. 1 (1970), entire issue.
     For radical approaches in England see, for example, D. Atkinson, *Orthodox Consensus and Radical Alternative, op. cit.*
     For radical approaches in Germany, mostly Marxist and upheld by the Frankfurt school, see the presentations in M. Jay, "Some recent developments in critical theory," *op. cit.*; D. Frisby, "The Frankfurt school; critical theory and positivism," *op. cit.*
     For France, see A. Touraine, *Pour la Sociologie* (Paris: Éditions du Seuil, 1974), especially Chs. 1 and 6.
     For Scandinavia, Holland, and Italy, see the materials cited in note 17 of Ch. 9.

35. A. Gouldner, *The Coming Crisis of Western Sociology, op. cit.*; R. Friedrichs, *A Sociology of Sociology, op. cit.*; D. Atkinson, *Orthodox Consensus and Radical Alternative, op. cit.*
     For illustrations of Birnbaum's concomitant commitment to radicalism and the tradition of critical sociological analysis, see N. Birnbaum, *Toward a Critical Sociology, op. cit.*; N. Birnbaum, "Sociology: discontent present and perennial," *op. cit.*
     For Bottomore's similar stand, see T. Bottomore, *Sociology as Social Criticism* (London: G. Allen and Unwin, 1974). See also, N. Birnbaum, "An end to sociology?", *op. cit.* and T. Bottomore (ed.), *Crisis and Contention in Sociology* (Beverly Hills and Los Angeles: Sage Publishers, 1970).

36. Some of these tribulations are fully illustrated in A. Gouldner's *For Sociology, op. cit.* especially Ch. 4 and 5. Gouldner's tribulations in *For Sociology* are reviewed by L. Coser

in *American Journal of Sociology*, vol. 80, No. 4, 1975, pp. 1009-1011 and P. Start, "Gouldner," *N.Y. Times* Book Review, Sept. 8, 1974.

Some of the broader significant problematics of Gouldner's "crisis" for sociological analysis are discussed in G. E. Swanson, "Interrogativi e perplessita sulla supposta decadenza della sociologia," *Rassegna Italiana di Sociologia*, Vol. 13, No. 4 (1972), pp. 637–647; John O'Neill, "Gouldner e la nuova sociologia," *ibid.*, pp. 665–679.

See also A. Touraine, *Pour la Sociologie, op. cit.*

37.   R. Quinney, "From repression to liberation: social theory in a radical age," *Theoretical Perspectives on Deviance*, edited by R. A. Scott and J. D. Douglas, p. 339. © 1972 by R. A. Scott and J. D. Douglas, Basic Books, Inc., Publishers, New York.

38.   A. Gouldner, *For Sociology, op. cit.*, Chs. 4 and 5.

39.   R. K. Merton, "Insiders and outsiders: a chapter in the sociology of knowledge," *The American Journal of Sociology*, Vol. 78, No. 1 (1972), pp. 9–47.

40.   For illustrations of this abdicative mode of discussion see, for example, D. Cohn-Bendit e. a., "Why sociologists?" *op. cit.;* J. Horton, "The fetishism of sociology," *op. cit.;* and most of the papers published in the issue of *Sociological Inquiry*, Vol. 40, No. 1 (1970).

41.   For an illustration of the radical sociology mode of analysis of power in the industrial-military complex see, for example, J. M. Schevitz, "The militarized society and the weapons maker," G. A. Miller, "Comments on the weapons maker," and J. M. Schevitz, "Reply to Miller," in *Sociological Inquiry*, Vol. 40, No. 1 (winter 1970), pp. 49–60.

For an interesting comparison to this mode of analysis, see also the discussions and analyses quoted in note 24 of this chapter.

42.   The increasing distrust of reason and its place in the conduct of human affairs is discussed by R. Bendix, "Sociology and the distrust of reason," *American Sociological Review*, Vol. 35, No. 5 (1970), pp. 831–843.

The minimization of the possibility of scholarly discourse as a result of closure into totalistic analytic, philosophical, or ideological paradigms is discussed by C. J. Lammers, "Mono- and polyparadigmatic developments in natural and social sciences," Institute of Sociology, University of Leyden, mimeo, 1973; the July-August, 1973, issue of *Sociologische Gids*, in which Lammers' stand is discussed by several sociologists from Holland and other countries; and J. D. Douglas, "The relevance of sociology," in J. D. Douglas (ed.), *The Relevance of Sociology* (New York: Appleton-Century-Crofts, 1970), pp. 185–233.

12

The Development of Sociological Analysis, Crises in Sociology, and the Structure of the Sociological Community

Crises in the Context of Patterns of Institutionalization

1. The analysis of the current "crisis" brings us back to some of the problems in the development of sociology that were posed in the beginning of our study: How is it possible to explain the paradoxical convergence of important openings and developments with the appearance of crises that might destroy the continuity of autonomous sociological endeavor? Is the convergence of these contradictory trends accidental, or is the combination related to inherent aspects of the sociological endeavor—at least in its development until now?

The latter conjecture gains support from the fact that the current crisis was not the first to emerge in the relatively short history of sociology. Indeed, rather similar, though perhaps less intensive or dramatic, crises developed, as we have seen,[1] in other periods of development—significantly enough, in periods which also produced some of the major breakthroughs in sociological analysis.

320

These crises occurred, as we have seen above, in connection with the breakdown of the positivist, idealistic, and evolutionary schools both in England and in France; with the upsurge of historicism and neo-Machiavellian schools, especially in Italy in the early twentieth century; with the discussion of Marxism that began late in the nineteenth century and continued in the early twentieth century, especially in Germany; and with the many controversies during the Weimar period among philosophical and ideological groups—between Marxist, conservative, and nationalistic groups, on the one hand, and between them and liberal camps, on the other. The discussions in such situations of crisis were characterized by a strong concern first, with the weaknesses of sociology, particularly the discontinuities in its development; and second, with the relationship between sociology and its "external" intellectual and institutional "neighbors."

The development of sociology does indeed show very marked discontinuities—evident above all in the extremely uneven patterns of development of different types of analysis and research, and in sizeable gaps between such developments in different periods and places. These discontinuities have been constantly evident. Not only have different sociological communities developed different traditions, more important, similar central problems in analysis have developed from different starting points, and their analysis has been pursued in different sociological communities without mutual awareness.

Such discontinuities in analysis can be found, as Raymond Boudon[2] has pointed out, not only in situations of low institutionalization, but also, as the recent developments analyzed in Chapters 9 and 11 have shown, where sociological work has attained higher levels of institutionalization.

To illustrate: the recent great upsurge of interest in equality, women, family, youth, and the poor was strongly related to current social and political concerns. The analysis of these aspects, however, was rarely related to earlier traditions—to Alexis de Toqueville's analyses of equality; to earlier sociological, anthropological, and ethnological studies of sexual mores; to the earlier analyses of low-income groups, or surveys of the living conditions of the poor. Similarly, studies of modernization which developed in the 1950s out of the great interest in problems of development were long dissociated from the traditions of comparative institutional analysis in sociology and anthropology.

Some of these "gaps" were gradually—though only gradually—closed. However, the very process of mutual discovery of the different sociological traditions studying the same problem often made the discontinuity even more visible.[3]

2.   The high degree of discontinuity in the development of analysis was due above all to the fact that any important problem could be formulated from several different points of analytic departure, and could be pursued without regard to similar or parallel formulations which had been derived from another departure point or component of sociological analysis. Each starting point or base of analysis could become a source for the development of new problems of research or of reformulation of old problems. Thus, the perception was often created of total novelty, difference or revolutionary thought.[4]

This discontinuity was also reinforced, as Boudon has rightly stressed, by several aspects of methodological development, especially the relationship between broader explicative paradigms, research programs, concrete research problems, middle-range theories, and descriptive analyses, and above all by the fact that while all these different types of analysis addressed themselves to similar problems, the analytical configuration of each approach was distinct from that of the others. The interrelationships among them, evident in the dearth of common systematic deductive propositions, were tenuous, and few could boast analytic or methodological sophistication. The combination of the multiple starting points and components of analysis, the intellectual role-orientations of sociologists, and the complicated and uneven relationships between different types or levels of analysis gave rise to the high degree of discontinuity in sociological theorizing.

Such discontinuity has not, perhaps, been unique to sociology. It may objectively be more widespread in other disciplines, such as philosophy, history, or political science. But the propensity to perceive this discontinuity as problematic; accept it as a problem to be solved; associate such perception and sensitivity with the relationship between sociology and other traditions and disciplines; and formulate these discontinuities and problematic intellectual relationships as crises of the discipline, seems to have been more prevalent among sociologists and to have had a stronger impact on the internal development of sociology than on other disciplines.

The reasons for the sensitivity of sociologists to such discontinuities are rooted in institutional and intellectual aspects of the development of sociology which have been analyzed above.[5] Above all, they are rooted in the fact that sociological theory and analysis was from its start an important part of a broader tradition of self-examination and self-inquiry and of the extension of the critical approach to the basic phenomena of human and social existence. The attainment of disciplinary distinctiveness did not mean a total separation from other parts of this critical scientific tradition.

As we have seen, this distinctiveness did not entail the development of problem areas entirely different from those of other disciplines. Rather, the attempts to at differentiation succeeded insofar as the different problems shared with philosophic, reformatory and ideological orientations or with other academic disciplines, were combined and transformed in terms of the specific analytic framework of the sociological *Problemstellung.* As a result, the distinctiveness of sociological analysis, as it gradually emerged in the periods of the Founding Fathers, was not attained either by the isolation of sociology from other intellectual traditions, or by a fully accepted division of scientific labor between it and these other disciplines. Thus it constantly competed with other intellectual traditions in attempting to provide the most powerful approach to both a scholarly and a critical analysis of social life, especially of modern social life. Hence during its formative phases, as well as its subsequent development, workers in sociology maintained close but problematic, ambivalent, and tension-ridden orientations to, and relationships with, other traditions.

The ambivalent orientation of sociologists to neighbouring intellectual traditions and academic disciplines was constantly reinforced by the multiplicity of starting points and components of sociological analysis, and by the fact that each component of sociological analysis was derived from other traditions. Because of this, each component could develop fairly independently of the others, maintaining or "reopening" relationships with "parent" or "sister" disciplines and orientations, often in such a way as to minimize its relationship to other components of the emerging sociological tradition itself. Hence, whatever the exact combinations of components of the sociological tradition were that crystallized in any concrete situation, tensions could always develop among them to revive orientations to other traditions or academic disciplines. These tensions and orientations were further reinforced by the fact that the multiplicity of analytic starting points and role orientations also involved relationships with different organizational settings, publics, and clienteles.

The Conditions of Development of "Crises"

3.   These aspects of the development of sociology explain the prevalence of discontinuity, the great sensitivity of sociologists to such discon-

tinuities, and the tendency to formulate such sensitivity in terms of sociology's relationship to other intellectual traditions and disciplines and as "crises" of sociology itself. Thus we see that the occurrence of such crises was not accidental or external, but inherent, although not necessarily predominant, in the development of sociology, at least until now.

However, while these institutional and intellectual processes provide the background conditions for the possibility of crisis, they do not explain either the concrete conditions under which such crises occur or their place in the development of sociological analysis. This is evident in the fact that sensitivity to external sources, and to discontinuities in their own discipline, though strong among sociologists, has not been consistently dominant in their self-conception, activity or in discussion. Similarly, openings to other intellectual traditions have generally been marginal to the central substantive discussions in sociology, existing as almost esoteric specializations in it or on its boundaries.

Only under special intellectual and institutional conditions have these sensitivities to internal discontinuity and the "external" relationships of sociology became more central in sociology and influenced the major pursuits in sociological analysis and research. These conditions can be specified in abstract terms. First, such sensitivity tends to develop among sociologists when in the intellectual development of the discipline, a close relationship exists between the reformulation of the central research problems of the time—class structure of modern societies, or the analysis of comparative institutions—and changes in sociological theories and paradigms. Second, such sensitivity tends to be greater when it is associated with the activation of different role-orientations of sociologists, such as the radical-critical or the practical orientation. Third, such sensitivity is greatest when any of these becomes linked to broader intellectual trends or social processes and movements which touch on crucial intellectual components of sociology—for example, the relative emphasis on its critical or scientific base.[6]

It is therefore no surprise that such sensitivity developed, above all, in those historical situations where critical junctures in the development of sociological theory became connected with great intellectual movements like positivism or Romanticism, or with changes in ideological perceptions of social reality which raised new themes of social protest. Thus, sensitivity to external sources developed in conjunction with the breakdown of the positivist, idealistic, and evolutionary schools and their impact on internal developments in sociology and social anthropology; the most important illustrations of this outcome are the sociological theories of Émile Durkheim, Max Weber, Georg Simmel, and Ferdinand Tönnies.[7]

Such sensitivity to the scientific nature of sociology, its boundaries, and its relationship to other disciplines developed also (though less intensively than in Germany) in the works of Vilfredo Pareto, Gaetano Mosca, and other Italian scholars in connection with the upsurge of historicism and neo-Machiavellian orientations in Italy in the late nineteenth and early twentieth century.[8] Similarly, a sensitivity to the academic standing, boundaries, and subject matter of sociology, as well as to its relationship to the major philosophic, political, and ideological movements of the time, developed in the first three decades of the twentieth century, and could be discerned in the formulations of the nature and direction of sociology in the works, among others, of Franz Oppenheimer, Werner Sombart, Robert Michels, and later of Alfred Vierkandt, Hans Freyer, Alfred Weber, and Karl Mannheim.[9]

Above all, such sensitivity became evident in the early and late 1960s in the controversies over the structural-functional model. The convergence of these internal controversies about theory with the new types of intellectual antinomianism of the student protest movement[10] gave rise to pronouncements about the necessity for the development of various "radical" sociologies, and to the contemporary outcry about crisis in sociology.[11]

It is in such situations that the impact of external intellectual and institutional factors impinge seriously on the various transitions, breakthroughs, and openings in sociological analysis. In all these situations, similar symptoms or manifestations of crises also developed—a sense of failure in sociology to live up to its scholarly and/or critical-intellectual premises, as evident in the discontinuities in sociological work; a continuous reopening of the problem of the intellectual identity and broader intellectual bases of sociology, including its ties with neighbouring disciplines; concern with the real and presumed, methodological and substantive weaknesses of sociological research and analysis in general, and the relation between theory and research in particular. Above all in such situations, disputes erupted over the possibilities of a value-free sociology, and continuous efforts were made to reexamine the major concepts of sociological analysis.[12]

The Impact of Crises on the Incorporation of Theory and on the Development of Sociology

4. The crucial importance of crises and of their conditions for the development of sociological analysis lies above all in their impact on the way theoretical changes or research programs are incorporated into the existing framework of sociological analysis.

First, as a result of such impingements and crises, central problems of sociological research are reformulated not only in terms of the internal problematics of sociology, but also in terms of the relationship of sociology to other disciplines. Internal developments in sociology are often confronted with those "external" intellectual traditions or academic disciplines which ordinarily are relegated to the periphery of sociological inquiry.[13]

Second, the tendency to combine internal with "external" discussions often produces a shift in the central preoccupations of sociologists. In their mildest form, these shifts result in temporary fads and fashions which move the center of sociological discourse from substantive research and theoretical analysis into marginal or external fields—social philosophy, philosophical self-examination of sociology and methodology. Instead of serving as catalysts of the major trends, these preoccupations "seize," as it were, the center of sociological endeavor. Discussions of such topics as the hidden dimensions of society, the philosophical or existential possibility or impossibility of pursuing sociological research, and the existential, personal, or social bases of the pursuit of such research, which in normal times accompany and leaven the interpretation of social phenomena, now become the central concern of the profession, replacing instead of aiding substantiative research and theoretical analysis.[14] This may lead to a sharp dissociation between methodological and philosophical analysis and empirical research. In extreme cases, the proclamation of general "principled" stands on these problems is taken as the main task of the sociologist, especially when the stand so adopted contains a denial—on philosophical grounds—of the objective validity of empirical research.[15]

The full impact of these developments on the incorporation of new insights into the framework of sociological analysis has been felt when they meld with another trend that tends to develop in such situations in sociological communities: the transformation of sociological "schools" into metaphysical and ideological sects, each with its own combined metaphysical, political, ideological, and analytic paradigms, and all developing strong symbolic closure and patterns of esoteric personal or sectarian discourse.[16]

Not all "paradigms shifts" and changes in research programs in sociology and social anthropology have been *so closely and directly* connected with the impingement of "external forces," Among the major explicative paradigms which emerged without the impact of outside forces have been (as was indicated in Chapters 5 and 6) the functional model in British social anthropology; the structural-functional model in sociology; and at least the initial developments of the exchange model and the conflict and symbolic interactionist models. Similarly, many more "restricted" research paradigms—such as those of "culture and personality" in its psychoanalytical and learning theory guises; the first studies of modernization; studies of stratification in general and of status incongruence in particular; a large number of the more recent shifts of emphasis in the sociology of religion from the earlier functionalist model; and many others have developed in isolation from external forces. They were, of course, greatly influenced indirectly by broader intellectual and social forces, but not by the direct impact of those external forces on sociological analysis that appear in association with "crises." Thus their incorporation into the existing sociological tradition was not, generally, accompanied by the symptoms of "crises"—even though there was no dearth of the "usual" doctrinal disputes between adherents of different models.

Once these paradigmatic shifts were "caught," however, in the web of external involvements, their entire mode of incorporation into the existing sociological tradition was transformed. This is attested to by the acrimonious sectarian debates which developed when such areas as modernization, political sociology and stratification, and many theoretical paradigms were related to political and ideological discussions, heightening sensitivity to the impact of these external forces on the format and direction of sociology.[17]

Such crisis influenced sociological work in two ways. On the one hand, it could undermine the distinctiveness and autonomy of sociological analysis, especially if patterns of discussions produced what Robert K. Merton calls the "insider-outsider" distinction in conduct of sociological inquiry[18]—that is, the assumption that only a member of given racial, ethnic, or ideological group can really understand phenomena concerned with such groups and even with social order in general. This development could produce balkanization and discontinuity in research. The chances of the abdication of autonomy were greater insofar as the sociological community was fragmented as a result of the processes associated with crisis, or its members tried to escape the challenge of crisis into philosophical meditation, dogmatic-metaphysical assertions about the nature of society and sociological inquiry, formalistic definitions of sociology, or pure technicism.

There could also be constructive outcomes of crises. These were manifest in the cases of some major analytic breakthroughs in the history of sociology; in the broadening of the scope of research related to such breakthroughs, in the development of sustained research programs, and in increasing mutual orientations among sociological groups and traditions. Although, as indicated, many shifts in paradigms and research programs took place through the internal momentum of sociological development, the situation of crisis also provided some of the most forceful challenges to the elaboration of the most powerful sociological theories or research programs—the theories of Durkheim, Weber, and Mannheim, the research programs of the Frankfurt school, and the more contemporary programs in stratification, health, sex relations, deviance, and modernization.[19]

The Structure of Sociological Communities and the Patterns of Absorbtion of "Crises"

5.   Whether the constructive or destructive possibilities were realized in crises depended not only on the pure intellectual content, the grandeur of the intellectual visions and paradigms, or on their relationship to research. It rested also on the combination of these intellectual aspects with institutional forces and settings.

The assurance of continuity of the constructive tendencies, above all the ability to form a base for sustained sociological activity, depended greatly on the ability of sociological communities to absorb external intellectual and institutional pressures, reformulate them in terms of their own analytic premises, and shape these influences through their internal momentum. The ability to absorb external pressure depended in turn on the intellectual and institutional structure of the respective sociological communities.

Systematic research on the interrelationship between these institutional patterns and the development of sociological analysis and research is still very much needed. Nevertheless, some preliminary indications bearing especially on the implications of these patterns for the understanding of crises in sociology may be attempted here.

The ability of sociological communities to absorb such impact depended above all on the degree of institutional autonomy and self-assurance they had attained, and on their consequent ability to generate continued sociological analysis and research.[20] Yet here, as our analysis has shown, sociology displays some peculiar characteristics.[21]

Continuing patterns of analyses and research programs could develop out of work based on any single component of research activity. Such a component might be philosophical concern and speculation, sociopolitical and comparative institutional analysis, statistical research, or field work. The continuity of any type of research was greater insofar as institutionalization was greater in terms of internal organizational continuity, the autonomy and solidarity of sociological groups, and intellectual and academic legitimacy. This was the case with the several traditions of empirical surveys which developed before World War I in England, France, Germany, the United States, and other countries; the traditions of "social biology" as it developed in England; the comparative historical work which developed in Germany until World War I and later in France; and the sociophilosophical speculations as they developed above all in Germany and to some degree in the United States in the first stages of the development of sociology.

However, unlike the case in disciplines like history or philosophy, continuity of research based on a single component was not ensured by institutionalization. Even when research was well institutionalized, there was little chance of maintaining its momentum as a continuing focus of broad sociological analysis—because such an emphasis was generally too narrow for the broader sociological *Problemstellung*. It is significant that in such institutionalized settings few reformulations of research problems were made in terms of the sociological *Problemstellung*, and few analytic innovations of wide or continuing influence took place.

Hence, although analysis or research based on a single component, notably various social surveys and exercises in social philosophy, could last in a segregated existence in an autonomous institutional setting, it could not become a focus of broader sociological work. If it tried to, unless it related itself to other components of sociological analysis, it could easily be undermined by the demands of other "external" intellectual traditions and, as a result, either disappear, be absorbed into these traditions or disciplines, or be transformed into purely technical services for administrators.

The continuity of sociological work, and the possibility of analytic and research innovation through its internal momentum, depended largely on the development of special mixes of several types of research and analysis and of role orientations of sociologists. The combination which has generally been most beneficial for continuity and innovation has been that of technical-professional research (e.g., field, comparative-institutional, or statistical research) with some orientation to broader "external" trends—philosophical, ideological, or intellectual—that is, mediated nevertheless by a very strong *internal* core of analysis focused on some aspect of the sociological *Problemstellung*. And the combination of role referents in these settings that has been most conducive to continuity has been a mix of broad intellectual and academic with some critical or professional orientations. Above all, the incorporation of these combinations in organizational and institutional bases ensuring stable sociological roles, career patterns, and professional identity has provided the best conditions for sustained sociological work.

The concrete organizational settings which were most conducive to continuous activity varied greatly at any time and at different stages of development. In the case of small communities of sociologists, the chances of development were greater insofar as they were at the margin of political, intellectual or academic settings yet somewhat segregated from them—oriented to but not highly dependent on them. Within such settings, the probability of innovations serving as bases for continuing analysis and research was greater, the more these scholars had strong orientations to multiple academic disciplines and intellectual settings—(e.g., journalistic, ideological, or political groups) but tried to free themselves from these groups to develop their own distinct orientation. Lewis Coser's analyses of the Forerunners and earlier Founding Fathers amply attests to the prevalence of this pattern.[22]

In the later stages of development, when sociologists were more oriented to emerging elements of their disciplinary tradition, the realization of such innovative possibilities depended much more on the concrete organization and institutionalization of this tradition. Above all, it depended on the degree to which ambivalence about various intellectual disciplines and neighbours of sociology was combined with the internal momentum of theory and research, institutional teaching, practical work, and some combinations of them

6.   Stable organizational settings that could accommodate the mixes conducive to sustained innovation were not easily attained.

Presumably, the academic framework should have provided the best setting for these constructive developments. Indeed, in the later stages of sociological development, in more dense sociological communities, the major constructive developments—breakthroughs to open-system approaches and strong research traditions and processes, did take place in universities or in associations between universities and research institutes which permitted the needed combinations of research components and role orientations.

But the mere acceptance of sociology in a university, often based on a narrow conception of sociological analysis, did not ensure the incorporation of these components. From the beginning of sociological work, various restrictions and confinements to a single component of sociological tradition, existed in academic settings as well as in nonacademic locales: research bureaus, philanthropic groups, groups of journalists, political-ideological sects, and intellectual groups.[23] The most prevalent restriction, especially in the earlier stages of development of sociology, was the dissociation of philosophical speculation from any type of research and particularly from empirical research. Another restriction developed in an opposite direction—in an emphasis on technical research against any broader theoretical orientation or institutional and comparative analysis. This situation was prevalent, as we have seen, in many research bureaus in Soviet Russia and Eastern Europe. Similarly, emphasis on the practical aspects of sociology could develop in academic departments—for example, in British universities which often neglected intellectual orientations in their training and activities. Other academic departments were relatively isolated from the publicist and critical tradition, as was true to some degree in large sectors of the American and in many European sociological communities, especially after World War II. Still other departments confined themselves to one approach or school. Some restrictions to one research paradigm developed, as we have seen, soon after World War II in some Scandinavian and American universities; other schools, like many Dutch universities, had much more varied areas of specialization and more theoretical paradigms but were more restricted in their intellectual orientations and role conceptions.

The best type of academic setting, from the point of view of the continuity and autonomy of sociological analysis, has on the whole been a university or institute in which one can combine teaching, on both graduate and undergraduate levels, with professional and broad intellectual orientations and organizational contacts. Such university departments, often in close relationship with broader professional or public agencies, have permitted the coexistence of a variety of mixes of sociological approaches—speculative, comparative, institutional, methodological—and a wide range of role-referents for sociologists.

These settings were provided between the two World Wars notably in the United States, to some extent in Germany, and in England (largely in social anthropology), and after World War II in the United States and to a lesser degree in England, Scandinavia, and Holland. It was in these locales that the most important research programs and paradigmatic shifts developed, largely through the internal momentum of sociological work. Among these, the most important were, as we have seen, the functional model in British social anthropology; the structural-functional model in sociology and at least the first post-World War II development of the exchange and conflictual models; many specific research programs, such as the "culture and personality" school in its psychoanalytic and learning theory guises; the first studies of modernization; studies of stratification in general and of status congruence in particular; a large number of the recent shifts of emphasis in sociology of religion away from the structural-functionalist model; and other developments alluded to above. These organizational settings contained those analytic-research and role orientation mixes that were most conducive to continuity and most able to absorb external pressures.

But not only were such academic settings late in the development of sociology and rare in its contemporary phases. Even when they did exist, they could be disturbed by external forces and the reactivation of latent components of the sociological role. These tendencies were often reinforced by the fact that the analytic starting points and role referents of sociologists often involved them with different organizational settings, publics and clienteles, which in turn could intensify role conflict and produce "closed" parallel markets for the different approaches.[24]

However strong these outside impingements, the internal structure of the various social settings of sociology also greatly influenced their response to these forces and affected the absorption of new intellectual and ideological influences. It could incorporate them in ways that broadened the sociological tradition, or in ways that threatened the distinctiveness of this tradition.

The Intellectual and Institutional Conditions of the Contemporary Argument About Crisis

7.   The relationship between institutional and intellectual conditions affecting the development of "crises" of sociology are well illustrated by the contemporary controversies analyzed in Chapters 8 through 11. The initial background of these controversies was the development of greater awareness of broader external and metascientific aspects of sociological analysis as against the segregated, specialized types of discussions that dominated the 1950s and early 1960s in the United States, and to some degree England, Holland, and the Scandinavian countries. These discussions had been based on a general acceptance of the professional commitment to research and to the academic core of sociology. They contained a strong, if often implicit, conviction of the possibility of its "neutral" application, and of *de facto* distance from outside intellectual, political, and institutional involvements and orientations. Institutionally, these orientations were accompanied by a steady development of all major aspects of the sociological endeavor, based on a strong central core of substantive specialization and research with strong institutional bases

in universities and research bureaus. Only in sociological communities like Italy, France, and to some degree Germany, where such institutionalization was weak, did there develop in the early postwar period a general, often radical, criticism of sociology and a more direct concern with its philosophical and ideological bases and presuppositions. But in all these communities, the weak institutionalization of sociology, and of research, teaching and applied work, and the concomitant dissociation between the centers of institutionalized sociology and the new philosophical approaches, made many debates seem remote and abstract, resembling the older *Methodenstreit* but lacking its force, and usually having but little impact on the conduct of research.

The shift from segregated discussions to the debates of broader scope which gave rise to the outcry about crisis developed from several institutional and intellectual trends impinging upon the structure of the sociological community. It was due first to the internal developments in sociology analyzed in Chapters 6, 7, 8, and 10, to trends which developed through the very success of sociology in terms of institutional and analytic advance, and the rise of a new generation of sociologists who could take these successes for granted and begin to question them. Thus, the change in the mode of discussion in and about sociology was strongly influenced by the increasing momentum of research, codification of fields, and by the development of research beyond the earlier stages of codification. The strengthening of sociological analysis was further displayed in the emergence of additional institutional clusters of sociologists—loci for the development of countermodels; the steady development of closed- and open-system paradigms, combined with research progress; and the aspiration to bring these areas closer to theoretical developments. All these factors raised the level of aspiration in sociology and provided a background for continual internal critical examination of the premises and achievements of theories and research programs, an examination that could easily lead to intellectual dissatisfaction.

Such dissatisfaction could be reinforced, paradoxically, by the strong institutionalization of sociology in universities and in major research centers. It may have been reinforced by the patterns of institutionalization of the theoretical approaches, for many approaches—some of the models and countermodels and fields of specialization (social psychology, small groups, demography, or mathematical sociology)—often found institutional bases and could develop into dense clusters and networks. These clusters, however, were unevenly distributed among academic settings, creating a feeling of disarray. In this way they sharpened for many sociologists, especially the younger generation or those close to the centers of sociological analysis, the sense of a lack of systematic and analytic unification, consistency, and continuity, compared with their hopes for a more unified discipline.[25]

These internal criticisms were reinforced by intellectual and institutional trends which affected the public and professional standing of sociology. With the institutionalization of sociological activity, sociologists and the broader public inspected the claims of sociology to contribute to social change and a better society, and to provide critical direction or technical guidance. Professional and lay communities became aware of the societal and political implications of research and the influence of sociologists on public opinion. The criticism of sociology and the ethical problems of research were underscored by the issues raised by the participation of sociologists in policy-making research.

Of special importance was the outcry about the development of sociology in a technocratic direction, as its activities became enmeshed in governmental and business enterprise. The conception of professional autonomy of the late 1940s and early 1950s that had assumed distance from direct political involvement, stressing purely "technical" and academic professional involvement, was no longer acceptable.

Sociologists became more sensitive to demands for a closer relation of their work to social problems and pressures from varying publics for changing commitments to the study of social problems. These trends intensified the influence of new publics who could undermine the legitimacy of dominant academic-professional orientations. Dormant or segregated role orientations, especially the critical role orientation, came back to the center of self-perceptions, reactivating or intensifying conflicts between various role orientations. Thus, an additional push was given to the critical reexamination of many premises of sociology and of self-conceptions of sociologists.[26]

The tendency to critical examination was intensified by intellectual trends which developed slowly from the early 1950s, gathering momentum in the mid-1960s. First was the critical examination of the relevance of scientific progress to the welfare of mankind. A new, searching look at the place of science was taken in the early post-World War II period. The necessity for this was first voiced in the *Bulletin of Atomic Scientists;* later it became much more intensified and was closely related to the broader problems of the place of science in the contemporary community, of the possible limits of reason, and of the validity of science as the basis of the major values of society. Whatever the impact of these discussions on other sciences, it touched one of sociology's nerves and questioned its standing in the intellectual tradition.[27]

From the mid-1960s, these discussions were intensified by the reopening of protest orientations toward "post-industrial" society and to international events and trends, which in extreme cases attacked Western culture itself. Of crucial importance were the internal upheavals in the United States on race, poverty, and the Vietnam War. These upheavals spread throughout the world, becoming most fully articulated in the West, and in Asia, Africa, and Latin America, in the outbursts of intellectual antinomianism, student protest, leftist radicalism and sophisticated and "crude" Marxism.

The broader scope of the sociological community, and its entry into the more central areas of intellectual and academic life, made sociology especially sensitive to the trends of protest and intellectual antinomianism that, with the massive expansion of student populations, swept over Western universities from the middle of the 1960s. This sensitivity was probably reinforced by the fact that, as Lipset has shown, students of sociology, and their departments, tended to exhibit social characteristics predisposing them to radicalism.[28]

The impact of these circumstances was reinforced by the unequal and uneven institutionalization of different parts of the national and, more important, the international sociological community, and by the fact that the developments within the centers of Western sociology were paralleled and to some degree reinforced by those in most countries of the Third World.

8.   The outcries and discussions about the crisis of sociology displayed all the elements characteristic of the situations mentioned above. But in the contemporary setting, the convergence of three trends has created a paradoxical constellation of the elements of "crisis."

The very features in the contemporary setting that created both greater density of the sociological community and a higher level of institutionalization seem also to have increased first, sociologists' vested interests and dependence on ensuring their own followings; second, the possibility of close relationships with central political movements as well as centers of economic and political power; and third, their possible submergence in larger movements or centers of power, as part of their ideological or technical apparatus.

Within such settings, the intensive preoccupation with external metaanalytical problems and above all the combination of this preoccupation with political involvement created a "nihilistic" atmosphere challenging the validity not only of selected aspects of sociological work, but of the entire enterprise. Many contemporary critics of sociology did not base their criticisms on criteria derived from other intellectual disciplines, even philosophy or history, but used ideological and political considerations.

At the same time, the larger, denser, and more highly institutionalized sociological communities also had more diversified ties to different intellectual academic settings, a strong internal core of academic research, a high degree of autonomy of resources, and an openness to new problems. The greater strength and momentum of analysis and research, density of the sociological community, and communication among its members also stimulated unprecedented examination of sociological analysis, theory, and methodology.

This examination may still open up many new avenues of development and growth. More than in earlier times, it is in the power of the sociological community (or communities) to draw strength from the intellectual turmoil in which it has caught itself; to overcome the negative potential of this turmoil and to maximize its constructive possibilities. Its success, however, depends largely on its ability to forge an open, critical, and scholarly identity and to withstand the pressures which can undermine it.

The Reactions of Sociological Communities to "Crisis"

9.   The contemporary constellation of these elements, the contemporary perception of crisis, posed for the sociological community a far more difficult, but potentially fruitful challenge than earlier declarations of crises. The outcome of crises, however, in terms of constructive or destructive developments, has varied greatly. We have few organized data, much less systematic research, about the conditions that have produced different outcomes; the present situation, moreover, is in constant flux. Nevertheless, some preliminary hypotheses may not be out of place.

A cursory, and admittedly superficial view indicates that the direction and consequences of the crisis were influenced by the strength of external forces, the structure and internal strength of the sociological communities, and the interaction between these two.[29]

In addition to the intellectual and institutional forces analyzed above, several external forces were important in this period. Most important, the sociological communities increased in quantity and density without corresponding institutionalization of their own control over resources, their academic and professional legitimation, or their ability to foster professional identification and develop continuing career patterns. It seems to have been above all the growth in numbers of students, changes in the student-teacher ratio, and pronounced shifts in the respective ages of students and teachers which markedly reduced the age gap between them, that undermined whatever stability of career patterns had been attained in sociological communities, and that weakened, at least temporarily, the academic socialization and identification of sociologists.

The most important aspect of the internal organization of sociological communities was the incorporation of mixes of different components of sociological work and role orientations. These mixes, as we have seen, were most conducive to the continuity of sociological activity and the creative absorbtion of outside influences.

These two factors, the strength of organizational settings with "good" mixes of sociological work and role orientations, and their undermining by the processes analyzed above, had different conjunctions in the sociological communities. Of course, the strength of incursions could be entirely independent of any internal aspects of the sociological community, determined almost entirely by external demographic, social, and political factors. But their impact differed greatly among sociological communities.

These differences can best be discerned in the stronger centers of research in the West, and to some degree in Japan. While the impact of "crises" on these centers was, for a time, quite forceful, both the impact and outcome were to a large degree influenced by the relative internal strength of these communities. The institutional settings least able to withstand external pressures and absorb new developments constructively were those in which sociological activity was based only on one work component or role referent, or on restricted intellectual orientations. Initial weakness in the face of these pressures tended to be greater insofar as the different types of restrictiveness reinforced each other—for example, when closed philosophical attitudes were combined with closed or discrete analytic approaches and with an emphasis on a purely critical-political role; or when emphasis was placed on technical research with practical "engineering" orientations, or on journalistic research with a purely ideological stance; or where the relations between all these strong traditions and research were weak. This inability to withstand pressure was reinforced if ties between theory and research were weak in terms of prevailing expectations in the sociological community.

Certain structural aspects of the sociological communities, and of universities and research bureaus in particular, were also important in influencing the types of reactions to external pressures. The ability to react constructively to pressure was weaker where emphasis was placed mainly on undergraduate studies, or where there was little contact between undergraduate or graduate teaching and practical work or research.

Although the specific importance of each condition and of their combined effect must still be systematically investigated, preliminary observations show that sociological communities which were restrictive, and which tended at first to belittle the impact of these external forces, often succumbed under "crisis" to various fads or fashions in sociological analysis or moved in one of several directions weakening the distinctiveness of sociological analysis.

Thus the ability to absorb the impact of crisis was generally weak in sociological communities in France, Germany or Italy, which had few institutions teaching sociology on both undergraduate and graduate levels, or connecting teaching with practical orientations, but which did have strong emphases on the ideological and philosophical aspects of sociology. In all these communities, the tendency to abdicate the distinctiveness of sociological analysis was, at least initially, the greatest. But even in many of these centers, important differences developed between stronger departments and research bureaus, which tried to absorb the impact of the crisis in a constructive way, and the wider student body and, often, large parts of departments of sociology which, at least at first, succumbed to the impact of these crises by accepting fads and the identification of sociology with ideological and political movements.

Yet even some stronger, fully institutionalized centers of research moved toward temporary abdication of research: in Holland, where heavier emphasis was placed on technical or practical, rather than intellectual, aspects of research; and in the Scandinavian countries, which had a relatively narrow research paradigm. In England, the reaction to crisis was most intense in undergraduate departments which were dissociated from graduate study and often where teaching was divorced from research. There it gave rise to relatively acrimonious disputes, and to the development of fads. At least some sectors of these sociological communities, however—several universities in Scandinavia, including Bergen, Uppsala, and Geteborg, and several departments in England, which had strong traditions of research with broader orientations, could absorb crisis in a way that permitted the sociological tradition to develop. Similarly, the stronger connection between graduate and undergraduate study and between these studies and practical work in some Dutch universities furthered the development of nuclei with more constructive reactions to these impingements, beginning in the early 1970s.

Within the United States, with its more variegated types of sociological communities, where there was some openness to the wider implications of sociology and a stronger grounding in research, constructive tendencies did prevail in many places after the initial surrender to the outcry of crisis.

It is difficult to estimate the impact of the outcries of crisis on sociological work in the Communist countries. On the one hand, the growing interest in the West in ideological Marxism could easily reinforce the official dogmatism and supervision of sociology in these countries. On the other hand, however, the opening up of discussions in the Marxist camp in the West could also reinforce some of the more dissident trends in the East and hence, paradoxically, the autonomy of sociological work and orientations within Communist countries.

The bifurcation of small, strong nuclei attempting to react to crisis constructively in terms of the distinctiveness of sociological analysis, as against a much wider tendency to abdicate this distinctiveness, can be found also in many of the countries of the Third World. But here the situation was complicated even more by several factors. In these countries, the weak and very restricted institutionalization of sociological work, combined with steady growth in quantitative density of the sociological community, and with the fact that sociologists faced the dilemma to define their roles and activities not only in terms of the international scholarly community centered in the West, but also in terms of national needs, pressures, and developments. These problems were intensified by the fact that the role of the sociologist as defined in terms of some Western experience—especially the mixture of academic and the professional orientations—lacked institutional anchorage and could contradict the definition of the intellectual's role in another culture.

These trends were also reinforced in these communities by the ideologization of intellectuals within them and their dissociation from, and rebellion against, the centers of the West.

These problems and demands became more strongly articulated as a result of the patterns of development in post-World War II sociological centers outside Europe and the initial reaction to these developments. The development of these centers created a feeling of dependence upon the Western and European centers in terms of resources and as the basic reference for groups of local scholars, influencing not only standards of scholarly work but the definition of problems and the techniques of research. After the first phase of acceptance of these models from the West, this situation produced a sense of inappropriateness, alienation, and imposition, and ultimately a demand to redefine the "dependent" place of Third World academics within the international scholarly community. At the same time the tendency to authoritarian regimes of the Right or the Left in many of these countries undermined the independence of academic institutions and of centers of sociological work.

All these trends made the centers of sociological work in these countries even more susceptible to outcries of crisis. Beyond a few strong nuclei of independent work, these centers were even less able to resist the impact of crisis.

Not surprisingly, it was above all on the international scene, where the institutionalization of sociological work was lowest, that the highest degree of ideologization of sociological disputes developed—a trend which was reinforced by meetings among sociologists from all sociological centers with those from Eastern Europe. Indeed, it was in the international settings that the tendencies to abdicate the distinctiveness of sociological analysis became most prominent.[30]

All these are very preliminary indications of the conditions which generated, in different sociological communities, varying patterns of response to outcries about crisis in sociology. Only further detailed researches can indicate more systematically the exact importance of different conditions, including the crucial importance of individual or collective academic entrepreneurs, in influencing the outcome of these developments.

Institutionalization and the Sensitivity of Sociologists to External Influence

10.   The preceding analysis brings us to one of the major points of dispute among sociologists about the nature of the sociological enterprise, its development and institutionalization. The crux of the dispute is whether some special features of the institutional and intellectual aspects of sociological work analyzed above, especially the sensitivity to external forces with its concomitant internal discontinuities, will, as Merton seems to intimate, disappear with the institutionalization and "maturity" of sociology, or whether, as Reinhard Bendix implies, they will remain with us, if not forever, then for a long period of time.[31]

Merton's approach seems to be supported by the fact that the various conditions conducive to discontinuity in sociological analysis, and to intensification of the relationship between such discontinuities and openness to "external" intellectual factors, have indeed developed most visibly in relation to the slow pace of institutionalization of sociology in the nineteenth and twentieth centuries, and to the long period of its differentiation from other disciplines.[32]

Moreover, as Merton has shown, some of the disputes about sociology are not dissimilar to those which characterized the earlier phases of development of the natural sciences.

Yet our analysis, and, in fact Merton's later analyses of some aspects of "crisis" in sociology,[33] indicate that the various discontinuities and their derivatives are characteristic of more than the initial stages of sociology. They erupted again, in somewhat different form but with undiminished intensity, during the recent period of greater institutionalization. They developed in fact, simultaneously with increasing institutionalization —with greater continuity in many fields of research, with closer relationships between research programs and middle-range or more general theories, and with greater momentum and vigor in the development of paradigmatic models and research programs.

Yet, even in these recent developments, the internal momentum was only one source of innovation or reformulation of problems of research and analysis. A very large portion of these innovations and reformulations was also due, perhaps to an even greater degree than before, to the reactivation of various external, intellectual and ideological sources, and to the very intensity of the activation of different role-orientations of sociologists, especially the critical component.

Thus the preceding analysis indicates that while the specific focus of the discontinuities and sensitivities of sociological work to external factors changes with the level of institutionalization of sociological activity, these "crises" may become even more intense in periods of increasing density and institutionalization. In some way, they seem to be given in the sociological enterprise as it has developed.

It may well be that we are witnessing one illustration of the possibility that different scientific and scholarly traditions may develop not only different degrees, but also different patterns, of institutionalization. As far as sociology is concerned, these specific patterns may change in the future, but only if the specific conditions of sociological work analyzed above weaken or disappear. So long as they continue, even if changing their concrete expression, one may hypothesize that sociologists will continue to be sensitive to these external impingements, and will continually pose before the sociological community the necessity of coping with them—hopefully in a constructive way.

The development of sociology so far has indicated that such sensitivity to external forces need not be detrimental to the sociological analysis, though it does create the various discontinuities analyzed above. Indeed, most attempts to deny these external forces have tended until now to impede the ability to deal constructively with such impingements and have had, from the point of view of furthering sociological analysis, rather negative results.

The possibility of constructive development in sociological analysis has been predicated until now on the ability to translate or transform external developments into the analytic and conceptual framework of the sociological *Problemstellung* and its internal momentum of research. The central core of such developments was the continuing elaboration and combination of explicative paradigms and research programs oriented to aspects of this *Problemstellung,* open to different external influences, but not identified with any of them.

The ability to effect such "translations" or "transformations" has been, in turn, continuously dependent upon the intellectual and institutional factors which we attempted to analyze above. But no such combination was ever fully assured of continuity. What may have been a proper "solution" under certain circumstances could prove inappropriate or inadequate under new conditions. Each new social or cultural situation which has impinged upon the development of sociology has provided a challenge to redefine and restructure many of its conceptions, tools, and approaches.

It is only insofar as these challenges have been constructively dealt with from within its central core that the continuity of sociological analysis—of its own scholarly-critical tradition and its potential contribution to the growth of that broader tradition of critical scholarly evaluation grounded in the trust of reason—could be assured. The maintenance and nurturing of the ability to cope constructively with these problems is the greatest challenge facing the sociological community now, and probably the greatest in the history of its development.

Notes

1. These "crises" have been analyzed in greater detail in Chs. 2, 3, and 5.

2. R. Boudon, "The sociology crisis," *Social Science Information,* Vol. 11, Nos. 3–4 (1972), pp. 109–139.

3. As an illustration of discontinuity, see for example H. P. Dreitzel (ed.), *Family, Marriage and the Struggle of the Sexes* (New York: Macmillan, 1972).

    For a radical's critique of the tendency of radical sociology to cut itself from the sociological tradition, see N. Birnbaum, "Sociology: discontent present and perennial," *Social Research,* Vol. 38, No. 4 (1971), pp. 732–750.

    For a similar critique, but from a more "liberal" point of view, see A. H. Barton, "Empirical methods and radical sociology: a liberal critique," in J. D. Colfax and J. L. Roach (eds.), *Radical Sociology* (New York, London: Basic Books, 1971), pp. 460–477.

4. On this see R. Klima, "Theoretical pluralism, methodological dissension, and the role of the sociologist: the West German case," *Social Science Information,* Vol. 11, Nos. 3–4 (1972), pp. 69–108; C. J. Lammers, "Mono and polyparadigmatic developments in

natural and social sciences," Institute of Sociology, University of Leyden, The Netherlands, mimeo, 1973; R. Boudon, "The sociology crisis," *op. cit.*

5. See above all Ch. 3, as well as the materials presented in Chs. 2 and 5.

6. Some of these points have been taken up by A. Pizzorno, "Una crisi che non importa superare," in P. Rossi (ed.), *Ricerca Sociologica e Ruolo del Sociologo* (Bologna: Il Mulino, 1972), pp. 327–357.

   Fuller illustrations can be found in F. Jonas, *Geschichte der Soziologie* (Hamburg: Rowohlt Verlag, 1968), 4 vols.

7. On Durkheim and Weber for this point of our analysis, see Chs. 2 and 4. and especially: T. Parsons, *The Structure of Social Action* (New York: Free Press, 1968), especially Vol. 1, Ch. 12 and Vol. 2, Ch. 18.

   On Weber see also A. Giddens, *Politics and Sociology in the Thought of Max Weber* (London: Macmillan, 1972).

   On Simmel see L. A. Coser, *Masters of Sociological Thought* (New York: Harcourt, Brace, Jovanovich, 1971), pp. 177–215; D. Levine (ed.), *Georg Simmel on Individuality and Social Forms* (Chicago: University of Chicago Press, 1971).

   On Tönnies see A. Mitzman, *Sociology and Estrangement* (New York: Knopf, 1973), pp. 39–131.

8. On the controversies as related to Pareto and Mosca, see the materials in F. Jonas, *Geschichte der Soziologie, op. cit.,* Vol. 3, and the bibliography there; and especially, Norberto Bobbio, *Saggi sulla Scienza Politica in Italia,* (Bari: Latrize, 1969), especially Chs. 3, 4, 7, 8, and 10.

9. See our analysis in Ch. 5, above, and the following:

   On Sombart, A. Mitzman, *op. cit.,* pp. 135–264.

   On Mannheim, E. Shils, "Mannheim, Karl," in *International Encyclopedia of the Social Sciences,* Vol. 9 (New York: Macmillan, 1968), pp. 557–562.

   On the whole period of the 1920s and 1930s in Germany, see R. König, *Studien zur Soziologie* (Frankfurt am Main und Hamburg: Fischer Bücherei, 1971), pp. 9–37.

   Some of the major expositions of this period have been incorporated in many of the essays in A. Vierkandt, *Handwörterbuch der Soziologie* (Stuttgart: F. Enke Verlag, 1931).

   On the Frankfurt school, see M. Jay, *The Dialectical Imagination* (Boston: Little, Brown, 1973).

10. On the theoretical controversies see details in Chs. 8, 10 above.

    On intellectual antinomianism and student protest see, from among the many works, S. M. Lipset, *Rebellion in the University: A History of Student Activism in America* (London: Routledge and Kegan Paul, 1972); S. N. Eisenstadt, "Generational conflict and intellectual antinomianism," in P. Altbach and R. S. Laufer (eds.), *The New Pilgrims, Youth Protest in Transition* (New York: David Mackay, 1972), and the other materials in this, as well as many other collections on this topic.

11. R. W. Friedrichs, *A Sociology of Sociology* (New York: Free Press, 1970); A. W. Gouldner, *The Coming Crisis of Western Sociology* (New York, London: Basic Books, 1970).

    For a critical review of these works, see J. Ben-David, "The state of sociological theory and the sociological community: a review article," *Comparative Studies in Society and History,* Vol. 15, No. 4 (October 1973), pp. 448–472; see also: J. D. Colfax and J. L. Roach (eds.), *Radical Sociology, op. cit.;* S. N. Eisenstadt, "Some reflections on the crisis in sociology," *Sociological Inquiry,* Vol. 44, No. 3 (1974), pp. 147–157.

12. Illustrations of these outcries have been documented in detail in Chs. 9 and 11, above.

13. For some illustrations see T. Schroyer, "A reconceptualization of critical theory," in J.
     D. Colfax and J. L. Roach (eds.), *Radical Sociology, op. cit.*, pp. 132–148; J. Horton, "The
     fetishism of sociology," *ibid.*, pp. 171–193; N. Birnbaum, "Sociology: discontent pres-
     ent and perennial," *op. cit.;* S. J. Bodenheimer, "The ideology of developmentalism:
     American political science's paradigm—surrogate for Latin American studies," *Ber-
     keley Journal of Sociology*, Vol. 15 (1970), pp. 95–137; and in greater detail the materials
     in Chs. 9 and 11, above.

14. The centrality of these topics in the present sociological discussions is illustrated by the
     great output of works which deal with them. See for example J. D. Douglas (ed.), *The
     Relevance of Sociology* (New York: Appleton-Century-Crofts, 1970); J. Horton, "The
     fetishism of sociology," *op. cit.;* E. Topitsch, *Sozialphilosophie zwischen Ideologie und
     Wissenschaft* (Neuwied & Berlin: Luchterhand, 1966); T. Adorno et al. (eds.), *Der
     Positivismusstreit in der Deutschen Soziologie* (Neuwied & Berlin: Luchterhand, 1969); W.
     Hochkeppel (ed), *Soziologie zwischen Theorie und Empirie* (München: Nymphenburger
     Verlagshandlung, 1970), especially pp. 13–48, 135–154, 179–195; A. Giddens (ed.),
     Positivism and Sociology (London: Heinemann, 1974); P. Rossi (ed.), *Ricerca Sociologica e
     Ruolo del Sociologo, op. cit.;* J. Goudsblom, *Belans van de Sociologie* (Utrecht: Het Spec-
     trum, 1974), especially Chs. 1–3; E. Topitsch, *Logik der Sozialwissenschaften* (Köln:
     Kiepenheuer & Witsch, 1972), Parts 2, 4, 8.
         For an interesting illustration of the increasing concern with somewhat marginal
     problems, see also John O'Neill, *Sociology as a Skin Trade* (London: Heinemann, 1972).

15. See for instance R. Quinney, "From repression to liberation: social theory in a radical
     age," in Robert A. Scott and Jack D. Douglas (eds.), *Theoretical Perspectives on Deviance*
     (New York: Basic Books, 1972), pp. 317 ff.; and the essays in W. Hochkeppel, *Soziologie
     zwischen Theorie und Empirie, op. cit.*, especially E. Topitsch, "Sackgassen des engage-
     ments," pp. 135–144 and K. Lenk, "Werturteilsfreiheit als fiktion," pp. 145–154; A.
     Touraine, *Pour la Sociologie* (Paris: Éditions du Seuil, 1974), especially Chs. 1 and 6.

16. The debates among German sociologists illustrate this tendency well. See R. Klima,
     "Theoretical pluralism, methodological dissension, and the role of the sociologist: the
     West German case," *op. cit.*
         For a Dutch assessment see R. F. Beerling, *Sociologie en Wettenschaptscrisis* (Amster-
     dam: Boon Meppel, 1973); S. N. Eisenstadt, "Some reflections on the crisis in sociol-
     ogy," *op. cit.;* the July-August issue of *Sociologische Gids* (1973) pp. 255–269.

17. For the area of modernization see, for example, S. J. Bodenheimer, "The ideology of
     developmentalism," *op. cit.;* G. Omvedt, "Modernization theories: the ideology of
     empire?" in A. R. Desai (ed.), *Essays on the Modernization of Underdeveloped Societies*, Vol.
     1 (Bombay: Thacker, 1971), pp. 119–137; A. R. Desai, "Need for reevaluation of the
     concept," *ibid.*, pp. 458–474; E. de Kadt and G. Williams (eds.), *Sociology and Develop-
     ment* (London: Tavistock, 1974); S. N. Eisenstadt, *Tradition, Change and Modernity* (New
     York: Wiley, 1973), Chs. 1 and 5.
         For political sociology see, for example, Dusky Lee Smith, "The sunshine boys:
     toward a sociology of happiness," in J. D. Colfax and J. L. Roach (eds.), *Radical
     Sociology, op. cit.*, pp. 28–44; and the following articles in *Sociological Inquiry*, Vol. 42,
     Nos. 3–4 (1972): P. M. Hall, "A symbolic interactionist analysis of politics," pp. 35–75;
     R. Moss Kanter, "Symbolic interactionism and politics in systemic perspective," pp.
     77–92; P. M. Hall, "The negotiation of identities: ego rejects alter-casting or who is a
     liberal?" pp. 93–99.
         In the field of stratification see, for instance, James Stolzman and Herbert Gamberg,

"Marxist class analysis versus stratification analysis as general approaches to social inequality," in *Berkeley Journal of Sociology*, Vol. 18 (1973–1974), pp. 87–105.

For the theoretical paradigms see details in Chs. 9, 11, above.

18. R. K. Merton, "Insiders and outsiders: a chapter in the sociology of knowledge," *The American Journal of Sociology*, Vol. 78, No. 1 (1972), pp. 9–47.

For a similar point see J. D. Douglas, "The relevance of sociology," in J. D. Douglas (ed.), *The Relevance of Sociology, op. cit.*, pp. 185–233.

19. Such constructive possibilities have been documented in greater detail above in Ch. 11.

20. These points have been made in a general but very forceful way, above all by E. Shils, in "Tradition, ecology, and institution in the history of sociology," *Daedalus*, Vol. 99, No. 4 (fall 1970), pp. 760–825; E. Shils, "The trend of sociological research," paper read at the 8th International Congress of Sociology, Evian, 1966.

They have also been documented in many works, as, for example, T. Clark, *Prophets and Patrons: The French University and the Emergence of the Social Sciences* (Cambridge, Mass.: Harvard University Press, 1973); P. Abrams, *The Origins of British Sociology: 1834–1914* (Chicago: University of Chicago Press, 1968), pp. 8–153.

For fuller documentation see Chs. 2, 5, and 6, above.

21. These peculiar characteristics of the development of sociology have been documented in greater detail above, especially in Chs. 2, 5, and 6.

See also E. Shils, "Tradition, ecology, and institution in the history of sociology," *op. cit.*; L. Coser, *Masters of Sociological Thought, op. cit.*; A. Oberschall, "The institutionalization of American sociology," in A. Oberschall (ed.), *The Establishment of Empirical Sociology* (New York: Harper & Row, 1972), pp. 187–251; P. Abrams, *The Origins of British Sociology, op. cit.*; T. Clark, *Prophets and Patrons, op. cit.*

22. L. Coser, *Masters of Sociological Thought, op. cit.*; E. Shils, "Tradition, ecology, and institution in the history of sociology," *op. cit.*

23. See the documentation above, in Chs. 2, 5, and 6.

24. On this see Sections 1, 2, above.

25. Some of these clusters are discussed in N. C. Mullins and C. J. Mullins, *Theories and Theory Groups in Contemporary American Sociology* (New York: Harper & Row, 1973); but see also the reviews of this book in *Contemporary Sociology*, Vol. 4, No. 3 (May 1975), pp. 223–226.

26. Illustrations of this can be found in B. Schäfers (ed.), *Thesen zur Kritik der Soziologie* (Frankfurt: Suhrkamp, 1969); Y. Lochen, *Sociologens Dilemma* (Oslo: Gyldendal Norksverlag, 1970); L. Gallino, "Crisi della sociologia, ricerca sociologica, e el ruolo del sociologo," in P. Rossi, *Ricerca Sociologica, op. cit.*, pp. 301–322; R. Friedrichs, *A Sociology of Sociology, op. cit.*; R. F. Beerling, *Sociologie en Wettenschaptscrisis, op. cit.*

27. R. Bendix, "Sociology and the distrust of reason," *American Sociological Review*, Vol. 35, No. 5 (1970), pp. 831–843.

28. S. M. Lipset and E. C. Ladd, "The politics of American sociologists," *American Journal of Sociology*, Vol. 78, No. 1 (July 1972), pp. 67–104.

29. The following discussions are mainly based on personal, albeit continuing, observations of the sociological scene. They should be viewed as tentative indications for further systematic research.

30. This can be best seen, for instance, in the many highly politicized declarations and papers presented to the 1974 Congress of Sociology in Toronto.

For analysis of some trends in international sociology see W. M. Evan, "The International Sociological Association and the internationalization of sociology," *International Social Science Journal,* Vol. 27, No. 2 (1975), pp. 385–397.

31. For these points of view of Merton and Bendix see R. Bendix, "Sociology and ideology," pp. 173–187; R. K. Merton, "The precarious foundations of detachment in sociology: observations on Bendix's 'sociology and ideology,'." pp. 188–199, and R. Bendix, "Comment," pp. 200–201, in E. A. Tiryakian (ed.), *The Phenomenon of Sociology* (New York: Appleton-Century-Crofts, 1971); See also, Paul Starr, "The edge of social science," *Harvard Educational Review,* Vol. 44 (November 1974).

32. These aspects of the development of sociology have been discussed at length above, in Chs. 2, 4, 5, 6, and 9.

33. R. K. Merton, "Structural analysis in sociology," in P. Blau (ed.), *Approaches to the Study of Social Structure,* (New York: Free Press, 1976), pp. 21–53.

13

The Broadening of the Sociological Tradition
Some Preliminary Indications

The Reopening of the Problem of Social Order in Contemporary Theory

1. In Chapter 10, we analyzed the major openings between the main analytic approaches in contemporary theoretical discussions of sociology, and their relation to developments in different areas of research. We also analyzed the potentially constructive divergences between these approaches and gave some indications how these might broaden the sociological tradition and sharpen its tools of analysis. In this chapter we will outline one constructive direction.

The refinement of the sociological tradition and its tools in the contemporary scene, as with other breakthroughs in sociological theory, involved three lines of analysis. These lines were: first, the reopening of the problem of social order as analyzed and "solved" in the predominant explicative paradigms and sociological theories; second, the reanalysis of the basic components of social life and their interrelationships; and third, the analysis of the ways in which the social mechanisms relating these components "solve" the problem of social order and, in a flexible and differentiated way, the structure, stability, change, and variability of different types of societies.

The reexamination of the problem of social order took place through a further exploration of the basic insight of the sociological tradition: that the key problem of social order, the original Hobbesian problem, was rooted not in a presocial "state of nature" but in the very construction of organized social and cultural life and the division of labor; and above all in the confrontation between the organizational givens of the social division of labor and multiple individual goals.

The classics of sociology had recognized that given this confrontation, social order could not be assured without mechanisms explaining the structure and continuity of social interaction, groups, and societies. The "answers" to this problem in the classics, as Parsons has forcefully analyzed them for the Founding Fathers in *The Structure of Social Action*, [1] centered on the relationships between the organizational and interactional aspects of social action—that is, the institutional mechanisms of social division of labor—and the symbolic or value elements of social action and behavior.

In explaining the working of such mechanisms of the division of labor as the market, contract, social control, and the like, the classic approaches had stressed the symbols of collective identity and the principles of legitimation of social activities, interests, and power. The crucial contributions were, as we have seen, Durkheim's analyses of precontractual norms and mechanical solidarity and its symbols, and Weber's analyses of the major types of legitimation of interests and of different types of social order. [2] Contemporary theoretical developments went beyond the classics in several ways, largely by extending the analysis of organizational aspects of the institutional order—that is, the structure and working of institutions and organizations, and the processes of social interaction.

The great contribution of the structural-functional school [3] was to elaborate the various mechanisms of social structure and the social division of labor. Starting from the general properties of mutual orientations of actors in terms of "pattern variables", it moved to the analysis of social systems with their needs and exigencies, the analysis of roles and role structures, institutional spheres and different types of allocative mechanisms operating within them, and of the general media of exchange.

These analyses have greatly enhanced our understanding of the nature of social structure; of the relationships between social roles and positions and institutional structure; of the ways in which positions are distributed in collectivities according to institutional "needs" and spheres, on the one hand, and basic primordial qualities or criteria of achievement, on the other hand; and how in this way the ownership and control of resources are distributed in social structure. In other words, these analyses have enhanced our understanding, in Peter Blau's nomenclature, of the "parameters of social structure" and its working.[4]

The major contributions of the conflict and exchange approaches were, as we saw in Chapter 10, the analysis of the principles of interaction and exchange between individuals and collectives. The symbolic interactionists and, to some degree, the ethnomethodologists paid special attention to the processes through which the "meanings" of different situations of interaction are constructed.

All these approaches, in line with the classical approaches, recognized that the institutional order incorporates the possibility of disorder and therefore stressed the importance of normative elements in upholding institutional arrangements. Yet the ways in which the relationship between the normative and organizational aspects of institutional life were analyzed in these approaches came increasingly to seem inadequate in the theoretical disputes analyzed in Chapters 9 and 10. They were seen as too general and unspecific to explain the problem of social order in general, and, more precisely, the continuity, changeability, and variability of different types of societies and patterns of social behavior. In the latest theoretical controversies, these analyses were even charged with regressing from the insights of the Founding Fathers, Marx and Weber.[5]

The inadequacies of the various explanations were manifest in the blind spots of the various analytic approaches.[6] The common denominator of these blind spots was the explanation of the relationship between the normative and organizational aspects of social life and was seen by critics to lie in two common assumptions: first, that the norms assuring the maintenance of social order on any level of interaction can be derived directly from general value-orientations or from systemic exigencies of social groups or interaction; and second, that these norms and rules are equally valid or silent on every level of social interaction.

Thus exchange theory acknowledged normative elements and rules through its emphasis on the principles of distributive justice. But these were taken as given in any situation of interaction, and the process of their construction was not analyzed.

Structural-functional analysis undertook extensive analysis of the spheres of institutional life "belonging," as it were, to the normative order: ascriptive communities, cultural symbols, the entire apparatus of pattern-maintenance. But these were subsumed, or were seen as subsumed, under the broad categories of value orientations and norms, which were seen as equally applicable to every level of social action, and as given, rather than as variables to be explained.

Symbolic interactionists and ethnomethodologists did probe in great detail the process of constructing meaning in social situations. But they neglected to combine this analysis with examination of the structural aspects of social life. Second, they seem to have assumed that the construction of meaning takes place in the same way on all levels of social action and organization. Third, they did not explain continuity or stability of meaning in social situations.

The structuralist-symbolic approach stressed heavily that the key to social order, its "hidden" or "deep" structure, lies in the symbolic realm. Yet it has failed to specify the mechanisms connecting these principles to the organizational aspects of social life.

Whatever the validity of the critical interpretations of these approaches—at best they were only partially true—they have reopened the problem of social order in contemporary sociological theory and analysis. By doing so they have made it necessary, as was the case with the classics of sociological theory, to locate the problem of social order in a wider analytic framework that indicates how potential areas of disorder and conflict in institutional life are rooted in the "givens" of human existence. They have also necessitated a more systematic exploration of the areas of potential disorder inherent in the organizational aspects of social division of labor and social interaction, which are not regulated by the "usual," or "routine" norms and rules that exist on all levels of interaction.

Finally, they demand the exploration of social mechanisms that will explain more differentiated types of relations between the basic components of social order (individuals, societies, culture, and the environment) and between them and the systemic aspects of social order, than did the prevalent theoretical approaches. In the following pages we will present some suggestions for possible approaches to these problems.

The Roots of the Problems of Social Order: The Biological Endowment of Human Beings and the Construction of Human Environments

2.   The potentiality of disorder and conflict in organized social life is rooted, above all, in aspects of the human biological endowment and the way in which they influence the relationship between humans and their environment.

From a biological and ethological point of view, the distinctive characteristic of the humans as a species lies in the fact that beyond a certain minimal base, the range of stimuli to which they respond has little genetic predetermination; the range of behavior that can be learned is broader than with other species and in many ways different. To quote Ernest Mayer, "The human genetic endowment constitutes an open program, that is, one which allows for appreciable modifications, for additional inputs, during the lifespan of its owner, i.e., during the process of translation into phenotype."[7]

The specifically human consequence of this open program is man's capacity to create major aspects of his environments—to create and re-create, to construct, the very stimuli and objects of learning that human beings respond to.

This construction of the environment is effected by the imposition on it of arbitrary forms,[8] particularly symbolic communication and various technologies. This combination creates the specifically human environments—both "material" and "symbolic." Patterns of technology and symbolic communication are accumulated and transmitted through nongenetic—that is, social and cultural—processes. Through these patterns, such activities as signalling, on the one hand, and toolmaking, on the other, which are found among many other species, are transformed into their specifically human forms.

But the combination of symbolic communication and technology which constitutes the human response to the "openness" of its biological program does not create a closed, fixed environment for the species or for any human society. The very construction of a human environment generates a new level of openness. This openness is evident above all in the fact that while the foci, modes, and rules of structuring the human environment—the arbitrary forms imposed on its objects through language, toolmaking, and social organization—are common to the entire human species, the details of any specific pattern and structure are not predetermined by generic rules, tendencies, or categories of language, technology, and organization. The crystallization of these activities is made possible only through their unfolding in concrete interaction in specific cultural, social and ecological settings which themselves are not "fixed." Hence any such concretization is changeable and continually changing, varying from one group to another, and within the same group at different times. For all these reasons, the construction by humans of their environments always contains uncertainty and unpredictability.

Such uncertainties and unpredictabilities, however, are not mere "objective" "external" conditions to be "discovered" by scientific analysis. It is basic to the human condition that the very process of symbolic communication and its combination with technology generates, or is closely related to, awareness of uncertainty and predicament. This consciousness stems from the discrepancy, or "empty space," between the human tendency to structure its activities and environment and the nongivenness of the contents of that structure. The awareness of empty spaces is intensified by the fact that, because of the multiplicity of symbolic modes in the human repertoire, such as the aesthetic or religious, or of media and technologies, any concrete activity may be organized in many different ways. No one of these ways is fully predetermined either by the genetic endowment of the actors or by the limits of the environment. Thus in all human societies, the uncertainties derived from the openness of the biological program and the construction of the human environment constitute a major focus of conscious concern and activities.

This concern centers on the major dimensions along which the internal and external environments are structured: the shaping of individual personalities; the constant interaction among people; their interaction with the external or natural environment; the structuring of the symbolic environment; and most important, the interaction among these activities. More concretely, these concerns center on the uncertainties or predicaments produced by the possible randomness and changeability of people's goals and activities; the lack of fixed, given regulation of human endeavor and the consequent uncertainty about controlling impulses and activities; the changeability of the environment of any individual, group, or society and the potential instability of any framework of interaction; and the scarcity of valuable resources, including human time and energy in the face of consciousness of death and the potential endlessness of human striving.

It is through the confrontation between the central predicaments and dimensions of the structuring of human environments (i.e., the shaping of personality, social interaction, and interaction with the natural environment) that the major objects and processes of the structuring of human activities are transformed from "natural" problems into cultural predicaments. They become objects of conscious concern which takes the form of questions about the nature of human life, social interaction, material and transcendental reality, and the relationship between all of these as they affect man's fate and possible salvation in the light of his own finitude.

In all human societies, concern with these predicaments gives rise to activities evident primarily in the spheres of symbolic expression, religion, philosophy, science, and art, which attempt to cope with, and overcome, these uncertainties. In all these spheres of human creativity, the central predicaments are the starting points for the construction of a meaningful environment. This symbolic environment is created by the attribution of meaning to these tensions in terms of the broad symbolic concerns of human existence, above all those defining the relationships between man, nature, and culture; between human existence and the transhuman, "religious" realms, between the quest for this-worldly activity and the search for salvation. The provision of meaning in turn entails relating these predicaments to basic "givens" and problems of human, biological existence: differences in age and the process of aging; the facts of birth and death; sexual differences and powers; physical differences among men; vulnerability to the natural forces of the environment and the futility of attempts to master them; the problem of consciousness of death.

Such structuring, whose details vary with type of activity and culture, provides a basis of meaningful order and "solution" of these predicaments. In one sense, of course, these tensions are never resolved; they are a constant, inherent, part of human reality which can never, except in utopian dreams, be eliminated. However, various cultural models transpose these problems to new levels of symbolic structuring which provide a measure of order, continuity, and meaning, some of these investing even disorder with at least partial meaning.

Such solutions, nevertheless, cannot be complete and hence completely satisfying. Their partiality is evident in the fact that utopian orientations, aiming at the unrealisable eradication of all these problems and tensions, are a basic element in all human societies and cultures.

The Problem of Social Order: Indeterminacies in the Relations between Actors, Goals, and Resources and the Predicaments of the Social Division of Labor

3.   The problem of social order, rooted in these predicaments of human existence, is also a focus of conscious concern, and of efforts to "solve" or "overcome" it, in all human societies. The basic existential dilemmas become manifest in social life because of the great interdependence of human beings and the consequent universality of the social division of labor; and the lack of fixed specification for the mode of division of labor through genetic programming, or through general rules or tendencies in the construction of symbols and technologies.

The organizational structure and mechanisms of the division of labor do not assure smooth interaction or the continuity of social units and frameworks.

The lack of assurance of harmony and continuity is evident in several indeterminacies that are inherent in any regular social interaction. These indeterminacies produce unpredictability in human behavior and are in turn exacerbated by the very construction of the organizational frameworks and mechanisms of the social division of labor that attempt to reduce them.

Because they are rooted in the universality of human interdependence combined with the non-specification of any specific division of labor, these closely related indeterminacies are built into any continuing social interaction. They inhere in the three important components of interaction: the relationship between actors, whether individuals or collectivities; the relationship between them and their goals; and the relationship between actors and their goals, on the one hand, and the resources at their disposal (including activities of other actors) on the other.

The first indeterminacy, the relationship among participants in any situation of interaction, is manifest in the lack of specification of the range of actors who are admitted to a situation—that is, of the boundaries of interaction and of criteria of participation (membership) in it.

The indeterminacy in the relationship between actors and goals is manifest in the lack of genetic specification of universal or general human goals and of goals that can or should be sought by participants in any particular situation of social interaction.

Indeterminacy in the relationship between actors and resources is manifest in the lack of fixed specification of the range of access of different actors to the major resources which are being produced, exchanged, and distributed in continuous interaction.

These indeterminacies develop on all levels of social interaction, from the most fleeting and informal to the morst organized. On micro and macro levels alike, they generate a basic unpredictability in human behavior and in social interaction.

Given the nature of human construction of its environments, which entails the social division of labor, and the awareness of inherent uncertainty generated by the process of construction, any long range predictability of social behavior and continuity of a social framework can be assured only through the development of stable mutual trust. This provides a meaningful framework for continuing obligation.

Such trust, in its turn, can be assured only by two developments: organizational arrangements providing frameworks and mechanisms for relatively continuous interaction; and a symbolic structuring of situations of interaction which provide meaningful definition of these situations in terms of the basic predicaments of human life and social organization.

The crucial problem of social order lies in the fact that the frameworks of *meaningful* obligations and trust are not provided by the *organizational* frameworks and mechanisms of social interaction and the social division of labor. It is true that the mechanisms of interaction and the division of labor (so exhaustively analyzed by the structural-functional, exchange, and symbolic interactionist schools) do provide the organizational means and frameworks for long-range social interaction, thus creating some predictability and continuity of social interaction. Nevertheless, the predictability of social behavior inherent in these structures and mechanisms cannot provide the type of meaningful definition which ensures the continuity of this interaction. On the contrary, not only does organization itself fail to solve the problems of potential disorder created by the basic indeterminacies of action. In a sense it exacerbates them, transposing these exigencies from organizational givens into foci of conscious concern that are formulated in symbolic terms, and emphasizing even more the possibilities of disorder, arbitrariness, and randomness in social life and organization.

These disruptive possibilities are rooted in the fact that in any given setting, a combination of conflict and cooperation develops among different groups and actors over the production, distribution, and use of resources. Therefore, the sustained functioning of any mechanism of the division of labor gives rise to attempts, by different actors, to seize access to resources and positions and promulgate rules that will support and perpetuate such arrangements. But, while these rules may produce stability in interaction, they are usually perceived as arbitrary, coercive and unjust. Thus they may generate a perception of ambiguity and disorder among actors. As a result, they cannot provide the bases of trust among participants in these relationships, and they generate built-in instability in the social relations they structure.

Such possibilities of instability and disorder, and the perception of arbitrariness, are exacerbated by the indeterminacies inherent in the basic organizational exigencies of social interaction, and of the organization of collectivities, institutions, and macrosocietal orders. In the construction of collectivities, institutions, and macrosocietal orders, these indeterminacies emerge because the goals and needs of any group and of their members are never simply given. The specific contents of these needs must be defined concretely in each instance, and in any group differences of opinion or interest always develop on defining each need concretely. Similarly, the different needs of any group are never completely compat-

ible, and tensions may exist among them, about evaluation of their relative importance, or about their compatibility with the "private" goals of
the individuals participating in the group.

Out of this arbitrariness and built-in instability, perceptions emerge in
all societies of the tensions inherent in social life, and of the predicaments
in the organizational aspects of the division of labor.

The most important of these symbolic tensions, which are found in all
societies and cultures, are those between hierarchy and equality; between
the pursuit by actors of instrumental and adaptive goals and the maintenance of a more general order and meaning; between competition,
struggle, authority, and power on the one hand, and solidarity and participation in a meaningful order on the other; between exploitation and
relatively just distribution of resources and positions; between human
spontaneity and the restrictiveness of any social organization or cultural
prescription.

The inherence of these tensions in social life generates the predicaments inherent in the organizational aspects of the social division of labor,
namely, that they do not provide for:

1. Assurance against uncertainty and risks in institutional life;
2. Assurance that one will take care of the recognized organizational
needs of the collectivity and of collective security;
3. The articulation or implementation of collective goals;
4. The attainment of some measure of individual and collective pride
and identity and a sense of participation in a meaningful social and
cultural order; and
5. The development and maintenance of feelings of mutual trust among
members of a collectivity.

*The Quest for Meaningful Order in Social Life and the Problems of
Setting Ground Rules of Social Interaction*

4.   The attempt to overcome these predicaments, to establish and
maintain meaningful social order and participation in it, is in any interaction, from the most fleeting to the most formal, an important goal that
transcends the various discrete goals of power, wealth, and prestige that
have been so strongly emphasized in sociological literature.

To understand the ways in which this quest is exhibited in social life, it
may be worthwhile to rephrase the preceding argument. In the language
of game theory, the argument states that the organizational aspects of

institutional life, and the various principles of exchange and interaction among individuals, so heavily stressed in the major theoretical approaches, may provide the basic mechanisms for the flow and exchange of resources and some concrete principles of such interchange. They do not, however, provide the ground rules of social interaction. To quote Buchler and Nutini, "The ground rules . . . structure the basic frameworks within which decision-making in different areas of social life is possible and, second (albeit here already in different degrees in different societies or parts thereof) some of the broad criteria that guide choices among the options which such frameworks allow."[9]

Thus the effort to overcome the predicaments of social organization, and to sustain meaningful order, takes the form of a quest for ground rules, or parameters, of social order. To provide long-range predictability of social interaction, these ground rules structure their environment symbolically to limit the range of possible "solutions" to the indeterminacies and arbitrariness inherent in social interaction, and invest these "solutions" with meaning in terms of proper answers to the tensions of human and social existence.

Accordingly, in all social situations, interaction develops which generates the ground rules that structure these indeterminacies and predicaments. The most important ground rules of social interaction, or parameters of social order, are those which portray or provide images, prototypes and specifications of:

1. The range of the goals or desiderata which are permitted to those participating in such situations, and the combination of such discrete goals into broader styles of life.
2. The concomitant symbolic and institutional boundaries of these collectivities—primarily through specification of the attributes of social and cultural similarity which define the criteria of membership in different collectivities—that is, those who may participate in any given interaction. Establishing attributes of similarity involves the definition of the contents of the sociocultural order, rules of access to them, and their legitimation in terms of a broader charismatic conception of order or appropriateness. These attributes also provide the starting points for defining the criteria of membership in various collectivities and for specifying the conditional and unconditional obligations involved in participation.
3. The rules of distributive justice and equity, which are seen as appropriate and binding with regard to distributions of the rights and obligations in the settings of interaction.

4. Criteria regulating access to resources and their use in different social settings and institutional spheres.

5. The definition of the broader purpose or meaning and collective goals of any interaction or collective activity, and the closely related definition of the relative importance of different societal "needs" within it.

6. Legitimation of such institutional complexes in terms of the prevalent criteria of justice, equity, and broader societal goals.

These ground rules "structure" and give order to the basic indeterminacies inherent in relationship among the components of social interaction. Thus they partly resolve the predicaments of the organization of the division of labor.

To demonstrate: the first ground rule, which specifies the range of the goals permitted to those participating in such situations, structures the indeterminacy between actors and goals. Those ground rules which specify the symbolic and institutional boundaries of these collectivities structure the indeterminacy of relationships among actors. The rules of distributive justice and equity, and the criteria of regulation of access to resources and of their use, structure the indeterminacy between actors, goals, and resources. The definition of the broad purpose and meaning and collective goals of any interaction or collective activity, and the legitimation of such institutional complexes, structure the potential arbitrariness inherent in the relationship between the various indeterminacies analyzed above as they crystallise in the basic predicaments of the organizational aspects of social interaction and the division of labor.

It is through the specification and institutionalization of these ground rules of social interaction that the uncertainties inherent in the organizational aspect of social division of labor are to some degree overcome and the possibilities of trust and predictability created. Although these problems and uncertainties are not abolished, they are transposed to a new and different level.

5.   Though leaning heavily on classic and contemporary sociological approaches, this discussion has tried to analyze in greater detail the areas of potential disorder which are built into the organizational aspects of social life. By stipulating the major types of ground rules of social interaction, it has identified and specified the nature and scope of the "precontractual" and legitimizing dimensions of social life through which the problems of social order are apparently resolved.

However, as the recent theoretical controversies have so clearly indicated, no institutional arrangements can be taken for granted. It is not enough, therefore, to provide closer specification of the nature and scope of these precontractual elements, or ground rules of social interaction, in social life. Beyond that one must also analyze the social processes through which these ground rules of social interaction are selected, institutionalized, and maintained. Here a set of questions arises which, at this stage of theoretical development, presents a major challenge for sociological analysis and research. These questions are: How are the contents of these ground rules of social interaction shaped? How are these rules concretely set up and institutionalized? What is their relationship to the routine aspects of social interaction? What is the nature of the mechanisms through which these different levels of institutional life are connected and maintained?

To answer these questions it is necessary to develop an approach more differentiated than those of the classic and contemporary analyses, which try to solve the problem of social order by providing "total" explanations in terms of their respective "base" or assumptions. It must go beyond the assumptions in current approaches in analyzing the relationships between the components of social order (individual, society, and culture), and between the organizational, symbolic, and "psychological" dimensions of human activities; and in identifying the mechanisms which structure these relationships. Such an analysis may compensate for the blind spots of these approaches, providing a basis for constructive development in theory and analysis. In the following pages we would like to provide a preliminary outline of such an approach.

The Symbolic Dimension of Human Activity; Contents of the Ground Rules of Social Interaction and the Parameters of Social Order

6. We may start by inquiring about the contents of the ground rules of social interaction, or the parameters of social order. These, as we have seen, cannot be derived from the exigencies of social interaction or the systemic needs of groups. The search for the "roots" or "sources" of the concrete contents of the different ground rules brings us close to the attempts, most fully exemplified by the symbolic structuralists inspired by Lévi-Strauss, to derive the criteria of ground rules, and of the deep or hidden structure of social organization, from the symbolic or cultural sphere of human activity.

The close relationship of the ground rules of social interaction to the symbolic dimension of human activity is borne by the fact that even the most superficial look at the contents of these ground rules—the rules of membership in collectivities, access to and control over resources, and symbols of collective identity—shows that they are very closely related to, or expressed in, various symbols. These symbols in turn are related to basic existential problems and to the tensions and problems inherent in organized social life.

However, unlike what many structuralists have assumed, these symbolic orientations do not, as general rules or properties of the human mind, influence the concrete crystallization of the ground rules of social interaction through a process of direct emanation.

The actualization of these presumably basic qualities or tendencies of the human mind, and the mastery over self and environment that they imply, are not simply given in the natural unfolding of these qualities. Rather, as Jerome Bruner has observed in several cognitive domains,[10] these tendencies of the mind are concretized through constant interaction with the various environmental forces and settings which in themselves have been constructed by human activity, and without which the very unfolding of such capacities is impossible. In each area of human activity, these capacities are concretized in terms of the specific premises and schemata of the area and of the symbolic orientations most relevant to it. This applies also, of course, to the construction of the social order. Thus, unlike the pure structuralists and more in line with scholars like Geertz, Turner, Beidelman, and Leach.[11] our analysis indicates that it is important to specify, first, which aspects of symbolic orientations are most relevant for constructing the contents of the ground rules; and second, the nature of the concrete institutional mechanisms through which they become operative in social life.

Both classic and recent sociological research provide important perspectives on these problems. They suggest, albeit roughly, some of the most important symbolic problems that are especially relevant to understanding the construction of a meaningful social order.*

As indicated above, these problems can be divided into two broad sets. One is concerned with the existential problems of human "cosmic" existence, the other with the specific symbolic evaluation of the exigencies of social life. Within each set, several problem areas can be distinguished.

In the first set, dealing with "cosmic" problems, the first problem area, is the evaluation of the primordial "givens" of human life: age, sex, the

---

* It is not claimed here that these constitute an exhaustive list of the cultural orientations which are significant from the point of view of social relations. It is only a tentative list of some orientations which were found to be of significance in the analysis of some important aspects of institutional analysis.

process of growth and aging, the bodily givens of human life and their relationship to mental capacities; and the definition of the relative importance of different dimensions of social existence, (political, economical, and ritual) and of different dimensions of temporality (past and future) as the meaningful foci of human existence, personal and social identity, and the quest for "salvation."

The second problem area within the set of "cosmic" problems focuses on the definition of the interrelationship between the cosmic and social (including political and economic) orders, their relative distinctiveness and autonomy, and their mutual relevance. This area can include several more specific problems, such as: the definition of the contents and attributes of these orders, their symbolic parameters; the ways in which their relationship is perceived; the degree of their autonomy and mutual relevance; the nature and degree of tension between them and the ways of resolving tension; and the relationship of such resolution to the main dimension of human existence and the focus of salvation.

The third problem area in this set is that of the relationship between social actors (group and individual) and the cosmic and social orders. The first subproblem is the nature of access of different social actors to these orders and their major attributes, above all the degree to which the major contents of these orders are seen as accessible directly to all individuals and groups, or only to some specific categories of actors or roles who act as mediators for other groups. The second subproblem is the nature of the actor's obligation to these orders, especially whether they are viewed as mere resources for other activities and goals, or can demand, that is —have claims on one's resources. The third subproblem is the degree to which individuals or groups see themselves as passive recipients or active participants in the creation of these orders and perceive the possibility of changing them. Fourth is the perception of man's degree of control of his fate—his social and natural environment, and the concomitant type and degree of responsibility for maintaining these orders.

The second major set of problems involves the symbolic evaluation of the social order. Here, two broad areas can be distinguished. The first problem area focuses on modes of converting resources into patterns of socially and culturally defined goals and activities.* The first subproblem is the relative emphasis on consumption of resources as against their long-term investment in more distant goals. This distinction applies not only to material or discrete commodities and goals, like wealth and power,

---

* These problems are closely related to, but not entirely identical with, the pattern variables analyzed by Parsons and Shils in their analysis of value orientations.

but to modes of orientation and participation in collectivities or cultural orders. Second is the subproblem of emphasis on discrete goals as against the tendency to combine them into a broader "meaningful" pattern.

The second problem area in the second category—symbolic definition of the social order—involves symbolic evaluation of the major organizational exigencies of interpersonal and social relations, above all those related to basic dilemmas of social life. These include hierarchy as against equality; conflict or harmony; individual or community; and the relative emphasis on power, solidarity, or instrumental inducements as major orientations to social order.

7.   These themes and problems are related to the quest for social order at all levels of social interaction, ranging from informal interpersonal relationships, through formal and institutional settings, to the construction of the macrosocietal order. On all levels, the provision of answers to these problems provides the starting point for the symbolic construction of social reality and the basis for a meaningful social and cultural order, as well as participation in it. Those answers are also the bases for bringing people's discrete social activities into patterns of meaningful experience which encompass crucial spheres of social and cultural life; and for developing and maintaining personal lives in some relation to these orders.

The answers to these problems, as they are constructed in social life or in other fields of activity, such as philosophy and art, may take three complementary forms. First, they provide symbolic models of the sphere of activity, in our case the social order. Second, they provide the principles or codes for structuring activities in any field; in our case these are ground rules of social interaction, or the parameters of social order. Third, they provide symbols which concretize the relationship between these codes and models and their actualization in specific situations.

In every society, different models of the cosmic, cultural, and social orders are constructed, ranging from models of interpersonal relationships to those of the macrosocietal order. These models define the cognitive and evaluative parameters of cultural and human reality. By offering answers to the predicaments of human existence, they provide a cognitive and evaluative map of the social and cultural world, and a guide for evaluation and choice among patterns of behavior.

Such models may be constructed according to the major types of cognition and of symbolic orientation. They may be religious, magical, philosophical, aesthetic, or scientific. They may be expressed in a great variety of cultural forms—myths, epics, tales, formalized works of art, or more popular versions of art and systems of belief. They are also pervasive in less differentiated patterns of private aesthetic, religious, or philosophic constructions of social and cultural reality. As Clifford Geertz has shown, they infuse the world of "common sense."

The number of models prevalent in a group or society, or even held by an individual, may vary greatly. In any society or subgroup, varied models of social and cultural life are articulated and formalized in different degrees. They vary also in the degree of pervasiveness, acceptance, and dominance in a society. Different models may be activated in different situations, though some are generally accepted as the more prevalent and binding ones in a society, cultural tradition, or sector. Private models of individuals and groups in a society may be similar to, or differ from, official constructions.

The second major way in which the answers to symbolic problems impinge on social life is through the provision of the principles which structure the frameworks of activity. These are the criteria for the parameters of social order or the ground rules of social interaction. The aspect of symbolic orientations most relevant to the choice of criteria for ground rules of social interaction, is the crystallization of these orientations into specific patterns of codes, which connect the contours of institutional order with answers to basic symbolic problems of human and social existence. Such codes are not merely general value orientations. They are much closer to what Weber called *Wirtschaftsethik*—generalized modes of "religious" or "ethical" orientation to specific institutional spheres and their problems, the evaluation of these spheres, and the provision of guidelines for their organization and for behavior within them in terms of the "proper" answers to major existential problems.[12]

Some important indications about the ways in which different constellations of these codes affect the construction of ground rules have been presented in comparative studies of modernization. Further work is necessary, however, and the exploration of this problem is a major task for analysis and research.

The various patterns of codes are closely related, of course, to the basic models of cultural order, but they are not identical with them. In a way, the models symbolize the basic and institutional implications of codes. They are, however, more closely related to the concretization of codes in specific social settings, and they involve a strong element of closure. Any closure involves the necessity to apply sanctions to enforce the norms through which these models are actualized in social life. Hence, it gives rise to strong ambivalence. This ambivalence is most fully and dramatically expressed in special social situations: in plays, public displays, private encounters, jokes depicted in various types of myths and plays. It tends, however, to be most fully articulated in special communicative situations and ritual occasions which are closely related to individual and collective *rites de passage,* rituals of birth, initiation, wedding, and death in individuals' lives.[13]

The Institutionalization of Ground Rules of Social Interaction

8.   Whatever the exact relationship between models of social and cultural systems and systems of codes, on the one hand, and the ground rules of social interaction, on the other, the contents of the ground rules do not emanate directly from the contents or dynamism of symbols. Hence we must deal with the nature of the processes of social interaction through which they are set up.

The answers to this question in approaches which stressed the negotiability of institutions, notably the exchange and symbolic interactionist models, were deficient in failing to distinguish processes through which these ground rules, as distinct from routine types of social interaction, are set up and maintained. Although the "routine" activities and the construction of ground rules of social interaction both involve production, distribution, and consumption of material or symbolic resources, they differ in the ways in which they regulate or structure the exchange of resources, in the nature of the actors who engage in these activities, and in the "tempo" or pacing of their activities.

"Routine" or organizational exchange and interaction is undertaken largely by individuals acting in their private capacity or as representatives of existing collectivities and their specific goals and interests. They engage in *ad hoc* or regular exchange of free and simple basic resources: wealth, services, power, esteem. By contrast, interaction oriented to setting up ground rules of social interaction focuses on potential long-range commitments and readiness to forgo some of the benefits and risks inherent in direct exchange.

Thus the setting up of ground rules of social interaction involves not only the exchange of the "simple" or "basic" resources, but above all the interchange and conversion of these resources with symbolic orientations. Such interchange involves the combination of 1) structuring control of relatively long-range distribution of major types of resources with 2)construction of the meaning of the situations of social interchange. This construction of meaning is not, however, "free-floating," as symbolic interactionists and ethnomethodologists sometimes portray it. It is, rather, closely interwoven both with the symbolic realm, from which possible meanings are derived, and with the organizational aspects of institutional order.

The readiness to accept definitions of social situations, implied in the construction of ground rules of social interaction and the obligations accruing to them, entails renunciation by the participants of some of the possibilities of direct and free use of their resources, especially their power; a concomitant readiness to permit investment of some of these resources in maintaining a broader conception of social order and its institutional derivatives and to refrain from using the resources beyond such specifications. This readiness has two complementary aspects. It entails the sacrifice by the more powerful actors of some of the immediate advantages they may potentially or actually possess, in favour of "lesser," or less immediate, advantages, such as the legitimation of their right to specify the broader goals of social order. On the part of those with fewer or more dispersed resources, accepting the rules means, first, giving up the possibility of using their own power or of opting out of any given situation; and second, investing some actors with the right to deal with the problems of the organizational aspects of social life, and hence to structure the range and base of trust and solidarity in the situation.

9.   Given that the basic function of the ground rules of social interaction is to "overcome," at least partially, the predicaments and uncertainties inherent in the social division of labor, it is natural that institutionalization of the ground rules should focus above all on setting non-market limitations and specifications for exchange of resources in social interaction.

The most important of these limitations is the *structuring of access* to the major types of markets existing in any framework of interaction; and of the possibility of converting resources exchanged in such markets. These limitations will vary for different groups and social categories.

A second limitation is effected through the setting up of *public goods*[14] —for example, provision by the government of defence or health services set up so that if one member of a collectivity receives them, they cannot be denied to other members. This limitation also sets the "prices" for various groups, of setting up such public goods, directly, or indirectly through taxation.

Third, such structuring of the flow of resources is manifest in the public distribution of private goods—that is, the direct allocation of services and rewards to different groups in terms of criteria differing greatly from those of pure exchange.

Fourth, closely related to the definition of public goods is the definition of the degree to which different groups, organizations, and institutional spheres enjoy *institutional credit*—the degree to which resources provided any group are not used in immediate exchange or in direct consumption, but are given to a certain degree unconditionally, providing that group or institution with what may be called "credit autonomy." This autonomy provides the base for the long-range functioning of the institution. Involved in the process of granting institutional credit is also the definition of the range and the long-term conditions of such credit.

The limitation of free exchange of resources, which is the major institutional derivative of the ground rules of social interaction, is effected through additional, quite complicated, mechanisms involving the specification of ascriptive titles and of limits of prestige[15] of different social categories and groups. These have yet to be studied in greater detail.

10.   The setting up of ground rules is undertaken and effected through interaction between two categories of actors. The first category includes elites who engage in enterpreneurial institutional activities,[16] and who are ready—or who give the impression of being ready—to use their resources for collective rather than private purposes. These groups articulate the models of social order, and set up norms and organizational frameworks. The other category includes those actors—individuals, social units, strata, groups and their representatives—who not only represent the direct interests of their respective groups but attempt to articulate the potential solidarity of such collectivities, and who are willing to invest resources and above all mutual commitments and support in frameworks of long-term interaction. They believe, or behave as if they believed, that through the acceptance of such obligations and their institutional implications, they will be provided with answers to the uncertainties and predicaments of social life.

The institutional ground rules crystallized in any concrete situation are set up and maintained through the interaction between conscious and unconscious coalitions of these different types of entrepreneurs—articulators of models of social and cultural order and of the solidarity of different groups, together with broader ecological, functional, and class groups.

The two types of actors—articulators of models of social and cultural order, and articulators of solidarity—are especially important because they create coalitions which differ from those studied in most coalition studies. These investigations have focused on the analysis of actors[17] who act *within* given frameworks of social interaction. These coalitions are usually composed of only one type of actors and of members related in symmetrical or assymetrical relations of power. The coalitions to which we refer are closer to the coalitions analyzed, for example, by S. M. Lipset and S. Rokkan in their analysis of the formation of European party systems.[18]

It is through the activities of such coalitions acting in special frameworks—institutional-ritual, legal and communicative, that the ground rules of social interaction are institutionalized and the interweaving of symbolic and organizational dimensions of social life takes place. This process characterizes all institutional spheres and the macrosocietal order.[19]

Such ground rules are not, however, given in any social situation, nor is their continuity assured. The maintenance of these ground rules and their major institutional derivatives depends on the constant control, by the coalitions acting within their institutional frameworks, of the flow of resources which are crucial to access to different "markets." The most important of these is control of the flow of information, its accumulation and the possible effect of this information, and of diffuse reservoirs of power in society, on the centers of the respective collectivities and on the positions defining the premises and symbols of the respective cultural and social orders. Second is control of access to positions which regulate the level of production, the principles of distribution of resources, and the conversion of economic resources into those of power and prestige. Third is control of access to those positions in the centers of society which control the setting up of reference orientations through which goals are internalized by individuals, and the communication processes which influence the levels of demand and evaluations of the social system by its participants.

The institutional derivatives of the ground rules of social interaction can be erected and maintained only insofar as the various elites who are the active partners in the coalitions analysed above can maintain control of their positions. Such control, however, is not given or assured in any situation of social interaction.

Ground Rules of Social Interaction as Principles of Deep Structure

11.   The special type of interaction and exchange through which the ground rules of social interaction are set up is closely related to the systemic qualities of societies. The institutionalization of these ground

rules provides what seem to be the principles of "deep" or "hidden" structures of social units. These are distinct from, but complementary to, their organizational structures.

This construction is effected through the concrete specification of the general needs or problems derivable from the organizational aspects of institutional life and the provision, by the respective entrepreneurs, of the major symbolic-institutional answers to them. That is, this construction defines the contents of these needs, the major relevant stimuli, and the patterns of response to them, since these aspects are not given either in the genetic endowment of people or in the organizational aspect of the division of labor.

It is the concrete specification of these ground rules that defines the range of concrete needs in a society, sets the boundaries of the environments for its respective groups, and defines the range of possible responses to the pressures of these environments.

The basic institutional derivatives of the ground rules, however, do more than specify the broad contours or boundaries of the social systems. By specifying the ways in which the basic societal functions of allocation, integration, and the like, are taken care of, they also influence the range of a society's systemic sensitivities. They influence the ways in which different systems cope with the range of problems to which they are exposed; the specific types of conflicts to which such systems are especially sensitive; the types of conditions under which the potential for conflict reaches levels that may threaten any society. Thus the rules influence the nature of the crises which may be generated within societies, and those to which they are especially sensitive, as well as the possible outcome of such crises—especially the modes of incorporating different types of demands, the degree of flexibility or rigidity in responding to them, the use of regressive or expansive policies in coping with them, and the potential direction of change within them.[20]

The ways in which the ground rules of interaction influence the dynamic qualities of social organizations show again that while a propensity to some systemic organization is given, in different degrees, in most situations of social interaction,[21] its concrete specification cannot be taken as given. This is generated and set up through special institutional processes.

As we have indicated, however, the maintenance and continuity of these ground rules, of the "deep" structure of social organizations and of their institutional derivatives, is not given or ensured either. Indeed, the very construction and institutionalization of such rules generates the potential for conflict and changes.

*The Ubiquity of Tension, Contradiction, Conflict, and Change in the
Construction of Social Order*

12. The potential for tension, conflict, and change is inherent in any concrete social setting, and above all in any macrosocietal order. The ubiquity of the tensions, conflicts, and contradictions that develop in any social order, and particularly within the macrosocietal order, is given in the fact that while institutionalization of ground rules of interaction copes with the problems of social order, it does not solve them. It only transposes them to a new level.

This is evident in the fact that within these orders there exists a continual tension between the tendency to closure, in any historical situation, of the concrete cultural and organizational possibilities which are available in it, and the tendency of many units and structures to maintain their own autonomy with respect to such closure.[22] A second source of tension resides in the fact that the institutionalization of the ground rules of social interaction always involves setting up and legitimizing differences and inequalities in the distribution of power, wealth, and prestige, and that this arrangement is always an outcome of struggle.

Thus, the institutionalization of the ground rules of interaction does not eliminate differences in power and access to resources or the exigencies of social organization. Rather, by assuring the possibility of mutual solidarity and long range mutual commitment and support, it regulates and legitimizes such differences. Through the specification and institutionalization of the ground rules, these various exigencies are symbolically and organizationally transposed to a new level creating meaning and order and the possibility of trust in social interaction, thus providing the precontractual and legitimizing dimension in social life.

But the institutionalization of the ground rules, with all the regulation of power it involves, is itself a focus of struggle. Because of this, the very construction and institutionalization of social order generates conflict and changes which are focused on the tension between the tendencies to closure and to openness in the construction of cultural and social life.

The tensions, or problems of social order, are most fully articulated in ritual and communicative situations, and in the symbols presented and played out in them. In these situations, the perception is most completely expressed that the order constructed through the specification and institutionalization of ground rules of interaction, especially through their "application" to concrete settings, is not simply or naturally "given." These situations indicate that while the ground rules do indeed provide structure to relieve the uncertainties inherent in interaction, they do not "solve" the problems generated by these indeterminacies, but transpose them to a level on which the potential for conflict and disorder is also given, but in a different way.

This potential is evident in several ways. First it is evident in the fact that any social order involves a plurality of actors—individuals and groups —who constantly struggle over differential control of "natural" and "social" resources. Second, these potential tensions and conflicts are exacerbated by the inherent characteristics of any institutionalized division of labor, particularly the distribution of individuals and groups among the basic institutional sectors, and the potential conflict between the different organizational prerequisites or needs in any institutional order.

Third, the development of tensions and contradictions is reinforced by the multiplicity of structural principles generated by the major types of symbolic orientations to the social order—that is, the major codes which are starting points for the structuring of ground rules, and by the fact that various orientations may be carried by different social actors and coalitions.[23]

These contradictions and conflicts are activated and intensified through several processes inherent in any social system, above all the shifts in relative power of groups, and in their attitudes towards the premises of the system, which are entailed in the continuity of any social system. The differences in power, wealth, and prestige which are legitimized by the institutionalization of ground rules of social interaction are never accepted to the same degree by all parts of society. The potential disagreements and conflicts are reinforced by the fact that the institutionalization of any social system, which involves attempts to mobilize resources, from fairly autonomous groups and individuals with different interests, in order to maintain its boundaries and the legitimacy of its symbols, necessarily generates constant shifts both in the balance of power among different groups and in their orientation to the existing system.

But while the propensities for conflict and change are inherent in the construction of any macrosocietal order, the intensity, location, and orientation of these conflicts and of propensity to change vary greatly among societies with different combinations of symbolic and structural-organizational properties.

They vary with the ways in which the symbolic orientations and codes are combined in a predominant cultural model and with the internal dynamism of these different codes. The nature and level of conflict vary also with the specific institutionalization of the basic derivatives of these codes, as influenced by the ecological and organizational settings of these societies.

These combinations of structural and symbolic characteristics vary greatly among societies and greatly influence the range of the environment these societies construct. They also influence the internal expansion of these societies, their propensity to develop, and their adaptibility to changing conditions and historical circumstances.

The Reopening of the Question of Social Order; the Broadening of the Sociological Tradition and a Possible Agenda for Sociological Analysis

13.   The preceding analysis has provided a preliminary delineation of the major problems of social order as they have developed out of the major theoretical controversies in sociology. It has specified, in greater detail than have classical and contemporary theoretical approaches, the areas of conflict, randomness, and potential disorder that are inherent in the organizational aspects of social division of labor and social interaction, and which are not regulated by the "usual," "routine" normative specifications and rules of these frameworks.

The analysis has also attempted to define the nature of the "precontractual" and legitimizing dimensions of social life, through which these problems of social order are seemingly resolved. Its central focus has been the construction of the ground rules of social interaction. It has indicated the difference between these dimensions of social life and the organizational and "routine" aspects of social interaction.

These general indications have opened up several new areas and problems of research which seem to us to constitute the most important challenges confronting sociological research at this stage of its development.

The most important of these problems are as follows:

First, how do different symbolic orientations influence the specific contents of the ground rules of social interaction affecting different levels and types of social organizations, from informal micro setting to the macrosocietal order? How are these orientations selected, and who are their carriers? That is, which types of entrepreneurs, groups, and coalitions choose and institutionalize different types of codes and ground rules? What are the concrete social mechanisms through which such orientations are connected in different situations with different ground rules?

Second is the nature of the institutional processes and mechanisms through which different ground rules and their institutional derivatives are established and maintained in various concrete situations. That is, what are the different types of mechanisms of interaction, and of restriction of the flow of resources, through which ground rules are institutionalized?

Third: What are the concrete criteria according to which the institutional derivatives of different types of ground rules—as for instance those pertaining to public goods, access to them, and institutional credit—are set up in different institutional spheres? How they are related to the distribution of power in different social settings?

Fourth: How do different ground rules influence the working of concrete social organizations? How do the two levels or types of social interaction, the "routine" and that oriented to setting up and maintaining the ground rules, impinge on each other?

Fifth: What are the different types of conflict and tension, and the potential and directions of change, generated in different kinds of social structures, both internally and through the impact of external, "international," forces?

All these problems can be identified on all levels of social life, from least structured to macrosocietal. The very specification of these problems, and the recognition that they can be identified on all levels of social life, entails extensive revison of many assumptions and perspectives in sociological analysis. On the macrosociological level it entails the recognition of the great variety of ways in which different coalitions may set up different types of macrosocietal orders, with different combinations of basic symbolic orientations and codes, ground rules of social interaction, and institutional derivatives. This approach, therefore, stresses the openness and specificity of different historical situations while permitting meaningful comparative analysis among them. In this respect, it goes beyond the assumptions of most prevalent comparative studies, especially those based on an evolutionary perspective.

On the microsociological level, this perspective entails the recognition of the variability of types of microsocietal settings and their relationships to the macrosocietal order. It revises some assumptions of sociological analysis, yet recognizes that the problems which arise out of such revision can be identified on all levels of social life and be analyzed in terms of different approaches. Each approach may concentrate on that level or aspect of institutional life and interaction it can best deal with. Accordingly, it can develop its own research program, working within the framework of a broader analytic conception of the problem of social order, yet without "total" incorporation into a new, unified paradigm.

The possibility of this broadening of the sociological tradition has developed, as we have seen, as a result of the theoretical controversies which began with the criticism of structural-functionalism by various countermodels. These models, despite the proclamation of many of their upholders, did not develop "total" alternatives to the structural-functional approach and its premises. From the beginning, they worked with some, at least, of the theoretical concepts and assumptions that were found also in the structural-functionalist model. Yet, by producing extensive changes in this model, they opened it toward the possible incorporation of the elements that they stressed.

In one way or another, all these approaches have accepted or incorporated the basic premises of the sociological tradition as developed by Tönnies, Weber, and Durkheim, and as crystallized in the structural-functional model in its varieties. They also incorporated several elements, especially the conflictual and historical elements of the open Marxist models, as well as parts of other paradigms, like that of the Chicago school or the phenomenological work of Alfred Schutz. Above all, most of these approaches also, on the whole, either accepted or assumed certain macrosocietal orientations and premises of the sociological tradition which were recrystallized in the work of the structural-functional school.

The transformation of these approaches from mutually exclusive models into different, yet mutually relevant, research paradigms with different emphases and research programs capable of enriching each other and the more general framework of sociological analysis, has taken place largely through the identification of the blind spots in different theoretical approaches, and through their comparison with research. All these developments provide the background for potentially constructive developments in sociological analysis. We have attempted to present the outlines of one approach in this chapter.

Whether these, or similar, constructive possibilities will be taken up, or whether sociology will abdicate its constructiveness and constructive potential depends not only on the intellectual availability of these alternatives. It rests also on the configuration, within the sociological community, of the intellectual and institutional trends analyzed above. Here lies the major challenge before sociology at this stage of its development.

Notes

1. T. Parsons, *The Structure of Social Action* (New York: Free Press [1937], 1968, 2 vols.

2. For Durkheim's analysis of precontractual norms and of mechanical solidarity, see E. Durkheim, *The Division of Labor in Society* (New York: Free Press [1933], 1964).

For Weber's analysis of the major types of legitimation, see the relevant materials from the collection *Max Weber, On Charisma and Institution Building,* edited by S. N. Eisenstadt (Chicago: University of Chicago Press, 1968), especially pp. 11–12; 46–65.

3. The contributions of the structural-functional model are discussed in detail in Ch. 7, above.

   The contributions of the exchange, conflict and other approaches mentioned below, are discussed in Ch. 8, above. See also the discussion in Ch. 10, above.

4. P. Blau, "Parameters of social structure," *American Sociological Review,* Vol. 39, No. 5 (October 1974), pp. 615–635.

5. These discussions have been analyzed in detail in Chs. 9 and 10, above.

6. For a fuller analysis of these blind spots, see Ch. 10, above.

7. E. Mayer, "Behavior programs and evolutionary strategies," *American Scientist,* Vol. 62 (November–December, 1974), p. 651.

8. R. L. Halloway, Jr., "Culture: a human domain," *Current Anthropology,* Vol. 10, No. 4 (October 1969), pp. 395–412.

9. I. R. Buchler and H. G. Nutini (eds.), *Game Theory in the Behavioral Sciences* (Pittsburgh: University of Pittsburgh Press, 1969), Introduction, p. 8.

10. J. S. Bruner, "On voluntary action and its hierarchical structure," in A. Koestler, and J. R. Smythies (eds.), *Beyond Reductionism—New Perspectives in the Life Sciences* (Boston: Beacon Press, 1969), pp. 161–191.

11. For the approaches of these scholars see Ch. 10, above.

12. For greater detail see S. N. Eisenstadt, "Post-traditional societies and the continuity and reconstruction of tradition," in S. N. Eisenstadt (ed.), *Post-Traditional Societies* (New York: Norton, 1974), pp. 1–27.

13. See in greater detail S. N. Eisenstadt (ed.), *Max Weber: on Charisma and Institution Building, op. cit.,* Introduction; T. Turner, "Groping for the elephant ritual, as process, as model, and as hierarchical system," in B. Meyerhoff (ed.), *Secular Ritual Considered* (forthcoming).

14. On the concept of public goods in relation to societal analysis, see A. Kuhn, *The Study of Society—A Unified Approach* (Homewood, Ill.: Dorsey, 1963); M. Olson, Jr., *The Logic of Collective Action* (New York: Schocken, 1968); O. E. Williamson, "Some notes on the economics of atmosphere," Fels Discussion Paper No. 29, Fels Center of Government, University of Pennsylvania, 1973; O. E. Williamson, "Markets and hierarchies: some elementary considerations," *American Economic Review,* Vol. 63, No. 2 (May 1973), pp. 316–325.

15. These concepts and mechanisms are elaborated in greater detail in S. N. Eisenstadt, "Prestige, participation, and strata formation," in J. A. Jackson (ed.), *Social Stratification* (Cambridge: Cambridge University Press, 1968), pp. 62–103; S. N. Eisenstadt, *Social Differentiation and Stratification* (Glenview, Ill.: Scott Foresman, 1971).

16. On the concept of institutional entrepreneurs see F. Barth, "Models of social organization," Occasional Paper No. 23, Royal Anthropological Institute of Great Britain and Ireland, 1966; S. N. Eisenstadt, *Essays on Comparative Institutions* (New York: Wiley, 1965), especially Chs. 1 and 12.

17. On the study of coalitions see, for instance, S. Groennings, E. W. Kelly, and M. Leiserson (eds.), *The Study of Coalition Behavior* (New York: Holt, Rinehart & Winston, 1970); J. S. Coleman, "Foundations for a theory of collective decisions," *American*

Journal of Sociology, Vol. 71, No. 6 (1966), pp. 615–627; W. Gamson, "Experimental studies of coalition formation," in L. Berkowitz (ed.), *Advances in Experimental Social Psychology.* Vol. 1 (New York: Academic Press, 1964), pp. 81–110.

18. S. M. Lipset and S. Rokkan, "Cleavage structures, party systems, and voter alignments," in S. M. Lipset and S. Rokkan (eds.) *Party Systems and Voter Alignments* (New York: Free Press, 1967), pp. 1–64.

19. Some of these aspects are explored in greater detail in S. N. Eisenstadt, "Structuralism and societal analysis," (forthcoming); and in S. N. Eisenstadt, "Anthropological analysis of complex societies: the confrontation of symbolic-structuralist and institutional approaches," in *Anthropology of the United States,* ed. by W. C. Sturtevant, a special publication of the Anthropological Association of Washington (forthcoming).

   On the concept of societal centers as related to these aspects see: E. Shils, "Center and periphery," in *The Logic of Personal Knowledge* (London: Routledge & Kegan Paul, 1961), pp. 117–131.

   On its elaboration in comparative analyses, see: S. N. Eisenstadt (ed.), *Political Sociology* (New York: Basic Books, 1970), the introductions.

20. For an attempt at the development of the relations between codes, ground rules of social interaction, and organizational problems in one type of society, see S. N. Eisenstadt, "Traditional patrimonialism and modern neopatrimonialism," Sage Research Papers in the Social Sciences, Studies in Comparative Modernization Series, No. 90–93, Vol. 1 (Beverly Hills, Cal.: Sage, 1973).

21. See among others G. E. Swanson, "Toward corporate action: a reconstruction of elementary collective processes," in T. Shibutani, (ed.), *Human Nature and Collective Behavior* (Englewood Cliffs, N. J.: Prentice-Hall, 1970), pp. 124–144.

22. This aspect is analyzed in greater detail in S. N. Eisenstadt, "Post-traditional societies and the continuity and reconstruction of tradition," *Daedalus,* Vol. 102, No. 1 (winter 1974), pp. 1–27.

23. These points have been elaborated in greater detail in S. N. Eisenstadt, *Tradition, Change and Modernity* (New York: Wiley, 1973), Part 3.

Name Index

Subject Index

Anthropology:
  debates and reorientations in, 231
Anti-systemic approach*:
  analytic blind spots of, 279
Aristotelian tradition, 61-62
  see also under Name Index: Aristotle
Asian mode of production, 262

Buddhism, 263
  see also under Name Index: Buddha

Chicago school, 156, 186, 187, 304-305, 373
Closed-systemic mode of explanation:
  analytic contributions, 96-101
  definition of, 90, 91
  illustrations of, 94, 95, 96
Coalition and network approaches, assumptions of, 85, 86
Codes, 363

Conflict (and power) approaches:
  analytic and research contributions, 277, 349
  analytic blind spots, 280
  assumptions, criticism of structural-functionalism, 197
  opening of to the symbolic dimension, 254
  opening of to the systemic dimension, 259
Crises in sociology, *see* Sociology, crises in
Culturalist approaches:
  as closed-systemic mode of explanation, 96
  assumptions of, 87
  illustrations of, 87-88

Darwinism, 27, 132
  see also: Social Darwinism
Discrete mode of explanation:
  definition of, 90
  illustrations of, 92, 93

---

note: "approach" denotes model or theory